GENETIC NARRATOLOGY

Genetic Narratology

Analysing Narrative across Versions

Edited by Dirk Van Hulle

https://www.openbookpublishers.com

©2024 Dirk Van Hulle

Copyright of individual chapters is maintained by the chapter's authors

This work is licensed under the Creative Commons Attribution-NonCommercial 4.0 International (CC BY-NC 4.0). This license allows you to share, copy, distribute and transmit the text; to adapt the text for non-commercial purposes of the text providing attribution is made to the authors (but not in any way that suggests that they endorse you or your use of the work). Attribution should include the following information:

Dirk Van Hulle (ed.), *Genetic Narratology: Analysing Narrative across Versions*. Cambridge, UK: Open Book Publishers, 2024, https://doi.org/10.11647/OBP.0426

Every effort has been made to identify and contact copyright holders of images included in this publication, and any omission or error will be corrected if notification is made to the publisher.

Further details about the CC BY-NC license are available at
http://creativecommons.org/licenses/by-nc/4.0/

All external links were active at the time of publication unless otherwise stated and have been archived via the Internet Archive Wayback Machine at https://archive.org/web

Any digital material and resources associated with this volume will be available at https://doi.org/10.11647/OBP.0426#resources

ISBN Paperback: 978-1-80511-399-7
ISBN Hardback: 978-1-80511-400-0
ISBN Digital (PDF): 978-1-80511-401-7
ISBN Digital eBook (EPUB): 978-1-80511-402-4
ISBN HTML: 978-1-80511-403-1

DOI: 10.11647/OBP.0426

This publication was made possible thanks to the support of the Flemish Research Council (FWO) and the Oxford Centre for Textual Editing and Theory (OCTET) in the context of the FWO project 'Creating Suspense Across Versions: Genetic Narratology and Stephen King's IT' (Grant G007422N).

Cover image: Louis Marcoussis, *Le Lecteur* (1937). Photo by Birmingham Museums Trust, Public Domain, https://dams.birminghammuseums.org.uk/asset-bank/action/viewAsset?id=8458&index=28&total=29&view=viewSearchItem
Cover design: Jeevanjot Kaur Nagpal

Contents

Acknowledgments　vii

Notes on Contributors　ix

1. An Introduction to Genetic Narratology: Geneses of Narratives and Narratives of Geneses　1
Dirk Van Hulle

2. Metagenesis: Manuscripts, and How Metanarration and Metafiction Contribute to Their Analysis　17
Karin Kukkonen

3. The Structures of Narrative Imagination: Reading an Outline of Theodor Fontane's Novel *Die Poggenpuhls* as a Test Case for Genetic Narratology　35
Matthias Grüne

4. A Lodger Returns: Change in Narrative Voice Across Epigenetic Versions and Works　55
Josefine Hilfling

5. Melville's Cancelled Note-to-Self: The Development of a 'Ragged' Narrative Across the Drafts of *Billy Budd*　73
Charles Mascia

6. 'The puzzle pieces fit too late': Posthumous Narratological Changes in Arthur Quiller-Couch and Daphne Du Maurier's *Castle Dor*　91
Claire Qu

7. Prototyping the Narrative Skeleton: Story Structure, Types of Narration and Vestigial Elements in the Genesis of James Joyce's 'Ithaca' Episode　111
Joris Žiliukas

8. Drafting 'Anon' and Killing Anon: Virginia Woolf and the
Genesis of English Literary Language   133
Joshua Phillips

9. Beckett's 'Arabian Nights of the Mind': Unnarratability,
Denarrat(ivisat)ion and Narrative Closure in the Radio Play
Cascando   151
Pim Verhulst

10. A Genetic and Biographical Analysis of Barbara Pym's
Companion Character   169
Jane Loughman

11. Also for Irony: Historical Realism and the Move of a Chapter
for the Final Version of *V.* (1963) by Thomas Pynchon   189
Luc Herman and John M. Krafft

12. You Don't Get Scared of Monsters, You Get Scared for People:
Creating Suspense across Versions in Stephen King's *IT*   199
Vincent Neyt

13. Genetic Narratology and the Novelistic Cycle across Versions   221
Lars Bernaerts

14. 'Indolence, interruption, business, and pleasure':
Narratological Rupture in *The Last Samurai*   241
Kaia Sherry

15. Nanogenetic Econarratology: Where Narratology Meets
Keystroke Logging Data   261
Lamyk Bekius

16. On the Value of Variants and Textual Genesis for Interpretation:
Some Remarks on a New Relationship between Historical-Critical
Editing, Genetic Criticism and Narratology   281
Rüdiger Nutt-Kofoth

Index   299

Acknowledgments

This volume originated in a 2023 conference on 'Genetic Narratology' at the University of Oxford (Jesus College, 23–24 February 2023). I would like to thank the fellows and staff at Jesus College and at the English Faculty for helping me host this conference. This publication was made possible thanks to the support of the Flemish Research Council (FWO) and the Oxford Centre for Textual Editing and Theory (OCTET) in the context of the FWO project 'Creating Suspense Across Versions: Genetic Narratology and Stephen King's IT' (Grant G007422N). I owe a debt of gratitude to Benjamin Helssen, Jana Wabbes, Adèle Kreager, Magda Verhaert, Michel Van Hulle, Sophia Bursey, Laura Rodríguez Pupo, Lucy Barnes, Jeevanjot Nagpal, Alessandra Tosi and the whole team at Open Book Publishers for helping to bring this publication to completion and making it available in Open Access.

Notes on Contributors

Lamyk Bekius is a postdoctoral researcher at the University of Antwerp as the University of Antwerp's coordinator of the CLARIAH-VL Open Humanities Service Infrastructure project and Platform{DH}, and as lecturer in the MA Digital Text Analysis. In 2023, she obtained her PhD at the University of Amsterdam and the University of Antwerp on the thesis *Behind the computer screens: The use of keystroke logging for genetic criticism applied to born-digital works of literature*, for which she also worked at the Huygens Institute (KNAW) in Amsterdam. Her research takes place at the intersection of genetic criticism, born-digital literary archives, keystroke logging and digital humanities.

Lars Bernaerts is an associate professor at the Department of Literary Studies, Ghent University (Belgium). Together with Hans Vandevoorde he coordinates the Center for the Study of Experimental Literature (SEL) which is part of the international research network ENAG. He is an editor of the *Online Encyclopedia of Literary Neo-Avant-Gardes* (www.oeln.net). His research and publications focus on narrative theory, modern Dutch literature, experimental fiction, and the literary radio play. Recent publications include co-edited special issues on literary representations of the internet in Dutch literature (in *Nederlandse Letterkunde* 28/2, with Siebe Bluijs and Inge van de Ven) and on the politics of form in literary neo-avant-gardes (in *Modernism/modernity* 8/1, 2023, with Vincent Broqua and Sabine Müller).

Matthias Grüne is an assistant professor at the University of Wuppertal, where he teaches Modern German Literature. After completing his doctoral project on Otto Ludwig's *Romanstudien* at the University of Leipzig, he worked in Leipzig as a research assistant on the DFG project 'Historisch-kritische Edition von Otto Ludwigs *Romanstudien*' before moving to the University of Wuppertal in 2018. His habilitation project focuses on literary representations of lived experience in German literature since the 18th century. His most recent book publications include the historical-critical edition of Ludwig's *Romanstudien* (2021), the anthology *Theodor Fontane und das Erbe der Aufklärung* (together with Jana Kittelmann; 2021) and the monograph *Realistische Narratologie. Otto Ludwigs* Romanstudien *im Kontext einer Geschichte der Erzähltheorie* (2018). Matthias Grüne is a board member of the Interdisciplinary Centre for Narrative Research (CNR) in Wuppertal and a member of the editorial board of *DIEGESIS, the Interdisciplinary E-Journal for Narrative Research*.

Luc Herman is Emeritus Professor of Narrative Theory and American Literature at the University of Antwerp. His publications include Gravity's Rainbow*: Domination & Freedom* (2013, with Steven Weisenburger), *Handbook of Narrative Analysis* (second edition, 2019, with Bart Vervaeck), *Becoming Pynchon: Genetic Narratology and* V. (2023, with John M. Krafft), and a variety of (often co-authored) essays in journals including *Narrative, Poetics Today, Style, Language and Literature, Critique,* and *Contemporary Literature*.

Josefine Hilfling is PhD fellow (2023–26) at the University of Copenhagen and at the Society for Danish Language and Literature, an independent research institution in Copenhagen, Denmark. Her research concerns the writing process of the Danish Nobel Prize-winning author Henrik Pontoppidan (1857–1943). She is also co-editor of the digital edition of Henrik Pontoppidan's three great novels *The Promised Land, A Fortunate Man,* and *The Kingdom of the Dead*.

John M. Krafft is Professor Emeritus of English at Miami University. He was a cofounder of the journal *Pynchon Notes* in 1979, and its coeditor and bibliographer until 2009. A series of essays coauthored with Luc Herman analyzing the evolution of Pynchon's *V.* from typescript to published novel culminated in their book *Becoming Pynchon: Genetic Narratology and* V. (2023).

Karin Kukkonen is Professor in Comparative Literature at the University of Oslo. She serves as director of LCE—Centre for Literature, Cognition and Emotions and leads the ERC Project JEUX—Literary Games, Poetics and the Early Modern Novel (2024–2028). Kukkonen specialises in the long history of the novel, cognitive poetics, manuscript genetics and narratology. She has published studies on the manuscripts of Frances Burney (in her monograph *How the Novel Found its Feet*, 2019) and on the manuscripts for the *Three Musketeers* (in *Orbis Litterarum*, 2019). In her most recent work, *Creativity and Contingency in Literary Writing* (forthcoming), Kukkonen develops a model for creativity in literature on the basis of literary theory, author interviews and manuscript analysis.

Jane Loughman graduated from Oxford University in 2023 with a Master of Studies in modern and contemporary literature. Her dissertation examined the resonant moods of Muriel Spark's early fiction and Ali Smith's *Seasonal Quartet*. The essay featured in this collection was adapted from a postgraduate assignment and was presented as an example of genetic criticism at the Barbara Pym Society's 2024 North American Conference. Before attending Oxford, she graduated from the Dual BA Programme between Columbia University (New York) and Trinity College Dublin, receiving two Bachelor of Art degrees in English. While at Columbia, she wrote a dissertation on Joyce Carol Oates's retellings of Henry James's *The Turn of the Screw* and was awarded the John Angus Burrell Memorial Prize for distinction in English literature. Jane now works in Dublin.

Charles Mascia completed his studies at McGill University (B.A.) and the University of Oxford (M.St.). In his postgraduate research, he wrote about descriptive style and the influence of Dutch painting in Willa Cather's historical fiction. He lives and works in London.

Vincent Neyt has a background in genetic criticism and digital scholarly editing. He is the technical developer of the Beckett Digital Manuscript Project (www.beckettarchive.org). In 2024 he completed the PhD *Turning the Thumbscrews Tighter: Suspense Across Versions in Stephen King's IT*, as part of a research project at the University of Antwerp funded by the Research Foundation of Flanders.

Rüdiger Nutt-Kofoth teaches German literature and scholarly editing at the University of Wuppertal (Germany). He has written and edited books and articles on German literature and on editorial theory and practice. He is the co-editor of *editio. Internationales Jahrbuch für Editionswissenschaft. International Yearbook of Scholarly Editing* and of the series *Bausteine zur*

Geschichte der Edition (Elements of a History of Editing). Furthermore, he is the *Sprecher* (chairman) of the *Arbeitsgemeinschaft für germanistische Edition* (Association of German Scholarly Editing).

Joshua Phillips is a Leverhulme Early Career Fellow at the University of Oxford's Faculty of English and a Junior Research Fellow at Jesus College, Oxford, where he is working on a project titled 'The Digital "Anon": A Digital Genetic Edition of Virginia Woolf's Final Essays'. He has published articles in *Textual Cultures* and *Woolf Studies Annual*, and contributed to *The Year's Work in English Studies*. His monograph, *Virginia Woolf and Futurity*, is under contract.

Claire Qu is a DPhil candidate at the University of Oxford, working on resource imaginaries in Gothic world literature. Her Master's dissertation explored overlapping concepts of the domestic and the colonial in Victorian ghost stories by British and Australian women, and her Honour's thesis analysed uncomfortable affects in *Melmoth the Wanderer*. Claire was introduced to the field of genetic narratology in a Master's subject on bibliographical studies, and her chapter in this volume stems from the coursework for that subject.

Kaia Sherry is a recent MSt graduate from the University of Oxford. Her research focused on 19th-century ephemera and affect, examining the works of illustrators including John Tenniel and Isaac Robert Cruikshank. She is now a recovering academic.

Dirk Van Hulle is Professor of Bibliography and Modern Book History at the University of Oxford, director of the Oxford Centre for Textual Editing and Theory (OCTET) and of the Centre for Manuscript Genetics at the University of Antwerp. With Mark Nixon, he is director of the MLA award-winning *Beckett Digital Manuscript Project* (www.beckettarchive.org), series editor of the series 'Elements in Beckett Studies', editor of the *Journal of Beckett Studies*, and curator of the Bodleian exhibition *Write Cut Rewrite* (Oxford, Feb 2024–Jan 2025). His publications include *Textual Awareness* (2004), *Modern Manuscripts* (2014), *Samuel Beckett's Library* (2013, with Mark Nixon), *The New Cambridge Companion to Samuel Beckett* (2015), *James Joyce's Work in Progress* (2016), *Genetic Criticism: Tracing Creativity in Literature* (2022), and *Write Cut Rewrite* (2024, with Mark Nixon).

Pim Verhulst is a postdoctoral researcher at the University of Oxford and the Vrije Universiteit Brussel. He has published articles in the *Journal of Beckett Studies* and *Samuel Beckett Today/Aujourd'hui*, and book chapters in *Beckett and BBC Radio* (2017), *Beckett and Technology* (2021), *Audionarratology* (2021), *Beckett and Media* (2022) and *Music and its Narrative Potential* (2024). He has co-edited *Beckett and Modernism* (2018), *Radio Art and Music* (2020), *Tuning in to the Neo-Avant-Garde* (2021), *Word, Sound and Music in Radio Drama* (2023) and *Beckett's Afterlives* (2023). His recent monographs, *The Making of Samuel Beckett's Television Plays* and *Radio Plays*, are forthcoming in the Beckett Digital Manuscript Project series.

Joris Žiliukas spent his undergrad years reading English and Italian at the University of Oxford. Returning to his interest in science, he also obtained a Master's degree in cognitive science in London. Joris is currently focusing on combining philosophy, mathematics, and biology to tackle questions in neuroscience.

1. An Introduction to Genetic Narratology: Geneses of Narratives and Narratives of Geneses

Dirk Van Hulle

A story to start with: once upon a time there was a block of white marble from Carrara. In 1408, the committee responsible for the decoration of the Duomo in Florence had decided to adorn the building's roofline with massive statues of biblical prophets and mythological figures. The slab of Carrara marble was destined to become one of these statues. The first sculptor to set to work on it was Agostino di Duccio. He received the commission to make a statue of the biblical hero David, who slayed the giant Goliath. Agostino started working on the legs first. But he abandoned the project. A second sculptor, Antonio Rossellino, was hired in 1476. Yet he, too, withdrew from his assignment, this time blaming the poor quality of the marble. The stone was exposed to the elements for the rest of the century, and it was not until 1501 that a new sculptor was found: the then 26-year-old Michelangelo. So far, the story has been one of laborious and slow progress, but in Britannica's narrative its ending is all of a sudden a fast-paced, one sentence apotheosis: 'Early in the morning on September 13, 1501, the young artist got to work on the slab, extracting the figure of David in a miraculous process that the artist and writer Giorgio Vasari would later describe as "the bringing back to life of one who was dead."'[1]

The 'miraculous' nature of this process is a persistent myth, reinforced by that other tale told of Michelangelo, who allegedly said

---

1   https://www.britannica.com/story/how-a-rejected-block-of-marble-became-the-worlds-most-famous-statue

that the sculpture is already complete within the marble block before one starts working on it; that one just has to chisel away the superfluous material. The story makes it seem as if any marble sculpture, even the famous statue of David, was just waiting to be liberated from a block of stone. He simply needed to extract what was already there in essence, as it were. This would imply a rather essentialist and deterministic view, as in the belief that things have a set of characteristics which make them what they are and that the task of the artist is their discovery. In fact, the statement attributed to Michelangelo is a way of moulding the creative invention into a discovery model, implying the pre-existence of the thing to be dis-covered.

Very often, however, that is not how the creative process works. The slow, difficult groping process of trial and error is easily forgotten after the fact, and replaced—with hindsight—by a narrative of 'eureka' instances and 'breakthrough' moments. The mythmaking mechanisms are part of the narrativising impulses we all tend to have—whether we are creative writers talking about their writing in retrospect or fans eager to aggrandise their literary heroes' genius.

It is good to be aware of these narrativising impulses. And in this respect, two subdisciplines may be of help: narratology and genetic criticism. On the one hand, narratology is defined by the Oxford English Dictionary as 'The study of the structure and function of narrative [...]; the examination and classification of the traditional themes, conventions, and symbols of the narrated story.' On the other hand, the study of creative processes is the province of genetic criticism. In combination with 'narratology', the adjective 'genetic' refers on the one hand to the genesis of narratives (the writing process of stories), but on the other hand also to narratives of this kind of genesis. That double focus is what this introductory essay wants to explore.

Genetic narratology combines methodologies of genetic criticism and narrative analysis. When Lars Bernaerts, Gunther Martens and I explored the possibility of such a combination in 2011 and 2013, we observed a general trend among narratologists to focus more on reception than on production. But we also discovered that in the past, quite a few narratologists had felt very comfortable using manuscript material in their arguments whenever they deemed it useful for their narrative analysis—Dorrit Cohn with Kafka, Franz Karl Stanzel with

Henry James, Gérard Genette with Proust, Philippe Hamon with Zola, Seymour Chatman with Virginia Woolf (2013, 303). The Oxford colloquium 'Genetic Narratology'[2] developed some of these earlier explorations of the possibilities to combine narratology with genetic criticism. They mutually enrich each other in all aspects of classical, structuralist narratology, which usually works with three large categories of narrative analysis: (1) *story*, consisting of 'actions', 'actants' and 'setting'; (2) *narrative*, encompassing 'time', 'characterisation' and 'focalisation'; and (3) *narration* (the ways in which the story is told), covering 'types of narrators' (intra-, extra-, homo-, heterodiegetic) and the 'representation of consciousness' (Herman and Vervaeck 2019, 42). Postclassical narratology has broadened the scope of this basic set of focal points in terms of intermedial, rhetorical, cognitive, feminist, queer, postcolonial, cultural, natural and unnatural narratology. David Herman defines postclassical narratology as a set of forms of narrative analysis that respect classical (mainly structuralist, text-oriented) narratology, but add contextual dimensions to it.[3] My suggestion is to add 'genetic narratology' to this list, and the present volume of essays is an attempt to show, by means of various examples ranging from the early nineteenth to the twenty-first centuries, how genetic criticism can enrich and refine narrative analysis, and vice versa. A genetic-narratological approach enriches the reading experience as it broadens the traditional focus on the product (the published text) to also include the process (the genesis of the text).

The devil's advocate might retort that genetic critics are thus using narratology as a crutch or a scaffolding which they can throw away when they do not need it anymore. This would suggest that genetic narratology might be only unidirectionally enriching; that genetic critics benefit from narratology but that this does not work the other way around. It is certainly true that genetic critics can use and apply

---

2   Several of the essays in the present collection originated in papers presented at this international colloquium 'Genetic Narratology' (Jesus College, Oxford, 23–24 February 2023).

3   David Herman in *The Living Handbook of Narratology*, https://www.lhn.uni-hamburg.de/node/38.html; see also Jan Christoph Meister, 'Narratology', https://www.lhn.uni-hamburg.de/node/48.html: 'Over the past twenty years, narratologists have paid increasing attention to the historicity and contextuality of modes of narrative representation as well as to its pragmatic function across various media.'

narratological models, such as the structuralist framework, because it offers a vocabulary for the phenomena we encounter in the manuscripts. But I do believe that the enrichment is mutual. It also works in the other direction: narratologists can use models from genetic criticism, because it offers a vocabulary and framework for the analysis of narrative across versions. For instance, one such framework is the triangular model of the dynamics between *endogenesis*, *epigenesis* and *exogenesis*. Endogenesis encompasses the 'inside' of the genesis, the chronological sequence of notes, drafts and other textual versions before the first publication. Epigenesis is the continuation of the genesis after publication. And exogenesis consists of the author's interaction with external source texts (for instance when they look something up in an encyclopaedia).

In addition to discussing the ways in which narratology can offer useful tools and vocabulary to examine the genesis of narratives using the tripartite structure of *story, narrative* and *narration* (Van Hulle 2022),[4] we could proceed in a similar way and examine how the genetic model of *endo-, epi-* and *exogenesis*[5] could—in its turn—be beneficial to narratology. Given the pioneering nature of this first full-length volume to merge genetic criticism with narratology, this collection of essays tries to find out if this exchange of methodologies and vocabularies can be mutually beneficial, and if that turns out to be the case genetic narratology can hopefully develop into something that is more than the sum of its parts, offering an innovative approach to understanding literature.

This introduction consists of two sections, one about studying 'the genesis of narratives', and one about the mechanisms behind the ways in which we inevitably make 'narratives of the genesis'. The first part of the essay focuses not only on the *narrated* but also on the *unnarrated*. While the first part discusses various methods of analysing the genesis of narratives, the second part examines narratives of the genesis. Very often, the writing process is the object of narrativisation. In interviews, letters or conversations, authors are invited to talk about the making-of. Due to numerous circumstances, certain elements of the writing process are emphasised, magnified, exaggerated, others are obscured or forgotten, either on purpose or by accident. This narrativisation

---

4   See especially the chapter called 'Genetic Narratology' in *Genetic Criticism: Tracing Creativity in Literature* (2022), 149–63.

5   See Karin Kukkonen's essay for an interesting fourth dimension to this approach.

of literary geneses is just as much the object of scrutiny in genetic narratology as the genesis of narratives. The second section of this introduction will therefore discuss how the genesis of narratives and narratives of the genesis relate to each other—a topic that will recur in several of the essays in this volume.

1. The Genesis of Narratives

The Narrated: The Telling of the Tale

Endogenesis: endogenetic narratology often analyses narrative elements across versions, comparing for instance a manuscript version with the published text. But even within one version, a comparison of subsequent writing layers (all the deletions, substitutions, additions within one document, as in Dorrit Cohn's analysis of Kafka's manuscript of *Das Schloss*) qualifies as endogenetic narratology. As a narratologist, Cohn was one of the first scholars to draw attention to a striking shift from first-person to third-person narration in the manuscript, preserved at the Bodleian Library in Oxford, not as part of a genetic analysis but as a narratological study. This already happens in the novel's opening sentence: 'Es war spät abend, wenn ich K. ankam' ['It was late in the evening when I K. arrived.'] (Bodleian, MS. Kafka 34, fol. 2v).[6] Again, the devil's advocate might argue that narratology only analyses one version at a time or one layer at a time; that there is not really a dynamic, temporal dimension. But Cohn gives narratological explanations for the change from first-person to third-person narration, trying to answer questions about free indirect style. With only a few minimal changes, Kafka manages to create a major stylistic effect: the impact of this shift from 'self-narrated monologue' to 'narrated monologue' (Cohn 1978, 169-70) is that the narrator is 'effaced', and the emphasis shifts to the experiencing character. In other words, a narratological argument is developed, not just for one layer and then for the next, but also for the narrative metamorphosis, for the change from one to the other. In

---

[6] The aim of the transcription conventions used in the present volume is to facilitate the reading by using as few diacritical signs as a possible, crossing out deleted passages and using superscript for additions.

Narrative Discourse Revisited, Gérard Genette discusses this example as a case of 'transvocalization'—shifts in voice from one version to another (1988, 109-11). In Kafka's manuscript, this transvocalization was remarkably easy, Cohn argues, because the original first-person narration was atypical, in the sense that the narrating 'I' completely gave way to the experiencing 'I'. It was 'a first-person narrative in grammatical form only, not in structure'; as a result, 'there was no obstacle whatever to the substitution of K. for ich in the manuscript' (1968, 33).

Epigenesis: The same principle of analysing narratives across versions can be applied to narratives across editions, if the genesis continues after publication, that is, if the author keeps making changes. Good examples are the various editions during the author's lifetime of Charles Darwin's *Origin of Species*; or Mary Shelley's *Frankenstein*. In the first edition, Frankenstein falls in love with his blood cousin Elizabeth Lavenza; in the 1831 edition, Mary Shelley turned her into an adoptive sister, to avoid any suggestions of incest. This change has an impact with regard to the actants and to some extent the characterisation. Sometimes an author destroys their manuscripts, but keeps making changes to every new edition of their work, as in the case of the Danish author Henrik Pontoppidan's novel *A Fortunate Man*, which makes it an excellent case study for epigenetic narratology (see Josefine Hilfling's contribution to this volume).

Exogenesis: Genetic narratology does not need to be limited to narrative analysis across versions. There is also an exogenetic dimension. With reference to characterisation, it is interesting to see how Alan Bennett gave shape to the character of the King in *The Madness of George III* by making detailed notes on Nesta Pain's *George III at Home* (1975). Or with reference to setting, in the case of *The Remains of the Day*, Kazuo Ishiguro took extensive notes from books on English country houses in the late 1930s, because this setting is such an integral part of the ideology. The butler's role in this chronotope is the central metaphor of the novel. Genetic narratology is interested in the role of this chronotopical metaphor in the creative development: was it the metaphor that triggered the narrative or was it the other way around? Was it the narrative that developed in such a way that gradually the butler's position turned into a metaphor for the average person's subservient position in global politics? It is not always clear what came first: was it the ideological idea that determined the setting, or was it the setting that led to a crystallisation of the ideology?

In addition to this primary triad of genetic dimensions, this volume of essays explores other avenues such as Karin Kukkonen's suggestion to take account of a work's metagenesis as a way of expanding the genetic dossier and contributing to a narratological understanding of metafiction. Genetic approaches to narratives will often concentrate on a work's macrogenesis (the genesis of a work in its entirety across multiple versions) or microgenesis (the revisions within one document or for instance the processing of one particular exogenetic source text)—see the essays by Matthias Grüne, Luc Herman and John M. Krafft, Charles Mascia, Vincent Neyt, Joshua Phillips, Claire Qu, Kaia Sherry, Pim Verhulst, Joris Žiliukas in this collection—but they can also include narrative analysis on the level of the nanogenesis, thanks to keystroke logging applied to born-digital work—see Lamyk Bekius's contribution to this volume—or on the level of the megagenesis, transcending the limits of a single work, encompassing for instance a whole cycle of novels or the recurrence of a certain narrative phenomenon such as a particular type of character in several novels by the same author—see the essays by Lars Bernaerts and Jane Loughman in this collection. In general, this is another opportunity to pay special attention to the oeuvre as a whole. Classical theories of both narratology and genetic criticism, as well as typologies of draft material (de Biasi 1996) tend to focus on the texts and *avant-textes* of single works. This is a plea to also take account of the oeuvre and the 'sous-oeuvre' (Van Hulle 2022, 113–19; 164)—the entire oeuvre's genetic dossier, including for instance notes, commonplace books, diaries, correspondence, marginalia in personal libraries and unpublished or abandoned works that did not make it into the author's official canon.

No matter on which scale these literary geneses are studied, they 'beckon the reader to investigate the messily unresolved inconsistencies and disunities that corrupt the text', as Charles Mascia notes with reference to the ragged narration in Melville's *Billy Budd*, referring to John Wenke's unsettling observation that, although a Genetic Text edition exists of this work (edited by Hayford and Sealts), 'as late as 2006 [...] virtually no *Billy Budd* criticism has made use of the materials of the Genetic Text' (Wenke 2006, 502; see Mascia's essay in this volume). That is why it is appropriate to conclude the present volume with an essay on the relationship between genetic narratology and scholarly editing by Rüdiger Nutt-Kofoth, who made an equally shocking observation regarding the relative neglect of genetic and historical-critical editions in German literary criticism and discusses the bidirectional interdisciplinary potential, in terms of both narratological considerations as a precondition for editorial decisions, and editorial representations as a basis for narrative analysis.

The Unnarrated: The Allure of the Untold

So far, to make the point about the mutual enrichment of narratology and genetic criticism, the focus has been on what is being narrated. But a field where genetic narratology becomes especially fascinating is the realm of the unnarrated. There is no shortage of negative designations in narratology. Brian Richardson introduced the notion of 'denarration' for narrative situations in which the narrator blatantly contradicts or denies what he has just told us (Richardson 2006, 87), as in the last lines of Beckett's *Molloy*: 'Then I went back into the house and wrote, It is midnight. The rain is beating on the windows. It was not midnight. It was not raining.' (Beckett 2009, 184); and Gerald Prince discusses the 'unnarratable' (for instance, when in certain periods the recounting of certain actions is taboo) and the 'disnarrated' (actions which do not happen in the world represented, but which are mentioned nonetheless). (Prince 1988, 3).[7]

The 'unnarrated', in contrast, consists of 'ellipses found in narrative', either 'inferrable from a significant lacuna in the chronology' or 'explicitly underlined by the narrator ("I will not recount what happened during that fateful week")' (Prince 1988, 2). This kind of ellipsis has a special allure. There is a fascination that emanates from the 'unnarrated'. And while 'unnarrating' or 'untelling' may sound weird, it does make sense as a verb in the sense of making something untold.

---

7   'For me, and to put it most generally, terms, phrases, and passages that consider what did not or does not take place ("this could've happened but didn't"; "this didn't happen but could've"), whether they pertain to the narrator and his or her narration [...] or to one of the characters and his or her actions [...] constitute the disnarrated. When I speak of the latter, I am thus referring to alethic expressions of impossibility or unrealized possibility, deontic expressions of observed prohibition, epistemic expressions of ignorance, ontologic expressions of nonexistence, purely imagined worlds, desired worlds, or intended worlds, unfulfilled expectations, unwarranted beliefs, failed attempts, crushed hopes, suppositions and false calculations, errors and lies, and so forth.' (Prince 1988, 3)

A good example can be found in Samuel Beckett's novel *Molloy*, written in French first and then translated into English by Beckett himself. At a certain moment, the narrator asks the rhetorical question: 'What then was the source of Ballyba's prosperity?' And he immediately adds: 'I'll tell you.' He then tries to present himself as an omniscient narrator, one who purports to give an 'authentic account of the actual experiences of individuals'—one of the 'various technical characteristics of the novel' according to Ian Watt (1957, 27). But then the narrator suddenly says: 'No, I'll tell you nothing. Nothing.' (Beckett 2009, 140)

Several pages further in the published text, there is another strange moment, when a character is introduced out of the blue and just as quickly abandoned again. He is called the 'Obidil':

> And with regard to the Obidil, of whom I have refrained from speaking, until now, and whom I so longed to see face to face, all I can say with regard to him is this, that I never saw him, either face to face or darkly, perhaps there is no such person, that would not greatly surprise me. (Beckett 2009, 170)

As a result, the textual surface is disturbed by these two anomalies: first, the narrator's announcement that he is going to tell us something which, on second thought, he doesn't do; and secondly the totally incongruous mention of a character called Obidil who does not feature anywhere else in the published text.

To scrutinise what is happening here, it is useful to know that while the eponymous character Molloy is the narrator of the first part of the novel, the second part is narrated by a man called Moran. Moran has been assigned to go and look for Molloy. Before he sets out, he describes the Molloy country, called 'Ballyba'. He talks about its geography and its agriculture, and then he starts explaining Ballyba's economy:

> D'où Ballyba tirait-il donc ses richesses? Je vais vous le dire.
> [What then was the source of Ballyba's prosperity? I'll tell you.]
> (Beckett 2009, 140)

In the manuscript, this is followed by a sizeable section describing Ballyba's remarkable economy, entirely based on the excrements of its citizens. According to Moran's account, the citizens' stools were the source of Ballyba's riches. Starting from the age of two, every citizen was to oblige the Market Gardening Organisation with a certain amount of faecal matter every year. All of this is taken very seriously, and recounted accordingly. To keep the faecal production at the highest level and producing primarily for the home market, travel abroad is strictly limited by the Organisation, headed by the Obidil, an official who is entirely dressed in white and who is the only one who can issue travel orders. The substantial fragment—more than a dozen handwritten pages—is meticulous in the scatological description of this economy. And it establishes a context for the mysterious character of the Obidil.

When Beckett had finished a typescript of his novel and had shown it to confidants, he decided to cut the passage. In grey pencil, he marks the start of the cut by means of an X in the right margin and a vertical line just after the sentence 'Je vais vous le dire', adding above the line: 'Non, je ne dirai rien.'—'No, I'll tell you nothing.' (BDMP4, FT1, 214r) In the printer's copy (kept at the University of Reading, UoR MS 5859, 214r), Beckett crossed out the whole passage with a big St Andrew's cross in blue pencil. If he had simply wanted to omit this ten-page passage, he could easily have done so without leaving any traces by starting the cut just *before* the question 'What then was the source of Ballyba's prosperity?' But he chose to let the narrator ask the question, say that he was going to tell us and then unsay his statement, leaving a textual scar and drawing attention to the unnarrated passage, so that the readers are left with the sense that they don't get to see everything.

Beckett deliberately gives us just enough tips to make us suspect a gigantic narrative iceberg underneath the textual surface—the underlying link between the two narrative anomalies. And this invisible iceberg turns out to be a biting satire of Ireland's religious, economic and political attitudes at the time. For Ballyba is said to be the region around the market-town of 'Bally', most probably inspired by the Irish name for Dublin, Baile átha Cliath, pronounced 'Bally ah cleeah'. Its self-sufficient economy based on its citizens' own faeces reads like a satire of Ireland's policy of economic protectionism in the 1930s, introduced by the Fianna Fáil government under Éamon de Valera. And the Obidil, the only person who can issue travel orders—dressed in white like a pope, deciding who goes to heaven and who doesn't—is an anagram (and a mirror image) of Libido. That underlying iceberg is the unnarrated. In this particular case, it turns the setting into a satirical chronotope, the ideological centre of the text. Most remarkable—both genetically and narratologically—is that Beckett decides to *take away* that centre; moreover, he does not take it away himself but makes his narrator decide to do so. In terms of narrative time, he moves from one extreme to the other on Mieke Bal's scale—between 'time of narration' and 'story time' (qtd. in Herman and Vervaeck 2019, 66; see also Bal 2017). In the manuscript, the narrative is 'paused' when Moran starts talking about the economy of Ballyba, which the reader does not really need in order to be able to follow the narrative of Moran's pursuit of Molloy. By cutting this bit, Beckett could have simply turned it into a continuation of the narrative (in the middle of Bal's scale, where 'time of narration' and 'story time' are more or less equal). But by making his narrator say 'No, I'll tell you nothing', he actually presents it as an ellipsis.

In terms of 'narration', it is important that he does not do so implicitly but *explicitly*. Beckett first styles Moran as a Balzacian narrator or storyteller, focused on the pursuit of clarity. His aim is what Beckett criticised in Balzac's treatment of characters, 'situating them in facts that will explain them' (Rachel Burrows's student notes, TCD MIC 60, 69). Against this background, it is telling that Beckett makes Moran undo or 'unnarrate' his explanation of Ballyba's economy, burying it, hiding it under the surface, obscuring it. Beckett's counterexample to Balzac was Dostoevsky, whose characters always seem to remain in the shadows (Gide 1923, 75; TCD MIC 60, 21). The unnarrated contributes to this feeling of obscurity. It makes the narrative less clear, but therefore more intriguing. Instead of Balzacian clarity, Beckett gives us a literary *clair-obscur*. The narrator first presents himself as the explainer, but then immediately becomes the teaser. No sooner has he whet the reader's curiosity than he frustrates it. If Beckett had made the cut *before* the question 'What was the source of Ballyba's prosperity?', the reader would have been blissfully ignorant; they would not even have been aware of any '*Leerstelle*' or 'gap of indeterminacy' in Wolfgang Iser's terms (Iser 1980). By making the cut *after* the question, readers are not blissfully but painfully ignorant; they are made aware of a gap. The narrator gestures towards something that is actually there but is not being told. What would the economy of Ballyba have been like? He invites us to fill the gap in whatever way we want. As genetically informed readers, we do find a suggestion (the narrator gestures in a certain satirical direction) but we also find the clear trace of a narratologically highly relevant act:

the conscious omission of this suggestion, as well as the deliberate trace of this act in the published text.

Playing the devil's advocate again, one could argue that taking this suggestion into account limits our reading experience. But the question is whether that is necessarily the case. As a general reader of the published text, one can read this passage as an invitation to fill the gap with whatever economy one can come up with. And it seems fair to say that not many readers, if any, would ever come up with an economy based on its own citizens' faeces. In that sense, taking the drafts into account can open up a reader's limited imaginative capacities and enrich their reading experience.

Genetic narratology is a form of framing. Usually, narratologists work with only one textual version—'the' published text. But if an author's drafts have been preserved, narratologists have the choice to frame the work in various ways. They can choose to work with the finished product only, but they can also frame the work differently and include the manuscripts in their narratological analysis.

2. Narratives of the Genesis

While genetic narratology is a form of framing, it also offers a vocabulary to enhance our awareness of this act of framing. Recounting the genesis of a literary work or any creative process is a narrative act in and of itself. A genetic dossier is often marked by several gaps and imperfections in the archival record. Even if the writing process has been recorded with keystroke logging software, there may be moments the author used another writing tool or accidentally forgot (or consciously decided not) to record a certain writing session. Genetic critics try to fill these gaps of indeterminacy by reconstructing the conditions of the creative imagination. The cognitive acts of inventing, undoing and revising can be hard to retrace. It is indeed impossible to enter the writer's mind after the fact, which is why Louis Hay advises critics to stick to the traces of writing: 'la trace, toute la trace et rien que la trace' ['the trace, the whole trace and nothing but the trace'] (Hay in Hay and Lebrave 2010, 154).

But these traces sometimes do give us clues as to what writers did not yet know at certain instances in the process. It is striking how many traces indicate second thoughts or moments the author changed their mind. While working on her last (unfinished) work, Virginia Woolf first wrote that 'Anon' dies, and then deleted this again 'as though not yet convinced of Anon's death', as Joshua Phillips notes (see his essay in this volume); in his plan for *Die Poggenpuhls*, the German novelist Theodor Fontane develops a scene that takes place on the day before a birthday, 'but Fontane is still unsure whose birthday' as Matthias Grüne observes (see his essay in this volume); in Melville's *Billy Budd*, the dramatisation of misreading and the problem of narrative access are themes that probably did not guide the narrative from its conception but 'emerged gradually', as Charles Mascia concludes (see his essay in this volume). Experienced writers like Stephen King even appear to count on this period of unknowing or this element of narrative ignorance as a measure of suspense, reasoning that 'if I'm not able to guess with any accuracy how the damned thing is going to turn out, even with my inside knowledge of coming events, I can be pretty sure of keeping the reader in a state of page-turning anxiety' (King, qtd. in Vincent Neyt's contribution to this volume).

Writers' own accounts of the writing process are fascinating documents that keep captivating readers' interest, as testified by the series of 'The Art of Fiction' interviews in *The Paris Review* that is still going strong after more than seventy years and more than two hundred and fifty interviews since 1953. But genetic narratology is not a form of intentionalism and the rule of thumb in genetic criticism is never to put full trust in an author's own retrospective statements about what they did or did not do during their works' genesis. This critical distrust is prompted by an awareness of the universal phenomenon of narrativisation. In the context of narratology, narrativisation is described by Monika Fludernik as a coping mechanism to deal with unfamiliar textual features, consisting of 'taking recourse to available, diverse interpretative patterns' and 'narrative schemata' (Fludernik 1996, 31; 34). But while this reading strategy describes a way of coping with strangeness in narrative fiction, reality—as is well known—is often even stranger than fiction. As a result, the phenomenon of narrativisation is—sometimes consciously, but very often inadvertently—applied to the strangeness and oddities of the creative process, imposing the framework of narrativity on the genesis to reduce its inconsistencies.

Samuel Beckett was aware of this phenomenon before it was made explicit and labelled as a narratological phenomenon, applying it in the first instance to the notion of the self. Especially in his novel *L'Innommable / The Unnamable*, he makes the character-narrator repudiate the self rather than being lulled into the belief that it can be grasped by imposing the framework of a narrative onto it (Van Hulle and Weller 2014; Bernaerts and Van Hulle 2013). Elsewhere in his oeuvre, for instance in the manuscripts of the radio play *Cascando* (see Pim Verhulst's essay in this volume), Beckett refers to his aim as conducting a story to the point of unnarratability—'jusqu'à l'inénarrable'. Fully aware of the universal impulse to—retrospectively—narrativise the strangeness of any work's genesis, I suggest we take this Beckettian objective as a motto for all our ventures into genetic narratology: while retracing the writing process will always involve a certain form of narrativisation, we can enhance our awareness of this mechanism and try to pinpoint moments of unnarratability rather than cover up or smooth out the strangeness of creative processes.

Works Cited

Bal, Mieke (2017), *Narratology: Introduction to the Theory of Narrative*. 4th edition (Toronto: University of Toronto Press).

Beckett, Samuel (2009), *Molloy*, ed. by Shane Weller (London: Faber & Faber).

Bernaerts, Lars and Dirk Van Hulle (2013), 'Narrative across Versions: Narratology Meets Genetic Criticism', *Poetics Today*, 34.3: 281–326, https://doi.org/10.1215/03335372-2325232.

Bernaerts, Lars, Gunther Martens and Dirk Van Hulle (2011), 'Narratologie en Tekstgenese. Een Terreinverkenning', *Spiegel der Letteren*, 53.3: 281–309.

Cohn, Dorrit (1968), 'K. enters *The Castle*: On the Change of Person in Kafka's Manuscript', *Euphorion*, 62: 28–45.

De Biasi, Pierre-Marc (1996), 'What Is a Literary Draft? Toward a Functional Typology of Genetic Documentation', *Yale French Studies*, 89: 26–58, https://doi.org/10.2307/2930337.

Gide, André (1923), *Dostoïevsky* (Paris: Plon).

Hay, Louis, and Jean-Louis Lebrave (2010), 'Lettres ouvertes: Une génétique sans rivages ? (par Louis Hay) Post-scriptum—L'ordinateur, Olympe de l'écriture ? (par Jean-Louis Lebrave)', *Genesis* 31, 151–55, https://doi.org/10.4000/genesis.386.

Herman, Luc and Bart Vervaeck (2019), *Handbook of Narrative Analysis*. 2nd edition (Lincoln, NE: University of Nebraska Press).

Iser, Wolfgang (1980), *The Act of Reading: A Theory of Aesthetic Response* (Baltimore, MD: Johns Hopkins University Press).

Melville, Herman (1962), *Billy Budd, Sailor (An Inside Narrative)*, ed. by Harrison Hayford and Merton M. Sealts (Chicago: University of Chicago Press).

Richardson, Brian (2006), *Unnatural Voices: Extreme Narration in Modern and Contemporary Fiction* (Columbus: Ohio State University Press).

Van Hulle, Dirk (2022), *Genetic Criticism: Tracing Creativity in Literature* (Oxford: Oxford University Press).

Van Hulle, Dirk and Shane Weller (2014), *The Making of Samuel Beckett's 'L'Innommable' / 'The Unnamable'* (London: Bloomsbury).

Watt, Ian (1957), *The Rise of the Novel* (Berkeley and Los Angeles: University of California Press).

Wenke, John (2006), 'Melville's Transhistorical Voice: "Billy Budd" and the Fragmentation of Forms', in: *A Companion to Herman Melville*, ed. by Wyn Kelley (Hoboken: John Wiley & Sons).

2. Metagenesis: Manuscripts, and How Metanarration and Metafiction Contribute to Their Analysis

Karin Kukkonen[1]

Introduction

'Reader, I married him'. This is perhaps one of the most famous sentences delivered in what narratology calls metanarration. Here, Jane Eyre turns to her audience and reminds them of the fact that she has been telling her own story, from hindsight, all along. The process of narration comes to the fore against the weave of the narrative itself. Metanarration is one of the ways through which fiction can reveal itself. Another more striking case would be metalepsis, namely, when characters leave their fictional worlds to interact with readers or authors. In *The Eyre Affaire* (Fforde 2001), Jane Eyre gets abducted from Brontë's novel. As she disappears from the manuscript, all mentions of her in all copies of the book turn blank. Novels reflect constantly on their own madness, challenging readers to meet themselves and their own preconceptions of the world through the tenuous truth-status and epistemic flexibility that comes with fiction (see Kukkonen 2020 for an extended version of

---

[1] Acknowledgements: this chapter draws on material from my monograph *Creativity and Contingency in Literary Writing* (forthcoming), and develops certain methodological and theoretical reflections around the notion of metagenesis from the book. Work on this chapter and the book was financed by LCE—Centre for Literature, Cognition and Emotions (FPIII, University of Oslo), and supported by exchanges in the LCE manuscript group. I would like to thank Stefka Eriksen and Stijn Vervaet, as well as Dirk Van Hulle and the reviewers of this volume, for their comments on earlier versions.

this argument). This quality of literature is fully realised in postmodern metalepsis, such as *The Eyre Affaire*, but it can also be found throughout realist texts, such as *Jane Eyre*, where it more commonly takes the form of metanarration. Metanarration refers to narrators drawing attention to their own telling or writing, while metafiction is a larger term that also includes instances where narratives represent characters crossing the boundaries of the text, such as in metalepsis.

The Eyre Affaire gives the manuscript a prominent role, and, as we shall see, the material written text also plays an important role in Charlotte Brontë's novels. The question arises, then, whether such instances of metanarration and metafiction can contribute to the project of a genetic, manuscript-oriented narratology, or whether such references to the madeness of the literary text are mere fictional invention? In this article, I propose to consider this question under the category of what I call 'metagenesis'. Metagenesis, I suggest, can be used to expand the genetic dossier and to bring manuscript genetics into further dialogue with narratology. It offers in particular the opportunity to draw on insights from embodied approaches to the study of narrative and literature, as well as bring manuscript genetics further into conversations around literary creativity. In the first section, I will define manuscript genetics and sketch out its place in an enlarged genetic dossier. In the second section, I propose an example analysis of two passages from Charlotte Brontë's writings to demonstrate how metagenetics works in practice. The third section, finally, addresses theoretical and methodological challenges that may arise from such a dialogue between manuscript genetics, narratology and literary studies, and proposes a number of ways by which they can be met.

Endogenesis, Exogenesis, Epigenesis—Metagenesis?

What are the elements that make up a genetic dossier, that is, the documentation of the process of writing that contributes to a genetic analysis of manuscripts? We start with endogenesis. Initially, we have the different drafts written by the author, any material trace of the author's revisions leading up to the moment when she designates the text as 'ready for print' (*'bon à tirer'*; De Biasi 1996). Charlotte Brontë's three novels published in her lifetime offer to my knowledge the only fair copy manuscripts for an endogenetic dossier. *Endogenesis* refers predominantly to processes of rewriting (Biasi 1996, 43). The circle can be widened with *exogenesis*. Here, draft manuscripts are complemented by other written documents surrounding the creative process, such as the author's notebooks, plans or copies of passages from other books. These documents make up the materials from which a broader analysis of the text can be developed, drawing on authors' formulations of ideas and plans that do not appear as variations to the final text but nevertheless contribute to its conceptual and practical emergence. Brontë, again, has not much to offer here, because her correspondence only rarely discusses the writing process or her plans and designs for writing. Pierre-Marc de Biasi (1996) takes the terms endogenesis and exogenesis from Raymonde Debray Genette (Debray Genette 1979; 1988, 24) but gives them a more specific, contrastive meaning, defining exogenetics as 'any writing process devoted to research, selection and incorporation, focused on information stemming from a source exterior to the writing' (43–44). De Biasi is quite clear in this specification that exogenesis needs to refer to written texts prepared by the author. The stuffed parrot that Flaubert apparently placed on his desk while writing 'Un Cœur Simple' does not qualify, and neither do the landscapes Flaubert had seen in the Near East (De Biasi 1996, 44–45).

The crucial point appears to be the written form here. Reading notes, plans in notebooks and copied out passages from other works, all fall under the category of 'exogenesis'. Arguably, the author (or one of their collaborators) needs to record, sketch out or write down the material and transform it into a written text. Dirk Van Hulle (2022, Ch.1.2.1) proposes to take the work of manuscript genetics beyond the moment when the text is published, and to include the work of editors, typesetters and translators. He calls this dimension of the genetic dossier *epigenesis*. All collaborators involved in the life of a text generate new versions, sometimes, because the work remains incomplete at the time of publication, for example, upon the death of the author, or because changes in the reception context make textual revisions necessary or desirable. Van Hulle's proposal links with John Bryant's notion of the 'fluid text' (2002), where different versions of a published text constitute a continuous development, especially after the text goes into print. They both argue that texts are anything but fixed after the moment when the author decides to give the manuscript into print, and show that the analytical methods from manuscript genetics also contribute to our understanding of the life of a text after publication. Van Hulle (2022), however, goes further than Bryant in highlighting the material and social dimension of epigenesis. Epigenesis underlines the importance of a consideration of the 'creative ecology' around a literary text. The 'creative ecology' unfolds in an author's library, her networks of collaboration, etc. In principle, it includes also Flaubert's stuffed parrot, as well as his pens and papers, as the material environment in which he composes his text, but also his collaborators. *Jane Eyre*, *Shirley* and *Villette* would be placed into the context of Brontë's desk and writing implements. Such an approach would easily go into dialogue with current work in book history, for example Barbara Heritage's (2021) investigation into Brontë's desk.

Where does metagenesis, that is, the literary text reflecting on its own making, come into the picture? Let us consider a case from *Villette*. After a description of something like a dream-state experienced by the narrator Lucy Snowe, we read: 'Cancel the whole of that, if you please, reader' (Brontë [1853] 2000, 57). Lucy Snowe makes an unusual request of her readers, namely, to 'cancel' the passage that they had just read. Would it not rather be the task of the author to 'cancel' the passage, while readers maybe could 'forget' it after reading? Does 'cancelling' a passage not require a direct intervention in the original manuscript? What is Brontë doing here? This statement has provoked some critical discussion in Brontë Studies and it has also drawn attention to the manuscripts for *Villette*. Lucy Hanks (2020) observes that Brontë had actually cancelled a passage just before that sentence in the manuscript; more so, that she did not merely strike through the words, but cut the sentence out from the paper. This is a case where I propose a metagenetic approach can be brought to bear most straightforwardly, since behind an explicit metanarrational statement in the novel hides a trace of the author's practice in the manuscript.

The ways in which *Villette*'s references to scissors and Lucy Snowe's strategic use of silences work together with the manuscript cancellations is not captured by endogenesis, exogenesis or epigenesis. I therefore propose to complement these dimensions of textual genesis with 'metagenesis', that is, the ways in which the final text reflects on the process of its making. Why introduce a fourth genesis with yet another Greek preposition? There are a number of answers to this question that I shall motivate and contextualise in detail throughout this paper. First, many texts explicitly reflect on the process behind them by referring to authors' practices and narrators' strategies. Indeed, I would argue that such a metafictional element is a general feature of literary fiction well beyond the historical confines of postmodernism. Manuscript genetics has so far rarely deployed this systematically as a resource in analysis. Second, writing a literary text involves creating an intimate connection between form and content. The literary text presents a design for readers' ongoing processes of meaning-making, where what readers read and how the text presents it, for example in the pacing of the narrative or focalisation, constantly inform one another. When looking at formal revisions, it is easy to forget the element of content that is transformed and nevertheless serves as an important anchor for authors' meaning-making. Third, while manuscript genetics works through the different versions of the avant-texte, it always (implicitly) compares them with the final version. This is necessary in order to establish how authors revise, what change counts as a revision or as a 'pentimento' (where early states are reinstated), and to establish an overall timeline in the writing process. The final manuscript, however, can also contribute to an understanding of how recursive loops in the writing process emerge, in which an idea that is located on the level of content (such as the name of a character) then feeds into a formal choice later on, or vice versa. These three answers are closely connected to one another and underwrite an understanding of creative writing as a recursive process, where authors keep revising.

A fourth answer relates to the importance of practice in the creative process. An author's practice is a complex configuration of actions. It includes an author's skill in using their writing implements, be they pen and paper, typewriters, or sound recordings. It also includes their skill in producing prose in a particular language, in spinning a narrative and in bringing the experience of a character into linguistic form. At the same time, the practice of an author also lies in risking the smooth performance of all these skills by seeking out contingent and unexpected ways of deploying them in order to generate the necessary creative energy (see Kukkonen, forthcoming). The issue lies in how to best reconstruct the practice of an author to bring to bear the evidence from manuscript genetics and in particular the 'creative ecology' or epigenesis (see Van Hulle 2022). A phenomenological approach may be possible for some cases, as Van Hulle (2017) suggests. However, one can also take into account how authors represent practices in the literary texts themselves, and moreover, how they talk about them in their interviews, author's notes and reflections around writing.

Metagenesis refers to the ways in which a text reflects on its own making, and it is linked to the other three dimensions of 'genesis' so far established. A metagenetic analysis needs to take into account how the final text contrasts, complements or mirrors what we can tell about an author's practices from the manuscript in an endogenetic analysis. A metagenetic analysis may also draw on exogenetic elements, as it connects with epigenesis through representations of environments and practices that constitute a 'creative ecology'. Indeed, it may be argued that the use of written language itself constitutes a 'creative ecology' that is predisposed for metagenesis (Clark 1998).

The initial proponents of genetic criticism position themselves clearly against any kind of 'psychology of creativity', exactly, because they draw on the concrete evidence of manuscripts. Still, they hold that studying manuscripts is often linked to the 'unconscious' of an author's work (see De Biasi 1996, 26). It sheds light on processes that authors are not aware of, and it draws out emergent developments in the composition of the literary work that do not merely instantiate an initial plan. Indeed, here, poststructuralist arguments about the 'death of the author' overlap with embodied arguments about 'material agency' emerging from the encounter between pen, paper and the author's hand (Bernini 2014). Rather than intentions preformed in the mind and then realised on paper, the approach from material agency suggests that intentionality arises in the encounter between writer and material environment. Approaching the writing process through metagenesis does not at all deny the pre-conscious, contingent and unexpected nature of creativity. Indeed, it finds it often emphasised. It is not unusual that authors express an inability to grasp exactly what happens when they write. However, when expository statements fail them, they can still make use of the affordances of fiction in order to bring their intuitions about their practice to paper imaginatively and make them available to readers.

Metagenesis, then, offers another way towards the ineffable in literary writing.

Two Metagenetic Sketches

What do Brontë's cancellations tell us about her writing process, and how can we read them in dialogue with the narratorial dynamics of the novel? Ileana Marin (2014) suggests that the cancellations by cutting into the paper reflect Brontë's efforts to censor herself, so that not even readers of the manuscript (very few, but personally known to Brontë) would be able to reconstruct what she had written. These gaps in narration are also palpable in the narration of Lucy Snowe, who, especially in the opening passages of the book often qualifies her statements with 'I could not say' or 'I do not know'. Lucy Hanks (2020) proposes a more 'productive' way of reading the silences, namely, that Lucy Snowe thereby places the need to fill in the gaps of the narrative on her readers. Brontë's narrator, in other words, empowers herself by essentially saying 'your turn' to her readers, prompting them into interpretative action. These interpretations draw evidence from the endogenetic and metagenetic dossier, but they perform not a complete manuscript analysis.

Let us look again at the passage I cited initially. 'Cancel the whole of that, if you please, reader—or rather let it stand, and draw thence a moral—an alliterative, text-hand copy—"Day-dreams are delusions of the demon"' ([1853] 2020, 57). Lucy Snowe actually stops the cancellation immediately, asking readers to 'let it stand', and supplying a different, moral inference. 'It' refers to a description of Lucy Snowe's mental state as a lush summer landscape. Soon enough, she needs to realise that she was mistaken. Instead of cancelling the memory, however, she proposes to note a 'moral' in 'text-hand copy', that is, in the hand of school children, learning their ABC with alliterative statements such as 'daydreams are delusions of the demon'. She asks us to overwrite the sensuous memory with the standardised and aesthetically unpleasing hand of taught at school, as well as a soul-deadening message. We can easily read here a metaphor of Lucy Snowe's profession as a school-teacher who would see many such corrections, and whose need to earn her money in this way keeps her (potentially) from unfolding herself fully. Yet, exactly in choosing to make the textual transformation palpable, Lucy Snowe also creates a sense of variants in readers.

Variants and variations are key terms in manuscript genetics. Different versions of the same text distinguish themselves through (1) variants on the level of individual words and phrases and (2) variations on the level of how meaning overall configures (see Ferrer 2016 for a discussion of that distinction). A variant replaces one word with another without necessarily changing the overall effect of the passage, while a variation requires to be read differently. The objection that it is almost impossible to identify a variant that is not also a variation puts a finger on the main point of the argument here. Any variant has the potential to turn into a variation. However, there are textual changes where the shift in meaning is fully formulated and fleshed out and where a variation is more easily identified. Brontë clearly provides an example of a variation here. The variation is charged by the fact that it is related back to the variant that gave rise to the reconfiguration in the meaning initially. Shifting the direction of transformation from variant to variation backwards is a hallmark of the interpretative processes on which metagenesis builds. It often foregrounds the material dimension of the manuscript in order to achieve this effect.

A full analysis of the *Villette* manuscript shows that when Brontë cancels, she actually uses strikethroughs more often than cuts, and that the cut cancellations are often linked to written revisions. Barbara Heritage (2021, 513) has established that Brontë very likely used not scissors but her quill knife in order to make the cut-cancellations in *Villette*. The precision of these revisions enables a second, more playful context in which we can read Brontë's practice in *Villette*. Consider another cancellation. In an allegorical dialogue between Reason and Imagination, we have two cancellations by knife on the same page, as well as several revisions by pen (BL Add MS 43481 f.113r). The first cancellation by knife has been repaired by glueing a piece of paper behind it, but curators have omitted to do so for the second cancellation, and you can read the words 'dashing against the panes' behind it (BL Add MS 43481 f.114r). The cancellation by knife has created a window onto the next folio. The phrase revealed, referring to rainfall, then seems to make its way into the revision earlier in the passage, where Brontë adds that Reason attacks her with 'savage, ceaseless blows', akin to the rain that 'dashes against the panes'. Brontë may well have used her knife as an aleatory tool in the revision process of *Villette*, revealing sentences not only in order to silence her narrator, but also in order to get inspiration from contingency.

Further examples can be found throughout *Villette*. A cut between the words 'a [ ] sober-sides' reveals the word 'mournful' (later crossed out) from the next folio, and the space between the words is then replaced with 'melancholy' (BL Add MS 43482, fol. 20r and fol. 21r). In her conversation with M. Paul, he complains that Lucy Snowe had 'inspired the highest hopes' thanks to her 'gravity, austerity and simplicity' (BL Add MS 43482, fol. 18r). The 'austerity' is a later revision that corresponds to 'had I not a bow of ribbon at my neck', which is revealed on the next page through the window made by a cut (BL Add MS 43482, fol. 19r). In other cases, multiple cuts are made on a page, opening further possibilities. When Lucy sits in reverie in the school room, contemplating her situation, we have a cut that reveals the phrase 'a human head', namely that of Mme Beck who is the object of description on the next folio (BL Add MS 43481, fol. 225r, fol. 226r). The 'human head' makes its way into the revision on the manuscript page, adding 'mock dry lips like baffling mirage', but is then deleted again by strike-through. The 'suffering' and 'agony' of Lucy in these scene comes to be contrasted by the 'communication of information' and 'perhaps she amused herself', referring to Mme Beck's habits of surveillance.

The playful approach to revealing what is on the next folio with knife cancellations[2] may have been inspired by what Brontë was writing. As Olga Springer (2020) remarks, *Villette* is full of oracular moments when characters read the future out of facial features, most strikingly when M. Paul's investigation of Lucy Snowe's face enables her to enter Mme Beck's school. We do not have a manuscript that is earlier than the fair copy for *Villette*, but arguably, drafts of these scenes had already been written when Brontë takes her quill knife to the fair copy, enacting her own oracle.

---

2   It is worth remembering that not all knife cancellations in *Villette* have stimulated revisions. Many of the cancellations with revision may have been motivated by the aleatory device, but then contingency did not reveal a relevant new phrase. The aleatory knife cancellations in *Villette* are playful throughout, however, removing the text from one page of paper in order to see what may lie beneath, sometimes turning to the silliness of cutting out a single dash (BL Add 43481, fol.122r).

Let us move to our second metagenetic sketch, which draws on a metafictional example. In *Shirley*, her second published novel, Brontë experiments with an omniscient third-person narrator and achieves an uneven result. In the initial passages, the narrator presents characters as if she pointed them out to readers—'You shall see them, reader' ([1848] 2007, 6)—and promises to narrate as if she and readers were both present in the scene: 'You and I will join the party, see what is to be seen, and hear what is to be heard' ([1848] 2007, ibid.). The third-person narrator is located in the fictional world and physically present, as the events take place. This is a strategy that is relatively unproblematic for first-person narrators like Jane Eyre and Lucy Snowe, but difficult for a third-person, omniscient narrator. In her juvenilia, Brontë solves the problem by having her narrators hide behind curtains or emerge from cup-boards,[3] but in her realist novels, such narratorial trickery does not work very well. Indeed, already in the juvenilia, Brontë appears to be aware of the problem. She writes in a short story called 'Strange Events',

> Whilst I was listlessly turning over the huge leaves of that most ponderous volume, I fell into the strangest train of thought that ever visited my mind [...] it seemed as if I was the mere idea of some other creature's brain [...] I felt myself raised suddenly to the ceiling, and ere I was aware, behold two immense, sparkling, bright blue globes within a few years of me. I was in a hand wide enough to almost to grasp the Tower of all Nations, and when it lowered me to the floor, I saw a huge personification of myself—hundreds of feet high—standing against the great Oriel. (Brontë [1830] 1987, 257–58)

Brontë's first-person narrator Charles Wellesley, a recurring narrator across her juvenilia, becomes aware of his nature as a creature of fiction. The realisation, however, interestingly does not lead to a metalepsis. Wellesley does not look up to behold Charlotte Brontë but to behold himself.

This is an interesting twist on what we know about the 'creative ecology' from which Charlotte Brontë's storytelling emerges. The Brontë siblings were presented with a box of toy soldiers by their father, which then turned into the protagonists for the game-play and

---

3   See Kukkonen (forthcoming) for a detailed discussion of how Brontë re-writes her juvenilia in *Shirley*.

for the narratives that make up the substantial body of the juvenilia of Charlotte, Emily, Anne and Branwell Brontë (see Ratchford 1949; Murray 1997; Gao 2021). Charlotte Brontë picks up a toy soldier who turns not only into her hero-protagonist, but very soon also into her narrator persona. Even the manuscripts of Charlotte Brontë's juvenilia are produced to scale for the toy soldiers: written in microscript on mini-folios the size of a large post stamp.[4] The creative process is tightly connected to the creative ecology of the Brontë nursery, where these toy soldiers would encounter, observe and communicate with one another. When she writes 'Strange Events' at age 13 Brontë already lays the finger on the problem of such a highly embodied approach to narration. The narrator always needs to be on the scene, and the only instance available to provide an outside perspective is he himself. For a novel like *Shirley*, with its historical scope and its double love story between two couples, a narrator modelled on a toy soldier would no longer suffice.

'Strange Events' as a metagenetic document can be placed in a productive dialogue with *Shirley*, because this is the novel where Brontë works through the problem of embodiment and the omniscient, third-person narrator (see Kukkonen, forthcoming, for a full discussion). A metagenetic analysis can throw light on how Brontë revisits her own narrative practice by reconstructing, as much as possible, the different material constellations available and imagined in the 'creative ecology' where she was working.

These two metagenetic sketches show, hopefully, the potential for manuscript genetics. Considering the ways in which literary texts reflect on their own making can easily direct attention in the analysis of the manuscript material, suggest what to look out for and provide a more holistic perspective of the creative process where both the material process of writing and revising the manuscript and the imaginative process of thinking up scenes and language for the narrative are entwined in a recursive process. It links imagined scenarios in the text with endogenetic (sketch 1) as well as exogenetic and epigenetic (sketch 2) dimensions.

---

4 See Kukkonen (forthcoming) for a full discussion of the ways in which the format of the mini-folios shaped Brontë's sense of narrative proportion and the plot of *Jane Eyre*.

Methodological Challenges and Opportunities

Metagenesis draws attention to what literary texts can reveal about the creative process behind them. It extends the genetic dossier by taking into account the literary texts themselves and other forms of writing where authors reflect on their creative work in literary form. Fictionalisations of extra-literary forms, such as imaginary interviews, or essays would also fall under this category.

An analysis starting from metafictional or metanarrative elements, I hope to have shown, has the potential to open new perspectives on the analysis of manuscripts. These are rooted in the dynamics of the creative process where writers produce not only words on paper but also build sentences and fictional scenarios that are closely entwined with one another. However, the approach comes not without its challenges, and as the case of *Villette* demonstrates, it may not be wise to take a narrator as a direct stand-in for the author. Also when Brontë's narrator invites readers to look over Louis Moore's shoulders as the teacher writes an essay about his feelings for Shirley, Brontë is in all likelihood not showing us how she herself wrote the passage. We can compare Brontë's (1997) own essays, written in French when she was a school teacher in training at the Hegers' school in Brussels with Shirley's essay on the 'Bluestocking' or with Louis' reflections, but these are by no means direct reproductions. The metafictional or metanarrative reflection does not provide a short-cut into genesis.

Indeed, the anecdotes and legends around authors' writing practices, as they emerge from contemporaries' testimonies and sometimes from their own writings, need to be compared analytically with the evidence from the genetic dossier. Charlotte Brontë, for example, has been influentially characterised as a 'trance-writer' by Sandra Gilbert and Susan Gubar in *The Madwoman in the Attic* (Gilbert and Gubar 1979, 311). The claim is based on the idea that Brontë wrote with her eyes closed. Gilbert and Gubar write: 'as [biographer] Winifred Gérin points out, the irregular lines of her manuscripts indicate that she did write in this way, a habit that Gérin suggests she adopted "intentionally the better to sharpen the inner vision and shut out her bodily surroundings"' (311–312). The claim is first made by Brontë herself in her diaries written at the boarding school Roe Head, and then taken up by Elizabeth Gaskell's seminal biography of Brontë ([1857] 1997) and reiterated throughout the research literature on Brontë's writing, including Lucasta Miller's iconoclastic *The Brontë Myth* (Miller [2001] 2020, 75). The manuscript evidence, however, tells a different story. Brontë claims indeed that she writes with her eyes closed in the self-reflective narrative from the Roe Head Journal, and some of the lines droop irregularly from around midway through the line, as if she had let her hand lead the way without looking (BPM Bon98[8]). The next line, however, follows the curve, and it is difficult to account for how Brontë would have adjusted that line without looking. Barbara Heritage, in her dissertation on the practices and expertise in book-making that went into *Jane Eyre* (Heritage 2014), challenges Gilbert and Gubar's assessment explicitly and suggests that Brontë should rather be understood as a 'craftswoman' who was very much in control of her work, and this is the evidence that we see in most of her manuscripts.

Writers' own statements about the writing process, just as much as fictional representations of them, need to be read against and with the manuscript evidence in a metagenetic analysis. Brontë may have indeed styled herself as a trance-writer who can write with her eyes closed, in order to suit particular expectations about female literary genius, or in order to claim artistic freedom for her practices.[5] (Indeed, many of the narratives in the Roe Head Journal play with the luxurious and sexually-charged settings of her earlier romances, which she abandons partly when turning to the realist novel *Jane Eyre*.) Brontë may even try out writing in this fashion to get a phenomenological 'feel' for such a practice. Such self-statements, just like the metafictional and metanarrative imaginings of writing, are therefore an important source for how writers think about the writing process and where the parameters of their practices are configured, and as such they should be considered in a metagenetic analysis.

---

5   This aspect of metagenesis overlaps with what Rüdiger Campe (2021) has called a 'Schreibszene', that is, a representation of a scene in which a character produces written discourse that is embedded in the media ecologies of the author, and that enables us to take into account the production of literary texts without falling back into the 'intentional fallacy', where every intention in the head of the writer is directly tracable on the page. Campe however remains very much in the context of discourse analysis informed by Kittler's *Aufschreibesysteme 1800/1900*.

In *Villette*, the knife cancellations relate in interesting ways to thematic concerns. The knife cancellations, I have argued, open windows into the next folio. That text can only be revealed if all the lines have the same distance from one another. Brontë indeed writes with very regular numbers of lines per folio sheet, which enables this practice. Arguably, she continued the practice of keeping the same number of lines on a folio in order to be able to calculate word counts for the three volumes of the three-decker novel that Barbara Heritage has established for her writing of *Jane Eyre* (2014, 58–59). It is this careful regularity that creates the material possibility for the aleatory use of the quill knife that brings contingency to the fore.[6] Metagenesis enables us to probe different writing practices authors may try out. Lucy Snowe describes her 'Creative Impulse' in terms of 'a strange hum of oracles' ([1853] 2000, 356; see Springer 2020, 158–62) when she reflects on her writing. That 'hum of oracles' may well have a material reality in her practice with the knife.

'Strange Events' imagines a scene where the character-narrator Charles Wellesley meets himself. It is not a scene where writing technologies play a role or where any text production is represented. Rather, the embodied situation underlying the material reality of the play practice from which Brontë's stories emerge gets reflected. The traces of this embodied situation then recur throughout Brontë's juvenilia and come to a creative crisis in *Shirley*. We do not have a complete endogenetic dossier for *Shirley*, so we do not know whether Brontë perhaps started writing in the first person, or whether she hesitated between different personal pronouns at stages that preceded the fair copy manuscript.[7] Metagenesis enables us to draw hypotheses about the gap here, taking into account the larger production of the author across her career, and the ways in which material elements of the manuscript and the imaginative element of the story that is written interact.

---

6   That playful approach is not yet noticeable in the *Shirley* manuscript, where Brontë also uses knives and (likely) scissors. In *Shirley*, there are fewer knife cancellations and more larger revisions, such as half a page being removed by cutting it off, while in *Villette*, there are many more cancellations made with greater precision. Ileana Marin (2014, 42) counts 27 cancellations in *Shirley* and 71 in *Villette*.

7   Incomplete narratives that Brontë writes around the same time as Shirley, such as the short story 'John Henry', start in the third person and then slip into the first (see Kukkonen, forthcoming).

Metagenesis does not assume a one-to-one correspondence between the practices that actually stand behind the text and the practices that it represents. Instead, it uses the strangeness of the fictional examples, such as Brontë's 'Strange Events', to bring development in the material writing process into relief and relate them to the imaginative dimension. It is exactly interested in how and why the material traces of the writing practices tell a different story from the imaginative constructs of characters and narrators talking about or enacting their practices.

Conclusion

Metagenesis cannot rely on these fictional representations alone. It needs to compare the imagined scene with the evidence in the manuscripts that are available. More likely than not, the practice represented will diverge from the practice we can reconstruct from the manuscript evidence. It underlines the importance of the empirical work of manuscript analysis, but it also shows the potential that lies in comparing how writers imagine writing with how they actually write. Writers arguably reflect on their process while writing, combining the material agency of interacting with pen and paper, with the epistemic agency of pacing their practice and also modelling it in fictional representations. The particular nature of literary manuscripts, where language both serves as the material substrate but also as the generator of imagined situations, enables such an approach where the material and the imaged can form a feedback loop.

Metagenesis takes seriously the dynamics of the creative process, where what I call 'mise-en-abyme models' often shape the creative process in tandem with the writing implements (see Kukkonen, forthcoming). Mise-en-abyme models include for example characters that serve as a proxy for writers' consciousness and choices of plot development. When Louis Moore writes his diary in *Shirley*, the character arguably serves as a proxy modelling the experience of the character. Throughout the juvenilia, Brontë writes not only the adventures of her protagonists, but also their dreams and reveries, as in the case of 'Strange Events'. Marco Bernini (2022, 25–28) suggests that Beckett provides a similar model for his own narration, for example in *Dream of Fair to Middling Women*, a posthumously published early work. My larger investigation into creativity in literary writing on the basis of manuscripts and interviews suggests that it is not coincidental that such mise-en-abyme modelling can be observed in authors as diverse as Brontë and Beckett. Creative writing itself is a recursive process, unfolding over a long time scale and across multiple different drafts, where authors' practices can start looping back and forth between concrete material engagements and imagination in written narratives (Kukkonen, forthcoming). Mise-en-abyme models arguably play an important role in keeping the creative process of writing a novel flexible and open-ended, and we also find their traces in the textual elements such as metanarrative commentary, metalepses and other metafictional elements. They offer another way for reconstructing writers' practices, not as a representation of what they actually did, but as an indication of the resonance space of creative possibility against which they make an ink stroke on the paper or take their quill knife to it.

Manuscripts Cited

British Library

Add. MS. 43481, Fair copy manuscript of 'Villette' Vol. 2, 1852, London: British Library.

Add. MS. 43482, Fair copy manuscript of 'Villette' Vol. 3, 1852, London: British Library.

Brontë Parsonage Museum

BPM Bon98(8), 'Roe Head Journal'. 14 October 1836, Haworth, Keighley: Brontë Parsonage Museum.

Works Cited

Bernini, Marco (2014), 'Supersizing Narrative Theory: On Intention, Material Agency, and Extended Mind-Workers', *Style*, 48.3: 349–66, https://doi.org/10.5325/style.48.3.349.

Bernini, Marco (2022), *Beckett and the Cognitive Method: Minds, Models and Explorative Narratives* (New York: Oxford University Press).

Biasi, Pierre-Marc De (1996), 'What Is a Literary Draft? Toward a Functional Typology of Genetic Criticism', *Yale French Studies*, 89: 26–58, https://doi.org/10.2307/2930337.

Brontë, Charlotte [1830] (1987), 'Strange Events by Lord Charles Wellesley', in: *An Edition of the Early Writings of Charlotte Brontë*, ed. by Christine Alexander, vol. 1, *The Glass Town Saga, 1826–1832* (Oxford: Blackwell).

Brontë, Charlotte (1997), *The Belgian Essays*, ed. and trans. by Sue Lonoff (New Haven and London: Yale University Press).

Brontë, Charlotte [1853] (2000), *Villette*, ed. by Margaret Smith and Herbert Rosengarten (New York: Oxford University Press).

Brontë, Charlotte [1849] (2007), *Shirley*, ed. by Herbert Rosengarten and Margaret Smith (New York: Oxford University Press).

Bryant, John (2002), *The Fluid Text: A Theory of Revision and Editing for Book and Screen* (Ann Arbor, MI: University of Michigan Press).

Campe, Rüdiger (2021), 'Writing; The Scene of Writing', *MLN*, 136.5: 971–83, https://doi.org/10.1353/mln.2021.0075.

Clark, Andy (1998), 'Magic Words: How Language Augments Human Computation', in: *Language and Thought: Interdisciplinary Themes*, ed. by Jill Boucher and Peter Carruthers, 162–83 (Cambridge: Cambridge University Press). https://doi.org/10.1017/CBO9780511597909.011.

Debray Genette, Raymonde (1979), 'Génétique et Poétique: Le Cas Flaubert', in: *Essais de Critique Génétique* (Paris: Flamarion).

Debray Genette, Raymonde (1988), *Métamorphoses Du Récit. Autour de Flaubert* (Paris: Seuil).

Ferrer, Daniel (2016), 'Genetic Criticism with Textual Criticism: From Variant to Variation', *Variants : The Journal of the European Society for Textual Scholarship*, 12–13: 57–64.

Fforde, Jasper (2001), *The Eyre Affair* (London: Hodder & Stoughton).

Gao, Timothy (2021), *Virtual Play and the Victorian Novel: The Ethics and Aesthetics of Fictional Experience*, vol. 127, *Cambridge Studies in Nineteenth-Century Literature and Culture* (Cambridge: Cambridge University Press).

Gaskell, Elizabeth [1857] (1997), *The Life of Charlotte Brontë*, ed. by Elisabeth Jay (London: Penguin).

Gilbert, Sandra M. (1979), *The Madwoman in the Attic: The Woman Writer and the Nineteenth-Century Literary Imagination* (New Haven: Yale University Press).

Hanks, Lucy (2020), 'Different Kinds of Silence: Revisions of *Villette* and the "Reader's Romance"', *Journal of Victorian Culture* , 25.3: 443–57, https://doi.org/10.1093/jvcult/vcaa010.

Heritage, Barbara (2014), 'Bronte and the Bookmakers: Jane Eyre in the Nineteenth-Century Marketplace', Doctoral Dissertation (Charlottesville, VA: University of Virginia). https://www.academia.edu/81020086/Bronte_and_the_Bookmakers_Jane_Eyre_in_the_Nineteenth_Century_Marketplace.

Heritage, Barbara (2021), 'Reading the Writing Desk: Charlotte Brontë's Instruments and Authorial Craft', *Studies in Romanticism*, 60.4: 503–22, https://doi.org/10.1353/srm.2021.0030.

Kukkonen, Karin (forthcoming), *Creativity and Contingency in Literary Writing* (Bloomsbury).

Marin, Ileana (2014), 'Charlotte Brontë's Busy Scissors Revising Villette', *Brontë Studies : Journal of the Brontë Society*, 39.1: 42–53, https://doi.org/10.1179/1474893213Z.00000000094.

Miller, Lucasta [2001] (2020), *The Brontë Myth* (London: Vintage).

Murray, Janet H. (1997), *Hamlet on the Holodeck: The Future of Narrative in Cyberspace* (New York: Free Press).

Ratchford, Fannie Elizabeth (1949), *The Brontes' Web of Childhood* (New York: Columbia University Press).

Springer, Olga (2020), *Ambiguity in Charlotte Brontë's Villette*, (Göttingen: V&R unipress).

Van Hulle, Dirk (2017), 'Cognition Enactment', *Samuel Beckett Today/Aujourd'hui*, 29.1: 185–98, https://doi.org/10.1163/18757405-02901016.

Van Hulle, Dirk (2022), *Genetic Criticism: Tracing Creativity in Literature* (Oxford: Oxford University Press). https://doi.org/10.1093/oso/9780192846792.001.0001.

3. The Structures of Narrative Imagination: Reading an Outline of Theodor Fontane's Novel *Die Poggenpuhls* as a Test Case for Genetic Narratology

Matthias Grüne

1. Introduction: From Story to Discourse

The aim of this article is twofold: on the one hand, I will propose a close reading of a genetic document on a narratological basis. I will thus use narratology as a reading strategy (cf. Van Hulle 2022, 149) to gain insights into the creation of a literary text—in my case a novel by the German author Theodor Fontane (1819–98). In this respect, 'genetic narratology' is to be understood as a combination rather than a fusion of genetic criticism and narratology. On the other hand, I will explore whether the analysis of a text type which is not commonly object of narratological research can add new perspectives to narratological debates. The question here is whether one can also speak of 'genetic narratology' in a narrower sense, i.e. as a designation of a differentiated field of narratological expertise that is aligned with, and enriched by, the study of genetic research.

For this purpose, I will focus not on an entire 'genetic dossier', but on a single text consisting of two handwritten pages. It is a plot outline that Fontane wrote between the end of 1891 and the beginning of 1892 in preparation for his novel *Die Poggenpuhls* [*The Poggenpuhl Family*].[1] The

---

[1] The manuscripts are in the possession of the Stadtmuseum Berlin and have the inventory number V 83/9,05-02v_002a (for the notes on chapters 1 to 4) and

novel was published in the journal *Vom Fels zum Meer* from October 1895 to March 1896 and as a book edition at the end of 1896, but the published text as well as other documents from the genetic dossier remain in the background here. The main reason for this narrow focus is that it helps to balance the genetic and the narratological aspects of the research. Studying the genesis of a text from the first idea to the final stylistic touches is primarily a genetic task, and compiling a dossier requires specific knowledge of the author's manuscripts and working methods. By selecting a single document that represents a particular stage of the genetic process, I aim to move away from the typical questions of genetic research such as what external events might have influenced the author, how the plot developed over several years, or what led the author to delete one passage and retain another. Instead, attention is drawn to the structural patterns that govern the narrative imagination in order to access (by means of classical narratology) a more general level of composition which is not affected by the decision for or against a single variant.[2]

The object that makes such a structural analysis possible is anything but spectacular. As already mentioned, it is merely an outline of the planned novel *Die Poggenpuhls* that Fontane jotted down in the beginning of his work on the project. The text divides the novel into eleven chapters. The sheets with the notes on chapters 1 to 4 and on chapters 8 to 11 have been preserved because Fontane later used the reverse side of the paper for an elaborated draft of the novel. The notes on chapters 5 to 7 have been lost. However, what makes the sketch, even in its fragmentary form, particularly interesting for narrato-genetic research is that it can be read as a kind of vertical cut through the compositional process, revealing different phases in the creation of the narrative. First and foremost,

---

V 67/864,2.5.2_07v (for the notes on chapters 8 to 11). All the following quotes from the plot outline are taken from the manuscripts. In her edition of the novel, Gabriele Radecke offers a (almost complete) linear transcription of the outline (Fontane 2006, 181–84).

[2] In this narrow focus, my approach differs from that of Michael Scheffel (2022), whose interest lies in the narratologically grounded reconstruction of the genesis of a literary work (*Werk*). Furthermore, my analysis does not presuppose any in-depth knowledge of Fontane and his writing practice. For a comprehensive insight into Fontane's working style, see Gabriele Radecke's (2002) study of the novel *L'Adultera*, which traces the formation of narrative structures across drafts and variants. For a more general overview see McGillen (2019).

the list of chapters represents what could be called the skeleton of the novel: a sketch of the general course of the plot, its starting and ending points, the connections between chapters, decisive plot twists, etc. But this list contains text passages that already go beyond a mere outline. Fontane inserts authorial comments in which questions of the narrative development are addressed. The text therefore shows direct traces of the narrative imagination *in actu*. Moreover, the list partially merges into the narrative unfolding of a storyworld. The authorial discourse then becomes the speech of a narrator and even integrates passages of dialogue.

Following Pierre-Marc de Biasi's (1996, 34–35) typology of genetic documentation, the manuscript thus bridges two phases and operative functions of the textual genesis: it ranges from the pre-compositional phase and the structuring of the story elements to the compositional phase and the textualisation of the narrative. Applying narratological terms, one could say that the text occupies a middle position between the presentation of a story and the elaboration of discourse. Unlike a mere summary, the outline provides insight into the artificial construction of the narrative and the distribution of the attention; it documents, for example, the decision to use letters to convey parts of the story, and even anticipates the character's dialogue. But it is still a plan for a narrative that has not yet been worked out, and the narrative discourse remains fragmentary. From a genetic perspective, therefore, it makes sense to drop the distinction between story and discourse and to use a triadic model instead. In the following, I will distinguish between story, plot and discourse, all three of which are understood in terms of textual genesis. They thus refer to the compositional process of creating a narrative and denote different stages of narrative composition.

This understanding differs not only from the binary distinction, but also from the common parallelisation of the distinction between story and discourse with that between content and form. Discourse here is not to be understood as any form of a text that has a rudimentary narrative structure (i.e. presents a sequence of events). Rather, it refers to what Franz Stanzel (1986, 37) calls a 'form of mediacy', that is, an intentionally elaborated textual design that has the purpose of transmitting a story by means of narration and dialogue. Thus, there could be textual representations of a story or a plot without discourse, although these texts certainly have a form.[3] From this genetic approach, *story* refers to a mere sequence of events and the associated set of elements of a storyworld (i.e. characters, places). It is the product of invention or research and could draw on the cultural inventory of story patterns (i.e. myths, motifs, etc.). A textual representation of a story could be, for example, a short synopsis, a collection of motifs or a list of characters, such as the one that exists from the early phase of Fontane's work on the *Poggenpuhls* (cf. Fontane 2006, 174–76). The *plot*, in turn, is the result of compositional decisions about the specific arrangement of the story elements, for example with regard to the dramaturgy, the suspense or the layout of the mediation structure.[4] An outline or a scenario could be seen as a textual representation of a plot. *Discourse*, finally, emerges from the process of textual elaboration when the author's summarising, commenting and discussing utterances are transformed into the speech of a narrator and dialogue. Systematically, the elaboration of the discourse represents the last stage of text genesis;[5] text types in which

---

3   In relation to text types such as synopses or summaries, Stanzel (1986, 30–37) speaks of a 'zero grade of mediacy'. His discussion of Henry James' notebooks, in which he shows how a higher degree of 'mediacy' is successively achieved in the course of the creative process, is indeed an early and impressive example of the potential of combining narratology and genetic analysis.

4   A representation of plot might thus already show traces or anticipations of the 'form of mediacy' as is it the case in Fontane's outline; but the design of the discourse remains abbreviated and punctual. In this perspective, plot is the intermediate state of composition between the gathering of story elements and the elaboration of the discourse. This makes it difficult to link certain compositional facets and decisions to a stage of narrative transformation. For example, the use of perspective or focalisation may already be implied in the outline of a plot (cf. Schmid 2010, 195). For genetic narratology, a gradual distinction between the three stages seems appropriate, depending on the degree of elaboration and narrative complexity. The complex history of the term 'plot' within the field of narratology cannot be traced here. My conceptualisation is based on a general pre-understanding that sees plot as 'something more complex' (Dannenberg 2005, 435) than story and, following Karin Kukkonen (2014), as part of the author's design: 'If one conceives of plot as part of the authorial design [...], then it becomes the means through which authors interest readers, keep their attention as the narrative unfolds and bring it to a surprising yet possibly satisfying conclusion. Such authorial design prefigures the mental operations which lead readers to a meaningful narrative' (Kukkonen 2014, n. pag.). This conceptualisation differs from Chatman's (1978, 43) understanding of plot as story mediated through discourse.

5   Of course, corrections related to the story (e.g. inventing new episodes) or to the plot (e.g. rearranging the events) can be made at any time in the actual creative process, even after the publication.

it becomes accessible are usually elaborated drafts and, of course, published narratives.

In the following analysis I will focus on a document that can be read as a representation of a plot. As already mentioned, this intermediate position makes the document a particularly attractive object for genetic research into the structures of the narrative imagination. The term 'narrative imagination' here denotes the creative activity set in motion to produce a narrative.[6] It refers to the whole set of compositional operations and decisions, from the invention of story elements to the arrangement of the plot and the elaboration of the narratorial discourse. In my discussion, I will focus on three structural features that I consider important for the dynamic progress of the narrative imagination in Fontane's text. These are the orientation towards a scenic organisation, the integration of details and the development of the narratorial discourse by approaching the character's perspective.

2. Plotting a Realistic Novel

In the outline, Fontane uses the form of a numbered list to structure the plot. The chapter segmentation is a basic but formal feature of the outline which does not say much about the regularities that apply to the transformation of story elements into a narrative arrangement. More important for the inner structure of the plot is that the document reveals the importance of orientation sequences. As content of the first chapter Fontane simply states: 'Einleitungskapitel. Wohnung. Die Menschen' ['Introductory chapter. The flat. The people in it'].[7] There is obviously no action in this chapter; it must serve some other purpose than to initiate the sequence of events. Instead, the main goal seems to be to introduce the reader to the specific setting of the novel. The establishing of a particular spatio-temporal environment precedes the representation of character's actions. This hierarchy is also reflected in the order of the elements: first comes the spatial environment, then the people in it. The narrative attention moves from the outside to the inside, from the setting to the characters.

---

6   The term is still relatively uncommon in narratology, but has a place in research on biographical and everyday narratives (cf. Andrews 2014).
7   All translations from the German text are mine, MG.

The creation of a particular setting is a central architectural element of the realist novel. The outline shows how this narrative convention already shapes the imagination of the story and the plotline. In this case, an entire chapter is reserved for what is known in film theory as the 'establishing shot'. Furthermore, explicit setting markers are also found in the following chapter summaries: 'Der 2. Januar früh. Rosalie geht durch die Schlafstube' ['Early on 2 January. Rosalie walks through the bedroom'] (chapter 2), 'Um 4 Uhr kommt Leo' ['At 4 o'clock Leo comes'] (chapter 3), 'Am andern Tag der Geburtstag' ['On the other day the birthday'] (chapter 4). All these short orientational sections are placed at the beginning of the chapter entries, which indicates that the change of setting is usually accompanied by the beginning of a new chapter. However, there are examples of spatio-temporal interruptions within a chapter. The entry for the fourth chapter states that the male protagonist Leo first goes for a walk with his sisters on the boulevard 'Unter den Linden' (in the centre of Berlin), then returns to his family's house 'Um 9 Uhr' [at 9 o'clock] and begins a conversation with the housekeeper Rosalie in the kitchen. As in the other examples, the time indication is remarkably precise.

These setting markers illustrate not only the author's interest in a clear timeline for his story, but also the 'scenic' structure of the plot. As Monika Fludernik (1996, 142–53) points out in her book *Towards a 'Natural Narratology'*, the scenic organisation of the story is a core feature of the so-called realist paradigm. While many pre-modern novels tend to build the narrative as a sequence of micro-episodes, realist texts slow down the pace by establishing larger episodes with clear markers for the beginning and the end of the situation. Instead of moving quickly from one event to the next, the narrative expands the representation of how characters act, speak and feel within the framework of a particular setting.[8] Thus, this kind of narrative puts emphasis on the orientational segments of the plot, which mark the opening of a new scene. Fontane's outline reflects this emphasis through the quantity and relative precision of the spatio-temporal markers. They establish a sequence not so much of events as of scenes, which can be expanded as the genetic

---

8 On Fontane's tendency to think in terms of scenes and situations, both in the collection of his material and in the conception of his narratives, see also Hehle (2023).

3. The Structures of Narrative Imagination   41

process continues. The scenic architecture of the plot functions both as a limitation and as a stimulus for the narrative imagination, as a glance at Fontane's notes to the third chapter can illustrate:

> Um 4 Uhr kommt Leo. Droschke. Rosalie lief hinunter, den kl[einen] ^{Offiziers-} Koffer zu holen. Leo kommt. Der Kaffetisch. Gespräch. 'Ja, Kinder eigentlich habe ich Hunger. Sieben Stunden und blos in Kreuth (?) eine belegte Sem[m]el'. Die Entenleber. Der nächste Tag muß Lulus Geburtstag sein oder noch besser der Alten Geburtstag. Abendspaziergang mit zwei Schwestern. Kommt zurück. Gespräch mit Rosalie. Primel. ^{Pralinés etc} Hildebrandtsche Pfeffernüße oder Mehlweißchen.[9]

> [At 4 o'clock Leo comes. The cab. Rosalie ran down to fetch the small ^{officer's} case. Leo is coming. The coffee table. Conversation. 'Yes, my dears, I am actually hungry. Seven hours and only a bread roll in Kreuth (?)'. The duck liver. The next day must be Lulu's birthday, or even better, the old woman's birthday. Evening walk with two sisters. Comes back. Conversation with Rosalie. Primrose. ^{Pralines etc.} Hildebrandt's peppernuts. Mehlweißchen.][10]

According to this summary, the chapter consists of two scenes, or more precisely, two conversation scenes since the only event mentioned in both cases is the conversation between the characters. The first scene is preceded by an abbreviated description of Leo's arrival. An interesting detail is that Fontane uses the narrative (i.e. past) tense for the information that the housekeeper Rosalie goes down to fetch the suitcase ('Rosalie lief hinunter'), but then switches back to the present tense ('Leo kommt'). The effect is that the singular use of the past tense characterises Rosalie's action as a past event in relation to Leo's arrival in the room. It is part of a broad orientation segment which highlights the beginning of the actual scene, the family's conversation at the coffee table. Although the topic of this conversation doesn't seem to be very spectacular—everyday talk about the food during the trip and the plans for the dinner ('Entenleber')—Fontane already inserts a line of character's speech. He seems to expand the scene almost automatically. The character's speech is followed by an authorial remark noting an

---

9 In my transcription of the manuscript, square brackets are used for resolved abbreviations. The question mark in the quotation above is part of Fontane's text.

10 'Mehlweißchen' are a type of biscuit. The name describes that they look 'white like flour'.

apparently spontaneous idea: the next day must be the birthday of one of the characters, but Fontane is still unsure whose birthday. Although this idea probably occurred to him at that moment, he immediately transposes this invention into another scene, a conversation between Leo and Rosalie about possible birthday presents.

In his revision of the document, Fontane elaborates on the first of the two scenes in several marginal notes. In doing so, he switches almost entirely into character speech:

> Legt Paletot ab, schnallt den Säbel ab, zupfte sein Waffenrock zurecht:
> 'Na, Mutter ^Kinder, da wär ich ^nun mal wieder. Wie findet ihr mich.'
> O wunderbar
> Danke schön. So was ~~erquickt~~ ^thut im[m]er ^wohl wenns auch nicht wahr ist;
>
> [He takes off his paletot, unbuckles his sabre and adjusted his tunic:
> 'Well, mother ^my dears, here I am again. What do you think'.
> O wonderful
> Thank you. That ~~is~~ ^does always ~~refreshing~~ ^good, even if it's not true;]

The dialogue continues for a while. And Fontane is already working on the fine details, thinking it important, for example, that Leo ate not a simple bread roll on his journey, but a roll topped with anchovy. Almost everything that is said is irrelevant to the story of the novel. Nevertheless, Fontane devotes himself to elaborating the dialogue early on. It seems that this is not just a coincidence, but also has to do with the realistic structure of the text. The balance between interest in the individual scene and interest in the plot as a whole shifts in favour of the scene in a realistic novel. The scenic structure invites the reader to immerse themselves in the scene and to some extent forget that it is part of a plotted novel. In the same way, Fontane also tends to immerse himself in the elaboration of scenes, regardless of whether the events in them are relevant to the progress of the plot or not. On the basis of the spatio-temporal framework initially established, the scene is developed not so much by conceptual considerations—for example, about important outcomes of the conversation—but rather through the more or less free (that is, free from the function of advancing the course of events) unfolding of the dialogue itself.

In Fontane's outline, the scene is a central narrative structuring unit that shapes the structure of the plot and directs the narrative imagination in certain directions. In order to identify this structure, narrato-genetic analysis can draw on a concept that has already been introduced into narrative theory. Yet despite Fludernik's impulses, 'scene' and 'scenic narration' have rarely been the subject of narratological investigation. It is possible, then, that genetic narratology offers a platform to further illuminate the heuristic potential of the concept.

3. Imagining the Superfluous

The examples given above draw attention to another aspect that governs the structure of the narrative imagination in Fontane's outline, namely the abundance of detailed information. Like 'scene', the concept of 'detail' is frequently used, but is rarely the subject of theoretical reflection. The most prominent contribution to a narratological theory of detail comes from Roland Barthes (1968), who is known to be particularly interested in those details that (supposedly) do not fulfil any function in the narrative context and should therefore be regarded as actually superfluous luxuries. Fontane's multiple corrections, which specify the topping of Leo's roll, can probably be regarded as such a case: 'Seit 1 Stunde nichts als ein ~~belegter~~ ^Sardellen^ Sem[m]el, ~~und dann belegt~~' ['Nothing but a ~~topped~~ ^anchovy^ bread roll for 1 hour~~, and then with topping~~'].

Barthes treats details like this as phenomena that appear on the surface of the narrative tissue ('la surface du tissu narratif'; 1968, 84). He does not examine their genetic development. However, he does briefly address genetic processes in his essay: in Flaubert's laborious revisions of descriptive passages, he recognises the alignment of narrative with the older, pre-realist principle of beautiful style (86). In his revisions, Flaubert would not be concerned with referential accuracy, but with the most aesthetically convincing formulation. But the superfluous detail does not serve the beauty of the style. According to Barthes, it is merely meant to denote 'reality'. For this 'reality effect', it is actually irrelevant which object is mentioned, as long as it appears functionless. Why spend a lot of corrective effort on something that is more or less arbitrarily interchangeable anyway? The functionless detail in Barthes' sense is an element that seems to be added to the narrative in the phase of textual elaboration and that should leave hardly any traces in the genetic process.

Genetic narratology, in turn, looks through the textual surface of the (finished) narrative and asks when the superfluous actually emerges in the course of the genesis. Fontane's 'Sardellen-Semmel' is an example of how such a detail can be worked out surprisingly early in the genetic process. But perhaps even more surprising are the details mentioned in the summary to the third chapter. As a reminder, Fontane records here possible birthday presents for old Mrs Poggenpuhl:

> Der nächste Tag muß Lulus Geburtstag sein oder noch besser der Alten Geburtstag. Abendspaziergang mit zwei Schwestern. Kommt zurück. Gespräch mit Rosalie. Primel. ^{Pralinés etc} Hildebrandtsche Pfeffernüße oder Mehlweißchen.

> [The next day must be Lulu's birthday, or even better, the old woman's birthday. Evening walk with two sisters. Comes back. Conversation with Rosalie. Primrose. ^{Pralinés etc.} Hildebrandt's peppernuts or Mehlweißchen.]

It is noteworthy that these details do not appear as part of a character's speech or the narrator's discourse. Fontane lists them as if they were events of the story; as if it really mattered for the outcome of the narrative whether the gift was primroses, pralines or peppernuts from Hildebrandt's manufactory. The superfluous details are already included in the textual fixation of the plot; they are not mere additions by the author to colour the narrative discourse. In a way, this contradicts the opposition between the supposedly functionless detail and the narrative structure that Barthes highlights. For it seems that these elements can already take on a function in the process of creating a realistic storyworld.

In the search for this structural function, one has to look more closely at the intended effect of realistic texts. According to Barthes' concept of 'reality effect', the main aim of realist writing is to make the recipients believe the text world to be true. The emphasis in this understanding is on the referential claim of the text and the principle of *celare artem*, the concealment of art. In contrast to this conception, both nineteenth-century poetics (cf. Grüne 2018) and modern, especially cognitive approaches to literary theory (Fludernik 1996; Kukkonen 2019) describe the primary aim of realistic texts as animating the recipient to immerse themself in the world designed by the text. The impression of being embedded like the characters in a concrete, sensually tangible reality is thus most important. And when it comes to the superfluous detail, its function is not to signify reality, but *this* reality, that is, a particular situation in which the characters are mentally and physically embedded.

The presence of supposedly superfluous details in early drafts and plot outlines leads once again to the assumption that similar processes underlie the imagination of the narrative and its reception. Like the orientation towards a scenic arrangement, the fixation on small details helps the narrative imagination to proliferate. Information about 'anchovy bread rolls' or a regional peppernut product triggers the illusion of being embedded or even embodied in a concrete and tangible situation not only in the course of reception, but already in the author's creation of the narrated world.

The casual integration of such elements (at all stages of the genetic process) also says something about the anthropology underlying the text. The realist gaze is primarily directed at the everyday world: it captures the extent to which the ordinary objects and routines of everyday life shape the nature of human beings. Everyday objects and practices can thus become the very subject of the narrative. A good example of this particular perspective can be found at the beginning of the entry for the second chapter. The first half of the chapter is devoted to the morning routine of the housekeeper Rosalie. Of course, none of the activities are important events in the conventional sense. Nevertheless, they are listed in detail in the summary:

> Der 2. Januar früh. Rosalie geht durch die Schlafstube. Einheizen. Reinemachen. Abwischen. Frühstück schon geholt. Das Wasser bullert. Die Damen stehen auf.

> [Early on 2 January. Rosalie walks through the bedroom. Heating up. Cleaning. Wiping. Breakfast already fetched. The water is bubbling. The ladies get up.]

Not only the finished narrative but also the outline of the plot 'wastes' space and time on the information about what Rosalie does first and that the water is boiling. The importance of this information lies not in its functional value for the story, but in its reality-creating character: that is, it helps to develop a mental image of a concrete world, both in the process of reception and in the process of creation. It is crucial that these elements do not lose their incidental character, as their presence does not have much influence on the course of events; and yet they are integrated into the structure of the narrative from the very beginning.

It is precisely this mixture of apparent casualness and indirect structural significance that allows these elements to become symbols without disturbing the illusion of a concrete reality. In the present case, it is interesting to note that the symbolic use of details is not yet indicated in the plot outline. It is only in the more elaborate drafts or in the published novel that these connections become apparent. There we read, for example, that when the housekeeper dusts the pictures in the flat every day, she always drops the picture showing the family's hero, a Prussian officer who had distinguished himself in a battle during the Seven Years' War (Fontane 2006, 15). The symbolic meaning of the detail, the criticism of an outdated aristocratic and Prussian pride, is obvious, but the symbolism seems 'natural' and unforced precisely because it is linked to a supposedly marginal act like daily cleaning. Another example is the aforementioned detail of the 'Hildebrandtsche Pfeffernüße' ['peppernuts from the Hildebrandt company']. This detail actually appears in the finished novel, though not in the place indicated in the sketch, but in a later chapter. In a discussion about the social value of names, the protagonist Leo refers to the company *Theodor Hildebrands*, which has existed in Berlin since 1817. He points out that the symbolic capital of a name is no longer a privilege of the aristocratic class. On the contrary, the importance of the family name is fading and the brand name is taking its place. The aristocratic elite is being outplayed by the social and financial power of capitalist bourgeoisie. A similar development, Leo believes, can be observed in the field of art. In terms of public awareness and recognition, brand names easily surpass the artist's name:

> Nehmen wir [...] beispielsweise den großen Namen Hildebrand. Es gibt, glaub' ich, drei berühmte Maler dieses Namens, der dritte kann übrigens auch ein Bildhauer gewesen sein, es thut nichts. Aber wenn irgendwo von Hildebrand gesprochen wird, wohl gar in der Weihnachtszeit, so denkt doch kein Mensch an Bilder und Büsten, sondern bloß an kleine dunkelblaue Packete mit einem Pfefferkuchen obenauf und einer Strippe drum herum. (Fontane 2006, 64)

> [Let's take [...] the great name Hildebrand, for example. There are, I believe, three famous painters of this name, the third may have been

a sculptor as well, it makes no difference. But when Hildebrand is mentioned somewhere, especially at Christmas time, no one thinks of pictures and busts, but only of small dark blue packages with a gingerbread cake on top and a ribbon around it.]

We do not know whether Fontane was already thinking of giving the 'Hildebrandtsche Pfeffernüße' a symbolic meaning when he wrote his outline. However, it is obvious why he succeeds so easily in attaching subtle symbolic references to supposedly superfluous details of the storyworld: because these details are always present and already integral components of the plot. They do not have to be invented for this purpose.

4. The Birth of the Narrator

With 'scene' and 'detail', two terms have been discussed so far that do not belong to the inner circle of narratological terminology. The next section turns to a far more prominent notion, as it deals with the emergence of a narrator figure in Fontane's manuscript. As already mentioned, the plot scheme does not represent a zero grade of mediacy in every respect, because it shows rudiments of a mediated (i.e. narrative) discourse as well as a dialogue. What Stanzel (1986, 33) notes about the notebooks of Henry James also applies to this text: along with the contours of the plot, the figure of the narrator is already vaguely visible. This process of a slow emergence of the narrator's voice from the author's text could become one of the most interesting and promising fields of investigation for genetic narratology. In the following, I will use the term 'narrativisation' to describe this process.

In modern narratology, this term was coined by Monika Fludernik (1996) who uses it as a kind of specification of the broader concept of 'naturalisation'. While naturalisation describes a strategy of coping with strange or unfamiliar aspects of a text 'by taking recourse to available, diverse interpretative patterns' (31), narrativisation refers to those cases in which this process is carried out 'by recourse to narrative schemata' (34). In other words: narrativisation describes a reading strategy that consists of imposing the framework of narrativity on a text in order to reduce its strangeness.

> When readers are confronted with potentially unreadable narratives, texts that are radically inconsistent, they cast about for ways and means of recuperating these texts as narratives—motivated by the generic markers that go with the book. They therefore attempt to re-cognize what they find in the text in terms of the natural telling or experiencing or viewing parameters, or they try to recuperate the inconsistencies in terms of action and event structures at the most minimal level. This process of narrativization, of making something a narrative by the sheer act of imposing narrativity on it, needs to be located in the dynamic reading process where such interpretative recuperations hold sway. (Fludernik 1996, 34)

Genetic narratology gives the concept of narrativisation a different but in some ways complementary meaning compared to Fludernik's approach. Instead of the 'dynamic reading process', the dynamic of production comes to the fore, and thus the question of which textual strategies the author uses to make 'something a narrative'. This does not correspond to Hayden White's (1980, 6) understanding of narrativisation as the act of imposing the form of a story on the raw material of (historical) events. Rather, this conception comes close to what Stanzel (1986, 37) describes as the search for and successive development of a 'form of mediacy', i.e. a specific shaping of the narrative discourse that includes, for example, the choice of narratorial perspective. The process of elaborating a narrative profile is likely to involve the activation of general as well as historically specific schemata associated with the concept of narrativity, for example, generic patterns or narrative conventions like the use of a figural perspective. Genetic research can identify which concrete textual strategies are used to create a certain 'form of mediacy' and which of these compositional choices are likely to be related to historically specific conceptions of narrativity.

The emergence of a narrator's speech and a characteristic narrative attitude from the author's conceptual notes can first be considered on a grammatical level. Referring to a concept of Käte Hamburger, Stanzel (1986, 32) speaks of the 'tabular present' as a characteristic of the conceptual text. The present tense is indeed the predominant tense used in Fontane's outline, as the examples quoted above have shown. Furthermore, in some sentences a verb is omitted altogether or Fontane uses infinitives without any tense marking, as in the (already quoted) beginning of the entry to chapter 2:

3. The Structures of Narrative Imagination 49

> Der 2. Januar früh. Rosalie geht durch die Schlafstube. Einheizen. Reinemachen. Abwischen. Frühstück schon geholt. Das Wasser bullert. Die Damen stehen auf.
>
> [Early on 2 January. Rosalie walks through the bedroom. Heating up. Cleaning. Wiping. Breakfast already fetched. The water is bubbling. The ladies get up.]

Although, grammatically, this text excerpt clearly does not yet constitute narratorial speech, it does already exhibit a more complex degree of narrativity. This is not because the events mentioned can be brought into a meaningful connection and in this respect form a minimal story, as this applies to the entire plot sketch. Rather, the point is that these lines display an increased degree of what Fludernik calls 'experientiality' (1996, 28–30): the impression of being situated in a specific spatio-temporal context. It has already been emphasised that the integration of details and casual actions obviously serves to accentuate the specificity of a situation in order to foster the narrative imagination. For the same reason, the text already tends to convey experientiality in many places, even where it does not yet show the grammatical characteristics of a narrative. Sometimes the experiential quality of the text can be detected in the lexis. In the example given, Fontane uses the expression 'Das Wasser bullert' ['The water is bubbling'], which not only informs us of the fact that the water is boiling, but also phonetically represents the sensual quality of the process. In terms of style, it corresponds more to the vocabulary of the simple housekeeper, so that Fontane approaches the linguistic perspective of the character through his choice of words.

All in all, it seems that Fontane automatically approaches the character's perspective when working on the plot—even before the elaboration of the discourse begins. The reason for this inclination lies in the poetological premise that immersion in the narrated world is a central aim of the literary text. This tendency also explains the abrupt shifts from the author's text to the narratorial discourse which sometimes occur in the middle of a sentence:

> Nach Lulus Brief an Leo, wird gepackt, Therese wollte in Trauer reisen, gab aber nach, weil es doch Nacht sei.
>
> [After Lulu's letter to Leo, they pack, Therese wanted to travel in mourning, but gave in because it was night after all.]

The first part is still in the 'tabular present', the next part already uses the past tense and in the last section the narratorial character is also underlined by the use of indirect speech. It is noticeable that the use of the past tense is often connected with dialogue passages. The development of the narratorial discourse then begins either directly before or after the character's speech. In this marginal note (already discussed), Fontane switches from mere enumeration to narration and then to dialogue:

> Legt Paletot ab, schnallt den Säbel ab, zupfte sein Waffenrock zurecht: 'Na, Mutter ^Kinder, da wär ich ^nun mal wieder. Wie findet ihr mich'.
>
> [He takes off his paletot, unbuckles his sabre and adjusted his tunic: 'Well, mother ^my dears, here I am again. What do you think'.]

In such passages, a gradual transformation can be observed from the author's text, which lists the plot elements, to a narrator's text, which tells a story. In this process, the voices of the author, the narrator and the characters can merge in a way that comes close to the phenomenon of free indirect discourse. In the following example, Fontane describes how the Poggenpuhl family decides who should buy the mourning clothes for their uncle's funeral. The text oscillates between narratorial discourse, author text and figural speech:

> Sie gingen in ein Mourning-Geschäft. Ja wer? Lulu wollte, Lulu versteht es am besten. Aber Therese bestand darauf, daß ihr das zufalle. 'Hochzeit kann Lulu besorgen, Trauer besorge ich'. 'Nun mit diesem Rollentausch bin ich zufrieden'.
>
> [They went to a mourning store. Well, who? Lulu wanted to, Lulu understands best. But Therese insisted that it was up to her. 'Lulu can do the wedding, I'll do the mourning.' 'Well, I'm happy with this change of role'.]

The passage begins with a narratorial statement that they went to the mourning store. But then the narration stops and someone asks: 'Well, who?'. The same question arises for the reader: who is speaking? Is the author correcting himself because he finds it unlikely that the whole family is there? Is it the narrator addressing a fictional reader? Or is this sentence to be understood as an abbreviated character speech because the following dialogue discusses precisely this very question?

In his analysis of James' notebooks, Stanzel (1986, 34–36) discusses similar instances of free indirect speech and interprets them as anticipating the 'narrative situation', in this case the figural narration, which is finally realised in the finished text. In Fontane's work, however, things are somewhat different: free indirect speech is occasionally used in his novels, but not particularly extensively; none of his novels presents a consistent figural narration. In this case, too, the scene is presented in the finished novel as a simple narratorial account without traces of free indirect discourse (Fontane 2006, 102). And this is not an isolated case; Walter Hettche (2003) has pointed out that Fontane's drafts sometimes contain advanced narrative forms, such as free indirect speech or interior monologue, which, however, are transformed into more conventional forms of presentation in the course of the genetic process. As for *Die Poggenpuhls*, a glance at the published text reveals a similar picture. The above-mentioned discussion between the characters is reduced to a single sentence by the narrator, who remarks that 'man sich untereinander dahin geeinigt hatte, daß Therese in die Stadt fahren und dort die Trauergarderobe besorgen solle' ['they had agreed that Therese should go to the city and get the mourning clothes'] (Fontane 2006, 102). It seems reasonable to assume that the appearance of more complex forms of representation in the outline is less an anticipation of the future 'narrative situation' than an unintended consequence of the effort to get closer to the characters' perspective of experience. For in Fontane's creative process, partial immersion in the concrete world of the characters functions as an essential stimulus for the narrative imagination.

5. Conclusion

My reading of a plot outline of Theodor Fontane's novel *Die Poggenpuhls* was intended as a test case for narrato-genetic research. The aim was not to give an exhaustive account of the entire genesis of a novel, but to gain insight into the structural conditions of the narrative imagination— understood as the creative activity of inventing, arranging and elaborating a narrative—on the basis of a single document. The narratological toolkit has proved suitable for drawing attention to these structural features that underlie individual compositional decisions and corrections. With regard to Fontane's outline, the concept of 'scene' was useful to describe a characteristic feature of the plot design and to explain the emergence of precise spatio-temporal information even at a relatively early stage of the genetic process. The narratological debate about the function of 'details' (or lack thereof) provided a framework to illuminate how attention to supposedly superfluous story details already structures the writing of the plot outline. Finally, the narratological distinction between several instances of utterance (author, narrator, character) paved the way for the analysis of the intermingling of authorial (i.e. factual) text with the fictional discourse of narrator and characters. In all these aspects, one can notice a strong tendency on the part of the author to put himself in the situation of his characters, which is obviously an important stimulus for the unfolding of the narrative imagination.

Narratology can thus become a powerful tool for genetic research to shift the focus of attention from individual textual changes to their systematic connections. However, the essay also discussed the extent to which narratology, for its part, can benefit from contact with genetic criticism. In some respects, the analysis has indeed pointed the way to a genetic narratology in the narrower sense. The discussion of the distinction between story and discourse, which is at the heart of narratology, is perhaps the clearest illustration of the benefits of taking a genetic perspective into account: within the framework of this approach, a triadic distinction between story, plot and discourse has been proposed, which breaks away from the form/content dichotomy and instead relates the three categories to different phases of textual genesis. In this way, it becomes possible to relate them to real textual documents rather than treating them as purely virtual entities. In other conceptual fields, too, a genetic narratology can develop a specific profile. For example, the notion of narrativisation has been reconceptualised in the discussion, in order to capture not only the reader's application of cognitive schemata, but also the formation of the narratorial discourse in the course of the genetic process. These examples show that it is not far-fetched to think that engaging with genetic research and material can lead to a further development of the narratological toolkit.

Works Cited

Andrews, Molly (2014), *Narrative Imagination and Everyday Life* (Oxford: Oxford University Press).

Barthes, Roland (1968), 'L'Effet de Réel', *Communications*, 11: 84–89, https://doi.org/10.3406/comm.1968.1158.

Chatman, Seymour (1978), *Story and Discourse: Narrative Structure in Fiction and Film* (Ithaca, NY and London: Cornell University Press).

Dannenberg, Hilary P. (2005), 'Plot', in: *Routledge Encyclopedia of Narrative Theory*, ed. by David Herman et al. (London and New York: Routledge), 435–39.

De Biasi, Pierre-Marc (1996), 'What is a Literary Draft? Toward a Functional Typology of Genetic Documentation', trans. by Ingrid Wassenaar, *Yale French Studies*, 89: 26–58.

Fludernik, Monika (1996), *Towards a 'Natural Narratology'* (London and New York: Routledge).

Fontane, Theodor (2006), *Die Poggenpuhls. Roman*, ed. by Gabriele Radecke (Berlin: Aufbau).

Grüne, Matthias (2018), *Realistische Narratologie: Otto Ludwigs 'Romanstudien' im Kontext einer Geschichte der Erzähltheorie* (Berlin and Boston: De Gruyter). https://doi.org/10.1515/9783110541502.

Hehle, Christine (2023), 'Situation/Szene', in: *Theodor Fontane Handbuch*, ed. by Rolf Parr et al., vol. 2 (Berlin and Boston: De Gruyter), 1047–51.

Hettche, Walter (2003), '"Die erste Skizze wundervoll". Zu einem Kapitel aus Theodor Fontanes Roman Vor dem Sturm', in: *Schrift—Text—Edition. Hans Walter Gabler zum 65. Geburtstag*, ed. by Christiane Henkes et al. (Tübingen: Niemeyer), 213–20.

Kukkonen, Karin (2014), 'Plot', in: *the Living Handbook of Narratology*, ed. by Peter Hühn et al. (Hamburg: Hamburg University). https://www-archiv.fdm.uni-hamburg.de/lhn/node/115.html.

Kukkonen, Karin (2019), *4E Cognition and Eighteenth-Century Fiction: How the Novel Found its Feet* (Oxford: Oxford University Press).

McGillen, Petra S. (2019), *The Fontane Workshop: Manufacturing Realism in the Industrial Age of Print* (New York and London: Bloomsbury Academic).

Radecke, Gabriele (2002), *Vom Schreiben zum Erzählen. Eine Textgenetische Studie zu Theodor Fontanes 'L'Adultera'* (Würzburg: Königshausen & Neumann).

Scheffel, Michael (2022), 'Wege zu einer Genetischen Narratologie oder: Von der Geburt und dem Abenteuer der Geschichten am Beispiel von Werkgenesen des Autors Arthur Schnitzler', *DIEGESIS. Interdisziplinäres*

E-Journal für Erzähl-forschung/Interdisciplinary E-Journal for Narrative Research, 10.1: 49–72, https://www.diegesis.uni-wuppertal.de/index.php/diegesis/article/download/424/608/.

Schmid, Wolf (2010): *Narratology: An Introduction*, trans. by Alexander Starritt (Berlin and New York: De Gruyter).

Stanzel, Franz K. (1986), *A Theory of Narrative*, trans. by Charlotte Goedsche (Cambridge: Cambridge University Press).

Van Hulle, Dirk (2022), *Genetic Criticism: Tracing Creativity in Literature* (Oxford: Oxford University Press). https://doi.org/10.1093/oso/9780192846792.001.0001.

White, Hayden (1980), 'The Value of Narrativity in the Representation of Reality', *Critical Inquiry*, 7.1: 5–27, https://www.jstor.org/stable/1343174.

4. A Lodger Returns: Change in Narrative Voice Across Epigenetic Versions and Works

Josefine Hilfling

Introduction

The first edition of the Danish Nobel Prize-winning author Henrik Pontoppidan's major novel *A Fortunate Man* (*Lykke-Per* 1898a) opens with a chapter introducing the protagonist, Per Sidenius. In the second chapter, however, readers are suddenly confronted with the hitherto unknown characters Senior Boatswain Olufsen and his wife in Nyboder, Copenhagen. In the rather long second chapter, it seems for a while as if the protagonist is no longer the young Per Sidenius, but instead the retiree Olufsen. This is the impression readers initially get, until Per is reintroduced in the newly established context as a lodger at the Olufsens. Given Henrik Pontoppidan's working method, characterised by rewriting and revising his works after publication, creating new works from old ones, and changing plans and ambitions during the writing process, it becomes relevant to investigate where this new environment comes from and to investigate why Per becomes a lodger at the Olufsens.

A Fortunate Man (1898a-1904; 1905; 1907; 1918a; 1920a; 1931; 1937) is, like almost all Pontoppidan's works, told by a heterodiegetic omniscient narrator. However, a short section of the novel was originally published as part of the short story 'Fra Byen. Hjærtensfryd' ['Heart's Delight'] (1885a). This first edition of the short story is told by an unknown and barely present homodiegetic narrator, the lodger, but at the same time it possesses characteristics that are normally only seen in heterodiegetic omniscient narration. In the revised, second edition of the short story (1886) the narrator is changed to heterodiegetic, thereby matching the omniscient context. Due to this change of narrator, the lodger disappears from the text. Yet the change of narrator serves as a prerequisite for Pontoppidan's later incorporation of the story into the heterodiegetic context of *A Fortunate Man* (1898a).

It is not uncommon for authors in the writing process to change the narrative voice from homodiegetic to heterodiegetic (Van Hulle 2022, 157ff). To my knowledge, however, such a change has not been studied in the epigenetic phase of a work's genesis, that is the genesis of a work after the first publication (Van Hulle 2014, 97; 2022, 14ff). Likewise, homodiegetic narration resembling omniscient narration has been described by narrative critics anchored in single versions of texts (e.g. Skov Nielsen 2004; Shen 2013). Here it is studied across versions and works.

This essay gives insight into the origin and the genesis of a snippet of *A Fortunate Man* and offers an explanation to how and why Per became a lodger at Olufsens. An analysis of the change in narrative voice from the first to the second edition of 'Heart's Delight', where the most significant and influential changes are located, will show how little change it took Pontoppidan to change the narrative voice completely. From the analysis it will become apparent how the narrative voice that would dominate Pontoppidan's oeuvre (heterodiegetic, omniscient, past tense) was already present in his early writings—even when it was unintended. The analysis serves as an example of how the combination of genetic criticism and narratology can explain inconsistencies in single texts and across versions and works.

The Author Pontoppidan

Pontoppidan made his literary debut in 1881 during the so-called Danish modern breakthrough. He wrote, published and revised his works up until his death in 1943 (Stangerup 1977, 268ff). Writing and publishing over half a century, Pontoppidan can be classified as neither modernist, nor realist, naturalist, or romanticist. He wrote novellas, short stories, novels and newspaper articles but is mostly known for his three novels *The Promised Land* (*Det forjættede Land* 1891–95; 1898c;

1903b; 1918b; 1920b; 1938), *A Fortunate Man* and *The Kingdom of the Dead* (*De Dødes Rige* 1912-16; 1917; 1918c [1919]; 1922). In 1917, after having published the second, revised edition of *The Kingdom of the Dead*, Pontoppidan received the Nobel Prize in Literature, which he shared with another Danish author, Karl Gjellerup. Pontoppidan was awarded the prize 'for his authentic descriptions of present-day life in Denmark' (The Nobel Prize in Literature 1917). While it was not unjustified to award the prize to Pontoppidan for his depictions of Denmark at the time, this recognition provides only a simplified and insufficient interpretation of his oeuvre. In the Denmark he depicts in his works, we find people and their destinies, often described in a morbid but realistic way, shuttling between the dichotomies of religion and science, provincialism and metropolitanism, vanity and impermanence (Ahnlund 1956). These themes are indeed present in *A Fortunate Man*, and thematic germs, especially regarding the latter two dichotomies, can be traced back to 'Heart's Delight' (1885a), which was published twelve years earlier.

Pontoppidan's Working Method

Pontoppidan is known to have destroyed his manuscripts and to have revised his published works considerably through numerous later editions. This is also the case with both 'Heart's Delight' and *A Fortunate Man*. 'Heart's Delight' was published in three editions of which the first two differ significantly from each other.[1] *A Fortunate Man* was published in seven editions, of which especially the second and fourth editions contain significant variants (1905; 1918a). These epigenetic layers make it possible to trace Pontoppidan's creative process and the development of his work. Pontoppidan generally changed elements regarding the theme, motives, characteristics and descriptions (Behrendt 1971, 122ff; Kielberg and Rømhild 1997, 80f; Skjerbæk 1970, 59; Gottlieb 2022; Gottlieb and Rasmussen 2023, 48f, 60ff). Besides the change in narrative voice in 'Heart's Delight', there is one other case of change from first to third and back to first-person narration in the short story

---

1   The third edition (1888) is a reprint (with only some minor differences in the spelling) of the second edition, which is why I leave it out in this study.

'Af Pigen Marthas Historie' (27 August 1884), later published as a part of the novel *Ung Elskov* (1885b; 1906) (Behrendt 2006). As it appears, Pontoppidan tended to create new works from earlier published works by incorporating them into new narratives (Gottlieb and Rasmussen 2023, 57f; Haarder 2002, 27; Andersen 1917, 19; Behrendt 2003). The texts that he incorporated in his later works could thus be considered sketches related to the genesis of another work. Pontoppidan's oeuvre is intertwined and interconnected. *A Fortunate Man* is a single work, yet it is a complex one—a mosaic of works. One piece in this mosaic is the short story 'Heart's Delight'.

'Heart's Delight', First and Second Edition

The first edition of 'Heart's Delight' was published in the Nordic literary weekly *Hjemme og Ude* on 15 February 1885, only four years after Pontoppidan's debut as a writer. It was published under the pseudonym 'Urbanus' in the column *Fra Byen* [*From the City*]. At this time, Pontoppidan published under two pseudonyms: 'Urbanus' and 'Rusticus' (Behrendt 2018). The former he used for his publications on city life in Copenhagen, the latter for publications on country life. The first edition of 'Heart's Delight' is in the present tense, narrated by a homodiegetic narrator—an unknown lodger at the house of the Olufsens. The lodger is barely present as a character in the text, we do not even know whether they are male or female, but the story is, nevertheless, narrated by him or her. The story is set in an actual street in Copenhagen named after the lemon balm herb, which is nicknamed 'heart's delight'. It is a satire on life in the city and on the Olufsens and their many parties, celebrating not so much the official and religious holidays but their numerous private and self-invented occasions:

> [...] Aarsdagen for Kanariefuglen "Peter"s højtidelige Indlemmelse i Familien, endvidere Mindefest for Højbaadsmandens salig store Taa, som for tredive Aar siden blev klippet af for Bénedder, samt Madammens Kopsætningsdag, der gjærne indtræffer ud paa Foraaret (Pontoppidan 1885a, 249)
>
> [the annual celebration marking the solemn admission of "Peter" the canary into the family, furthermore, the commemoration of the day thirty years ago when Senior Boatswain Olufsen lost part of his blessed

big toe due to a severe bone infection, and the Madam's blood-letting day, which often occur well into the spring season][2]

As it appears, the Olufsens would use any event as an excuse to arrange a gathering—to eat and drink. The short story can be divided into two parts. The first part purports to provide a general description of how all their parties are held. Yet they are described with such accuracy that it can hardly serve as a general description. The second and longer part of the story contains a description of how one party, which differs from all the others, is planned and carried out.

The second edition of 'Heart's Delight' was published on 9 December 1886 as part of a collection of short stories by different Danish authors, entitled *Hjemmekinesere og andre Fortællinger* (Skjerbæk and Herring 2006, 66). In this edition, Pontoppidan does not mask himself behind a pseudonym. Instead, his name is explicitly listed in the index. Furthermore, the text is accompanied by a genre declaration, that is 'En Fortælling' ['A Tale']. The text is similar in its structure to the text in the first edition, but adjustments have been made. Text has been added, removed and revised. The number of deletions—or omissions—is greater than the number of additions. In that regard, the text has been shortened and tightened, which is typical of Pontoppidan's revisions (Skjerbæk 1970, 59). The most significant difference between the two editions is, as described, the voice, which changes from homodiegetic to heterodiegetic, along with a shift in tense from present to past.

In *A Fortunate Man*, the first and second parts of 'Heart's Delight' are incorporated into two different places and contexts of the work. The first part is located in the beginning of chapter 2, pages 55–58. The second part is located in the fourth chapter, pages 165–72.[3] In this essay, I will focus on the essential change of the narrator's voice in the first part of 'Heart's Delight'.

---

2   All translations of 'Heart's Delight' (1885a; 1886) and *A Fortunate Man* (1898a) are mine. I have found inspiration and support in Peter Larkin's English translation of the second edition of *A Fortunate Man* (Copenhagen: Museum Tusculanum Press, [1905] 2018) and received proficient advice from Jonathan Adams.

3   Both parts are incorporated into the first booklet of the first edition. Chapter 4 is the last chapter of the first booklet.

A Fortunate Man, First Edition

The first edition of *A Fortunate Man* was published in eight booklets over a span of six years (1898a-1904). It is a bildungsroman narrated by a heterodiegetic omniscient narrator chronicling the life journey of Per, the son of a rural clergyman. Per aspires to succeed as an engineer. However, the narrative transcends a mere career pursuit, interweaving a love story and an exploration of the fundamental meaning of life. The novel proposes that the quest for existential meaning cannot be found exclusively through the city's high society, material acquisitions, or professional aspirations. Instead, it suggests that true meaning must be found within oneself. The following recapitulation of chapters 1 and 2 sheds more light on the context in which the passage from 'Heart's Delight' is incorporated.

Chapter 1 sets the scene, describing the main character, Per, his family and the environment. Readers learn how Per feels estranged from his family and friends, and why he feels the urge to separate himself from the Christian home he is embarrassed to be associated with. Out of this far-from-easy, far-from-glamorous childhood emerges a dream of material success and recognition as an engineer in the Danish capital, if not in the whole of Europe. Per wants to distance himself from everything his life has been so far: Christianity, his family and the countryside of Jutland. The first chapter ends with a scene in which Per, at the age of seventeen, sails away from Jutland towards Copenhagen to embark on his studies at the Polytechnical Institute. Chapter 2 begins with a rather long passage of the hitherto unknown characters of boatswain Olufsen, his wife and their foster daughter and maid, Trine (1898a, 49–53). The introductory passage is an adaptation of two other, earlier publications 'Enetale 19. April' (19 April 1897) and 'Den sorte Aline. En fortælling' (1889). The adaptation of these texts is followed by what I have referred to as 'the first part' of 'Heart's Delight', introducing the main character Per, now a lodger at the Olufsens' (1898a, 56).

Change in Narrative Voice from 'Heart's Delight' to *A Fortunate Man*

Every version of the examined story contains a description that purports to specify not just one party but every party held at the Olufsens for the last forty years (1885a, 249; 1886, 47; 1898a, 55). Especially with a homodiegetic narrator, as in the case of the first edition, the description is too specific to be believable. Furthermore, the homodiegetic narrator conflicts with elements of omniscience. I do not argue, however, that this is a case of unreliability. Rather it is what James Phelan has defined as deficient narration (2017, 235). In both unreliable and deficient narration something is 'off-kilter', meaning that there is a disruption 'of the alignment of authors, narrators, and audiences that characterizes most reliable narration' (231). The difference is that unreliable narration is off-kilter intentionally whereas deficient narration is not (195). When readers recognise the narration of a text as unintentionally off-kilter, their expectations run counter to the progression of the story. Phelan describes how he identifies off-kilter elements in his reading of Joan Didion's publication *The Year of Magical Thinking* (2005):

> Why would I or any reader notice that this clause [in Didion's text] is off-kilter? Because of our unfolding responses to the progression. In my own experience, the clause seemed to jump off the page because it ran so counter to the expectations and desires I had developed by attending to the narrating-I's quest for something that could have made a difference. (Phelan 2017, 208)

The identification of the off-kilter elements depends on readers' expectations. Phelan distinguishes between three kinds of deficient narration: deceptive, inadvertent and intratextual (237). Deceptive and inadvertent forms of deficient narration concern nonfiction. Here the deficiency is measured in correlation with external facts. Intratextual types of deficient narration can relate to both nonfiction and fiction. Here the deficiency exists within the frames of the text. In Phelan's definition intratextual deficient narration 'reveals its deficiency through some inconsistency or other flaw in the overall design of the narration. To put it another way, intratextual deficient narration is deficient in relation to the terms set by its own larger narrative' (Phelan 2017, 236f).

In this analysis, I argue that the narration in the first edition of 'Heart's Delight' appears deficient because its homodiegetic narrator resembles an omniscient heterodiegetic narrator, recounting too many details. However, because the first edition already had features of an omniscient heterodiegetic narrative voice, the analysis will show that it only took Pontoppidan one omission to resolve the deficiency and change the narrative voice to heterodiegetic. The analysis is split into two parts focusing respectively on two discrepancies: 1) between the homodiegetic narrator and the features of omniscience; 2) between the homodiegetic narrator and the number of details offered.

1. The Lodger and Signs of Omniscience

The first sentence of the first edition of 'Heart's Delight' informs readers about the narrator's identity, the atmosphere and where the story is set. It provides information about the narrative situation, making readers expect a reliable, homodiegetic narrative: 'Der fejres aarlig mange Festdage hos min Vært, pensioneret Højbaadsmand Olufsen i Hjærtensfrydgade' ['Many festive days are celebrated annually at my host, retired Senior Boatswain Olufsen in Heart's Delight Street'] (1885a, 249). The homodiegetic narrator is the unnamed and unidentified lodger. There are no first-person singular references to the narrator themself, other than the possessive pronoun 'my' in 'at my host', and no further direct information on the character-narrator is offered. In the second edition of 'Heart's Delight', the little descriptive phrase 'at my host' is omitted: 'Der fejredes mange Festdage hos pensioneret Højbaadsmand Olufsen i Hjærtensfrydgade' ['Many festive days were celebrated annually at retired Senior Boatswain Olufsen in Heart's Delight Street'] (1886, 73). Since the omitted phrase is the only direct reference to a homodiegetic narrator in the first edition, it only takes a single omission to 'transvocalize' from homo- to heterodiegetic (Genette [1983] 1988, 109ff). The ease with which Pontoppidan accomplishes this resembles the genesis of another work. In her study of Franz Kafka's manuscript for *Das Schloß* (1926), Dorrit Cohn describes how Kafka employs a homodiegetic narrator, 'Ich', for the first 42 pages but then decides to change it to a heterodiegetic narrator, 'K' (1968, 29). Cohn argues that there were no obstacles in changing the narrator's voice because the text was 'a first-person narrative in grammatical form only, not in structure' (Cohn 1968, 33; Van Hulle 2022, 158). The same goes for the first edition of 'Heart's Delight' except it barely was a first-person narrative in grammatical form at all. When, twelve years later, 'Heart's Delight' is incorporated into *A Fortunate Man*, Per becomes a lodger at the Olufsens': 'Denne lystige unge Mand er Olufsens Logerende, den enogtyveaarige Polytekniker Sidenius' ['This merry young man is Olufsens' lodger, the twenty-one-year-old engineering student Sidenius'] (1898a, 56). To sum up, there is a movement from the first edition of 'Heart's Delight', where the narrator-character is an unknown and almost invisible lodger; to the second edition where the narrator-character is omitted and replaced with a heterodiegetic narrator; to *A Fortunate Man* where the heterodiegetic narrator introduces the protagonist Per as a (or maybe *the*) lodger.

A homodiegetic narrator's insight is normally limited to the character it represents, and what he/she can experience, recount and recollect (Prince [1987] 2003, 40). In contrast, an omniscient narrator possesses potential insight into everything at any given moment (Niederhoff 2013). Yet features of omniscience in homodiegetic narrative fiction are not unusual (Skov Nielsen 2004, 135f). The final three lines of the examined passage in the first edition of 'Heart's Delight' (1885a, 250) are a sign of a latent omniscient narrator: 'Endelig henad Morgenstunden sejler de hjemad, hver til sit, i en Lyksalighedstilstand, fra hvilken der endnu Dagen efter hviler et Skjær over dem, som fra en nedgaaet Sol.— —' ['At last, towards the morning hours, they sail homeward, each to their own, in a state of bliss, from which there still lingers a glow over them the next day, like that of a setting sun.— —'] (1885a, 250). There are several indications of omniscience in this passage. First, it describes how the guests go home in a state of pure happiness ('bliss'). This indicates that the narrator has insight into the guests' feelings. Second, the narrator has insight into the way the light falls upon not only one, but all the attendees' faces at the same time, the day after the actual parties. To possess this insight, the homodiegetic narrator would have to (always) be present at several different places at the same time. The quoted passage is adapted into the heterodiegetic narratives of both the second edition of 'Heart's Delight' and *A Fortunate Man*. The passage shows that there is an element of omniscience in all three versions of the story, but the context differs. In the first edition, the passage appears in the context of a homodiegetic narrator. In the second edition of 'Heart's Delight' and in *A Fortunate Man*, it appears in the context of a heterodiegetic omniscient narrator, where it does not come across as off-kilter.

2. Party in Plural

Another reason why the narrative comes across as deficient is due to the level of detail in the description of the parties, which—in combination with the homodiegetic narrator—appear unbelievable and off-kilter.

In both editions of 'Heart's Delight', the descriptions of the parties are meant to be general but are detailed to a degree that would make one suppose that it was a description of a single event rather than several events. A good example is the passage in which the narrator refers to a recurring exchange between Madam Olufsen and one of the guests, Riveter Fuss. After the guests have been seated and Madam Olufsen has placed the 'duck or ham roast' on the table, Fuss throws himself back in the chair exclaiming a joke about Madam Olufsen being a hen and the roast a giant egg she laid, whereupon she 'berates' him as 'an old fool' and invites the guests to 'treat her abode as if it were their own' (1885a, 149; 1886, 74; 1898a, 55). The accuracy in the description of the events would make it possible to recreate a typical party at the Olufsens'. It can be compared to an already tried recipe for how a party is held at the Olufsens'. But, as David Herman states, a recipe is not narrative (2002, 88). This impression of a narrative created from something non-narrative containing a description of a general phenomenon as if it were specific makes readers experience something in the narrative as off-kilter.

The accuracy and the number of details appear off-kilter in the first edition of 'Heart's Delight' due to the limits in the narrative voice of a homodiegetic narrator, but in the second edition of 'Heart's Delight' and in *A Fortunate Man* it is less so, because they are narrated by an omniscient heterodiegetic narrative voice. Furthermore, the number of details decreases in each of Pontoppidan's revisions. Below is an example from the same scene across the three different editions. In both editions of 'Heart's Delight' (1885a, 1886), time is referred to with exact time markers; in *A Fortunate Man*, the proceedings of the events depend to a higher degree on the causality of earlier events:

Paa Slaget sex aabner Olufsen Døren ind til "Salen", hvor Bordet staar dækket (1885a, 249)
[At the stroke of six Olufsen opens the door into the "parlour", where the table is laid]

Paa Slaget sex aabnede Olufsen Døren ind til "Salen" (hvor Bordet stod dækket) (1886, 47)
[At the stroke of six Olufsen opened the door into the "parlour" (where the table had been laid)]

Saa snart Gæsterne var bleven samlede inde i Gaardværelset, aabnede Højbaadsmanden egenhændig Døren ind til "Salen", hvor Bordet stod dækket (1898a, 55)
[Once all the guests were assembled in the back room, Senior Boatswain Olufsen, in person, opened the door into the "parlour", where the table had been laid]

Note the parenthesis in the second edition of 'Heart's Delight', '(hvor Bordet stod dækket)' ['(where the table had been laid)'] (1886). The text inside the parenthesis serves as the narrator's commentary clarifying Olufsen's use of the term 'parlour' to signify a room where the dinner table is set. This kind of explanatory narrator's comments can be found in both editions of 'Heart's Delight' but have been removed from the passage contained in *A Fortunate Man* (Behrendt 1971, 122f). In this regard, the heterodiegetic narrator in *A Fortunate Man* appears more neutral because this style of narration places less emphasis on the storytelling.

Another change that may contribute to making the narrative voice in the second edition of 'Heart's Delight' and the first edition of *A Fortunate Man* appear more neutral is the change from present to past tense. Present tense narration is not necessarily 'unnatural' in Brian Richardson's sense (2015). Yet in Pontoppidan's time, when epic preterite was the dominant form of narration, (homodiegetic) present tense narratives were not as 'conventionalized' (Skov Nielsen 2011, 85) as they are today. Therefore, if the second edition of 'Heart's Delight', narrated in the past tense, seems more neutral to its contemporary readers, it may have seemed even more so to readers in Pontoppidan's time.

It is the comprehensive recollection of events in the first edition, narrated in the present tense by a homodiegetic narrator, that appears off-kilter. In the two later versions, the inconsistencies are resolved thanks to the change to heterodiegetic narration, matching the already present elements of omniscience.

The Larger Narrative and Concluding Remarks

In the analysis above, I have studied the narrative conflicts in the first edition of 'Heart's Delight' regarding the homodiegetic narrator, the signs of omniscience and the unbelievable number of details used to describe plural parties but imitating a description of a single event. I have argued that the deficiency in the first edition is resolved in later versions due to, primarily, the single omission of the phrase 'at my host' in the second edition of 'Heart's Delight' and in *A Fortunate Man*.

The described changes in 'Heart's Delight' and *A Fortunate Man* signal changes in Pontoppidan's intentions, at least for that specific moment when they are made. In this genetic-narratological analysis, the knowledge of Pontoppidan's working method and the insight into his revisions in the three versions of the story can serve as a retrospective authorial confirmation: Pontoppidan's intuition that something is off-kilter in the first edition of 'Heart's Delight' confirms the narratological analysis of the deficiency.

In the earlier quoted description of deficient narratives, Phelan writes: 'intratextual deficient narration is deficient in relation to the terms set by its own larger narrative' (2017, 236f). What he means by 'larger narrative' is not unfolded. On the one hand, it could be the narrative presented at first, shaping readers' expectations; in that case, it is the omniscient, heterodiegetic elements that appear off-kilter. On the other hand, it could also be the narrative that takes up more of the actual space in the text; in that case, it is the homodiegetic phrase 'my host' that appears off-kilter. In 2006, the eminent Pontoppidan scholar Flemming Behrendt wrote that there is no first-person narrator in the first edition of 'Heart's Delight'. Fifteen years later, he corrected this mistake, identifying the narrating 'I' in the first paragraph (2021, 706). The fact that Behrendt overlooked the homodiegetic narrator and mistakenly concluded that there is none supports the argument that the homodiegetic narrator in the text is almost absent, to such a degree that it makes readers overlook it and therefore read the text without even finding the text deficient. This also goes some way towards explaining why the inconsistency was there in the first place: maybe Pontoppidan as his own first reader simply overlooked it.

In a manuscript study, we would be able to trace the genesis in the documents and observe where the inconsistencies appeared. In an epigenetic study such as this one, where the genesis is in print, it is only the result of the writing process that is left in the document. Therefore, the conclusions depend to a higher degree on interpretation. Still, it is possible to draw a few conclusions from this kind of epigenetic study. Pontoppidan's plan for, and concept of, *A Fortunate Man* changed both during the endo- and epigenetic writing process of the first edition (Pontoppidan in a letter to Otto Borchsenius, 3 July 1898). This working method suggests that Pontoppidan was not an author who made a thorough plan of his works beforehand. When he had just published the first booklet of the first edition, the ambition was to create a novel in six booklets published over two years, concerning five different homes in Denmark. One of these homes was the Olufsens'. By the time the first edition was finished, eight, not six, booklets had been published over a span of six, not two, years. The Olufsens' home does play a part in the novel. Still, it is not central to the story and its relevance is, perhaps due to the revisions and to the decreased importance of the foster child Trine (Gottlieb and Rasmussen 2023, 48), further reduced in the later, revised editions (1905; 1918a). This could indicate that the incorporation of 'Heart's Delight' in *A Fortunate Man* was not part of a great plan. Due to the context of the incorporation which followed two further incorporations of earlier works, Pontoppidan at this moment in the writing process had likely reread some earlier published works in search of texts that would fit in with the established narrative. Incorporating 'Heart's Delight' in *A Fortunate Man* may have reminded him of the homodiegetic narrator, the lodger, in the first edition of 'Heart's Delight', which possibly inspired him to turn Per into a lodger. Pontoppidan did not have much experience with writing first-person narratives. In his entire oeuvre, he mainly worked with heterodiegetic narrators. His apparent preference for heterodiegetic narrative voice is reflected in the lack of coherence in the first edition of 'Heart's Delight', but also in the genesis of the narrative voice across the versions of the story in 'Heart's Delight' and in *A Fortunate Man*.

In this essay, I have described how little revision it took Pontoppidan to change the narrative voice in 'Heart's Delight'. This was because the first edition already possessed characteristics inherent to omniscient narration. I have argued that the inconsistency in the narrative voice in the first edition of 'Heart's Delight' was unintended, and that the shift from a homodiegetic narrator to a heterodiegetic narrator in 'Heart's Delight' enabled Pontoppidan to incorporate the short story into *A Fortunate Man*. Removing the unidentified lodger and changing the narrator opened the door for another lodger at the Olufsens' in *A Fortunate Man*, namely, the protagonist Per Sidenius.

Works Cited

Ahnlund, Knut (1956). *Henrik Pontoppidan. Fem huvudlinjer i författarskapet* (Stockholm: P. A. Norstedt & Söners Förlag).

Andersen, Vilhelm (1917), *Henrik Pontoppidan: Et nydansk Forfatterskab* (København: Gyldendalske Boghandel).

Behrendt, Flemming [1964] (2003), *Pontoppidans omarbejdelser: Genetisk-tekstkritiske studier i forfatterskabet, især 1890-1908* (Henrik Pontoppidan Netstedet). https://www.henrikpontoppidan.dk/text/seclit/secboeger/behrendt/index.html#kap1IV.

Behrendt, Flemming (1971), 'Fra ledefigur til hovedperson: Om Lykke-Pers tilblivelse', in: *Omkring Lykke-Per*, ed. by Knut Ahnlund (København: Hans Reitzels Forlag), 103–24.

Behrendt, Flemming (2006), *Jeg lå i mit Vindue: En undersøgelse af Henrik Pontoppidans tøvende og eksperimenterende vej til 1980'ernes jeg-romaner* (Henrik Pontoppidan Netstedet). https://www.henrikpontoppidan.dk/text/seclit/secartikler/behrendt/jegfortaellere.html#note2.

Behrendt, Flemming (2018), *Meninger og holdninger (1994)* (Henrik Pontoppidan Netstedet). https://www.henrikpontoppidan.dk/text/kilder/boeger/meninger.html.

Behrendt, Flemming (2021, 2. e-book edition), *Livsrusen. En bog om Henrik Pontoppidan* (Gads forlag).

Bernaerts, Lars and Dirk Van Hulle (2013), 'Narrative across Versions: Narratology Meets Genetic Criticism', *Poetics Today*, 34.3: 281–326, https://doi.org/10.1215/03335372-2325232.

Cohn, Dorrit (1968), 'K. enters *The Castle*: On the Change of Person in Kafka's Manuscript', *Euphorion*, 62: 28–45.

Niederhoff, Burkhard (2011, rev. 2013), 'Perspective—Point of View', in: *The Living Handbook of Narratology*, ed. by Peter Hühn, et al. (Hamburg: Hamburg University). https://www-archiv.fdm.uni-hamburg.de/lhn/node/26.html.

Genette, Gérard [1983] (1988), 'Person (II)', in: *Narrative Discourse Revisited* (Ithaca, NY: Cornell University Press), 109–13.

Gottlieb, Katja (2022), *Smagssag. En editionsfilologisk undersøgelse af Henrik Pontoppidans Lykke-Per med særligt henblik på inspirationen fra Nietzsche* (Henrik Pontoppidan Netstedet). https://www.henrikpontoppidan.dk/text/undervisning/opgaver/eksempler/gottlieb_smagssag.html.

Gottlieb, Katja and Krista Stinne Greve Rasmussen (2023), 'Litteraturens mange versioner: Metodiske overvejelser for litteraturstudier og Henrik Pontoppidans Lykke-Per', in: *Boghistorie i Skandinavien*, ed. by Krista Stinne Greve Rasmussen, et al. (Aarhus: Aarhus University Press), 47–70, https://doi.org/10.2307/jj.3643869.5.

Haarder, Jon Helt (2002), 'Henrik Pontoppidan', in: *Danske digtere i det 20. århundrede*, vol. 1, ed. by Anne-Marie Mai (København: Gads Forlag), 11–30.

Herman, David (2002), 'Sequences versus Stories', in: *Story Logic: Problems and Possibilities of Narrative* (Lincoln, NE: University of Nebraska Press), 87–92.

Kielberg, Esther and Lars Peter Rømhild (1997), 'Efterskrift', in: *Det forjættede Land*, vol. 2, ed. by Esther Kielberg, Lars Peter Rømhild (København: Det Danske Sprog- og Litteraturselskab; Gyldendal), 11–188.

The Nobel Prize in Literature (1917), *NobelPrize.org*, The Nobel Prize in Literature 1917. NobelPrize.org.

Pontoppidan, Henrik (27 August 1884), 'Fra Landet: 2det Kapitel af Pigen Marthas Historie', in: *Ude og Hjemme*, 356: 525–26.

Pontoppidan, Henrik (1885a), 'Fra Byen. Hjærtensfryd', in: *Hjemme og Ude*, 20: 249–52.

Pontoppidan, Henrik (1885b), *Ung Elskov* (København: Gyldendalske Boghandels Forlag (F. Hegel & Søn)).

Pontoppidan, Henrik (1886), 'Hjærtensfryd', in: *Hjemmekinesere og andre Fortællinger* (København: N. C. Roms Forlagsforretning), 71–82.

Pontoppidan, Henrik (1889), 'Den sorte Aline. En Fortælling', in: *Folkets Almanak for det Aar efter Christi Fødsel 1890*, ed. by Niels Christian Rom and Christian Andersen Thyregod (N. C. Roms Forlagsforretning), 2–12.

Pontoppidan, Henrik (1891), *Muld. Et Tidsbillede* (København: P.G. Philipsens Forlag).

Pontoppidan, Henrik (1892), *Muld. Et Tidsbillede* (København: P.G. Philipsens Forlag).

Pontoppidan, Henrik (1892), *Det forjættede Land. Et Tidsbillede* (København: P.G. Philipsens Forlag).

Pontoppidan, Henrik (1893), *Det forjættede Land. Et Tidsbillede* (København: P.G. Philipsens Forlag).

Pontoppidan, Henrik (1895), *Dommens Dag. Et Tidsbillede* (København: P.G. Philipsens Forlag).

Pontoppidan, Henrik (19 April 1897), 'Enetale 19. April', in: *Politiken*.

Pontoppidan, Henrik (1898a), *Lykke-Per, hans Ungdom* (København: Det nordiske Forlag).

Pontoppidan, Henrik (1898b), *Lykke-Per finder Skatten* (København: Det nordiske Forlag).

Pontoppidan, Henrik (1898c), *Det forjættede Land* (København: Det nordiske Forlag).

Pontoppidan, Henrik (1899), *Lykke-Per, hans Kærlighed* (København: Det nordiske Forlag).

Pontoppidan, Henrik (1899), *Lykke-Per i det Fremmede* (København: Det nordiske Forlag).

Pontoppidan, Henrik (1901), *Lykke-Per, hans store Værk* (København: Det nordiske Forlag).

Pontoppidan, Henrik (1902), *Lykke-Per og hans Kæreste* (København: Det nordiske Forlag).

Pontoppidan, Henrik (1903a), *Lykke-Per, hans Rejse til Amerika* (København: Det nordiske Forlag).

Pontoppidan, Henrik (1903b), *Det forjættede Land* (København: Det nordiske Forlag).

Pontoppidan, Henrik (1904), *Lykke-Per, hans sidste Kamp* (København og Kristiania: Gyldendalske Boghandel; Nordiske Forlag).

Pontoppidan, Henrik (1905), *Lykke-Per*, Anden Udgave, Første-Tredje Del (København og Kristiania: Gyldendalske Boghandel; Nordisk Forlag).

Pontoppidan, Henrik (1906), *Ung Elskov* (København: Det Schubotske Forlag).

Pontoppidan, Henrik (1907), *Lykke-Per*, Tredje Udgave, Første-Tredje Del (København og Kristiania: Gyldendalske Boghandel; Nordisk Forlag).

Pontoppidan, Henrik (1912), *Torben og Jytte. (En Fortælling-Kres)* (København og Kristiania: Gyldendalske Boghandel; Nordisk Forlag).

Pontoppidan, Henrik (1913), *Storeholt. (En Fortælling-Kres)* (København og Kristiania: Gyldendalske Boghandel; Nordisk Forlag).

Pontoppidan, Henrik (1914), *Toldere og Syndere. (En Fortælling-Kres)* (København og Kristiania: Gyldendalske Boghande; Nordisk Forlag).

Pontoppidan, Henrik (1915), *Enslevs Død*. (*En Fortælling-Kres*) (København og Kristiania: Gyldendalske Boghandel; Nordisk Forlag.)

Pontoppidan, Henrik (1916), *Torben og Jytte*. (*En Fortælling-Kres*) [4. oplag] (København og Kristiania: Gyldendalske Boghandel; Nordisk Forlag).

Pontoppidan, Henrik (1916), *Favsingholm*. (*En Fortælling-Kres*) (København og Kristiania: Gyldendalske Boghandel; Nordisk Forlag).

Pontoppidan, Henrik (1917), *De Dødes Rige* (København og Kristiania: Gyldendalske Boghandel).

Pontoppidan, Henrik (1918a), *Lykke-Per*, Fjerde Udgave, Første-Andet Bind (København og Kristiania: Gyldendalske Boghandel).

Pontoppidan, Henrik (1918b), *Det forjættede Land* (København og Kristiania: Gyldendalske Boghandel).

Pontoppidan, Henrik (1918c), *De Dødes Rige* (København og Kristiania: Gyldendalske Boghandel; Nordisk Forlag).

Pontoppidan, Henrik (1920a), *Lykke-Per*, Femte Udgave, Første-Andet Bind (København og Kristiania: Gyldendalske Boghandel; Nordisk Forlag).

Pontoppidan, Henrik (1920b), *Det forjættede Land* (København og Kristiania: Gyldendalske Boghandel; Nordisk Forlag).

Pontoppidan, Henrik (1922), *De Dødes Rige* (København, Kristiania, London og Berlin: Gyldendalske Boghandel; Nordisk Forlag).

Pontoppidan, Henrik (1931), *Lykke-Per*, Sjette Oplag, Første-Andet Bind (København: Gyldendalske Boghandel; Nordisk Forlag).

Pontoppidan, Henrik (1937), *Lykke-Per*, Syvende Udgave, Første-Andet Bind (København: Gyldendalske Boghandel; Nordisk Forlag).

Pontoppidan, Henrik (1938), *Det forjættede Land* (København: Gyldendalske Boghandel; Nordisk Forlag).

Phelan, James (2017), 'The Implied Author, Deficient Narration, and Nonfiction Narrative: Joan Didion's *The Year of Magical Thinking* and Jean-Dominique Bauby's *The Diving Bell and The Buttery*'; 'Reliable, Unreliable, and Deficient Narration: Toward a Rhetorical Poetics', in: *Somebody Telling Somebody Else: A Rhetorical Poetics of Narrative* (Columbus: Ohio State University Press), 195-214; 230–8, https://doi.org/10.2307/j.ctv15rt209.15.

Prince, Gerald [1987] (2003), *A Dictionary of Narratology* (Lincoln, NE and London: University of Nebraska Press).

Richardson, Brian (2015), *Unnatural Narrative: Theory, History, and Practice* (Columbus: Ohio State University Press).

Shen, Dan (2011, rev. 2013), 'Unreliability', in: *The Living Handbook of Narratology*, ed. by Peter Hühn et al. (Hamburg: Hamburg University). https://www-archiv.fdm.uni-hamburg.de/lhn/node/66.html.

Skjerbæk, Thorkild (1970), *Kunst og budskab. Studier i Henrik Pontoppidans forfatterskab* (Odense: Gyldendal).

Skjerbæk, Esther and Thorkild, and René Herring (2006), *Henrik Pontoppidans forfatterskab: en bibliografi*, ed. by René Herring (København: Det Danske Sprog- og Litteraturselskab; Det Kongelige Bibliotek).

Skov Nielsen, Henrik (2004), 'The Impersonal Voice in First-Person Narrative Fiction', *Narrative*, 12.2: 133–50, 10.1353/nar.2004.0002.

Skov Nielsen, Henrik (2011), 'Unnatural Narratology, Impersonal Voices, Real Authors, and Non-Communicative Narration', in: *Unnatural Narratives— Unnatural Narratology*, ed. by Jan Alber and Rüdiger Heinze (Berlin and Boston: de Gruyter), 71–88, https://doi.org/10.1515/9783110229042.

Stangerup, Hakon (1977), 'Henrik Pontoppidan', in: *Dansk Litteraturhistorie*. 2nd edition, vol. 4, ed. by Hakon Stangerup et ál. (København: Politikens Forlag), 268-317.

Van Hulle, Dirk (2014), *Modern Manuscripts: The Extended Mind and Creative Undoing from Darwin to Beckett and Beyond* (London and New York: Bloomsbury).

Van Hulle, Dirk (2022), *Genetic Criticism: Tracing Creativity in Literature* (Oxford: Oxford University Press). https://doi.org/10.1093/oso/9780192846792.001.0001.

5. Melville's Cancelled Note-to-Self: The Development of a 'Ragged' Narrative Across the Drafts of *Billy Budd*

Charles Mascia

1. Introduction: 'The Presentation of Ambiguity'

In 1890, a *New York Times* reporter speculated that 'there are more people to-day who believe Herman Melville dead than there are those who know he is living' (*New York Times* 1890, 7). Melville's long fall into obscurity—after the commercial success of *Typee* (1846) or the controversy of *Moby-Dick* (1851)—was never corrected during the author's lifetime. When he died in 1891, he had been forgotten by American readers. However, Melville was working on something in his final years that would come to sharpen his legacy. In 1886, he had begun to compose a rough ballad, with a brief prose headnote, that was intended for publication in the verse collection *John Marr and Other Sailors* (1888). Yet Melville continued revising 'Billy in the Darbies' until his death. After five years, this ballad had transformed into a substantial novella of 351 leaves (Hayford and Sealts 1962, 224).[1] Unfinished and unpublished at his death, the manuscript was kept for two decades in a 'bread box' in the Melville attic. It wasn't until 1922 that the leaves of *Billy Budd, Sailor* (*An Inside Narrative*) were seen and hastily transcribed by the scholar Raymond Weaver (Parker 1990, 45). A version of the *Billy Budd* text was published for the first time in 1924. Despite being riddled with transcription errors that misinterpreted

---

1   Cited hereafter as "H&S."

Melville's notes, *Billy Budd*'s publication spurred a profound revival of interest in the author's work (76). By 1927 E.M. Forster had already praised *Billy Budd* in *Aspects of the Novel* (64). At mid-century, the New Critics had enshrined Melville as a centrepiece of the American canon, and identified *Billy Budd* as the text in which the author 'came to full mastery of himself' (73). These readers valued 'literary ambiguity' above all else, and Melville's novella was esteemed as a masterwork of this effect (77). But absent from these evaluations is the troubling fact that *Billy Budd* was never actually completed—and at times it is simply incoherent. This chapter attempts to resolve longstanding interpretative questions about how readers of *Billy Budd* might disentangle the errors of a dying man from the exquisitely enigmatic achievements of his art.

Briefly, the story is as follows: *Billy Budd* is a young seaman and figure of prelapsarian innocence, 'an upright barbarian, much such perhaps as Adam' (*BB* 2009, 288).[2] 'Of self-consciousness,' we are told, 'he seemed to have little or none' (288). The story of Billy's maritime career is both a finely wrought historical fiction and a warped retelling of man's fall from Eden. It is 1797, and Billy is impressed into the service of England's Royal Navy as a foretopman on the HMS *Bellipotent*. It is a dangerous time: the French Revolutionary Wars are ongoing, and recent mutinies have sent waves of paranoia through the Navy. In this perilous context, Billy is wrongfully accused of mutinous intent by John Claggart, the *Bellipotent*'s master-at-arms. Likened to a 'snake' throughout, the depraved Claggart harbours a mysterious, maniacal hatred for Billy and his innocence (332). Claggart makes his accusation before the ship's commander, Captain Vere, and Billy is called upon to speak for himself. Crucially, he suffers from an agonising stutter. In his shock at the baseless charge levelled against him, and in his frustration with his 'tongue-tie', Billy strikes his accuser a fatal blow (331). Captain Vere is sympathetic to Billy, having already divined his innocence of Claggart's

---

2   For the sake of clarity, I cite the standard reading text of *Billy Budd* as "BB." When referring to details from the story—in order to provide context, as I do here—I will cite from the OUP edition of *Billy Budd* (a 2009 reprint of the reading text edited by Harrison Hayford and Merton Sealts). However, when specifically referring to a detail of *composition* or of textual revision *in the manuscript*, I will cite the manuscript leaf number and the corresponding page number in Hayford and Sealts's 1962 Genetic Text edition, abbreviated as H&S.

charge. But Vere is also a pragmatic disciplinarian, and determines that 'the angel must hang' (333). Vere persuades a court of the ship's officers not to consider 'the essential right and wrong of the case', insisting that 'measured forms are everything' (335; 358). Thus, though the court recognises Billy's moral innocence, they agree he must be hanged for killing his superior officer. When Billy is executed the next morning, his inexplicable final words are 'God bless Captain Vere' (354). Described as a 'martyr' and illuminated from above by the light of the 'Lamb of God', the brutality of Billy's hanging is transfigured into a glorious ascension into the dawn sky (352; 354). In the remaining chapters, Billy's afterlife in memory is enumerated—revealing how variously and incorrectly others interpret his fate, therefore necessitating the 'inside narrative' we have been reading.

In the words of one 1924 reviewer, the novella is 'the last will and spiritual testament of a man of genius' (Murry, qtd. in Parker 1990, 58). But what does this testament mean? Nearly a century after the novella's publication, there remains no critical consensus on the answer to this question. Initial readings argued that *Billy Budd* revealed Melville's arrival at 'inward peace', his acceptance of both good and evil in the world (Freeman, qtd. in Parker 1990, 62). In this case, the novella is a work of 'brightness', affirming the glory of Christ by celebrating the 'complete triumph' of the 'utterly pure' at the moment of death, or transcendence (Murry, qtd. in Parker 1990, 60). Yet other readers of the time found only 'blackness and sadness' in the story (Forster, qtd. in Parker 1990, 64). By mid-century, critical focus had begun to emphasise the irony of the text's portrayal of Captain Vere. New readings suggested that he, as well as Claggart, is an oppressive figure of arbitrary evil. *Billy Budd* was thus deemed a miserable 'testament of resistance' against the tyranny of man and authoritarian regimes (Parker 1990, 75). Out of all these readings emerges the impossible question that continues to animate criticism: does Melville's text *endorse* Vere's harsh enforcement of the law despite his belief in Billy's innocence? Or does the text *protest* against the unjust moral inconsistency of these very laws and the society they represent? As Hershel Parker writes, *Billy Budd* is 'designed to force the reader to take one of [these] two mutually incompatible positions', each of which is supported by the story (98). Thus, Charles Olson remarks that 'the secret of Melville as artist [is] the presentation of ambiguity by the event direct' (qtd. in H&S 1962, 38).

Differently from other critics, I do not aim to dissolve Melville's ambiguous effects in favour of a definitive meaning. Rather, this chapter traces *how* certain ambiguities emerged in Melville's process of composition. In other words, I attend not to the text, but to the text's becoming. Excavating the genesis of the *Billy Budd* manuscript, I draw attention to the material traces of Melville's revisions, which serve as witnesses to his artistic process and shifting intentions. My simple rationale is articulated well by Dirk Van Hulle in *Genetic Criticism*: 'knowing how something was made can help us understand how it works' (2022, 75). Towards this end, I rely upon the Genetic Text edition of *Billy Budd*, compiled and edited by Hayford and Sealts, and upon the Fluid-Text Edition available on the Melville Electronic Library. These materials allow us to follow as Melville 'built up, piece by piece' the successive drafts of his work (de Biasi 1996, 29). Melville's five-year process of composition was anything but smooth. In John Wenke's words, it was a constant 'remaking [of] a text that intrigued, haunted and even baffled him. He was seemingly unable to recopy his manuscript without reconceiving parts of it' (1999, 502). The myriad ink and pencil inscriptions that record the 'writing movements' of this struggle are, of course, 'untraceable' in standard reading versions of *Billy Budd* (de Biasi 1996, 29). Thus, attending to the changing story in its fluid manuscript state is an invaluable way to 'validate' critical interpretations that would only otherwise be hypotheses (29).

A few questions guide this inquiry: Do Melville's revisions reveal that he had a clear, or consistent, sense of what was important in his story? How does his focus change as he writes? Do his late revisions inadvertently obscure the shape and tone of the narrative, or do they indicate a new stylistic impulse? How can we distinguish between the oversights or errors of an infirm artist and his intentionally ambiguous effects? Do the themes and aesthetic principles of *Billy Budd* guide Melville's composition, or do they emerge unforeseen out of the process of composition? Simple as they appear, these questions beckon the reader to investigate the messily unresolved inconsistencies and disunities that corrupt the text. These textual inconsistencies are all the more complex, and fascinating, because *Billy Budd* is a story about narrative disorder—a story that emphasises the unreliability of texts and the hazards of their interpretation. Indeed, Hershel Parker identifies a 'recurrent' theme in the text, of the tension between 'misconstruing and reading aright' (1990, 161). Barbara Johnson agrees that *Billy Budd* is Melville's 'study of the nature of reading' (1979, 587). She argues that the plot of the novella is founded on the dramatisation of the 'misreading of gaps in knowledge' (584). Lawrence Douglas observes, likewise, that *Billy Budd* is concerned with 'narrative access and historical misreading', and that the plot focalises the 'vulnerabilities' of 'narrative representation' by enacting a 'collapse' of the narrator's authoritative account into competing re-tellings (1994, 157; 151). Thus, for all the discord animating *Billy Budd* criticism, there seems to be some agreement that the misshaping of truth might be the central theme of the work. Despite this fact, no critical account of the genesis and evolution of this theme across Melville's successive drafts has yet been written. This chapter attempts to construct such an account.

In his revisions to *Billy Budd*, Melville increasingly cultivated textual disorder, creating a narrative of 'ragged edges' (BB 2009, 358)—or a narrative governed by the aesthetic principle that stories 'must in the end be both incomplete and unshapely, since truth is both elusive and intractable' (H&S 1962, 39). The novella's formal raggedness or its 'aesthetics of imperfection', as Hershel Parker writes, thus thematises its own narrative disorder, and the broader tendency of narratives to misrepresent what they describe (1990, 159). Following the growth of Melville's composition in the Genetic Text, I find that themes of misreading and ragged narration were not an intuitive or immediate principle guiding *Billy Budd* from its conception. Rather, my suggestion is that this emphasis emerged gradually, as a by-product of Melville's revisionary process, and only came to be inscribed as the definitive aesthetic and thematic crux of the text *in the latest stages of composition*.

I evidence this new claim by tracing the fluctuating form of the conclusion of *Billy Budd*. A one-sentence coda with a tidy allegorical moral initially resolves the narrative as a spiritual parable about the natural conditions of good and evil in the world. But later expansions heighten the story's ambiguity, by revealing the limitations of the narrator and by imposing the onus of interpretation upon the reader. The initial coda is then replaced with a new conclusion that shifts thematic focus by introducing texts-within-the-text staging the misrepresentation of Billy's fate by other narrators. Melville's addition here of an authorial comment on the 'ragged edges' of truth was, I show, a strikingly late development—and a striking contradiction of the closure of earlier drafts in favour of an explicitly incomplete narrative. Finally, I examine a late-draft cancelled note-to-self which reveals Melville identifying an unintended inconsistency, the result of his many additions, and choosing to preserve this textual disorder instead of correcting it. This crucial detail reveals that it was only belatedly that Melville chose to enhance his story's unshapeliness, emphasising the friction between competing narrations at the novella's 'ragged edge'.

Of course, in interrogating how *Billy Budd* was made, I necessarily call attention to the fact that the text was highly changeful, and also that Melville never completed the work—an issue thus far grievously overlooked by critics intent upon locating a coherence or 'organic unity' which is fundamentally absent from the manuscript (Parker 1990, 93). As a text 'not altogether finished', whatever emphases seem to surface in Melville's last-completed draft are necessarily unstable and partial (H&S 1962, 3). Parker goes so far as to say that any criticism which fails to account for the genesis of the text is 'simply not worth doing' (1990, 91) and, as late as 2006, Wenke is still able to remark that virtually no *Billy Budd* criticism has made use of the materials of the Genetic Text (2006, 502). My chapter is thus part of a burgeoning effort to right this critical wrong. I suggest that critics have overlooked the belated growth of this theme because Melville's aesthetic and narratological interest in raggedness appeared concurrently with many of the major textual inconsistencies that arose out of his middle-stage additions to the manuscript. As a result, critics have been quick to identify errors but have not fully accounted for Melville's intentional, ambiguous deployment of a 'ragged aesthetics'—defined by incompletion, contradiction and a stylisation of narratorial fallibility.

2. From 'innocence and infamy' to 'ragged edges'

In the early stages of composition, Melville ended *Billy Budd* with a one-sentence coda that articulates an unambiguous meaning: 'Here ends a story not unwarranted by what sometimes happens in this [undeciphered word] world of ours—innocence and infamy, spiritual depravity and fair repute' (leaf 344; H&S 1962, 422). Despite being partly illegible, the resonance of this untroubled prose is a clear moral: in 'this world of ours', composed equally of innocence and infamy, it is fated that Billy's goodness will be violently paired with Claggart's evil, and result in tragic consequences. In this version, as Wenke writes, 'Billy's hanging simply happens' and the story abruptly concludes as a universal spiritual parable (2009, 126). At this point in its genesis, Stage B in Hayford and Sealts's chronology, the text of *Billy Budd* was significantly shorter and its narrative had a different focus from that of the last-completed draft. At Stage B, *Billy Budd* concerns itself primarily with the allegorical conflict between Billy and Claggart. Much of the historical materials had yet to be written, and the crucial character of Captain Vere was not yet developed. At this point, 'Vere appeared only as the commander who witnessed the false accusation and the retaliatory blow and who thereupon, without ado, imposed the summary sentence of death by hanging. No issue was made of the execution' (H&S 1962, 6). Set at the end of this version of the story, this coda is a tidy resolution that adequately draws together the forces at play on the *Bellipotent*.

However, as Melville was transcribing fair copies, he couldn't resist being led 'into further revision and elaboration' (H&S 1962, 1). After extensive re-writing in fair copy Stages C and D, during which only slight additions were made, Melville embarked on a significant pencil-draft expansion. Stage X, the final major phase of wholesale composition, dramatically altered the focus of the story and more than doubled its length—from 150 leaves to some 350 (Parker 1990, 36–37). In this stage, Melville elaborated his external description of Captain Vere (ch. 6) and added a new section (ch. 7) conducting an inward analysis of this now 'exceptional character' (H&S 1962, 9). Most importantly, this stage saw the creation of the lengthy trial scene as well as a section (ch. 22) in which the narrator admits to having no knowledge of the content of Vere and Billy's last conversation (8–9). Melville also made a significant alteration to the scene of Claggart's death. Now the ship's surgeon, checking the corpse of the master-at-arms, speculates about Vere's sanity ('Was he unhinged?') and encourages readerly questioning about the Captain's powers of judgement (10–11). What is the effect of these changes?

Primarily, they 'transform Vere into a character whose importance equals—and according to some critics even surpasses—that of Billy and Claggart' (H&S 1962, 8). Such a transformation necessarily brings on a substantial shift in the thematic focus of the novella as a whole. Billy's hanging is no longer simply an event that happens, distilling the inherent spiritual conditions of the world. Instead, the nature of Billy's judgement and sentencing is shrouded in indeterminacy, and the story becomes animated by questions about *why* he is executed and *how* we are to interpret Vere's actions. In this way, the irresolvable mystery of particular human motives and actions becomes predominant, displacing the earlier allegorical focus. It is with this change that *Billy Budd* takes on its famous 'hermeneutical openness' (Wenke 2006, 502). These later revisions destabilised Melville's original one-sentence coda in a few different ways, and functioned to radically enhance indeterminacy and ambiguity.

First: the coda's assured authorial tone ('Here ends a story [...]'), which implies the narrator's mastery over his material, is profoundly undermined by the addition of ch. 22. In this section, Billy's sentence has been decided by the drumhead court, and Captain Vere then takes it upon himself to 'communicate the finding of the court to the prisoner' (leaf 285; *BB* 2009, 345). This is an important moment. Thus far, Vere has been characterised as a sympathetic 'father' to Billy (*BB* 332) yet he has also been insistent upon the brutal supremacy of 'military duty' over 'moral scruple' (341). This unresolved conflict in Vere's character is only heightened by this last meeting, as the narrator confesses that 'beyond the communication of the sentence, what took place at this interview was never known', and 'only conjectures may be ventured' (leaf 285; *BB* 346). Perhaps knowledge of this crucial exchange might have helped us to explain Billy's puzzling final words, a blessing of Vere, his executioner. In any case, this late addition to the text functions as a revelation of the limits of the narrator-historian's knowledge. Indeed, for Lawrence Douglas, this moment exemplifies a 'crisis in omniscience' (1994, 151). The narrator's admission that he has only partial knowledge of the events being described focalises the unreliability of the narrative at hand, and compromises our faith in the comprehensiveness or accuracy of tidy interpretative statements like the one-sentence coda.

Second: though Melville's late revisions relocate Captain Vere to the centre of the tale's moral puzzle, these revisions also declare a new unwillingness to interpret him. This enhances ambiguity and, again, weakens the narrative's earlier constructions of resolution or completeness. In the newly added sections of ch. 20 and ch. 21, in which the ship's surgeon speculates on whether Vere was 'affected in his mind', Melville initially adds a line in which the narrator declares: 'I for one, decline to determine' (leaf 237; H&S 1962, 382). Melville then changed his mind, and altered the line to read: 'Whether Captain Vere, as the surgeon professionally and privately surmised, was really the sudden victim of any degree of aberration, *every one must determine for himself* by such light as this narrative may afford' (leaf 237; H&S 382, my emphasis). This addition reveals Melville as his intentions for *Billy Budd* finally begin to make their sea-change. In the revised version of this line, the narrator makes explicit the limits of his own knowledge and implies that there is no stable, determinate, or resolved truth in the case of Vere and Billy. His initial statement of non-interpretation is thus replaced by an insistence that readers must each make of the story what they will. This is Melville, in contradiction of the straightforward meaning imposed by his earlier coda, encouraging 'the protean activity of hermeneutical pursuit' but also undermining 'the prospect of […] closure' (Wenke 2006, 507). Indeed, the singular moral theme of the coda has begun to be supplanted by Melville's interest in thematising not the meaning of Billy's story, but the hazards of reading it—and the hazards of any 'hermeneutical pursuit'.

With these revisions, Melville's story is no longer a matter of 'innocence and infamy' but of the ambiguous space between the moral poles of this formulation. This ambiguous space is precisely where the newly central character of Captain Vere is located. For this reason, as Parker writes, the coda becomes an 'unintelligible' conclusion when 'applied to the enlarged story' (1990, 63). Recognising this, Melville cancelled it from the text (H&S 1962, 422). The re-imagined conclusion makes crucial additions that indicate a late change in Melville's aesthetic and thematic intentions. The coda was replaced with a carefully paired triptych of chapters, intended to be read against one another. The narrative notes that 'though properly the story ends with' Billy's life, 'something in a way of sequel will not be amiss' (*BB* 2009, 358). That Melville's fiction now requires greater attention to what happens *after* Billy's death signals that the meanings or themes of the story likewise transcend the direct events of his life, and resonate in the ways Billy is narrativised in memory—the new focus of the conclusion.

This sequel of 'brief chapters' is prefaced by an entirely new addition to the text which announces to the reader Melville's late discovered thematic focus upon reading, misreading and the shaping of truth in narrative. He writes:

> The symmetry of form attainable in pure fiction cannot so readily be achieved in a narration essentially having less to do with fable than with fact. Truth uncompromisingly told will always have its ragged edges; hence the conclusion of such a narration is apt to be less finished than an architectural finial (*BB* 358).

Inscribed in the last stage of composition, this passage reveals the stark departure of Melville's later vision from his earlier intentions. Though of course it had now been erased from the text, readers tracing Melville's revisions will identify in this passage a clear repudiation of the emphasis that dominated the story's coda in earlier versions. Indeed, *Billy Budd* is no longer a 'fable' about the clash of 'innocence and infamy' or the tragic fate of a pure 'angel of God' (*BB* 2009, 333). With this late addition, *Billy Budd* becomes a story that is primarily to do 'with fact', and with what a narrative that aims to tell 'truth uncompromisingly' must look like. For Melville, as Hayford and Sealts write, 'such a narration *must* in the end be both incomplete and unshapely, since truth is both elusive and intractable' (H&S 1962, 39). This necessary unshapeliness, disorder and indeterminacy forms the proverbial 'ragged edge' of a truthful narrative—which *Billy Budd* now claims to be. Thus, in this passage, Melville announces that *Billy Budd* is formed by a 'ragged' style of narration, or for Parker an 'aesthetics of imperfection' (1990, 159). This announcement gives name and shape to the trend in Melville's late revisions towards greater ambiguity. It also warns the reader that *Billy Budd*'s final chapters will foreground this raggedness at the edge of its narrative. The resolution, Melville declares, must be incomplete or 'less finished' than the coda was. The belatedly realised emphasis of the novella is upon *how* readers should deal with the ragged edges represented by these chapters. By now, Melville is of course unwilling to offer us interpretative help.

3. Making Mistakes: The Becoming of an 'inside narrative'

But what, after all, makes these chapters 'ragged edges' to the story of *Billy Budd*? The first chapter is an account of Vere's death, the second is a naval newspaper's report of the events leading up to Billy's execution and the third is an elegiac ballad, supposedly written by a fellow sailor on the *Bellipotent*, which renders Billy as a heroic figure. The result of these chapters, in Barbara Johnson's words, is that *Billy Budd* ends 'not once, but no less than four times' (1979, 568). Indeed, Billy's hanging represents the 'proper' ending to the story (*BB* 2009, 358). Yet each one of these 'sequel' chapters introduces their own further endings, with their own distinct meanings and senses of resolution. This triptych is Melville's mode of 'fraying' the symmetry of the story, so that the drama of *Billy Budd* becomes that of the original story coming undone as it is re-told in alternate narrations (Johnson 1979, 569).

The first of these chapters, written in the very last stage of composition, depicts the death of Captain Vere after he is wounded in battle. Vere's last words are 'Billy Budd, Billy Budd', yet the narrative is explicit that 'these were not the accents of remorse' (*BB* 359). This new ending tantalises the reader with the prospect that a second death will reveal the moral attitude of the text, but it is only a detail that enhances irresolution and moral uncertainty. As such, it is further evidence of my claim that the 'calculated ambiguity' critics identify in *Billy Budd* was effected in Melville's latest revisions (Wenke 2009, 127). The second and third chapters share much in common with each other. The former chapter purports to be a transcription of an article in a 'naval chronicle' (*BB* 360). This article is the 'authorized' version of events, yet it presents an entirely distorted rendition of what transpired on the *Bellipotent*. In this narrative, Billy is the 'assassin', at the heart of a malicious 'plot', who stabs Claggart, his patriotic victim, to death (360). The third chapter is a 'rudely printed' ballad in which Billy himself is the speaker and the scene is the eve of his execution. Apparently written by a fellow sailor on the

Bellipotent, the poem mythologises and venerates Billy as a brave victim. In this narrative, as many critics have noted, Billy likewise 'ceases to be the recognizable character sketched elsewhere in the novella' (Douglas 1994, 157). The poet, presumably unaware of the stutter so crucial to the status of his innocence, depicts a Billy who is highly articulate, reflective and even capable of irony and poetic images—despite the fact that the narrator states early in *Billy Budd* that 'double meanings' are 'foreign' to his nature (*BB* 285). In the narrative that *Billy Budd* finally ends with, Billy himself has been 'converted into a monument' (361).

Different though they are, these last two chapters both centre the phenomenon of 'historical misreading' as the text's culminating thematic issue (Douglas 1994, 157). A faithful account of Billy that centres this issue of 'misreading' must take into account how Billy's life is distorted in historical memory. Of course, this is precisely what these chapters and their texts-within-the-text add to *Billy Budd*. In doing so, they introduce a necessary disunity, unshapeliness and disorder to the form of the whole narrative—and thus make up the 'ragged edge' of its truth. Together, these chapters 'problematize' the idea of narrative 'authority', and reveal that the truth of Billy's story is subject to infinite 'revision, displacement, and reversal' in narration (Johnson 1979, 569). Thus, in the final version of his indeterminate conclusion, Melville dramatises, above all else, narrative fallibility and inconsistency. But complicating our efforts to investigate this theme is the fact that, by the final stages of revision, more and more of Melville's own unintended errors were beginning to mar the manuscript.

The time has come to note the materiality of Melville's peculiar method of revision. In making his expansions to the *Billy Budd* text, Melville was constantly 'interpolating' new sections 'into parts already written' (Parker 1990, 100). He did so by messily pinning or pasting 'part-leaves' onto the 'whole-leaves' of the text (H&S 1962, 225). 'Some of these part-leaves', Hayford and Sealts report, 'bear passages Melville salvaged by clipping them from *earlier* leaves merely to avoid copying them. [...] Others bear revisions or insertions *later* than the copy stage of the leaves to which they are fastened' (225). So, fastened to the text of the manuscript (itself continually being re-copied) were layers of attached leaves, each leaf marking the insertion of external material into the text. These part-leaves, confusingly, might have been from any stage of the text's genesis—they might contain material from an earlier version of the text now re-inserted into the manuscript, or completely new material written at a much later stage than the composition of the whole-leaf and then inserted retrospectively, in lieu of re-transcribing. The manuscript Melville was working with was a sort of collage of leaves from different phases of composition. Of course, as I have discussed, each of these phases contained starkly different versions of the story and its characters. Thus, the *Billy Budd* text was itself riddled with literal 'ragged edges'. Unsurprisingly, as Melville was revising the narrative he often misread his own text. After all, 'all the time he was working on *Billy Budd*, Melville was old and tiring, and most of the time he was perceptibly weakening when not observably sick' (Parker 39). Particularly towards the end—after the major expansions noted above had inserted new material into the middle of the story—errors and inconsistencies began to emerge in the drafts, sometimes with significant consequences.

The drumhead court of officers summoned by Captain Vere, so crucial to the story's moral ambiguity, is a notable site of such errors. Early in Stage X, the court was composed of four men (H&S 1962, 179). Later, Melville inserted a new description into ch. 21 in which the court included only three men, and in which a 'lieutenant of minor grade' is replaced by a 'captain of marines' (H&S 262). In the fair copy which followed this emendation, however, Melville does not transcribe this change in full. He does write that there are three officers on the court, but (on leaf 275) the cancelled lieutenant still appears as a fourth member of the court and then even speaks in the proceedings (H&S 262). Inconsistencies like this one, to do with the number of court personnel and their identities, appear on half a dozen leaves and remain unreconciled in the manuscript. Furthermore, Melville's pencil revisions at this fair copy stage introduce crucial contradictions about whether Vere's calling of the court is in keeping with naval law or in contravention of it—obviously an essential detail when readers are tasked with interpreting the rightness of his actions. From an earlier draft (leaf 245) Melville notes Vere's actions are definitively 'not [. . .] at variance with usage' (H&S 263). But, later in his revisions, he pastes an insertion into the text that precedes this earlier-written statement with its contradiction: that it is thought 'the matter' of Billy's fate 'should be referred to the admiral' and not be handled solely by Vere (leaf 236; H&S 176). This inconsistency was not intentional; the evidence shows that Melville himself was unable to determine what the *actual* naval law of the time dictated, and that the text remained unsure on this point (H&S 176). As Parker writes, 'we are stuck with a text which is confused on precisely a point where we strongly want to know what the facts are' (138). Implicit in this comment is the fact that, in such a case, Melville's errors and oversights merge with the contrived ambiguity of the story in uncertain ways, and complicate our readings of that ambiguity. Such errors in Melville's revisions have led many critics to conclude that *Billy Budd* is simply a 'flawed product', an incomplete work which, in its semi-final form, 'does not in fact make sense' and is often so internally problematic as to frustrate all efforts at coherent interpretation (Parker 1990, 174–77).

But a final example in the manuscript that has thus far gone overlooked presents a striking problem for such conclusions about how *Billy Budd*'s unintended flaws should be understood.[3] Melville wrote the flawed news report of Ch. 29 very early in the genesis of *Billy Budd*—at Stage B, before the vast expansions of Stage X centred Captain Vere's character and focalised the issue of his interpretation. Because it was written earlier, this news report makes no mention whatsoever of Captain Vere, his critical role in Billy's judgement, the battle that followed Billy's execution, or Vere's death after being wounded in that battle (leaves 340–44; H&S 1962, 269). Eventually, Melville recognised this discrepancy. At the end of Stage X, he inscribed an instruction to himself in pencil at the top of leaf 340, the beginning of ch. 29. The note reads: 'speak of the fight & death of Captain Vere' (H&S 269, 420). Clearly enough, this reveals Melville identifying an inconsistency in his material—resulting from the changes to the middle of the narrative not yet being represented in the text of the narrative's end—and determining to correct this inconsistency by adding details on

---

3   Hayford and Sealts identify Melville's note-to-self as a 'point of genetic interest' (1962, 269) in their study, Parker reads it as a simple authorial oversight (1990, 160) and Wenke interprets the note's cancellation as straightforward evidence of Melville's intentional deployment of irony (2009, 141). These readings are valuable, yet they make only passing mention of the note-to-self, ultimately declining to imagine—as I do in this chapter –what sorts of wider compositional patterns or thematic evolutions this piece of evidence might help us to recognise across the genesis of the *Billy Budd* text.

Captain Vere. But Melville never made this correction; the news report attests only to 'John Claggart and *Billy Budd'* (*BB* 2009, 361). In fact, in the final 'late pencil' stage that preceded his death, Melville *cancelled* this note-to-self by drawing a line through his words. In doing so, he chose to preserve an instance of textual disorder and amplify the inconsistency of his own text.

The interpretative ramifications of this moment in the genesis of *Billy Budd* cannot be understated. The note-to-self and its cancellation crystallises how Melville's intentions evolved. In the simplest of narratological terms, we might say that this note and its cancellation captures *Billy Budd* as it accomplishes a long evolution across its genesis: a shift away from a primarily 'mimetic' focus upon the story's happenings, towards a more 'diegetic' focus upon both the 'narrators' themselves (now plural indeed), who 'place themselves between' the story and its readers, and upon the indirectness and uncertainty that are the product of their competing narrations (Herman and Vervaeck 2019, 15). Thus, this cancellation shows us two things. First, it confirms my claim throughout this paper that Melville's 'aesthetics of imperfection' and thematisation of the 'ragged edges' of truth was not an *a priori* principle governing his composition, but rather something that developed belatedly, becoming the text's primary focus at a *late stage* of composition. Second, the cancellation of this note indicates that Melville actually incorporated this unintentional inconsistency into the 'imperfect' narration of *Billy Budd*, such that an error became a component of its essential ambiguity. This instance demands a re-evaluation of the basic distinctions drawn by critics seeking to separate the incomplete, 'ragged' parts of Melville's final work from those parts which appear to be masterful and unmarred. With *Billy Budd*—a story about the fallibility of narrative—we cannot separate the unintended flaws of Melville's narrative from the disorder Melville intentionally cultivated.

4. Conclusion

The decision to cancel this note-to-self, and keep Captain Vere *outside* of the 'authorized' news report, is what justifies the novella's titular claim that it is an 'inside narrative' containing privileged information (Wenke 2009, 140–41). In defining itself as such, *Billy Budd* invites the reader to contemplate what it means for a narrative to be 'inside', as opposed to 'outside'—and what is revealed when a story allows authorship to bleed into the text from 'outside', such that the activity of narration 'belongs' within the narrative itself (Herman and Vervaeck 2019, 18). The story of *Billy Budd*, the novella's subtitle seems to suggest, will address these very questions of narrative access, limits and construction. It bears noting now, though, that this subtitle was only appended to the text, in pencil, sometime after the late revisions that began at Stage X (H&S 1962, Plate VI). This is to say that *Billy Budd* did not begin as an 'inside narrative'. Instead, as this essay has shown, Melville gradually discovered this theme in the multiplying leaves of his ongoing revisions, and made it his focus. Unfinished as it is, *Billy Budd* is the 'haunting story' of truth's elusiveness that Melville 'could not, or would not, bring to any kind of peaceful ease' (Wenke 2006, 511).

Building upon the crucial studies of critics like Hershel Parker and John Wenke, my chapter further demonstrates the essential role that the Genetic Text must play in all criticism of *Billy Budd*. With an unfinished work such as this, interpretations have an obligation to attend to the evidence of Melville's unfulfilled intentions. Otherwise, readers' understandings of the workings of the text are only partial, and end up like the distorted news report of *Billy Budd*. Naturally, this essay calls for further criticism to take this genetic approach and expand upon my findings. One such avenue might be found in Melville's much earlier novella, *Benito Cereno* (1855), which exhibits a similar narrative unshapeliness and likewise dramatises re-tellings of its own plot. Noting how formally similar this text is to *Billy Budd*, a comparison of the drafts and composition processes of both works might generate interesting questions, and answers, about the degree to which Melville's 'ragged' aesthetic was or was not a product of his infirmity late in life. Melville's eschewal of 'high finish' across his oeuvre requires a more comprehensive examination of both the contrived and accidental messiness that pervades his fictions—an examination that can only be conducted with a genetic framework (Wenke 2006, 501).

Works Cited

Denis, Claire, dir. (1999), *Beau Travail*. Directed by Claire Denis, performances by Denis Lavant, Grégoire Colin, Michel Subor, Paris: Pyramide Distribution.

Brodtkorb, Paul (1967), 'The Definitive *Billy Budd*: "But Aren't It All Sham?"', *PMLA*, 82.7: 602–12, https://doi.org/10.2307/461168.

Bryant, John (2002), *The Fluid Text: a Theory of Revision and Editing for Book and Screen* (Ann Arbor, MI: University of Michigan Press).

De Biasi, Pierre-Marc (1996), 'What Is a Literary Draft? Toward a Functional Typology of Genetic Documentation', *Yale French Studies*, 89: 26–58, https://doi.org/10.2307/2930337.

Douglas, Lawrence (1994), 'Discursive Limits: Narrative and Judgment in "*Billy Budd*"', *Mosaic: A Journal for the Interdisciplinary Study of Literature*, 27.4: 141–60, http://www.jstor.org/stable/24775803.

Genette, Gérard (1988), *Narrative Discourse Revisited* (Ithaca, NY: Cornell University Press).

Hardwick, Elizabeth (2000), *Herman Melville* (New York: Viking).

Herman, Luc, and Bart Vervaeck (2019), *Handbook of Narrative Analysis* (Lincoln, NE: University of Nebraska Press).

Hunt, Lester H. (2002), '"*Billy Budd*": Melville's Dilemma', *Philosophy and Literature*, 26.2: 273–95, http://doi.org/10.1353/phl.2003.0009.

Johnson, Barbara (1979), 'Melville's Fist: The Execution of "*Billy Budd*"', *Studies in Romanticism*, 18.4: 567–99, https://doi.org/10.2307/25600211.

"Literary Fame" (1890), in: *The New York Times*, 12 November 1890: 7, https://nyti.ms/3G1QxTP.

Melville, Herman (2009), *Billy Budd, Sailor, and Selected Tales*, ed. by Robert Milder (Oxford: Oxford University Press).

Melville, Herman (1962), *Billy Budd, Sailor (An Inside Narrative)*, ed. by Harrison Hayford and Merton M. Sealts (Chicago: University of Chicago Press).

Melville, Herman (2000), *Moby-Dick, Billy Budd, and Other Writings* (New York: Library of America).

Milder, Robert (1989), *Critical Essays on Melville's 'Billy Budd, Sailor'* (Boston: G.K. Hall).

Parker, Hershel (1990), *Reading 'Billy Budd'* (Evanston, IL: Northwestern University Press).

Schiffman, Joseph (1950), 'Melville's Final Stage, Irony: A Re-Examination of "Billy Budd" Criticism', *American Literature*, 22.2: 128–36, https://doi.org/10.2307/2921745.

Scorza, Tom (1979), *In the Time before Steamships: Billy Budd, the Limits of Politics and Modernity* (Dekalb, IL: Northern Illinois University Press).

Stritmatter, Roger, Mark K. Anderson, and Elliott Stone (2015), 'Melville's "Billy Budd" and the Disguises of Authorship', *New England Review*, 36.1: 100–31, http://www.jstor.org/stable/24772718.

The Melville Electronic Library: A Critical Archive. National Endowment of the Humanities, Houghton Library of the Harvard College Library, The University of Chicago, https://melville.electroniclibrary.org.

Van Hulle, Dirk (2022), *Genetic Criticism: Tracing Creativity in Literature* (Oxford: Oxford University Press).

Vincent, Howard P., ed. (1971), *Twentieth Century Interpretations of Billy Budd; a Collection of Critical Essays* (Englewood Cliffs, NJ: Prentice-Hall).

Wenke, John (1999), 'Complicating Vere: Melville's Practice of Revision in "Billy Budd"', *Leviathan*, 1.1: 83–88, muse.jhu.edu/article/491475.

Wenke, Johm (2009), 'Melville's Indirection: "Billy Budd," the Genetic Text, and "the Deadly Space between"', in: *New Essays on 'Billy Budd'*, ed. by Donald Yanella (Cambridge: Cambridge University Press).

Wenke, John (2006), 'Melville's Transhistorical Voice: "Billy Budd" and the Fragmentation of Forms', in: *A Companion to Herman Melville*, ed. by Wyn Kelley (Hoboken: John Wiley & Sons).

Wolff, Nathan (2020), '"Dead Then I'll Be": "Billy Budd" and the Death of Politics', *Leviathan*, 22.3: 3–24, http://doi.org/10.1353/lvn.2020.0029.

Woloch, Alex (2009), *The One vs. the Many: Minor Characters and the Space of the Protagonist in the Novel* (Princeton, NJ: Princeton University Press).

Yanella, Donald, editor (2002), *New Essays on Billy Budd* (Cambridge: Cambridge University Press).

6. 'The puzzle pieces fit too late': Posthumous Narratological Changes in Arthur Quiller-Couch and Daphne Du Maurier's *Castle Dor*

Claire Qu

'It is a curious coincidence that no poet, or shall we call him investigator, has ever lived to conclude this particular story.[1] His work has always been finished by another' (Quiller-Couch and Du Maurier 2004, 80). In this statement and several others of a similar kind, *Castle Dor* draws attention to its own layered construction as well as to the fragmentedness and multiplicity of the legend it is rewriting, that of Tristan and Iseult.[2] A novel begun in the 1920s by Arthur Quiller-Couch (known as 'Q') and posthumously completed by family friend, Daphne Du Maurier, nearly forty years later, *Castle Dor* recounts the re-emergence of the Tristan legend in Victorian Cornwall through the ill-fated affair between Amyot Trestane and Linnet Lewarne, and the gradual discovery of the links between their situation and that of the mythical lovers by Dr. Carfax, Ledru and Tregentil, characters with no exact counterpart in the original story. By comparing the manuscript of the novel with the published version, this essay attempts to survey the development of some of its narratological elements in the avant-texte, or its prior-to-publication form(s). Lars Bernaerts and Dirk Van Hulle's claim that 'genetic criticism's awareness of the diachronic dimension of writing is directly relevant to the project of narrative theory' is doubly

---

1 I would like to thank the President and Fellows of Trinity College, Oxford for giving me access to the Arthur Quiller-Couch archive.
2 I use the spelling 'Iseult' to maintain consistency with the spelling used by both authors of *Castle Dor*.

true in the case of *Castle Dor*, in which the 'diachronic dimension' spans the composition timelines of two authors working one after the other (2013, 285). This posthumous co-authorship adds further complexity to the narratological analysis of the novel in that Q and Du Maurier have their own non-teleological processes which, while independent of each other, necessarily intersect, not least because of the latter's explicit aim of maintaining Q's voice.[3] At the same time, both Q and Du Maurier's creative processes are constrained, to an extent, by the basic plot (and variations) of the Tristan legend. Some insight into the way each author works within these particular parameters to arrive at the published form of *Castle Dor* can be obtained by consulting its MS and other relevant archival materials.

Castle Dor's nature as a popular co-authored Arthurian adaptation makes it an unusual subject in the fields of both narratology and genetic criticism. Narratological studies of adaptations are, for the most part, concerned with adaptations across media[4] rather than retellings like Q and Du Maurier's work. The popular novel/adaptation is also generically distant from the proto- and high modernist texts that genetic critics typically focus on; witness Bernaerts and Van Hulle's list of landmark genetic critic-author pairings including 'Cohn and Kafka, Stanzel and James, Genette and Proust, Hamon and Zola, [...] [and] Seymour Chatman and Virginia Woolf' (2013, 303). This essay endeavours to partially fill these gaps, discussing the development of story, setting, narrative and characterisation (as in Gérard Genette's tripartite model [Herman and Vervaeck 2005, 41–42]) across the MS and published versions of *Castle Dor*.[5] Its analysis is limited by the extant archival materials; with only one MS version of Q's half-finished draft, no drafts by Du Maurier and no notes by either, it is impossible to arrive at a detailed reconstruction of the two authors' composition processes. A direct comparison of the MS to the published text, supported by

---

3   Du Maurier is quoted in a contemporary review expressing her hope that 'had (Sir Arthur) read what I had written, he would have turned to me [...] and murmured, "Well, child, you were more observant than I thought. This was happily done"'. (Hogan 1962).
4   See for instance Ton 2016; Alber 2017; Kukkonen 2011.
5   I omit the third layer of Genette's model, narration, as Du Maurier deliberately preserves and imitates Q's style, making only very slight changes in the narration of *Castle Dor*.

information from Du Maurier's letters, can nonetheless reveal the broad shape of her changes to Q's draft. The impression that emerges is of Du Maurier's careful carving away of digressions and tonal discordances in the MS.

Archival Materials and Versions

The following sections will use the *Castle Dor* MS as well as Du Maurier's letters to Foy and contemporary English and American reviews of *Castle Dor* to construct as accurate as possible an idea of Du Maurier's revision and continuation of Q's novel. All archival materials consulted are held at the Trinity College, Oxford Archive (TCOA), and are catalogued as follows:

1. The *Castle Dor* MS [DD36/A/14]
2. Du Maurier letters to Foy [within DD36/D/D]
3. Contemporary reviews of *Castle Dor* (newspaper clippings) [within D36/E/6 ('Miscellaneous items relating to Q')][6]

The MS itself comprises multiple versions of the prologue and first chapter and one version of the following twenty-two chapters. While I call chapters in the published version of *Castle Dor* 'chapter 1', 'chapter 2', etc., I give the MS chapters/versions the following names:

1. Loose unfinished prologue beginning 'A watcher of the stars' [P1]
2. Loose finished prologue beginning 'It happened to a watcher' [P2]
3. Loose finished prologue beginning 'A certain watcher of the skies', with annotations 'Chap. 1', '4 Copies', and 'By Sir Arthur Quiller Couch' [P3]
4. Unfinished prologue in 'For Foy' folder [P4]
5. Finished prologue in 'For Foy' folder [P5]

---

6 Many items in the archive are catalogued together, hence the designation 'within'. As I will not refer to any other materials than the ones listed, I will use the general reference numbers provided, and if need be, will describe individual items.

6. Chapter I, titled 'The Onion-Boy', section title 'Amyot and Amice', p. 1 (Q's pagination) [C1a]
7. Chapter I, titled 'The Onion-Boy', p. 1 (Q's pagination) [C1b]
8. Chapter I, titled 'The Onion-Boy', p.5 (Q's pagination) [C1c]
9. Chapter I, titled 'The Onion Boy', p. 5 (Q's pagination) [C1d]
10. Chapters II to XXIII [C2, C3, ...]

Whose Story?

Castle Dor has attracted much debate regarding the nature of its so-called 'originality'. Contemporary reviews and scholarly criticism tended to focus on comparing and evaluating—largely through speculation—Q and Du Maurier's respective contributions to the story. In *The Return from Avalon*, his study of modern Arthurian retellings, Raymond H. Thompson 'credit[s] Quiller-Couch with overall creative control of the novel from its inception to its posthumous completion' despite there being 'no evidence that du Maurier was working from any form of [...] plot outline' (Bunting 2013, 269). Considerations of the necessarily significant role of Arthurian source materials in shaping *Castle Dor*'s plot have been confined to passing judgements of the two authors' assumed levels of familiarity with the Tristan legend. One review presumes that 'Miss Du Maurier' would have been 'daunted by all [the scholarly] apparatus' of Q's beginning, and ascribes to this supposed perplexity her 'old-fashioned climax lack[ing] [the] finesse' of 'Q's theorem' (Curtis 1962). Competence in Arthurian scholarship and creative power are conflated here without any comment on the nature of their relationship. Du Maurier herself claims to have completed *Castle Dor* in a way that 'satisf[ied] [her] own sense of order' after having consulted 'every available volume on the legend of Tristan and Iseult from the London Library' (Du Maurier 1962). Her statement, though affirming her control over the novel's ending, also highlights the text's essential reliance on existing versions of the Tristan tale.

Story, then, constitutes a foundational aspect of *Castle Dor*—setting, specifically geography, is another, as will be discussed in the following section. In this respect, the novel falls into a category with adaptations, rewritings and even historical fiction, for which '[t]he 'fabula' or chronological sequence of events is especially relevant [...] [in providing] a chronology of events to [adhere to or] deviate from' to varying extents (Van Hulle 2022, 149). As Monika Fludernik argues,

> taking plot as the basic ground on which discourse builds is [...] not very convincing from a generative perspective. The situation is, however, very different if there already exists a prior textual source for the narrative, for instance another novel, a fairy tale, a history book, or if the core of the story is a historical sequence of events which has already been canonized. Under these circumstances, transformations do indeed take place on a prior event sequence (2010, 108).

For Q, beginning *Castle Dor*, and for Du Maurier, finishing it, the several versions of the Tristan legend, particularly the Béroul, Gottfried von Strassburg and Thomas poetic fragments (the first two mentioned by name in the novel), offer plot possibilities and constraints, both on a primary level, informing the chronological sequence of events in the novel, and, secondarily, as material for metafictional scenes in which certain characters discuss the correspondences between their experiences and the details of various Tristan romances.

The following table (see Fig. 6.1) shows, in chronological order, the major plot incidents of Q's MS, Du Maurier's version of *Castle Dor*, and the Tristan legend, as told in the texts of Eilhart von Oberge, Béroul, Gottfried and Thomas.[7] The novel, in both MS and published versions, keeps most of the major events of the legend, so that its quality as an adaptation of the latter is perceived by those passingly familiar with Arthurian romance, even setting aside the many diegetic discussions of the Tristan source texts in *Castle Dor*. Several of the events occur out of order in the novel, however, adding a sense of disorientation and uncanniness to the readers' and characters' sense of recognition; as Carfax notes towards the novel, '[w]e are seeing the past through the wrong end of the telescope', so that 'the puzzle pieces [...] fit[ ] too late' (Quiller-Couch and Du Maurier 2004, 252; 256). It may be due to this puzzle-like, '"piecemeal" construction of Arthurian legend—put together from "a narrative tradition of intertwined tales"', that this rearrangement of

---

7   Information on the Tristan romance is from Schoepperle 1913; Ditmas 1969; and Loomis [1963] 2012. Because of the many, often fragmented, versions, there is no single chronology of events; the table in Fig. 6.1 shows a chronology pieced together from several versions.

story elements does not compromise the recognisability of the novel's source material (Carroll 2022, 477–79).

Table 6.1 Major story elements in the *Castle Dor* MS and published text and in the Tristan legend.

Q's MS	Du Maurier's version	Tristan legend
Linnet marries Mark Lewarne, but their marriage remains unconsummated	Deborah Brangwyn takes her mistress' place in the marital bed on Linnet Lewarne's wedding night	Iseult heals Tristan's injury after his battle with Morholt
Linnet heals Amyot Trestane's injury after his struggle with Fougereau	Linnet heals Amyot Trestane's injury after his struggle with Fougereau	Iseult and Tristan accidentally drink the love potion meant for Iseult and King Mark
Linnet deliberately falls upon Amyot at the hay harvest; later she does not have to lie that she has been in no man's arms but Mark's	Linnet deliberately falls upon Amyot at the hay harvest; later she does not have to lie that she has been in no man's arms but Mark's	Brangwyn takes Iseult's place in the marital bed on her wedding night
Linnet gives Amyot the love potion	Linnet gives Amyot the love potion	The dwarf plots to expose Tristan and Iseult; they allay suspicions temporarily
Linnet and Amyot meet for a tryst	Ned Varcoe spies on Linnet and Amyot's tryst and reports it to Mark; Linnet protests her innocence	Iseult contrives to be carried by Tristan disguised as a pilgrim/leper so that she may truthfully say she has been touched by no man but him and King Mark
	Deborah betrays Linnet to Mark	Brangwyn betrays Iseult to King Mark
	Amyot arrives at the Indian Queen, disguised; Mary Bosanko follows	Tristan, disguised as a fool, seeks Queen Iseult

	Linnet, under a heavy sleeping draught, and Amyot, with an infected injury, travel separately to the hospital; Mary lies about Linnet's approach	Iseult of the White Hands lies to a poisoned Tristan about Queen Iseult's approach, not knowing the latter can heal him

Du Maurier's version mostly preserves the plot of Q's MS in the first half, where the two overlap; what small differences there are can be mainly attributed to the altered setting of the published version. The remainder of the novel's plot follows through to the end of the Tristan legend, despite the tension generated by Carfax's repeated reflections on the incompletion of Béroul and Gottfried's texts. Notably, both Q and Du Maurier place the drinking of the love potion sometime after signs of Linnet and Amyot's mutual attraction appear, whereas in the legend, the incident is clearly seen as the entire cause of Tristan and Iseult's illicit love and the origin of all the exploits and tragedy that follow. The downplayed significance of the potion in *Castle Dor* aligns the novel somewhat with Thomas' *Tristan*, which 'allow[s] no abatement of the spell imposed by the philtre', where Eilhart and Béroul both portray the potion's love effect as temporary and unnatural, even 'miserable' (Loomis 2012, 104). This decision at the plot level—the kind of 'transformation of a prior event sequence' that Fludernik refers to—allows Q and Du Maurier to render the tone of Linnet and Amyot's love different from that of their mythical models, without removing any key story elements from the sources of the legend.

Q's Geography and Du Maurier's Temporality

Another, equally important aspect of *Castle Dor*'s genesis is setting, not only in the general sense of a *'chronotope* [...] constitut[ing] the narrative and ideological center of [...] [a] text' in 'giv[ing] form to figures and actions' (Herman and Vervaeck 2005, 56–57, original emphasis), but also, more particularly, in the inspiration Q takes in local geography and, later, in the tonal shift resulting from Du Maurier's decision to change the novel's temporal setting from 1914 to the 1860s. The nostalgic, parochial quality created in large part by the Cornish backdrop of *Castle Dor* and its doubly retrospective evocation of the Middle Ages and the mid-Victorian period has led contemporary reviewers to call it 'an entertaining piece of romantic Victoriana' (Brett 1962). The effect is the product not of a romantic veneer applied to a nearly complete narrative, but of fundamental processes in the composition of the text. As the available evidence suggests, it was the discovery of Cornish geographical details pertaining to the Tristan legend that motivated Q to begin writing *Castle Dor*, retelling a story long in his consciousness. Du Maurier's temporal intervention, apart from smoothing out some tonal inconsistencies of the MS, helps to fully realise the Arcadian feeling already present in Q's draft.

Both the specific location and the type of landscape in which the events of *Castle Dor* take place are predetermined by the novel's source material. Of course, an adaptation of *Tristan and Iseult* does not have to adhere to the geography of the legend, but for Q, geography was the main point of interest. As he exults in a letter to his friend, H.F. Stewart:

> I have been spending time [...] writing a novel as well as my poor eyes will allow; and [...] renewing old explorations of the real scene of the Tristan and Iseult business. Yes, my boy—the real scene. Is there anything in the world jollier than happening on a little trifle of confirmatory evidence that has lain latent for hundreds of years and dodged the antiquarians? Last week when I was morally certain of where King Mark's castle must have stood, the farmer's wife at the manor farm below [...] got out some deeds and a map with the names of fields on it; and lo! The meadow exactly fitting my hypothesis was named 'Mark's Gate'. An adjoining small field, on which the postern should have opened, has for name 'Pilfer Parc'. *Plus ça change* ... (Letter to H.F. Stewart, 9 April 1925, qtd. Brittain 1947, 117)

A very similar passage appears in C11 of the MS, when Carfax and Ledru are visiting the Bosanko farm:

> Dr Carfax leaning across^(the shoulder of) M Ledru, bent and poring over the map, suddenly dashed a forefinger down it. –
>
> 'My God, man—look at that!'
>
> 'Hein?'

'Can't you see?—A field in the very place entered as "Mark's Gate"— "Mark's Gate—King Mark's Gate—Oh it's a clincher. And Woodgate would be t'other approach from the river, up through the plantations. Hey? & look here!'—he jabbed a thumb upon another ~~parcel~~ parcelled field on the large map—'"Pilfer Door"—and if we're right, just where a postern door would be. Plus ça change—Yes, "Pilfer Door" leading to an angle of Prior's Meadow Oh, this is glorious!' (DD36/A/14, C11, fols. 08r–09r)

A significant portion of the MS is devoted to such historical landscape features, either as scenes set amid them, as in MS C4, 'Troy River', and C5, '*Castle Dor*', or as characters' discussions of them, as in C9, 'A Discussion over Punch' and C11, 'Lantyan' (Du Maurier continues the trend in chapters such as chapter 23, 'Mary finds a champion, and Mr Tregentil takes tea at Lantyan', chapter 24, 'Plot and counterplot' and chapter 25, 'Castle-an-Dinas', all unfolding an exploration of castle-an-Dinas). The resulting entrenched rural-ness and enchanting sense of temporal suspension that comes with revived historical scenes takes *Castle Dor* out of the realm of the 'urban, bourgeois, contemporary, and realistic', the supposed domain of the novel; instead, like the typical romance, it offers 'wilderness, aristocracy, past times, and fancy' (Matthews 2009, ch. 24). Q and Du Maurier's faithfulness to the traditional landscape of the Tristan romance blurs some of the generic markers of the novel, imprinting *Castle Dor* with a dreamy sense of geographical and temporal dislocation.

It is this quality of detachment from the modern, cosmopolitan world that Du Maurier enhances with her alteration of the period in which *Castle Dor* is set. Though two MS versions of the prologue mention a 'War' (P2) or 'late War' (P3) following the events of the novel, exact dates are not mentioned until C18, which rather abruptly adds, after the scene of the lovers' littoral tryst: 'It was the night of July 29th 1914' (DD36/A/14, C18, fol. 5r). Du Maurier notes the disjunction between this strict imposition of dates in the latter part of the MS, apparently connected with the sudden emphasis on the war theme, and the timelessness of the beginning, wondering if 'there was a gap of time' between Q's composition of the two sections (Letter from Du Maurier to Foy, 15 July 1959, DD36/D/D fol. 1v). In a letter to Q's daughter, Foy, she muses:

> I do feel Book Two rather falls away, with your father concentrating so much more on the Bosankos and the children and then the hint of the war [...] That opening, and the Inn, and the river, the races, the air of mystery, all so good, but that dialogue is just not 1914 and to my mind never could be. I feel he began to force it out of its true context—the story, I mean, when he began to bring in the war. (Letter from Du Maurier to Foy, 15 July 1959, DD36/D/D fol. 01v)

The 'true context' of *Castle Dor*, as Du Maurier appears to be proposing, is pre-industrial—an echo, perhaps, of the summers of Q's youth, with their 'drenching sense of beauty', later to be deepened by the knowledge of their having been spent at 'the actual scene of the greatest of love stories, of Tristan and Iseult' (Quiller-Couch 2008, 65). Indeed, such an Arcadian atmosphere is hinted at throughout the MS, as in Amyot's assumption that 'behind everybody's thought while he is growing there must be a forest' (DD36/A/14, C14, fol. 06r; Quiller-Couch and Du Maurier 2004, 94). It is the clash between this sense of enchanting atemporality and the realism periodically breaking through the later MS chapters that Du Maurier avoids by removing the latter.

From C19 of the MS onward, war is worked into the plot of the novel, most prominently in C22, 'War', a chapter entirely devoted, as the title indicates, to patriotic discussions, with Amyot expressing a wish to enlist (DD36/A/14, C22, fol. 05r). The MS chapter concludes with a strange meditation on Amyot's national identity:

> 'But you are a son of France: one of her young seamen [...] I can give you the money to pay your way home & up to the barracks gate'
>
> 'I thank you M'sieur –'
>
> Amyot paused [...] Whilst he & Dr Carfax had stood in talk, women with handkerchiefs to their eyes had been running back past them [...]
>
> '– I had thought myself to belong to this country, Sir. I was never happy until I came to it' (DD36/A/14, C22, fol. 06r)

Du Maurier replaces the whole chapter with one more directly related to the Tristan legend. In this new chapter, Mark Lewarne visits Carfax in distress, having heard Ned Varcoe's report of Linnet's meeting with Amyot. The scene provides an opportunity to reference one of the many fits of suspicion King Mark suffers in the legend and to reinforce the significance of earlier events:

'Oh yes', she tells me, 'of course I've lain in another man's arms. I fell off the hay wagon at Mr Bosanko' 'and if the farm-hand hadn't caught me I'd have broken my ribs, so I can't swear no one's touched me but you can I?'

[...]

[Carfax] stood motionless, struck by a sudden memory [...] Did not a queen, centuries past, cover her guilt in the selfsame fashion? (Quiller-Couch and Du Maurier 2004, 143–44)

This substitution, the lengthiest change Du Maurier makes to the MS, not only alters the novel's temporal setting, moving it back from 1914, but also re-centres its emotional focus on the events of the Tristan tale. Whereas, in the MS, the war suddenly takes over as a catalyst for action and an anticipated major event in itself, Du Maurier's excision of references to it and complete re-writing of C22 [chapter 17], part of her attempt to restore the 'true (temporal) context' of *Castle Dor*, tightens the novel's plot.

This carving away of digressions meets tonal adjustment in Du Maurier's revision of C23, 'Duet of Passion'. Cutting nearly two pages from this final chapter in the MS, she reworks 'the love scene in the woods (Linnet talking about breaking from an egg, etc) [where it gets] rather too much. Here, of course, Father was brewing up for his 1914 war, and it all got very cosmic' (Letter from Du Maurier to Foy, 1 May 1961, DD36/D/D, fol. 01v).[8] In the lurid monologue that Du Maurier refers to, Linnet recalls not only the feeling of being imprisoned in 'an egg—yes, even so silly a thing as an egg', but also wonders, at length, 'if you & I have lived before—perhaps many times, to be be born again', and mentions visions of a foreboding woman whom Amyot, in an incongruous outburst of patriotism, claims as his 'mother ... France!' (DD36/A/14, C23, fol. 03r; 04r; 06r). Here, Q's novel becomes, as Du Maurier recognises, strangely 'cosmic' and war-oriented, detached from the lightness and local focus of the earlier chapters. It appears that Q's choice of temporal setting necessarily creates a heightened sense of drama which, in Du Maurier's view, sits oddly with the folk legend at

---

8   It is interesting that Du Maurier refers to Q as 'Father', given that she 'remained haunted by the power of the father' in both her writing and her personal life (Zlosnick and Horner 2009, 17).

the core of Castle Dor and with the jaunty tone established at the start of the novel. Together with Q's careful use of Cornish geography, Du Maurier's intervention sustains in Castle Dor an air of romance.

'A Certain Watcher': Narrative and Framing

How to sequence and focalise the story of *Castle Dor* is again a matter coloured by the fact of the novel's adaptation of mediaeval romance. As Inga Bryden points out, the nineteenth-century Arthurian revival, undergirded by '[t]he rehabilitation of relics (textual or archaeological)', brought with it an acute awareness of the mediacy of mediaeval history and literature: 'The process of historical recovery, whilst satisfying a need for sensuous experiences of the past, was itself a reminder of the *impossibility* of recreating a unified or definitive Arthurian past' (2005, 22, original emphasis). This 'piecemeal' quality (to use Shiloh Carroll's term again) is not, perhaps, easily reconciled with the multivalence and interiority of the novel, something which may be surmised from the MS evidence of Q's multiple attempts to frame the story and of Du Maurier's marshalling of his digressions. The palimpsestic quality of *Castle Dor* and the tension between its episodic and linear structural principles can be seen in a comparison between the MS and the published versions of the work.

As the five MS versions of the prologue suggest, the framing of *Castle Dor* gave Q some difficulty. This is not an uncommon situation, given the significance of narrative beginnings. 'An *incipit*', as Raymonde Debray Genette observes, 'is fundamentally different from an *explicit*, and all *incipit* studies fall prey to the same paradox: no matter how random it may be, an *incipit* always retains the character of being decisive and (in every sense) primordial' (2004, 70). The decisiveness of the *incipit* consists in its '"set[ting] up [of] the narrative parameters of fiction such as perspective, tone, and focus", and these initial parameters also "determine the conditions for closure"' (Leander, qtd. in Van Hulle 2022, 152). And yet, behind this decisiveness lies the 'tentacular' avant-texte (Debray Genette 2004, 72). In the case of *Castle Dor*'s prologue, the avant-texte, Q's MS versions, show the persistence of core elements, including the notion of three or four 'stages' of feeling, partially brought about by the landscape (and underscoring the sense of '[a]ll England' being 'a palimpsest' (P3), and the figure of an anonymous 'watcher of the stars' (P1, P2, P3) who, in P4 and P5 are identified as 'a certain Dr. Carfax' (DD36/A/14, P3, fol. 3r; P1–P5, fol. 01r). Otherwise, however, versions P1, P2 and P3 are markedly different from P4 and P5, and each version varies from the others in small details of phrasing.

The published text of *Castle Dor*'s prologue closely resembles P3, the only major changes being Du Maurier's specificity about the year ('in the early 1840s') and her cutting of the last third (Quiller-Couch and Du Maurier 2004, 3; D36/A/14, P3, fol. 03r). There is no apparent reason for this choice of P3 as the source for the published text apart from, perhaps, the fact that the former is the longest of the prologue versions and seems to be finished, ending with a bar beneath the writing. Du Maurier uses some sentences from the part of P3 that she cuts in the epilogue she writes, effectively reframing the narrative of *Castle Dor* according to her own taste rather than adhering strictly to Q's intended text, as indicated by the MS. The salient portion of the epilogue reads:

> From the minstrels down, great poet after great poet had attempted to explain the genesis of love and had failed; still it loomed large through their failures, asserting itself through them to be greater than any man's telling.
>
> Nurtured on this soil, his young eyes having fed on this very landscape, he had not been able to stay the repetition of one of the saddest love stories in the world. (Quiller-Couch and Du Maurier 2004, 274)

It is modelled closely on the corresponding section of P3:

> From the minstrels down, great poet after great poet had attempted to tell the ~~great~~ story & had failed; still ~~the theme~~ it loomed large through their failures, asserting itself through them to be greater than any man's telling. Well enough he knew it to be miles beyond his power: and yet he had been nurtured of this soil, his young eyes had fed on this very landscape. (DD36/A/14, P3, fol. 04r)

In saving this paragraph from P3 for the very end of *Castle Dor*, Du Maurier gives Q's message about the story being 'greater than any man's telling' more weight. Yet the changes she makes, from the position of the sentences to small alterations of phrases, shift the entire tone of the passage. Whereas Q's narrator is full of doubt, knowing the re-telling of the *Tristan* legend 'to be miles beyond his power', Du Maurier's, having already finished the story—having, indeed, 'failed' *not to tell* 'one of the saddest love stories in the world'—is overwhelmed not by the literary task, but only by the effort to 'explain the genesis of love', an impossible undertaking.

A subtle but important alteration Du Maurier makes to the focalisation of *Castle Dor* is her more consistent integration of Carfax's perspective, a point of view which, already in the MS, functions as a kind of proxy for that of Q and which Du Maurier sees as similar to that of 'Shakespeare's Prospero' (Bawden 2004, vi). To this end, she makes explicit Carfax's involvement in the birth of Linnet, something which might be inferred from the statement in P4 and P5 that 'a certain Dr. Carfax' was present upon *Castle Dor* 'on a summons that the mistress was crying-out' (DD36/A/14, P4 and P5, fol. 01r). Du Maurier confirms that the anonymous infant of the MS versions is, in fact, Linnet, first by stating that birth had taken place at the 'blacksmith's' and introducing Linnet as the daughter of 'a one-time blacksmith'—details not present anywhere in the MS—and, later, by having Carfax recall 'slapp[ing] the life into [...] [Linnet] some twenty years ago' (Quiller-Couch and Du Maurier 2004, 3, 7, 164). The revelation of his connection with Linnet anchors Carfax more firmly to the legend playing out around her. In chapter 11 [C14], Du Maurier again reinforces Carfax's centrality to the novel, inserting him in a scene from which he is originally absent. In the MS, Amyot's song is discussed by the harvesters:

> 'Now that's a funny thing,' observed old Tregenza [...] 'The lad seems to be spackin', and yet you and me Missus Emmet,'—he turned to an elderly harvest-woman, 'don't understand one word of it [...]' (DD36/A/14, C14, fol. 05r)

In Du Maurier's version, however, it is Carfax who reacts to the song, with a more troubled sense of something missed:

> Doctor Carfax, in the act of lighting his pipe, paused, and stared at the singer, allowing his match to go out.
>
> 'Would you mind repeating that?' he demanded slowly [...]
>
> Dr Carfax frowned [...] It was not the moment to pursue his line of inquiry, but he had been reminded, all too suddenly, of poor Ledru[.] (Quiller-Couch and Du Maurier 2004, 93)

At the end of the chapter, after Linnet's trick of falling off the hay cart into Amyot's arms, Carfax's voice is again inserted: '"Neatly manoeuvred," murmured Doctor Carfax' (Quiller-Couch and Du Maurier 2004, 97). With these few lines Du Maurier adds to the MS, the entire scene takes on a more detached, knowing tone. Echoing the prologue's set-up of watcher and watched, the re-focalised chapter more closely ties the main events of the novel with its frame, and emphasises Carfax's importance as a character whose observing thoughts constitute a major throughline of *Castle Dor*.

'Tristan the Fool'? The Characterisation of Amyot

In terms of characterisation, Du Maurier makes only a few small changes to the MS, taking care to preserve much of Q's writing. The one exception to this is her consistent revision of Amyot's character. These changes, though mostly small and localised, affect what is arguably the central aspect of the novel, aside from the matter of geography. Q portrays Amyot as a dim-witted boy, going so far as to ascribe animalistic attributes to him. The very first description of him in C1d compares his 'puzzled patient eyes' to 'those of a dog who has been chidden without understanding' (DD36/A/14, C1d, fol. 08r). Du Maurier alters this to 'fine brown eyes' (Quiller-Couch and Du Maurier 2004, 9). Other instances of changes in the same vein are given in the following table:

Table 6.2 Differences in the characterisation of Amyot between the MS and published text.

MS	Published version
'Hitherto—for save for a dumb-animal look—he had scarcely expressed his gratitude, she [Deborah] was rather doubtful of his wits or of any aptitude in him'. (DD36/A/14, C4, fol. 02r)	Excised (Quiller-Couch and Du Maurier 2004, 23)
'He still regarded this handsome taciturn boy as something of a half-wit.' (DD36/A/14, C4, fol. 05r)	Excised (Quiller-Couch and Du Maurier 2004, 24)

'Then perhaps you are not the half-wit I have been taking you for.' (DD36/A/14, C4, fol. 07r)	'Then perhaps you are not the dreamer I have been taking you for.' (Quiller-Couch and Du Maurier 2004, 27)
'Amyot kept beside him, faithful as a dog that trusts his master in a strange place, uncomprehending.' (DD36/A/14, C5, fol. 01r)	Excised (Quiller-Couch and Du Maurier 2004, 28)
'Amyot's face expressed nothing but an almost brutish puzzlement. He did not in the least understand what quest he was following.' (DD36/A/14, C5, fol. 02r)	'Amyot's face expressed nothing but puzzlement. He did not in the least understand what quest he was following.' (Quiller-Couch and Du Maurier 2004, 28)
'But Amyot had turned stupid. [...] "I was indeed expecting—something," he stammered. "I cannot tell what, monsieur."' (DD36/A/14, C5, fol. 05r)	'But Amyot had turned indifferent. "I had indeed expected—I cannot tell what, monsieur."' (Quiller-Couch and Du Maurier 2004, 30)
'"It was a very dangerous trick," he answered stupidly' (DD36/A/14, C15, fol. 03r)	'"It was a very dangerous trick," he answered firmly' (Quiller-Couch and Du Maurier 2004, 100)

The changes Du Maurier makes to Amyot's character, whether through excision or substitution of words and phrases, present him as decisive rather than simple. Without adding any descriptions of Amyot or passages from his perspective, Du Maurier adds depth to Q's somewhat two-dimensional hero, hinting at parts of his consciousness beyond the narrator's purview. Similar, though less prominent, changes are made to the characters of Mary [Molly]. While in Q's MS, Molly Bosanko (who becomes Mary in the published text), *Castle Dor*'s incarnation of Iseult of the White Hands, is quite an unlikeable child, Du Maurier's Mary has more of the unreadabillty of an adolescent. The alteration is again achieved through removal of sections of the MS which emphasise Mary [Molly]'s juvenility and unimaginativeness, such as the following:

> Johnny had become quite expert at this play, which the more matter-of-fact Molly could never master. She listened avidly: but her wind-ups were always disappointing, sometimes quite imbecile [...] (she could never invent). (DD36/A/14, C14, fol. 03r; 07r)

Q's characters, not unlike those from Arthurian legend, who 'frequently have very little interiority or clear motivation', appear to the reader mainly through their actions and simply represented thoughts (Carroll 2022, 477). By removing some of the explication of their feelings, Du Maurier is able to give them a degree of opacity that suggests a complexity more typical of characters in a novel than those in a legend. Without any major changes or additions of her own (in the section of the *Castle Dor* that corresponds to the MS), Du Maurier hints at the superficial nature of the narrative layer through which the characters are presented. The sense of their interior lives, inaccessible beneath the narrative surface, is perhaps partially attributable to this real suppression of descriptions from the MS.

Conclusion

Castle Dor is somewhat unusual in its compositional process, both its authors being constrained by the story and setting of the Tristan legend and Du Maurier having, additionally, to consider Q's MS. This essay has used the *Castle Dor* MS to reveal an earlier stage of this process, and, comparing it to the published version of the novel, has shown how Du Maurier's alterations to its temporal setting, narrative framing, focalisation and characterisation smooth out tonal conflicts, increase thematic cohesion and suggest greater character complexity than in the MS. Her changes, however, seem mainly to intensify or extend aspects already present in the MS. In light of this, her contribution appears to be in distilling Q's ideas and modes of expression rather than in exploring further creative possibilities for an Arthurian adaptation. It is quite possible that, in other instances of posthumous completion, the completing author diverges more from the originating author's writing, and these cases would also make for interesting studies. Narratological formations may not always be the work of a single author, and in each case of co-authorship, the nature and results of the collaboration will be different. A genetic approach helps to shed some light on these nebulous processes, exposing the changing content and form of a text across time and, perhaps, in the hands of various authors.

Works Cited

Alber, Jan. (2017), 'Narratology and Performativity: On the Processes of Narrativization in Live Performances', *Narrative*, 25.3: 359–73, https://doi.org/10.1353/nar.2017.0019.

Bawden, Nina (2004), Introduction, in: *Castle Dor*, by Arthur Quiller-Couch and Daphne Du Maurier (London: Virago Press), v–viii.

Bernaerts, Lars and Dirk Van Hulle (2013), 'Narrative across Versions: Narratology Meets Genetic Criticism', *Poetics Today*, 34.3: 281–326.

Brett, David, 'Daphne can give 'Q' the 'U' Appeal' [Review], Manchester Evening News, 6 April 1962, Trinity College Oxford Archive (TCOA), D36/E/6.

Brittain, F. (1947), *Arthur Quiller-Couch: A Biographical Study of Q* (Cambridge: Cambridge University Press).

Bryden, Inga (2005), *Reinventing King Arthur: The Arthurian Legends in Victorian Culture* (Aldershot and Burlington, VT: Ashgate).

Bunting, Kirsty (2013), '"The imprint of what-has-been": Arthur Quiller-Couch, Daphne Du Maurier and the Writing of *Castle Dor*', *Cornish Studies*, 21.1: 260–75.

Carroll, Shiloh (2022), 'Arthur in Modern Fantasy Literature', in: *The Arthurian World*, ed. by Victoria Coldham-Fussell et al. (London: Routledge), 477–87, https://doi.org/10.4324/9781003255475.

Curtis, Anthony, 'Lovers' Tale Retold' [Review of *Castle Dor*], Sunday Telegraph, 8 April 1962, Trinity College Oxford Archive (TCOA), D36/E/6.

Debray Genette, Raymonde (2004), 'Flaubert's "A Simple Heart," or How to Make an Ending: A Study of the Manuscripts', in: *Genetic Criticism: Texts and Avant-Textes*, ed. by Jed Deppman et al. (Philadelphia: University of Pennsylvania Press), 69–95.

Ditmas, Edith Margaret Robertson (1969), *Tristan and Iseult in Cornwall: A Twelfth-Century Romance by Beroul Re-told from the Norman French* (Gloucester: Forrester Roberts).

Du Maurier, Daphne (1962), 'Finishing a Romance' [Article], Sunday Telegraph, 1 April 1962, Trinity College Oxford Archive (TCOA), D36/E/6.

Du Maurier, Daphne, Letters to Foy Quiller-Couch, Trinity College Oxford Archive (TCOA), DD36/D/D.

Fludernik, Monika (2010), 'Mediacy, Mediation, and Focalization', in: *Postclassical Narratology: Approaches and Analyses*, ed. by Alber, Jan and Monika Fludernik (Columbus: Ohio State University Press), 105–33.

Herman, Luc and Bart Vervaeck (2005), *Handbook of Narrative Analysis* (Lincoln, NE and London: University of Nebraska Press).

Hogan, William (1962), 'Miss Du Maurier Assists a Master', San Fransisco Chronicle, 12 February 1962, TCOA D36/E/6.

Kukkonen, Karin (2011), 'Comics as a Test Case for Transmedial Narratology', *SubStance*, 40.1: 34–52, https://doi.org/10.1353/sub.2011.0005.

Loomis, Roger Sherman [1963] (2012), *The Development of Arthurian Romance* (Minneola, NY: Dover Publications).

Matthews, David (2009), 'Scholarship and Popular Culture in the Nineteenth Century', in: *A Companion to Arthurian Literature*, ed. by Helen Fulton (Oxford: Wiley-Blackwell). https://doi.org/10.1002/9781444305821.ch24.

Quiller-Couch, Arthur [1944] (2008), *Memories and Opinions: An Unfinished Autobiography* (Cambridge: Cambridge University Press).

Quiller-Couch, Arthur, '*Castle Dor*' Manuscript, Trinity College Oxford Archive (TCOA) DD36/A/14.

Quiller-Couch, Arthur, and Daphne Du Maurier [1962] (2004), *Castle Dor* (London: Virago).

Schoepperle, Gertrude (1913), *Tristan and Isolt: A Study of the Sources of the Romance*, vol. 1 (Frankfurt a.M. and London: Joseph Baer and Co.; David Nutt).

Ton, Jan-Noël (2016), *Transmedial Narratology and Contemporary Media Culture* (Lincoln, NE: University of Nebraska Press).

Van Hulle, Dirk (2022), *Genetic Criticism: Tracing Creativity in Literature* (Oxford: Oxford University Press). https://doi.org/10.1093/oso/9780192846792.001.0001.

Zlosnick, Sue and Avril Horner (2009), 'Myself When Others: Daphne du Maurier and the Double Dialogue with "D"', *Women: A Cultural Review*, 20.1: 9–24, https://doi.org/10.1080/09574040802684780.

7. Prototyping the Narrative Skeleton: Story Structure, Types of Narration and Vestigial Elements in the Genesis of James Joyce's 'Ithaca' Episode

Joris Žiliukas

Where is the 'skeleton' in 'Ithaca', the penultimate episode of *Ulysses*? The 'Organ', assigned to the episode in the Gilbert schema Joyce devised in 1921, promises structure and stability. This assurance is, however, undermined once the reader discovers a second, earlier schema, which instead designates the episode's organ as 'Juices'. In a 1920 letter to Carlo Linati, Joyce included this list of correspondences and describes it as a 'sunto-chiave-scheletro-schema' ['summary-key-skeleton-scheme'] (*SL*, 270–71).[1] Here the Italian word for 'skeleton' again seeks to provide stability, but whatever was 'skeletal' about the 1920 schema was apparently not stable enough to survive into 1921, and 'Ithaca' had its 'Organ' reassigned from 'Juices' to 'Skeleton'.

All this to say that it is not always advisable to put blind faith in Joyce's own explications. The tantalising concreteness of the schemata overshadows the fascinating implication that Joyce changed his mind as he worked. Michael Groden and A. Walton Litz have written about Joyce's creative practices, both distinguishing between 'Early' and 'Late' stages of writing, with Groden proposing a third—'Middle'—stage (Litz 1974; Groden 1977). Each stage is characterised by different approaches to writing, and the late stage overturned the entire novel, along with producing the final episodes. With the expensive purchase of Joyce's

---

1 For abbreviations see the list of Works Cited.

manuscripts by the National Library of Ireland in 2002, a wealth of early drafts has become available, making possible a micro-scale investigation of the genesis of 'Ithaca' through manuscript evidence. The manuscript containing the draft of 'Ithaca', referred to as the 'proto-text' or as the 'proto-draft',[2] is especially enlightening, as it was composed in the intervening months between the Linati and Gilbert schemata, promising to render visible the growth of the skeleton.

The proto-draft is written out in page-long stretches of questions and answers, the stylistic calling card of 'Ithaca', and contains various additions in the margins. The writing is so tight that Joyce used multi-coloured crayons to divide up and cross out separate sections as they were reused in the following drafts. The episode is often described as a 'catechism' for its question-and-answer routine, but, in this state, it is more akin to a colourful pile of LEGO bricks. These 'bricks' are not yet arranged, nor is the 'building set' complete. The draft stage that follows, the Rosenbach fair copy, is roughly twice as long with 66% more questions and answers, and the 1922 text is three times as long (Madtes 1983, 36).

The most salient structural feature Joyce worked out during the movement from the disjunct proto-draft to the tightly woven fair copy is the narrative. All three of its levels—narrative text, narration and story, to use Mieke Bal's (2017) terminology—are subject to substantial reshaping. The story is brought into existence from nothing, and the time and place are made consistent and clear. This is done by rearranging the textual 'blocks', i.e. the question-and-answer pairs. Joyce arranges coherent sections into a plot, whereas disparate blocks congeal into new scenes. The 'skeleton'—a chronotope, narrator, fabula, beginning and ending which support the text—comes into view.

On the other hand, Joyce also develops strategies which work to 'undo' whatever progress this narrative makes. Terence Killeen notes that, despite the narrative's 'impressive mastery of facts', most of what is narrated 'is oddly disappointing' (2022, 278). What Killeen and others find disappointing is brought about by 'disnarration' and 'the unnarrated', that is, hypotheses, implausible tales and omissions (Prince 1988). These techniques counteract, remain silent on, and digress from

---

2   Respectively by *James Joyce Digital Archive* and Crispi, 2015.

the fabula, unmaking 'Ithaca' as it is being made. While traces of these are present in the proto-draft, their fleshed-out versions in the fair copy afford unique insight into how such strategies were utilised to 'take apart' the narrative skeleton.

Rather than a comparison of two drafts, like the confrontation of 'Juices' against 'Skeleton' as the organs of 'Ithaca', this essay aims to describe the creative process the comparison reveals, in the vein of genetic criticism. Dirk Van Hulle argues that this revelation emerges from 'the tension between the concrete objects of manuscripts that have been left behind and the abstract retrospection to reverse-engineer the process that produced them' (2022, 138). By reading the proto-draft and the fair copy as traces of the operations that produced the final version of 'Ithaca', it is possible to interrogate Joyce's work in a way which dissolves (or at least remedies) the ambiguities created by 'skeletal' interpretations of the novel, such as the schemata provide. Instead of accepting 'Skeleton' as the 'Organ' that 'Ithaca' represents, we can ask how it got there, and how (and when) it is meaningful for reading the episode.

Genetic criticism allows for more than simply re-tracing what is found in the published text—it also casts light on the significance of what is left behind. As a writer, Joyce tended to add disproportionately more than he would take away (Madtes 1983, 35), and therefore textual units that remain confined to the proto-draft appear especially significant. Some paragraphs are recycled in such a way as to become almost unrecognisable or are left behind only to be re-added at a later stage. Here I lean heavily on what Van Hulle calls 'vestigial' writings. A writer's unused notes, while 'purposeless from a teleological point of view', are still 'crucial [...] in the study of creative writing processes' (2022, 170). These elements do not appear in the final version, and thus have no 'end' (teleological) goal, but they still contribute to the final 'shape' of 'Ithaca'. Returning to the skeleton metaphor, these vestigial 'bones' highlight how the episode's structure works precisely by virtue of not fitting the final design.

Though this essay mainly focuses on the proto-draft and the fair copy, it occasionally references later drafting stages, particularly the first typescript and its extracts. With reference to narratology and looking through a genetic lens, it is shown how the development of narrative contributes to the effect, that is, the poetics, of the episode, and how, in its yet-undeveloped form, the proto-draft was used to work out important aspects of narrative for the final version.

The Structure of the Story: Assembling the Narrative Skeleton

Studying the composition of 'Ithaca' means studying the composition of *Ulysses* as a whole. It was the last episode to be written but appears as the second-to-last in the novel. In several letters dating to the end of 1920 and the beginning of 1921, Joyce mentions the final part of *Ulysses* as being 'sketched' (*LIII*, 31) or 'in part written' (*LII*, 459). None of these sketches are known to be extant, but the letters testify that Joyce's conception of the final episodes changed drastically during the process of writing. 'Ithaca', one of the episodes he refers to as 'very short' (*LIII*, 31) and written in a 'quite plain' style (*LI*, 143), turned out to be disproportionately long and, as A. Walton Litz notes, the novel's 'climax' of 'stylistic development' (1974, 386).

Joyce did not work on 'Ithaca' in isolation from other episodes. Michael Groden notes that in 'the last stage', that is, while writing 'Circe' through 'Penelope', Joyce 'returned to the early- and middle-stage episodes and revised them considerably, almost always by adding' (1977, 166). In a letter to Harriet Shaw Weaver, dated 7 August 1921, Joyce writes of fleshing out 'Ithaca' and beginning 'Penelope'. This marks a break from work on the episode, which began in February. It also marks the transition into the following drafting stage, as Joyce notes in the letter that 'Ithaca' now needs to be 'completed, revised and rearranged'. From that point Joyce often accompanies mentions of 'Ithaca' with plans to 'put [...] into shape' (*LIII*, 48) and 'put in order' (*LIII*, 49). In his letters, Joyce punctuates the switch between 'writing' and 'putting in order' or 'rearranging', suggesting the proto-draft and fair copy belong to different stages of composition with different goals.

It is important to note that there is no way to show, nor is it likely, that the proto-draft is a direct genetic antecedent to the fair copy draft. Luca Crispi notes that the 'relatively stable manner' of the text in the fair copy means that Joyce likely 'revised and expanded' some sections 'on one or more missing intermediary manuscripts' (2015, 205). While this sounds alarming—how is it possible to analyse missing material?—in reality, the discovery of additional manuscripts would only increase the resolution of the analysis. For now, we must carry on with what is available, being careful to not make too many assumptions.

The versos of the folios in the proto-draft notebook were initially left blank for later insertions (*JJDA* 'Draft Analysis Ithaca'). The writing is marked up with three colours of crayon: blue is used to demarcate the divisions between paragraphs, which Joyce later crossed out in blue, red and green colours to note their being incorporated into the following draft (Van Hulle 2021, 170). The writing continues until the second-to-last recto. Most pages have ample insertions on the verso, but for the last two. This suggests that the manuscript was a stop along the way to a more developed draft. Joyce uses it to flesh out ideas and copy in material, but moves on before 'finishing it'—the writing stops arbitrarily.

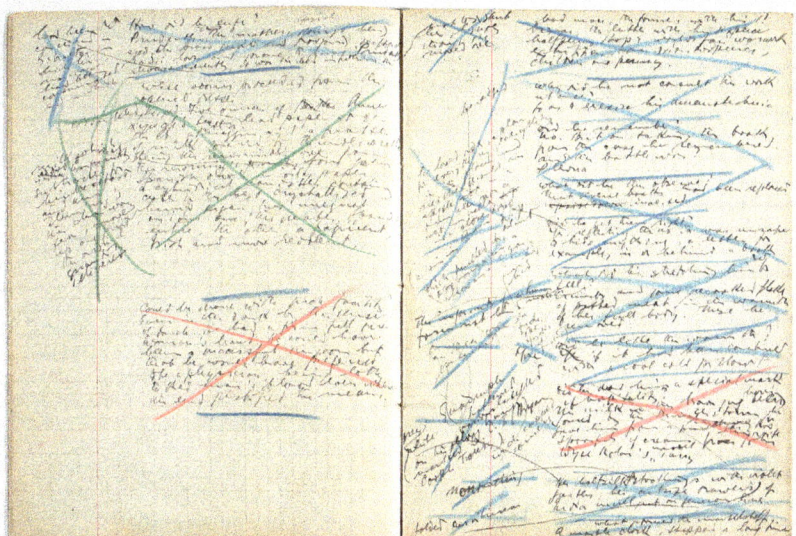

Fig. 7.1 Folio 7v and 8 of *NLI 13* (James Joyce, Partial draft: 'Ithaca', National Library of Ireland, MS 36,639/13, https://catalogue.nli.ie/Record/vtls000357810/, reproduced courtesy of the National Library of Ireland). Note the consistently widening margin with additions on page 8. Further additions, one of them marked with siglum 'W', made on 7v.[3]

---

3   I wish to thank James Harte (NLI Special Collections) for granting the rights to reproduce these pages (personal correspondence 4 April 2024).

The previous description of the proto-draft as a pile of LEGO bricks turns out to be a powerful metaphor that renders visible the text in motion. The 'bricks' in question are paragraphs, their boundaries coinciding with the question-and-answer pairs inherent to a catechetical form. Daniel Ferrer and Jean-Michel Rabaté analyse paragraphs 'in Expansion', noting their 'relative stability' (2004, 142) in Joyce's *Ulysses* and *Finnegans Wake*. The paragraph break is of special interest to Ferrer and Rabaté since it lies between 'linguistic' and 'iconic' divisions (2004, 135), that is, between the grammatically necessary border of a sentence and the arbitrary end of a page. Paragraph breaks bear properties of both fixity and arbitrariness:

> They are deliberate and somehow gratuitous because, as we have noted, they are prescribed by no clear rule. Above all, they are not a separation from the exterior but an inner separation. We are therefore dealing with a border, but an attenuated border, less irrevocable than the others. (Ferrer and Rabaté, 2004, 135)

Yet here the border is not 'attenuated', nor 'less irrevocable'—in the proto-draft, Joyce forcefully demarcates the paragraphs with crayon (see Figure 7.1). This separation allows us to consider each question-and-answer paragraph as a textual 'unit' or 'block' that is moved around in the process of rearrangement. But, as we will see, even these forceful graphical divisions are not as final as they seem—as Ferrer and Rabaté note, '[the paragraphs] show themselves to be open to fissures, scissions, and doubling' (2004, 142).

Despite making up half the length of the fair copy, the proto-draft covers much of the same material. That is, if we rearrange the textual blocks—the question-and-answer pairs—to match the ordering of the fair copy, the resulting distribution is surprisingly even from start to end. The fair copy has many additional blocks, but these are inserted consistently in between the proto-draft ones. The average 'gap', that is, the number of blocks inserted between subsequent ones, is around two, with the most common value being one, and extremes of ten and twelve. Regarding structural matters, Joyce had almost everything he needed before moving onto the next drafting stage. Whichever way he proceeded—either rearranging blocks and then writing insertions or writing them as he was rearranging—the basic structure of the episode results directly from proto-draft material.

7. Prototyping the Narrative Skeleton

This material is highly unordered, however, as can be seen in the illustration below.[4] The column on the left represents four sections that begin the proto-draft. On the right are the same blocks, but in the way they are ordered in the fair copy:

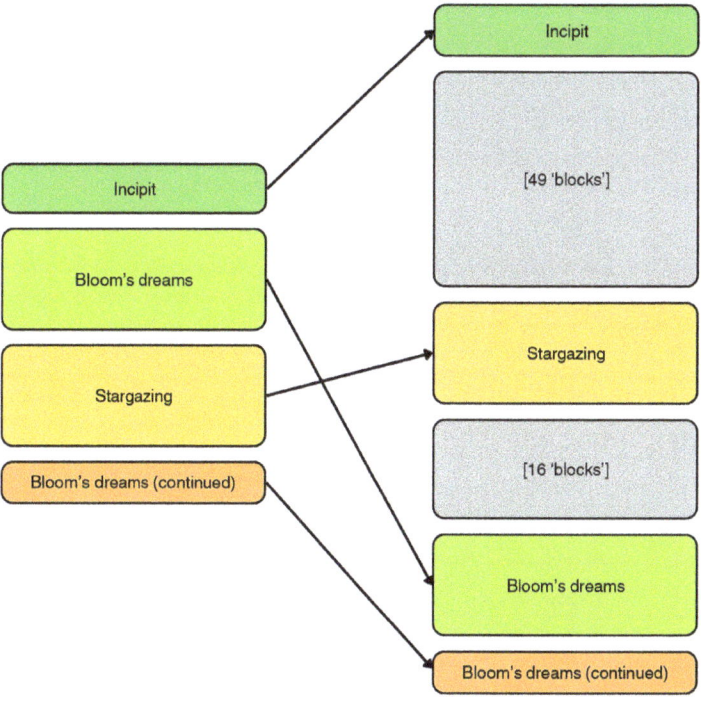

Fig. 7.2 Schematic illustration of text rearrangement and expansion from the proto-draft to the fair copy. Blocks on the left represent the content and ordering of the opening folios of the proto-draft, on the right these are rearranged, or interspersed with additional content.

The first four thematic sections of the proto-draft (the blocks on the left in Fig. 7.2) are rearranged in the fair copy (the blocks on the right) and spaced out by material taken from later in the proto-draft, or newly

---

4   I thank Dirk Van Hulle for the suggestion of this visualisation.

inserted. Thus, for instance, 'Bloom's dreams' jump over 'Stargazing' to form a coherent segment.

Despite some sections, such as Bloom's dreams of a country house or the stargazing, being maintained intact, the rest is rearranged according to non-obvious principles. Two scholars who have commented on the proto-draft's structure, Luca Crispi and Philip Keel Geheber, also call it 'non-sequential' (Crispi 2015, 182) and 'disordered' (Geheber 2017, 70). This also applies to the episode's narrative. The key events of the fabula are present—Bloom and Stephen arriving at 7 Eccles Street, drinking cocoa, urinating in the garden, Stephen leaving, Bloom re-entering the house and going to bed—but they are not presented in that order. Though the incipit of arriving home is in place, Stephen leaves around a quarter of the way through, reappearing in later questions, and Bloom goes to bed after a third of the chapter. In order to see how the narrative was constructed, it is necessary to investigate how the textual units were rearranged.

The establishing of a narrative sequence is the most significant structural change the proto-draft undergoes before it takes its shape in the fair copy manuscript. In fact, the linear structure the episode acquires is so rigid that Joyce wrote the fair copy in five parts, alternating between two notebooks, and had it typed piecemeal without fear of needing to backtrack to rearrange the narrative sequence. Even though the fabula is the main thing established, this happens alongside narration and narrative text—here narratological analysis helps us distinguish what exactly was being moved, and what happened to tag along, so to speak. Two examples will demonstrate how this stability was achieved: large, preconceived sections were moved into a fixed order and at the same time expanded, while disparate textual units pertaining to the same topic or narrative strand were brought together to constitute new sections.

The first section, describing Bloom's and Stephen's journey home, confined to folio 2r (*Proto*), remains essentially fixed, providing both the first events of the fabula and the incipit of the narration. As we turn the page, the narrative thread is severed—3r and 2v are a digression into a description of Bloom's dream countryside home. Folio 4r contains another question belonging to Bloom's dream section, prompting several later additions on 3v that are marked for insertion right after it. The most substantial section on fol. 4r, however, is the one that marks Stephen's departure and prompts Bloom's solitary cogitations on loneliness and space. Most notable is that in the proto-draft, Bloom sees 'the heaventree' and 'the lamp by her [Molly's] bedroom window' (*Proto*, fol. 4r) alone, unlike in the fair copy (*RB*, 15)—Joyce had not yet worked out (or made explicit) Stephen's presence in these blocks. These three sections end up far apart in the fair copy ordering: the incipit remaining fixed, Bloom's dreams are placed later in the draft and joined together, whereas the paragraphs on astrology now take place between Stephen and Bloom drinking cocoa and Bloom returning inside, alone (see Figure 7.2). The already formed sections provide the backbone for the reordering of the rest—later on in the proto-draft, when Joyce decides that Stephen and Bloom urinate together (*Proto*, fol. 11r), he reprises the motif of the light in Molly's window (*Proto*, 10v) and inserts it in the middle of the stable astrology section in the fair copy (*RB*, 15).

Stephen's presence in the proto-draft is instead built up gradually and disparately and only made continuous in the fair copy draft. First Joyce compares Bloom and Stephen's ages on fol. 7r (*Proto*), then a page later Bloom is made to forego his special cup as a sign of hospitality to Stephen. On fol. 10r Bloom imagines Stephen is quietly composing a poem in his head, but only on fol. 11r is the later context of drinking cocoa established. The question and answer about their sitting positions, one of the earliest in the fair copy, is the last in the proto-draft. In this case, Stephen acts as the backbone—his presence, strewn all about the proto-draft, is made to coagulate into a new section. Instead of combining blocks pertaining to the same event, Joyce collects all the blocks involving Stephen as an actor.

At this point we should ask how this rearrangement was motivated, as it makes sense that Joyce had some conception of what the episode should be. Litz provides a rationale for the episode's structure:

> Clearly, he [Joyce] conceived of 'Ithaca' as a series of scenes or tableaux, not unlike the narrative divisions in 'Circe', and on the early typescripts he blocked out these scenes under the titles 'street', 'kitchen', 'garden', 'parlour', 'bedroom'. We may consider the 'narrative' development of 'Ithaca' under these headings, since each scene builds to a revealing climax which forwards our understanding of both Bloom and Stephen. (1974, 398)

The 'typescripts' Litz is referring to are an extract of the episode prepared specially for Valery Larbaud. Joyce refers to them in a letter dated 30 October 1921: 'My typist has sent you extracts (of course uncorrected) from the beginning and middle of *Ithaca*. In a few days she will send you extracts from the end' (*LIII*, 51). This typescript, containing one question and answer per page, was prepared partly from what was already typed, partly directly from the fair copy manuscript (*JJA* v. 16, x–xi). The 'titles' which Litz is referring to are written in pencil, in Joyce's hand according to Peter Spielberg (1962, 70–71), on pages where a change of scene occurs (*TSE*, 215; 216; 238; 248; 269). Curiously, the last title, 'bedroom', is only found on the carbon copy of the typescript. Since we know the episode already had its final narrative shape in the form of the fair copy manuscript, it is difficult to tell whether these 'tableaux' were a guiding principle Joyce followed as he composed, or whether he gravitated towards such an arrangement only as he was working out the structure of the episode. Van Hulle documents a similar phenomenon in the case of the chronotope in Kazuo Ishiguro's *The Remains of The Day*, calling it a 'chicken-or-egg' question (2022, 151). Since Joyce wrote the designations only after finishing the episode, it is unclear which conditioned which.

With the benefit of having access to the proto-draft, it is possible to draw stronger, but less specific principles for rearrangement. Instead of trying to apply an idealised, evenly divided schema in retrospect, we can try to reason about what kind of reordering the text necessitates. For example, Stephen's explicit or implied presence in certain units means that they must be moved before his departure. Sure enough, in the fair copy, we only find two references to Stephen post-departure, both in Bloom's retelling of his day to Molly. Likewise, the existence of sections which remain stable points to Joyce having preconceived ideas about structure, but some developments happen only as he was writing them out, such as the idea of Bloom and Stephen urinating in the garden while gazing at the stars. The combination of shared agents or topics brought certain blocks together, but a picture which could then be subdivided into 'tableaux' possibly only arose when Joyce was already finished with the reordering.

On a final note, it is interesting that some small and well-defined sections need no rearrangement—they are already explicitly ordered in the proto-draft. When returning to make additions in the margin or on the verso, Joyce often marks them with sigla to signal the precise place of insertion. Mostly this is confined to clauses within textual units, but sometimes Joyce marks entire question-and-answer pairs to be included before or after others. The insertion of 'Could he foresee himself?' on fol. 3v (*Proto*), marked to be inserted after the 'Bloomville' question, maintains its ordering in the fair copy (*RB*, 17). Likewise, Joyce inserts the final paragraph on fol. 4v right after the final one on fol. 5r (*Proto*), and the ordering is the same in the fair copy (see Figure 7.3). Another example is Joyce adding the 'How did he enter?' question on fol. 7v (*Proto*), but marking it for insertion on fol. 8r between 'Did he set them right?', referring to resetting inverted books, and 'What did his stretching limbs feel?' The sequence is now solidified—Bloom resets the books, enters the bed and then stretches. We can distinguish more than just sections which are either preconceived or unordered, since there are also new inventions which Joyce felt he needed to mark right there on the page.

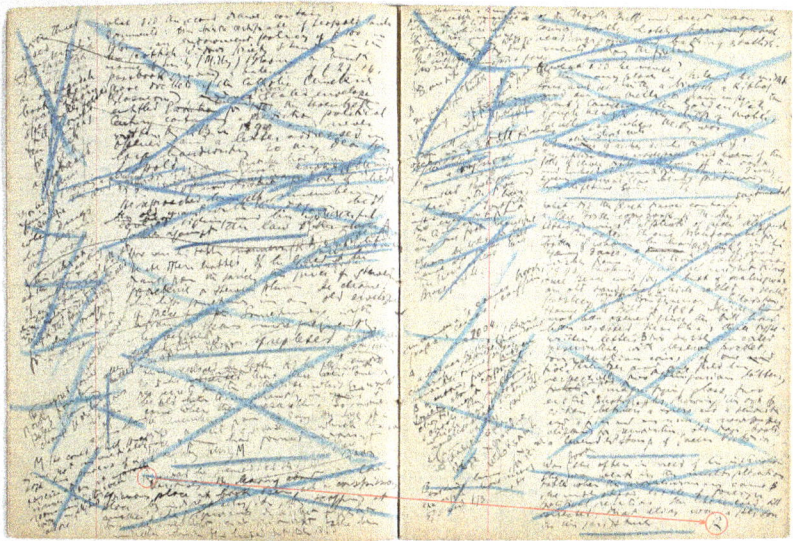

Fig. 7.3 Addition on 4v in *NLI 13* (James Joyce, Partial draft: 'Ithaca', National Library of Ireland, MS 36,639/13, https://catalogue.nli.ie/Record/vtls000357810/, reproduced courtesy of the National Library of Ireland), marked to be inserted after final block on fol. 5r. Red marking (my own) highlights the siglum 'R' used to mark place of insertion.

This suggests that the proto-draft, though 'rudimentary' (Crispi 2015, 205), is perhaps not so 'non-sequential' as Crispi describes it. He notes several instances of sections maintaining coherence (2015, 182; 205) and comments on how 'unusual' they are. The evidence of Joyce working out certain ordering explicitly on the proto-draft manuscript refines the picture. Copying in old material and writing new, Joyce was working in the context of both chance and structure. While the entire draft appears chaotic, it is no surprise that some blocks naturally inspired others and therefore they maintain their ordering during the movement to the subsequent drafting stage. Perhaps it is more accurate to say that the proto-draft was composed non-sequentially, or without a clear structure in mind, since the process of writing, inevitably, conditioned a sort of structure on the physical document.

Establishing narrative structure in 'Ithaca' can be seen as a process whose principles developed alongside the actual writing of the text. As Joyce gathered material in the proto-draft, it began to take shape right there on the page, with some sections clearly predestined to be self-standing, and others slowly elaborated over the course of writing. The view that Joyce had the episode laid out from the start, proposed by Litz, conflicts with the unstructured nature of the proto-draft and Joyce's post-hoc scribblings on the typescript. On the other hand, the draft is not as 'non-sequential' as it first appears to Crispi and Geheber, as here and there it does show some strong structuring that persisted into the next drafting stage, sometimes even enforced graphically during a round of additions to mark that the material is already being structured in a non-arbitrary way. Joyce imbues the material with a narrative stability that makes the fair copy text cohere, but this proves to be only a starting point for a different kind of narrative development.

Disnarration and the Unnarrated: Taking the Skeleton Apart

Constructing a coherent fabula and chronotope was clearly a priority for Joyce, but not the only one. As noted by Richard E. Madtes, around a third of 'Ithaca' was written in additions to the typescripts and proofs (1983, 36). As the episode expanded, its fabula remained the same, but the narrative effect changed significantly. Most of the work that resulted in 'Ithaca' being named the 'ugly duckling' of the book took place at this later stage—the first reference to the epithet appears in a letter to Weaver dated 25 November 1921 (JJC), just as Joyce was revising the episode's typescript. Though the effect achieved by this expansion develops mostly in the typescripts and proofs, it is possible to trace the genesis of the narrative strategies at play to the proto-draft and fair copy.

'Ithaca', in the end, takes the route of anti-narrative. Take, for example, Karen Lawrence's analysis: 'Just as we are hoping for the resolution of the plot, then, the narrative opens up to include almost everything imaginable' (2014, 192). Narrative is undone by its own mirror image, the hypothetical, which Gerald Prince christens the 'disnarrated' and defines as 'events that *do not* happen, but, nonetheless, are referred to (in a negative or hypothetical mode) by the narrative text' (1988, 2). Having arranged the 'real' fabula, the chain of cause and effect which drives the narrative to its end, Joyce was free to open many branching narratives situated in the hypothetical and the negative.

The hypothetical is not as developed in the proto-draft as it is in the published version, but we can retrace the textual sites where it is expanded in later writing stages. One key event in the fabula is Stephen declining to stay the night at Bloom's house, which mirrors Bloom declining to have dinner at the Dedalus household twelve years earlier. While Bloom's refusal is already laid out on fol. 12r (*Proto*), in the proto-draft Stephen leaves without first having refused to stay. The first trace of what would become the symmetrical response appears on fol. 14r:

Would they meet?

He wondered. He had no son. [...]

Joyce continues with Bloom's circus story—this story immediately follows the expanded version of those three short phrases in the fair copy (*RB*, 12). Then, Bloom and Stephen discuss possible locations for 'Italian instruction', 'vocal instruction' and 'intellectual dialogues' (*RB*, 11) that are 'unlikely to take place' (Killeen 2021, 271). By introducing Stephen's denial, Joyce opens up the possibility of him accepting, and thus creates a rift into the disnarrated, which is expanded with plans that will not be realised. As the most important plot event in 'Ithaca', Stephen's declining to stay is fittingly downplayed.

There are also small and significant changes from the indicative to the conditional, which again underline Joyce's intention to understate and disnarrate. The question which prompts Molly's list of lovers appears in its simplest form in the proto-draft: 'He [Bloom] smiled?' (*Proto*, fol. 11r). The version which appears in the fair copy, and is brought forward unchanged into the published version, is cast into the hypothetical: 'If he had smiled why would he have smiled?' (*RB*, 27). Even an insubstantial smile, seen by no one, is dedramatised and rendered purely mental, reflecting the episode's tendency to narrate more of what does not happen, instead of sticking to what does. Simple additions like 'Duel he wd not' (*Proto*, 14) not only add to characterisation, as is one of the functions of disnarration according to Prince (1988, 4), but also work against the fabula by drawing textual and narrative attention away from it. Prince paraphrases Claude Bremond: 'every narrative function opens an alternative, a set of possible directions' (1988, 5). Joyce exploits this feature of narrative events to its fullest extent in 'Ithaca' by prioritising a non-linear web of hypotheticals instead of cause-and-effect narrative.

Killeen describes the episode as producing 'the effect [...] of beings looking down from the heavens, from an enormous distance, on the affairs of humans, indifferent to the phenomena which they merely observe and report' (2021, 276). This results from the tension between focalisation—'the relation between the vision and what is seen, perceived' (Bal 2017, 133)—and the unnarrated. Prince defines the unnarrated as 'ellipses [...] inferable from a significant lacuna in the chronology' (1988, 2). A genetic reading, especially of an early manuscript, affords a luxury unavailable to other readings: the ability to distinguish between lacunae to be filled in and the unnarrated. Graphically, there is little difference between a dash which signifies a halt in narration, and a placeholder dash, destined to be filled in in making a fair copy, rendering the wording precise. In the proto-draft, these two overlap, and it is therefore possible to trace the development (or undoing) of the unnarrated.

For instance, returning to Molly's 'list of lovers' on fol. 11r (*Proto*), we can see that 'the most famous list in *Ulysses*' (Kenner, qtd. in Crispi 2015, 264) is little more than five names and eight dashes:

> It amused him that each man fancied himself the first to enter the breach whereas he was the last of a series through Penrose, -- -- -- --, Bloom, Holohan, Bodkin, Mulvey, -- -- -- --

Crispi comments that 'the list's trajectory suggests that it was never intended as an accurate enumeration of Molly's lovers, few as they actually are' (2015, 265). Furthermore, Crispi asserts that the dashes are 'merely reminders to fill in the names later on' (2015, 265). Here the early state of the proto-draft confirms a certain reading by underlining the relative unimportance of the elements to the form, the unnarrated is dissipated.

The effect is different when considering Bloom's thoughts as he enters the bed. On fol. 7v (*Proto*) Joyce writes the following:

How did he enter?

Prudently. [...] it was the bed in which she –

Then in the margin he adds:

had been conceived [...], in which her marriage had been consummated and in which [blank]⁵

Crispi notes that, at first leaving 'the point incomplete (or simply unstated)', Joyce's later addition again leaves 'the rest of the line unfinished' (2015, 264). The unnarrated creeps into the working draft, as if Bloom were subconsciously blocking thoughts about Boylan sleeping with Molly. The line is finished in the fair copy: it becomes 'the bed of conception and birth, of consummation of marriage and breach of marriage, of sleep, of death' (*RB*, 26). Again, the unnarrated becomes narrated, but here it subtly alters the focalisation, shifting it away from Bloom and closer to Killeen's 'beings looking down from the heavens'.

Through the expansion or elaboration of the techniques of disnarration and the unnarrated, 'Ithaca' loses much of its capacity for signification on a 'human' level. Disnarration ceaselessly directs narration away from the fabula, on which it prefers to remain silent, while the unnarrated is systematically removed and thus the tension that arises from focalisation and narration—the excitement and mystery of not being told everything that is seen—is destroyed. The narration of the unnarrated closes off possibility, the opposite of disnarration's plunge into every possibility. The skeleton, as much as it is an organ where each bone has its right place to give a supporting structure for

---

5   Here, the preferred reading is Crispi's instead of *JJDA*.

the rest, is taken apart and rendered useless by these techniques which condition this 'most detached' and 'indifferent' episode.

Vestigial Structure

Up to this point, the reading of the proto-draft has been teleological. That is to say, the forces structuring and, at the same time, undermining its structure were considered keeping in mind a telos, an 'end goal'—the structure and effect of the fair copy draft. But this is only one side of the coin, which presupposes publication, or at least the next drafting stage, before it actually happens. In this case it presupposes the very document of the fair copy before its creation—our reading of the proto-draft may be influenced by 'prescient' knowledge of the fair copy. In order to read, to repeat Van Hulle's usage of Ernst Haeckel's term, dysteleologically (2022, 168), we have to pay attention to the purposes a draft serves for itself, or how its purpose changes up to the point when the next drafting stage takes place.

In any draft, material not carried over into the next drafting stage has dysteleological properties. Van Hulle proposes to label such material 'vestigial' (2022, 170). But he also notes that vestigial material '*had* a purpose at some point or at some stage in the evolution of the work' (2022, 172). Examining the proto-draft, we find material that was reused in different shapes, partially recycled, or entirely scrapped. Some material provides concrete examples of an idea being worked out in multiple forms before becoming stable, or, more intriguingly, of how the 'telos' changes between different drafting stages. By examining these 'vestigial bones' (Van Hulle 2022, 170) which do not fit the final design, a more ambiguous, differently shaped 'Ithaca' will be shown.

Joyce wants to write about Bloom shaving but keeps changing his mind on what exactly to write. The topic is brought up a total of three times in the proto-draft, each time receiving different treatment. The first time it is an aside to a thematically separate paragraph, prompted by comparison of women to stars, and from then comparing men and women: 'man not knowing the pleasure of hair combing, woman not knowing the luxury of a cool shave' (*Proto*, fol. 3v). The second appearance seems unprompted and even isolated from other blocks in on the verso of fol. 7r:

> Could he shave with such felicity?
>
> Even in the dark by the sense of touch. He had a firm full sure woman's hand. He could have been a successful surgeon but that he would have preferred to be a physician, being loath to shed men's blood even when the end justified the means.

Here Bloom's hand is compared to a woman's and his hypothetical career as a surgeon is mentioned, but the context of comparing men and women of the previous instance is missing. The third time shaving is brought up appears the most cogent and developed (*Proto*, fol. 15r)—it is also the clear antecedent of the version found in the fair copy (*RB*, 5). None of these appear in the context in which the shaving block ends up—alongside Bloom boiling water for the cocoa to have with Stephen. Though some of the material ends up being used, other parts, such as the reference to shaving, fall away like scaffolding, and the block is moved into a context which does not resemble what prompted the question in the first place.

Another example is the reprise of the 'Throwaway' narrative. In the proto-draft, a block disconnected from the surrounding ones tells of Bloom rediscovering the winner of the race in Ascot:

> What did he discover from this connection?
>
> Opening the paper ~~the~~ at the ~~telegraph~~ by special wire page he found that the Gold Cup race at Ascot had been won by a dark horse Throwaway at 20 to 1. (*Proto*, fol. 11v)

This story strand runs throughout the novel and is mentioned in nearly every episode, so naturally 'Ithaca' references it as well. Strangely enough, if we turn to the fair copy, the block is absent. Instead, the story has now morphed into one of Bloom's 'rapid but insecure means to opulence', i.e. cheating by receiving 'a private wireless telegraph' (*RB*, 19) with the results of the race ahead of time. In this version, the cup is won by 'an outsider at odds of 50 to 1 3 hr 8 p.m at Ascot (Greenwich time)' (*RB*, 19). It is apparent that the 'Throwaway' version provided the inspiration for Bloom's scheme in the fair copy—words like the struck-out 'telegraph', or 'wire' and 'dark horse' are echoed in 'wireless telegraph' and 'an outsider'. Even though the 'Throwaway' story itself is not found in the fair copy, it provides the vocabulary and the impetus to generate a different narrative. It is not found in the fair copy but is necessary for its creation.

Except both the unused shaving and Throwaway material do end up being used, just not in the fair copy. In the drafting stage following the fair copy, the typescript, Joyce immediately re-adds both the original 'Throwaway' story, the comparison of Bloom's hand to a woman's and his potential as a surgeon (*TS*, u21, 747; *TS*, u21, 746). Though both blocks end up having an 'end goal', their way into the text is not straightforward. Even more, this is a direct result of the fissile nature of paragraphs, as pointed out by Ferrer and Rabaté above. Here we see different teloi fighting for centre stage. Gabler notes that the production of the fair copy that was to be typed up was a rushed process due to tight deadlines and Joyce's wish to have the episode read in Larbaud's séance (*JJA* v. 16, x). As noted in the first section, the fair copy appears to be the result of Joyce's repeated wish to put 'Ithaca' 'in order', and here is evidence that this goal was pursued even to the temporary detriment of textual stability. Joyce ended up foregoing some material in order to get the 'skeleton' in place, with a clear eye where to put the material back in once the typescript was done. The material is vestigial with regard to establishing structure, but once that goal is achieved, it can enter back into play.

This force disrupts straightforward consideration of the episode as an 'evolving' organism. Though it is clear that the proto-draft was reordered with a view to establish narrative coherence, and that Joyce expanded the hypothetical and unnarrated dimensions in order to undermine the significance of the fabula, some other processes do not follow the straight path towards their goal, nor do they always have one. The shaving block eventually 'found its way' into the published version, but not without a substantial detour and temporary 'vestigial' status. It is precisely the fact that the block was unnecessary that underlines what goal Joyce had in mind while writing the fair copy—a narratively stable text he could later add to.

Conclusion

The genesis of the narrative structure of 'Ithaca' involved several different lines of development which interact to support or undermine each other. At the same time as the fabula is set in place, disnarration steers the reader away from it; as soon as we spot a repeating narrative motif, such as the 'Throwaway' story, we also find out that it was wholly unnecessary to the 'skeleton', only re-added after the structure was established. We can trace the evolution of 'Ithaca' and see how it achieves its effects of distance and detachedness via textual accretion, but also recover lacunae which had to be filled in. The incredible heterogeneity of the writing process seems to rear its head as soon as any generalising assumption is made, showing the text-in-progress to be both unstable, not yet settled, as well as rigid, already conceived, even 'a projection into the future' (Van Hulle 2022, 171).

The most obvious conclusion to make is that the 'skeletal' model of structure does not work to describe 'Ithaca'. A skeleton is a collection of bones, where each bone fits with others in a predetermined way, whereas the episode is constructed from blocks which can be inserted any way around, and, as seen in the final section, often are. 'Ithaca' may have a story, a backbone which drives the narrative forward, but it cracks and groans under the weight of the episode's style and ever-expanding paragraphs. The schemata restrain the novel's motility—only by cracking open the bones of the 'skeleton' is it possible to get to the episode's 'Juices', as is the designated 'organ' in the Linati schema.

Returning again to the schemata investigated at the beginning, a broader question may be asked—what do we need them for? Killeen notes that, due to discrepancies, 'the [Gilbert] schema's authority is slightly compromised' (2021, xv), but he still reproduces it at the end of his introductory *A Reader's Companion to James Joyce's 'Ulysses'*. The OWC edition of *Ulysses* instead chooses to reproduce both alongside the 1922 text—a pleasure which readers at the time of publication did not get to enjoy, as the first schema was printed only in 1931. The schemata close the text off; in order to open it back up it is necessary to ask, why do the schemata give different 'organs' for the same episode?

That question, inevitably, leads back to the text, itself existing in many iterations. The proto-draft cannot easily be read as a narrative, nor is it meant to be treated as one. Being aware of its reordering undermines its stability, but also opens it up anew, this time to the reader instead of the writer. Perhaps it is the possibility of moving along with the text, rather than leaning on calcified structures like the schemata, that can bring the reader closer to *Ulysses*.

List of Abbreviations

JJC	*James Joyce Correspondence*, ed. by William Brockman et al., jamesjoycecorrespondence.org
JJDA	*James Joyce Digital Archive*, ed. by Danis Rose and John O'Hanlon, jjda.ie
LI, LII, LIII	Joyce, James (1957-1966), *Letters of James Joyce*, ed. by Stuart Gilbert, Richard Ellmann and James Fuller Spoerri, 3 vols. (London and New York: Faber & Faber; Viking).
NLI 13	Joyce, James, MS. 36,639/13, Partial Draft: 'Ithaca', National Library of Ireland.
Proto	Joyce, James, MS. 36,639/13, 'u17.1 (proto-text)', in: *James Joyce Digital Archive*, ed. by Danis Rose and John O' Hanlon, transcription of National Library of Ireland, https://jjda.ie/main/JJDA/U/ulex/s/s11d.htm.
RB	Joyce, James, 'Ithaca' Blue and Green MS., 'u17.2 (Rosenbach)', in: *James Joyce Digital Archive*, ed. by Danis Rose and John O' Hanlon, transcription of Rosenbach Museum, https://jjda.ie/main/JJDA/U/ulex/s/s12d.htm.
SL	Joyce, James (1975), *Selected Letters of James Joyce*, ed. by Richard Ellmann (London: Faber & Faber).
TS	Joyce, James, MS. V.B.15.c, 'u17.3 (Gabler-B)', in: *James Joyce Digital Archive*, ed. by Danis Rose and John O' Hanlon, transcription of University at Buffalo Libraries, https://jjda.ie/main/JJDA/U/ulex/s/sd3.htm.
TSE	Joyce, James (1977), '"Ithaca" Typescript Extracts', in: *Ulysses, Vol. XVI: "Ithaca" and "Penelope": a Facsimile of Manuscripts and Typescripts for Episodes 17 and 18*, prefaced and arranged by Michael Groden, James Joyce Archive (New York: Garland Pub.), 215–290.

These works are cited in parentheses without author or date information for readability.

Works Cited

Bal, Mieke (2017), *Narratology: Introduction to the Theory of Narrative*, trans. by Christine van Boheemen (Toronto: University of Toronto Press).

Crispi, Luca (2015), *Joyce's Creative Process and the Construction of Characters in Ulysses: Becoming the Blooms* (Oxford: Oxford University Press). https://doi.org/10.1093/acprof:oso/9780198718857.001.0001.

Ellmann, Maud (2008), '*Ulysses*: The Epic of the Human Body', in: *A Companion to James Joyce*, ed. by Richard Brown (Malden, MA and Oxford: Wiley-Blackwell). https://doi.org/10.1002/9781405177535.

Ferrer, Daniel and Jean Michel-Rabaté (2004), 'Paragraphs in Expansion', in: *Genetic Criticism: Texts and Avant-textes*, ed. by Jed Deppman, Daniel Ferrer and Michael Groden (Philadelphia: University of Pennsylvania Press).

Fludernik, Monika (1986), '"Ulysses" and Joyce's Change of Artistic Aims: External and Internal Evidence', *James Joyce Quarterly*, 23.2: 173–88.

Gabler, Hans Walter (1984), 'Afterword', in: *James Joyce, Ulysses: A Critical and Synoptic Edition*, vol. 3, ed. by Hans Walter Gabler, Wolfhard Steppe and Claus Melchior (New York and London: Garland Pub.), 1859–1908.

Geheber, Philip Keel (2018), 'Filling in the Gaps: "Ithaca" and Encyclopedic Generation', *James Joyce Quarterly*, 55.1/2: 59–78, https://doi.org/10.1353/jjq.2017.0029.

Groden, Michael [1977] (2014), *Ulysses in Progress* (Princeton, NJ: Princeton University Press).

Joyce, James, MS. 36,639/13, Partial Draft: 'Ithaca', Dublin: National Library of Ireland.

Joyce, James (1977), '"Ithaca" Typescript Extracts', in: *Ulysses, Vol. XVI: "Ithaca" and "Penelope": a Facsimile of Manuscripts and Typescripts for Episodes 17 and 18*, prefaced and arranged by Michael Groden, James Joyce Archive (New York: Garland Pub.), v. 16, 215–90.

Joyce, James, MS. 36,639/13, 'u17.1 (proto-text)', in: *James Joyce Digital Archive*, ed. by Danis Rose and John O' Hanlon, transcription of National Library of Ireland, https://jjda.ie/main/JJDA/U/ulex/s/s11d.htm.

Joyce, James, 'Ithaca' Blue and Green MS., 'u17.2 (Rosenbach)', in: *James Joyce Digital Archive*, ed. by Danis Rose and John O' Hanlon, transcription of Rosenbach Museum, https://jjda.ie/main/JJDA/U/ulex/s/s12d.htm.

Joyce, James, MS. V.B.15.c, 'u17.3 (Gabler-B)', in: *James Joyce Digital Archive*, ed. by Danis Rose and John O' Hanlon, transcription of University at Buffalo Libraries, https://jjda.ie/main/JJDA/U/ulex/s/sd3.htm.

Joyce, James (1957–1966), *Letters of James Joyce*, 3 vols., ed by. Stuart Gilbert, Richard Ellmann and James Fuller Spoerri (London and New York: Faber & Faber; Viking).

Joyce, James (1975), *Selected Letters of James Joyce*, ed. by Richard Ellmann (London: Faber & Faber).

Joyce, James (2023), *Ulysses*, ed. by Jeri Jonson, New edn. (Oxford: Oxford University Press). https://doi.org/10.1093/owc/9780192855107.001.0001.

Joyce, James (1993), *Ulysses*, ed. by Hans Walter Gabler, Wolfhard Steppe and Claus Melchior, afterword by Michael Groden (New York: Vintage Books).

Killeen, Terence (2022), *Ulysses Unbound: A Reader's Companion to James Joyce's Ulysses*, New edn., prefaced by Colm Tóibín (London: Penguin Books).

Lawrence, Karen [1981] (2014), *The Odyssey of Style in Ulysses* (Princeton, NJ: Princeton University Press). https://doi.org/10.1515/9781400855773.

Litz, A. Walton (1974), 'Ithaca', in: *James Joyce's Ulysses: Critical Essays*, ed. by Clive Hart and David Hayman (Berkeley: University of California Press), 385–407.

Litz, A. Walton (1961), *The Art of James Joyce: Method and Design in Ulysses and Finnegans Wake* (London: Oxford University Press).

Madtes, Richard E. (1983), *The "Ithaca" Chapter of Joyce's Ulysses* (Epping: Bowker).

Prince, Gerald (1988), 'The Disnarrated', *Style*, 22.1: 1–8.

Spielberg, Peter (1962), *James Joyce's Manuscripts and Letters at the University of Buffalo: A Catalogue* (Buffalo, NY: University of Buffalo).

Van Hulle, Dirk (2022), *Genetic Criticism: Tracing Creativity in Literature* (Oxford: Oxford University Press). https://doi.org/10.1093/oso/9780192846792.001.0001.

8. Drafting 'Anon' and Killing Anon: Virginia Woolf and the Genesis of English Literary Language

Joshua Phillips

Drafting 'Anon'

In the final year of her life, as the nascent European fascism of the 1930s bred the all-out global conflict of the 1940s, Virginia Woolf's thoughts turned to the past and she began work on three historical projects. Note, began: Woolf would not live to finish her novel *Between the Acts*, edited and published posthumously by her husband Leonard Woolf in 1941, only six months after her death in March of that year, nor her memoir, 'A Sketch of the Past', which first saw print in 1976, edited by Jeanne Schulkind (second edition 1985). Nor would she finish her literary history, which she provisionally titled 'Turning the Page' or 'Reading at Random', but which is better known today by the dual title of 'Anon' and 'The Reader', due largely to Brenda Silver's 1979 edition of the drafts (Silver 1979). This essay discusses the last of these projects to see print, Woolf's unfinished history of English literature. This essay posits that the drafts dramatise the work of genetic narratology, and doubly so. In this essay, I trace the birth and death of Anon, Woolf's figuration for the oral ballad tradition that prefigured and made possible literature in English and English literary language. The narrative Woolf crafts to explain or explore the genesis of English literary language is complicated by the state of the drafts in which we encounter this narrative. Or perhaps it is more accurate to use the plural, 'these narratives', instead. Put simply, there is not one single draft essay titled 'Anon', nor one titled

'The Reader'. Rather, the essays exist as a panoply of holograph and typescript drafts that echo and mirror and repeat and respond to one another. These draft pages bear witness to Woolf's process of drafting and redrafting, of thinking through her distinctive vision of literary history as she wrote. The drafts at once reconstruct the process by which English literature developed and require readers to perform a similar act of reconstruction in order to find their footing in Woolf's richly perplexing corpus of documents.

This essay investigates the development of Anon, Woolf's figuration for the anonymous oral tradition which gave rise to and made possible English as a literary language. First, it gives a brief overview of the corpus of drafts Woolf left at the time of her death. It then zooms in to examine various renditions of the moments at which Anon emerges and when Anon is killed. It reads across these variants, tracing the ways in which Woolf theorises and re-theorises the development of English literature and of English literary language as she drafts and redrafts the primal scene(s) of English literary history.

In the draft fragments, Woolf inscribes a radical literary history. It is not one rooted in the banner names of early English literature, in the writings of singular named authors such as Chaucer or Langland; nor is it rooted in authors known pseudonymously by their works, such as the Beowulf-poet or the Gawain-poet. Rather, Woolf's literary history finds its origins in the radically communal 'nameless vitality' of Anon, and in the oral tradition that precedes, prefigures and makes possible English literature. Woolf's narrative is complicated by the messy textuality of the drafts, but in very broad brushstrokes, early English literary language is for the birds. The anonymous oral tradition emerges from the primeval forests of Britain, from the 'innumerable birds' that sang in their 'matted boughs'. In this fragment, designated as M.53, Woolf writes that this birdsong was 'heard only by a few skin clad hunters in an occasional clearing'. From this moment of aesthesis comes the 'desire to sing', and 'by degrees, the clearing becomes larger; the birds fewer; and the human voice sung instead' (M.53, fol. 1r). Anon emerges from this prehistorical avian mimicry, but he dies at the inky hands of William Caxton—in some fragments, at least.[1] In others,

---

1   Although the narrator of *A Room of One's Own* (1929) 'venture[s] to guess that Anon, who wrote so many poems without signing them, was often a woman'

it is the printing press that ensures Anon's persistence: we can only know anonymous, pre-print works because they have been printed. The mode of anonymous co-creation that Anon represents, however, persists for some centuries in the early modern playhouse, which Woolf theorises as a contact zone between audience and playwright, where the voice of the audience shapes the plays in a kind of feedback loop—although curiously actors are rarely to be found in Woolf's history of the early modern stage. But even this mode of co-creation declines. What emerges in the place of this anonymous subjectivity is a mode of subjectivity predicated on the act of reading silently, to oneself. Woolf's narrative ends (or, at least, is permanently forestalled by her death) in the first half of the 1600s with the closing of the theatres and the publication of Robert Burton's *The Anatomy of Melancholy*. These two events, according to Woolf, give rise to modern subjectivity as she conceived of it. This is a mode of subjectivity premised not on the radically communal songs of Anon but rather on what she calls the 'theatre of the brain', a theatre that is seen by the mind's eye, experienced in solitude. (M.110, fol. 5r).

As I said at this essay's outset, Woolf did not leave behind her a single completed draft of an essay called 'Anon', nor one called 'The Reader'. Instead, she left a corpus of draft fragments. The earliest documents date to 1937 and take the form of loose-leaf reading notes gathered together into a volume titled 'Reading at Random', which Woolf kept from 1937 onwards (Woolf 1937). After this, Woolf began to draft longhand, in the eighth and final volume of a series of notebooks which she had kept for some decades, bound herself and given the overall title 'Articles, Essays, Fiction and Reviews' (M.1-8, 1–10). The final volume of this series contains some 71 pages of writing towards the project, divided into ten fragments which range from half a page to fifteen pages in length. These manuscript drafts are interspersed between other drafts of contemporaneous essays and short fictions. None of them is dated, although Woolf titled one 'Anon' and two as 'The Reader'. There are also 181 pages of loose-leaf material, thirty of which are handwritten (three fragments, corresponding to M.45–47) and the remainder of which is typewritten (twenty-seven fragments). Woolf collected these in three

---

(Woolf [1929] 1993, 45), Woolf only ever uses the masculine personal pronoun 'he' to refer to Anon in these drafts. I follow this usage and refer to Anon as male.

Lifeguard Multigrip folders, somewhat like a modern ring-binder, each of which bears a variant on the title 'Turning the Page' (Multigrip Folders 1, 2 and 3). When these documents acceded to the New York Public Library's Henry W. and Albert A. Berg Collection of English Literature, the drafts were removed from these folders and curated into a bifurcated archive. Drafts of 'Anon' are catalogued as M.45 through M.54 (the latter of which is a composite collection which I believe is comprised of eleven distinct sub-fragments), while drafts of 'The Reader' are catalogued as M.108 through M.113. This division is perhaps arbitrary: Woolf did not tend to title or date the loose-leaf fragments, while subject matter is not necessarily a reliable guide to whether a fragment should be considered a draft of 'Anon' or 'The Reader'.

Although Woolf had a lifelong interest in literary history and had expressed a desire to write a history of English literature that would 'go through English literature like a string through cheese' in a diary entry of 13 January 1932, she only worked on material in this corpus towards the very end of her life (Woolf 1977, 4; 63).[2] The very earliest fragment to bear a date is M.45, which is dated 24 November 1940—some six months before her death (M.45, fol. 2r). M.45 is a handwritten document that she evidently began to type up later that day: the typescript draft M.53 bears the same date, and their openings are near-identical, though they start to diverge as Woolf continues to type. Because of the lack of definitive identifiers, any detailed composition history must remain speculative for now, although this does not preclude the kind of paleological detective work Lawrence Rainey undertook to establish a timeline for the composition of *The Waste Land* (2005, 29–46). For now, however, I want to bracket off the search for a genesis of the 'Anon' drafts in favour of a search for the genesis of Anon, the unnamed poet-singer who Woolf uses as a figuration for the oral ballad tradition that preceded and made possible English as a literary language. The next section of the essay works to trace the beginnings of English literary language in the 'Anon' fragments through the emergence of Anon from Britain's prehistory and his possible demise.

---

2   For a more detailed account of the diary entries and letters that prefigure and discuss this project, see Phillips 2022, 207–8.

Killing Anon

Anon was dead to begin with. Perhaps. This section of the essay reads across the variant fragments of Woolf's 'Anon' drafts. It investigates Anon's emergence from the primeval treetops of prehistoric Britain, and his multiplicity of deaths, first when Caxton begins printing works in English, and then (only somewhat) more decisively in the seventeenth century. In so doing, I hope to provide less a definitive biography of Anon, but rather to show the ways in which Woolf wrote and rewrote, worked and reworked her narrativisation of the origins of English literature. Both of these origins, Woolf's genesis of English literature and the genesis of these documents, are hard to pin down. They exemplify what Raymonde Debray Genette describes as the 'paradox' of the genesis. All searches for the moment when a work's genesis begins 'fall prey to the same paradox', Debray Genette writes in her 1984 study of the twelve draft endings of Gustave Flaubert's 'Un Cœur Simple' ('A Simple Heart'). Regardless of 'how random' the moment at which a work begins may be, 'an *incipit* always retains the character of being decisive and [...] primordial' (2004, 70). Searching for a work's moment of genesis, Debray Genette argues, is searching for a moment that is at once arbitrary—the moment a writer has an idea and writes it down or otherwise leaves a material trace of this thought—and originary. This section of the essay demonstrates the ways in which Woolf dramatises this paradox (whether intentionally or not) in the 'Anon' drafts.

Anon first appears in hindsight, some five pages into the first, untitled, draft in this corpus, M.1-8-1: Woolf discusses the diaries of Philip Henslowe, a major funder of the early modern stage, and asks 'But how far was the ~~author~~ playwright in 1570 separate from Anon the minstrel, the ballad singer?' (M.1-8-1, fol. 6r). Anon appears overleaf also, though Woolf only approaches his voice obliquely, through the works of Thomas Malory. She writes:

> It is in Malorys
> pages that we hear the ~~anonymous~~
> half conscious voice of anon it
> telling his tales to the noble & the peasant:
> reminding them of the ~~very~~ old Kings &
> Knights who ~~lived~~ went their ways through the
> wild woods seeking adventure (M.1-8-1, fol. 7r)

In neither case are Anon's words heard directly. In the first case, Anon is cited as an example of something separate from the nascent early modern stage, while in the second, readers do not quite hear Anon, his name left uncapitalised as though not yet a proper noun. The voice of Anon (or perhaps the voice of anon) is not directly heard, but rather it is a voice preserved in the works of another, named, author.

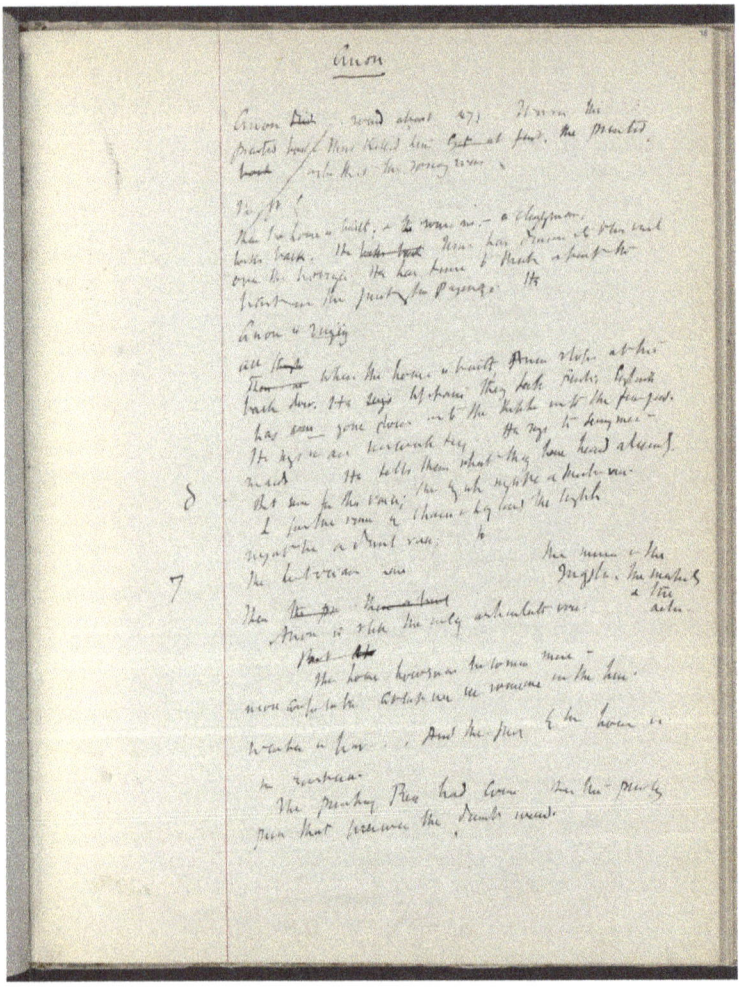

Fig. 8.1 Woolf, Virginia (1940), 'M.1–8. 2 of 10. Anon. Holograph. In [Articles, Essays, Fiction and Reviews], Vol. 8 [1938-9], fols. 78–102. 13p'. (New York Public Library), Henry W. and Albert A. Berg Collection of English Literature, Berg Coll. MSS Woolf, fol. 1r. © Society of Authors.

In the next draft, the first that Woolf titled 'Anon', Woolf approaches Anon directly, writing the sentences 'Anon ~~died~~ round about 1477. It was the printed book that killed him', as part of a paragraph at the top of the folio that is scored through (see Figure 8.1), while at the bottom of the folio are the sentences 'the Printing Press had come. It is the Printing Press that preserves the dumb world' (M.1-8-2, fol. 1r). We see here in its earliest form a tension or paradox that animates the 'Anon' fragments: the tension between Anon's death as printing technologies arrive in England and the preservation of his voice through printed works. In this variant, Anon's death is deleted though still legible. Woolf writes that Anon died, then scores through the word 'died', presumably *currente calamo*, and then later scores through the entire paragraph as though not yet convinced of Anon's death.

Woolf begins to write about Anon's death before she does his birth: the final lines of a later notebook draft narrate the moment when Anon is not just killed, but when he is 'dead forever' as the curtain rises on *The Tempest* (M.1-8-4):

> The play has killed the stage. The stage has
> become too small to act the drama.
> Perhaps, after centuries, the play will
> renew itself with Mozart in the Magic Flute
> or with Beethoven in [Fidelio]. It never
> lived again in England. The book after that
> takes the place of the play
> & the   Anon is dead forever. (M.1-8-4, fol. 9r)

In this variant, the sentence which reports that Anon is not just dead, but that he is 'dead forever' is cramped, squeezed in at the very bottom of the folio. The paragraph above does not discuss Anon: he is only invoked at its close as though he has disappeared entirely from view and very nearly from memory, only to be remembered and his passing marked at the final possible moment.

The first loose-leaf handwritten draft, M.45, is titled 'Anon' and dated 24 November 1940. This fragment narrates the slow birth of English literary language from the primeval forests of prehistoric Britain, and Anon's voice is to be heard 'singing out of doors' (M.45, fol. 3r). Woolf does not immediately connect the human voice that is to be heard in the primeval forest with the voice of Anon until the typescript fragment

M.48, when she scores through descriptions of this voice as 'like a birds voice, singing out of doors' in pencil before making clear that this voice was 'the voice of Anon' (M.48, fol. 1r). Returning to M.45, Woolf names Anon's killer: 'it was Caxton who killed Anon by giving him a name. It was Caxton made Anon some one apart from his song [...] The song became author became alone responsible' (M.45, fol. 6r). In this variant, Caxton kills Anon not by printing his words but through the act of naming, setting a name to what had hitherto been anonymous.

The next fragment, M.46, develops narratives of Anon's birth and Anon's death, though with subtly different language from earlier drafts in both cases. Anon appears first in a curious aporia: the fragment starts with the sentence 'He'—perhaps referring to Anon and perhaps someone else—'has emerged then from the sufficiently from the past forest & from the floods, from the to be seen [...] in outline'. Anon here is knowable insofar as he begins to shed his anonymity, begins to take on characteristics that can distinguish him: he becomes 'a man with a mastiff, with a garden' and 'his name may be [William] Harrison, it may be Paston' (M.46, fol. 1r).[3]

Later in the fragment, Woolf writes: 'Anon died round about 1477. It was the printed book with the author's name attached that killed him. After that the audience was separate from the singer' (M.46, fol. 4r). Here, it is not the song that becomes separate from the singer, as was the case in M.45, but the audience that becomes separate from the singer. In M.46, anonymity is not a matter of responsibility but of mode of communication and of iterability. Once words are printed, they can be consumed by an audience (whether read aloud to others or silently

---

3   William Harrison (1534–93) was an English priest best known for his 'Description of England', published in 1577 as part of *Holinshed's Chronicles of England, Scotland, and Ireland*. Woolf took notes from Harrison's 'Description' in preparation for this project (Woolf 1937, fols. 1r, 2r). She most probably read the 1877–81 three volume edition (ed. Frederick J. Furnivall), the first two volumes of which she had in her library (King and Miletic-Vejzovic 2003). Paston is a reference to the Paston family and their surviving letters, initially published in 1787 as *The Paston Letters*. Woolf wrote about the specifically non-literary qualities of the *Paston Letters* in her essay 'The Pastons and Chaucer', which she published as part of the first volume of *The Common Reader* (1925; cf. Woolf 1986a). The Woolfs had both volumes of a 1924 Dent two-volume edition of the *Paston Letters* in their library (cf. King and Miletic-Vejzovic 2003), but in his edition of Woolf's essays, Andrew McNeillie notes that she began reading the letters in January 1922, prior to the Dent edition being published.

to oneself) distanced from the writer or singer by space and by time, and the same words can be consumed again and again in a manner that perhaps anticipates Jacques Derrida's figuration of the written signifier as iterable in 'Signature Event Context' (Derrida 1988, 7). In M.46, the printing press kills Anon by severing the audience from the moment of literary production.

Woolf again makes explicit that Anon is born in the forests of prehistoric Britain in a later fragment, M.50, in which she tells us that 'The voice that broke the sielnce [sic] of the forests was the voice of Anon', and further on we read that 'It was the printing press [...] that killed ~~finally was to kill~~ Anon. But it was the press also that preserved him' (Woolf 1940d, 1r; 4r). The opening of M.53 appears to be a typescript variant of M.45. As I discussed above, both documents bear the same date, and it is likely that Woolf started work on this typescript immediately after writing M.45. The variant of Anon's slow emergence from Britain's primeval forests presented in typescript in M.53 is drawn from M.45. However, the typescript presents a version of Anon's death which is identical to that in M.46 (quoted above). M.53 is not just a redraft of M.46 but becomes somewhat of a composite document that bears witness to Anon's continually changing life story, and to the continually changing conceptual parameters of Woolfian anonymity.

Anon recedes from view as Woolf's narrative progresses through the centuries. Having died in 1477 at the inky hands of William Caxton, Anon is mentioned less and less frequently, and he tends to be discussed as a way of contrasting the new episteme inaugurated by the arrival of print with the earlier, pre-print world. Despite this, anonymous modes of co-creation persist well into the seventeenth century. Woolf describes the early modern playhouse as a contact zone of sorts between playwright and audience, wherein the voice of the audience shapes the plays in a kind of feedback loop.[4] But even this mode of co-creation declines and dies out. The first of the handwritten 'Reader' fragments, M.1-8-5, opens with the question 'At what point is the reader born?' In a passage dense with deletions, Woolf describes the 'faculty, the power' that the reader holds to 'make ^visible^ out of print ~~ho~~ men, countries, [...] warm bodies'. (M1-8-5, fol. 1r). This is a faculty that develops concurrently

---

[4] Curiously actors are rarely to be found in Woolf's history of the early modern stage, and when they are, they are not seen acting.

with Elizabethan drama: overleaf Woolf writes that the 'extraordinary intensification' that leads to the decline of anonymous co-creation and the rise of the readerly subject 'comes fitfully: we note a passage that ~~seems~~ [...] flits through Marlowe; it is in the Revengers Tragedy. ~~Their~~ It is in words like Heywoods: oh God ~~or in the~~ & of course finally in Shre'. (M.1-8-5, fol. 2r). The next manuscript fragment of 'The Reader' asks a similar question, 'At what point in the Elizabethan drama is the reader born?' but locates the answer not in the works of the playwright but in the manifold physical differences between the early modern playhouse and the scene of reading. The passage continues to ask, 'At what point do we cease to be aware of the trumpet & the flag; of the audience drawing up the poetry like a sheet of paper drawing up a fire', and at what point the audience of this flame-like poetry recedes, and the poetry itself becomes 'detached, reading in a room alone' (M.1-8-6, fol. 6r).

The penultimate handwritten 'Reader' fragment, M1.8–9, begins not with a question but with an answer, perhaps to the questions posed in 1.1-8-5 and -6. The answer is not a confident one, however. It is littered with deletions, and Woolf scores a single, straight line through the entire paragraph: 'We can suppose that the ~~reader~~ ^{reading public} ~~came into existence some four hundred~~ years ago; when the ~~playhouse could no longer hold the play~~'. Here, however, Woolf introduces another reason for the decline of the mode of anonymous co-creation that she theorises took place in the Elizabethan playhouse. The reader 'came into existence', Woolf writes, '~~when~~ ^{in the first place} the playhouse was shut [...] & in the second the play ~~became~~ outgrew the theatre' (M.1-8-9, fol. 1r). Woolf traces the decline of anonymous co-creation in these manuscript fragments, but her originary figuration for this mode of co-creation, Anon, is far from the scene. In the typescript 'Reader' fragments, however, we find that rumours of his death may have been exaggerated as Woolf revives Anon only to kill him off for good.

In M.111, Set 2 of 3, anonymity is worn away slowly as '[t]he curtain rises upon play after play. Each time it rises upon a more detached, a more matured drama'. As time goes on, and the curtain rises to reveal Shakespeare's continuing career, the play

> outgrow[s]
> the uncovered theatre where the s n beats and the rain
> pours. That thetare must be replaced by the

> thestre of the brain. The playwright is replaced by the man
> who writes a book. The audience is replaced by the reader.
> Anon is dead. (M.111-2, fol. 2r)

In M.112, Set 1 of 3, meanwhile, it is not the audience whose character changes but that of the playwright: 'by degrrees [*sic*]', Woolf writes, 'the dramatist sheds his anonymity. He separates himself from his audience' (M.112-1, fol. 1r). The next 'set', meanwhile, is perhaps less concerned with the subjectivity of the literary object's creator or its consumer, and more concerned with the form of the object itself: we read that 'the play never again fitted the stage completely in England. The book after Shakespere [*sic*] takes the place of the play. And Anon is dead forever' (M.112-2, fol. 1r; 2r).

If Anon's first death is swift, tied to the singular historical moment at which Caxton first impressed inked plates of type onto paper, Anon's second death is lingering and uncertain. We have seen that in earlier manuscript fragments of 'The Reader', Woolf does not link the death of Anon to the slow decline of anonymous co-creation. Rather, this link is only made explicit in some of the final typescript fragments. But Woolf expresses hope that this death is not final and that Anon, or at least a mode of anonymous subjectivity can be revived through a process of historically aware aesthesis.

In the opening paragraphs of M.45, the earliest of the loose-leaf drafts, Woolf writes that 'Now & then, by choosing a view carefully', if we 'eclipse a chimney or bungalow we can still see a flat ^{reed whispering} ~~weed~~ fen' (M.45, fol. 2r). M.52, one of the typescript 'Anon' drafts, contains a variant on this. Woolf writes 'Now and then, by choosing a view carefully to shut out a chimney or a bungalow, we can still see a fragment of what they saw-- a flat fen, reed whispering, water logged; or a down covered with turf only' (M.52, fols. 1r; 2r). In M.53, the next fragment, though, Woolf revisits and revises this language, substituting the nonspecific pronoun 'they' for the singular proper noun 'Anon'. The revised passage reads:

> By choosing a vuew carefully to shut out a chimney or a
> bungalow we can still see what Anon saw-- the bird haunted
> reed whispering fen; the down covered with turf, and the
> scar long healed over the moor, over the down, along which
> Anon came when he made his journeys. (M.53, fol. 2r)

Woolf posits the mode of anonymous subjectivity that Anon represents as a once-and-future mode of being, as recoverable if we cultivate a sensibility that allows us to do so. This is a crucial part of Woolf's historiography. Woolf does not turn to literary history at this moment as a way of looking back into a bygone past, a past without chimneys or bungalows. Rather, her history is future-oriented. Anonymity becomes a once-and-future subjectivity that can be recruited as part of the 'mental fight' Woolf called for in 'Thoughts on Peace in an Air Raid' (1940): a way of 'thinking against the current, not with it'. (Woolf 1986b, 243).

This section of the essay has traced variations of Anon's birth and death through the fragments of Woolf's literary history. It did so with the intent of demonstrating just how intensively Woolf wrote and rewrote her story of the genesis of English literary language, just how frequently she revisited and revised the foundations upon which English literature was constructed. The next section of the essay asks what this panoply of beginnings might tell us about the conceptual resources of genetic narratology.

Reading 'Anon'

The previous section of the essay read across the 'Anon' and 'The Reader' fragments in order to trace the slow birth and multiple deaths of Anon. It found that drawing definitive conclusions from the fragments is no easy feat. M.112, Set 3 of 3, ends with the observation that, after the birth of the reader, 'We are in a world where nothing is concluded' (M.112-3, fol. 3r). This is an apt guide for the corpus of documents themselves. Another fragment of 'The Reader', M.111, Set 1 of 3, provides an apt figuration for these documents. In this passage, Woolf talks about the peculiar quiddities of reading Shakespeare:

> But Shakespere has nosuch appeal to the reader-writer.
> His styles are too innumerabel. Perhpas then he is chiefly
> used for more general piposes--when the ink has gone dry
> upon the pen to revive the sense of langauge; or to
> testify, when words seem motinless, to the enormous
> possibilities of speed. One reading always supersedes another.
> Thus the truest account of reading Shakespere would be
> not to write a book with a beginning middle and end;
> but to collect notes, without trying to make them
> consistent (M.111-1, fol. 1v)

The drafts do not resemble a 'book with a beginning middle and end'. To give an account of them that treats them as such is to elide what makes them quite so distinctive. Instead, reading the fragments is more an act of curation, of gathering, of 'collect[ing]' without trying to ensure that the collected or gathered material is 'consistent'. Woolf's account of the experience of reading Shakespeare differs from the experience of reading Woolf's own writing insofar as, for Woolf, '[o]ne reading' of Shakespeare 'always supersedes another'. I do not believe that this is quite the case with Woolf's fragments. Rather, in this corpus, narrative—such as the biography of Anon I tried to sketch earlier in the essay—and other phenomena become emergent properties that can only be grasped as Woolf works and reworks phrases, tropes, figurations from fragment to fragment. The drafts call for a mode of reading that is attentive to the materiality of the drafts and to their nature as draft writing without obvious teleology, or perhaps even dysteleologically (cf. Van Hulle 2020). They call for a mode of reading that negotiates between the variants of Woolf's narrative(s) and which is alive to the implications of these differing accounts—in other words, they call for genetic reading.

As Dirk Van Hulle demonstrates, genetic narratology is a form of postclassical narratology, one that always involves evaluation and negotiation. The 'parties' to this negotiation are the text, the reader, the author image and the context. Genetic criticism, the study of a text's genesis, adds to this narratological negotiation by transforming the text into a 'dynamic succession of versions' unfolding diachronically (Van Hulle 2022, 163). The corpus of drafts this essay has discussed at once affirms and complicates Van Hulle's figuration of genetic narratology as an expanded postclassical narratology. It affirms it insofar as my reading has sought to negotiate between variants; it complicates it insofar as my reading demonstrates that the drafts engage in an auto-negotiation, rewriting and writing one another over and over. The fragments afford a vivid insight into Woolf's slow thinking-through of English literary history. In so doing, they show the affordances of genetic narratology and the resources it can provide for reading literary drafts.

Works Cited

Debray Genette, Raymonde (2004), 'Flaubert's "A Simple Heart," or How to Make an Ending: A Study of the Manuscripts', in: *Genetic Criticism: Texts and Avant-Textes*, ed. by Jeb Deppman, Daniel Ferrer, and Michael Groden (Philadelphia: University of Pennsylvania Press), 69–95.

Derrida, Jacques (1988), 'Signature Event Context', in: *Limited Inc*, trans. by Samuel Weber (Evanston, IL: Northwestern University Press), 1–24.

King, Julia, and Laila Miletic-Vejzovic (2003), *The Library of Leonard and Virginia Woolf: A Short-Title Catalog* (Pullman, WA: Washington State University Press).

Phillips, Joshua (2022), 'How Should One Read "The Reader"? New Approaches to Virginia Woolf's Late Archive', *Textual Cultures*, 14.2: 195–219, https://doi.org/10.14434/tc.v14i2.33658.

Rainey, Lawrence S (2005), 'Eliot Among the Typists: Writing The Waste Land', in: *Modernism/Modernity*, 12.1: 27–84, https://doi.org/10.1353/mod.2005.0049.

Silver, Brenda R. (1979), '"Anon" and "The Reader": Virginia Woolf's Last Essays', *Twentieth Century Literature*, 25.3/4: 356–441.

Van Hulle, Dirk (2020), 'Sheherazade's Notebook: Editing Textual Dysteleology and Autographic Modernism', *Modernist Cultures*, 15.1: 12–28.

Van Hulle, Dirk (2022), *Genetic Criticism: Tracing Creativity in Literature* (Oxford: Oxford University Press).

Woolf, Virginia (1937), 'Reading Notebook 37: "Reading at Random"' (Sussex: The Keep), Monks House Papers, SxMs-18/2/B/2/C, http://www.woolfnotes.com/notebook-display/?pdb=37.

Woolf, Virginia (1938a) 'M.1–8, 1 of 10. [The Great Elizabethan House, Penshurst...]. Holograph. In [Articles, Essays, Fiction and Reviews], Vol. 8 [1938–39], Pp. 60–76. 9p.' (New York Public Library), Henry W. and Albert A. Berg Collection of English Literature, Berg Coll. MSS Woolf.

Woolf, Virginia (1938b), 'M.1–8. 2 of 10. Anon. Holograph. In [Articles, Essays, Fiction and Reviews], Vol. 8 [1938–39], fols. 78–102. 13p.' (New York Public Library), Henry W. and Albert A. Berg Collection of English Literature, Berg Coll. MSS Woolf.

Woolf, Virginia (1938c), 'M.1–8, 4 of 10. [Anon: The Loves & Hates of the Elizabethans Themselves...]. Holograph. in Back [Articles, Essays, Fiction and Reviews], Vol. 8 [1938–39], fols. 8–16. 9p.' (New York Public Library), Henry W. and Albert A. Berg Collection of English Literature, Berg Coll. MSS Woolf.

Woolf, Virginia (1938d), 'M.1–8, 5 of 10. The Reader. Holograph. In Back [Articles, Essays, Fiction and Reviews], Vol. 8 [1938-39], fols. 17–20. 4p.' (New York Public Library), Henry W. and Albert A. Berg Collection of English Literature, Berg Coll. MSS Woolf.

Woolf, Virginia (1938e), 'M.1–8, 6 of 10. [The Readers Faculty Is a Queer One...]. Holograph. In Back [Articles, Essays, Fiction and Reviews], Vol. 8 [1938-39], fols. 21–26. 6p' (New York Public Library), Henry W. and Albert A. Berg Collection of English Literature, Berg Coll. MSS Woolf.

Woolf, Virginia (1938f), 'M1–8, 9 of 10 The Reader. In Back [Articles, Essays, Fiction and Reviews], Vol. 8 [1938-9], fols. 34–36. 3p.' (New York Public Library), Henry W. and Albert A. Berg Collection of English Literature, Berg Coll. MSS Woolf.

Woolf, Virginia (1938f) 'M.1–8. [Articles, Essays, Fiction and Reviews].' (New York Public Library), Henry W. and Albert A. Berg Collection of English Literature, Berg Coll. MSS Woolf.

Woolf, Virginia (1940a), 'M.45. Anon. Holograph Fragment, Unsigned, Dated Nov. 24, 1940. 11 fols.' (New York Public Library), Henry W. and Albert A. Berg Collection of English Literature, Berg Coll. MSS Woolf.

Woolf, Virginia (1940b), 'M.46 [Anon]. Holograph Fragment, Undated. 9 fols.' (New York Public Library), Henry W. and Albert A. Berg Collection of English Literature, Berg Coll. MSS Woolf.

Woolf, Virginia (1940c), 'M.48. Anon. Typescript Fragment, with the Author's Ms. Corrections, Unsigned and Undated. 2 fols.' (New York Public Library), Henry W. and Albert A. Berg Collection of English Literature, Berg Coll. MSS Woolf.

Woolf, Virginia (1940d), 'M.50. Anon. Typescript Fragment, with the Author's Ms. Corrections, Unsigned and Undated. 9 fols. Paginated 1–9.' (New York Public Library), Henry W. and Albert A. Berg Collection of English Literature, Berg Coll. MSS Woolf.

Woolf, Virginia (1940e), 'M.52. Anon. Typescript Fragment with the Author's Ms. Corrections, Unsigned and Undated. 19 fols. Paginated [1]–19, Wanting p. 5, 14 (Two p. 15).' (New York Public Library), Henry W. and Albert A. Berg Collection of English Literature, Berg Coll. MSS Woolf.

Woolf, Virginia (1940f), 'M.53: [Anon]. Typescript Fragment, with the Author's MS Correction, Dated Nov. 24, 1940, 26 fols.' (New York Public Library), Henry W. and Albert A. Berg Collection of English Literature, Berg Coll. MSS Woolf.

Woolf, Virginia (1940g), 'M.110 [The Reader]. Typescript Fragment, with the Author's Ms. Corrections, Unsigned and Undated. 5 fols.' (New York Public Library), Henry W. and Albert A. Berg Collection of English Literature, Berg Coll. MSS Woolf.

Woolf, Virginia (1940h), 'M.111 [The Reader]. Set 1 of 3. Typescript Fragment, with the Author's Ms. Corrections, Unsigned and Undated. 8 fols.' (New York Public Library), Henry W. and Albert A. Berg Collection of English Literature, Berg Coll. MSS Woolf.

Woolf, Virginia (1940i), 'M.111 [The Reader]. Set 2 of 3. Typescript Fragment, Unsigned and Undated. 4 fols.' (New York Public Library), Henry W. and Albert A. Berg Collection of English Literature, Berg Coll. MSS Woolf.

Woolf, Virginia (1940j), 'M.112 [The Reader]. Set 1 of 3. Typescript Fragment with the Author's Ms. Corrections, Unsigned and Undated. 5 fols.' (New York Public Library), Henry W. and Albert A. Berg Collection of English Literature, Berg Coll. MSS Woolf.

Woolf, Virginia (1940k), 'M.112 [The Reader]. Set 2 of 3. Typescript Fragment, Unsigned and Undated with the Author's MS. Additions. 2 fols.' (New York Public Library), Henry W. and Albert A. Berg Collection of English Literature, Berg Coll. MSS Woolf.

Woolf, Virginia (1940l), 'M.112 [The Reader]. Set 3 of 3. Typescript Fragment, Unsigned and Undated. 3 fols.' (New York Public Library), Henry W. and Albert A. Berg Collection of English Literature, Berg Coll. MSS Woolf.

Woolf, Virginia (1940m), 'Multigrip Folder: "Spare Sheets T of P" (2)' (New York Public Library), Henry W. and Albert A. Berg Collection of English Literature, Berg Coll. MSS Woolf.

Woolf, Virginia (1940n), 'Multigrip Folder: "Turning the Page" (1)' (New York Public Library), Henry W. and Albert A. Berg Collection of English Literature, Berg Coll. MSS Woolf.

Woolf, Virginia (1940o), 'Multigrip Folder: "Turning the Page" (3)' (New York Public Library), Henry W. and Albert A. Berg Collection of English Literature, Berg Coll. MSS Woolf.

Woolf, Virginia (1977), *The Diary of Virginia Woolf*, 5 vols., ed. by Anne Olivier Bell and Quentin Bell (London: Penguin).

Woolf, Virginia [1925] (1986a), 'The Pastons and Chaucer', in: *The Essays of Virginia Woolf*, 6 vols., ed. by Andrew McNeillie and Stuart N. Clarke (London: The Hogarth Press), 20–38.

Woolf, Virginia [1940] (1986b), 'Thoughts on Peace in an Air Raid', in: *The Essays of Virginia Woolf*, 6 vols., ed. by Andrew McNeillie and Stuart N. Clarke (London: The Hogarth Press), 242–48.

Woolf, Virginia (1989), 'A Sketch of the Past', in: *Moments of Being*, ed. by Jeanne Schulkind (London: Grafton Books), 69–173.

Woolf, Virginia [1929] (1993), 'A Room of One's Own', in: *A Room of One's Own and Three Guineas*, ed. by Michèle Barrett (London: Penguin), 3–104.

Woolf, Virginia [1941] (2011), *Between the Acts*, The Cambridge Edition of the Works of Virginia Woolf, ed. by Mark Hussey (Cambridge: Cambridge University Press).

9. Beckett's 'Arabian Nights of the Mind': Unnarratability, Denarrat(ivisat)ion and Narrative Closure in the Radio Play *Cascando*

Pim Verhulst

According to narratologist Brian Richardson, Samuel Beckett 'almost single-handedly created a theater of narration' (1988, 202). Largely abandoning dialogues after *Waiting for Godot* and *Endgame*, turning to monologues with plays such as *Krapp's Last Tape*, *Happy Days* or *Play*, and increasingly in later stage works from the 1970s and 1980s, Beckett indeed challenges the commonly held assumption that theatre is a mimetic, not a diegetic genre. This achievement extends to the radio plays that he embarked on in the 1950s and 1960s, particularly *Cascando*, written in French in 1961 and translated into English by the author in 1962. This chapter aims to illustrate how a study of its surviving draft material can inform a narratological analysis of Beckett's last radio play. I will begin by discussing how its abandoned false start foregrounds notions like 'narration' and the 'unnarratable'. Next, I will argue that the genesis of *Cascando* is marked by a shift from 'denarration' to the more radical act of 'denarrativisation', which at the same time coincides with a transmedial shift from text or script to audio recording. Lastly, I will adopt a more intertextual approach to explore how the radio play deals with 'narrative closure' in relation to the *One Thousand and One Nights* (also known as the *Arabian Nights*) and Marcel Proust's *À la recherche du temps perdu*. The goal of the chapter is to demonstrate that genetic narratology can be applied not just to the 'endogenesis', but also the 'exogenesis' and 'epigenesis' of a literary work, i.e. its writing process, the external source material it uses, and its post-publication afterlife, which comprises translations as well as revised editions. By combining these three levels, it becomes possible to understand how Beckett's initial attempt to narrate the unnarratable gradually evolved, across versions, from a creative dead end into a never-ending story.[1]

The 'Unnarratable'

Cascando as we know it was preceded by a false start of three paragraphs, written down and cancelled again on the verso of the radio play's first manuscript page. These paralipomena are fascinating in that they explicitly thematise the act of narration. As the first paragraph reveals, the notion of telling an 'histoire' or 'story' was present from the outset:

> ... le moyen d'achever cette histoire, qui est achevée en ce sens, que le corps dont c'est l'histoire, et la conscience dont c'est l'histoire, ayant été conduits, l'un et l'autre, jusqu'à l'inénarrable (BDMP12, FM2, fol. 01v)[2]

> [... the way to finish this story, which is finished in the sense that, the body of which this is the story, and the mind of which this is the story, have been conducted, the one and the other, to the point of the unnarrable.][3]

The *Larousse* dictionary defines the term 'inénarrable' as 'd'un comique, d'une extravagance extraordinaires, difficiles à décrire' ['exceedingly extravagant or ludicrous, difficult to describe']. The implication is that any attempt to describe a body or mind exhaustively, in the finest possible detail, is a ludicrous, hyperrealist or hypermodernist endeavour. At the same time, it relates the goal of the monologue to the 'inexpressible', or

---

1 Although I am aware that radio drama is a hybrid genre (see Verhulst 2024), existing as both a sound recording and a script, for the purpose of this genetic analysis I will restrict myself to the textual dimension of Beckett's *Cascando*. For an audionarratological analysis of the radio play that focuses on the narrative aspects of voice and music, see (Verhulst 2021).

2 This shorthand notation refers to the forthcoming online digital genetic edition of the Radio Plays (no. 12) in the Beckett Digital Manuscript Project (BDMP). 'FM' stands for French manuscript and 'FT' for French typescript, followed by the number of the document in the genetic sequence of drafts and the page. By analogy, 'EM' stands for English manuscript and 'ET' for English typescript.

3 All omitted passages that were not rendered into English by Beckett are my own translation. For the sake of legibility, I have not crossed out the entire transcription of every paragraph, only the words that Beckett deleted within them, before he cancelled the whole page. In the transcription conventions of the BDMP an 'x' marks an illegible letter, deletions are crossed out and additions are in superscript.

the Beckettian 'ineffable', which is another term for 'l'inénarrable' or the 'unnarratable', i.e. that which cannot be put into words.

The second deleted paragraph, which introduces a protagonist, appears to question the paradox inherent in the attempt to reach beyond words by means of words, the narrating voice asking itself how it can possibly achieve such an objective:

> ~~ce c ... corps~~ ... et ^{la} conscience de Madame Veuve Thomas narrée jusqu'à l'inénarrable comment en achever l'histoire de Madame Veuve ~~Thomps~~ Thomas de son corps de sa conscience (BDMP12, FM2, fol. 01v)
>
> [... and the mind of the widowed Mrs Thomas narrated to the point of the unnarratable, how to finish the story of the widowed Mrs Thomas, of her body and her mind]

The third and last cancelled paragraph then extends the problem to all bodies and all minds:

> ~~... à tous ces corps~~ ... à toutes ces consciences ... amorcer à tous ces corps ... à toutes ces consciences ... en dehors ... de leur mortalité ... et avec le mien ... la mienne ... quel autre ... point en commencer ... toutes ces vies ... très longues ... quoi que l'on ... dise ... ~~toute~~ $^{toutes\ les\ pensées}$ ... ~~l'idée~~ il me semble que ... j'estime que ... ~~l'~~ ^{les} allées et venues ... $^{toutes\ les\ allées\ ...\ et\ venues}$ ... toujours mal placée ... même ailleurs ... ou plus chassé ... chassé ailleurs ... ~~xxx de ça~~ ... tous c^{l}es mots ... ah les mots ... aux autres ... à part soi ... amochés ... toujours amochés ... quoi que l'on dise ... (BDMP 12, FM2, fol. 01v)
>
> [... on all those minds ... get started on all those bodies ... all those minds ... aside from ... their mortality ... and with mine ... mine ... which other ... no point to begin ... all those lives ... very long ... no matter what you ... say ... all those thoughts ... it seems to me that ... I believe that ... the comings and goings ... all those comings ... and goings ... always wrongly put ... even elsewhere ... no longer hunted ... hunted elsewhere ... all those words ... ah the words ... to others ... to oneself ... messed up ... always messed up ... no matter what you say ...]

This statement could be read as a radical negation of the very possibility to narrate fictional characters and their attributes. It implies that the validity or veracity of such a story would be restricted to the narrator, revealing more about the narrating voice than who the story is about, the latter being just a construction of that higher-level agency, assimilating its characteristics. Near the end of the third paragraph, an even greater problem is broached, one that undermines every type of narrative, even in the first person. It is typical of Beckett's fascination with the language scepticism of Fritz Mauthner and his book *Beiträge zu einer Kritik der Sprache* (1901–02).[4] Written or spoken narratives must inevitably resort to language as a means to tell stories, but words always fall short of their goal, so that every verbal narrative is doomed to fail or 'mess up'. Having deconstructed the most basic assumptions of storytelling in just three short paragraphs, at the outset of the monologue, the voice concludes it is pointless to even try.

With these false starts, Beckett had written himself into a proverbial corner. In a next step, after striking out the three paragraphs with a large St Andrew's cross, he first sketched a framework, on separate sheets of paper, into which the monologue could be embedded. Then, he put the same compactly formulated idea into practice, but now for a more prolonged and sustainable narrative. Again, it would undergo heavy revision, across about a dozen versions in French and half as many in Beckett's English self-translation of the radio play, comprising loose-leaf manuscripts, notebooks, typescripts, proofs and various publications in magazines as well as collected editions.

Denarration

For the framework of *Cascando*, Beckett devised several layers or levels of narration. On the one hand, we are confronted with a more traditional character called Opener, and on the other we have two audio channels referred to as Voice and Music. Opener has a story of his own to relate, in which he mostly divulges information about himself and his surroundings, but he is also tasked with activating Voice and Music, sometimes together, at others separately. Opener functions as a first-person intradiegetic narrator of his monologue, or what Brian Richardson, in his terminology for the narratological analysis of drama, calls a 'generative narrator'. Such an entity 'narrates what is happening or will happen on stage and functions as a kind of stage director in deciding what will happen next' (1988, 258), and thus 'generates a

---

4 For a comprehensive overview of the Beckett-Mauthner connection, see (Van Hulle 2011).

fictional world [...] in a manner similar to that of an omniscient narrator' (2001, 685). However, this does not entail that he is also the narrating instance of Voice, let alone of Music. Opener constantly repeats that he merely 'opens' ('j'ouvre') and 'closes' ('je referme') the two channels, thus rejecting all responsibility for what they bring forth and denying that they emanate from his own mind. For example, about the Voice he observes 'Aucune ressemblance' (Beckett 2009b, 57)—'No resemblance' (Beckett 2009a, 90)—meaning that it sounds entirely different from his own, which indeed it does in the existing radio recordings of *Cascando*. In the manuscript, he still referred to Music explicitly as 'et ça [...] c'est ma musique, ça?' (BDMP12, FM1, fol. 04r), before this remark, too, was obscured in the first typescript to 'Et ça [...] c'est de moi aussi?' (FT1, fol. 04r), leaving open the option that Voice and Music represent or symbolise something else still, for example reason and emotion.[5]

The Voice becomes a first-person narrator in its own right, be it on a lower diegetic plane than the frame story and apparently unconnected to the narrator of that higher level. In turn, the monologue of Voice, as 'opened' by Opener, consists of two further strands: a rather straightforward story about a character called 'Maunu' ('Woburn' in English) and a somewhat more erratic or repetitive string of phrases in which the Voice encourages itself to finish the story of Woburn—the latter thus offering a meta-reflection of sorts on the former. These two strands Beckett developed independently, on separate sheets of paper, designated in the draft versions of *Cascando* as the 'Histoire' ('Story') and the 'Soi' ('Self') elements. Similar to the relationship between Opener and the two audio channels, Voice lacks agency over the subject of its narrative. Roger Blin, who played Ouvreur in the French radio production, referred to Voice as a narrator who describes with difficulty, out-of-breath, that which he can only see vaguely: 'Narrateur qui décrit péniblement, en haletant, ce qu'il ne voit que de façon floue' (qtd. in Mélèse 1966, 113). Indeed, Woburn is constantly on the run, pursued by Voice, who believes it will catch up with him and bring the narrative to a

---

5   Tom Vandevelde (2013) provides a helpful overview of recent developments in narrative approaches to drama, also using *Cascando* as a case study, although he conflates theatre with radio drama, the latter of which can be more adequately analysed using audionarratology (see Huwiler 2005; Mildorf and Kinzel 2016; Bernaerts and Mildorf 2021) as well as transmedial narratology (see Ryan 2004; Ryan and Thon 2014; Thon 2016).

halt. However, unable to view the character clearly or read his mind, this lower-level narrator does not seem to be of the traditional omniscient type either. *Cascando* thus enacts the earlier mentioned impossibility of narration as a game of cat and mouse between Voice and the protagonist. Woburn exists only because he is told into being by Voice, yet Voice has no control over the protagonist, leading to an impasse that locks narrator and protagonist in shared impotence, reflected on the upper-level narrative echelon by Opener, who finds himself in a similar role with regard to Voice.

The drafts of *Cascando* offer several explanations as to why Woburn, despite being a character in a story, manages to escape the grasp of the narrating Voice, of which I will only discuss one example in this chapter, as a representative case of many similar ones. The first possibility is related to Beckett's attempt, in the early drafts of *Cascando*, to link the pursuit of Woburn directly to that of the self, which is notoriously elusive in his work. For this theme, Beckett created a subdivision within the overarching 'Soi' element, splitting it up into 'Soi 1' and 'Soi 2'. In the manuscript, as well as some of the earlier typescripts, Voice still identifies openly as Woburn and claims it is trying to speak about itself. In the third typescript, Beckett even amplified the crossed out 'je me serai dit' with the more explicit 'c'est moi' in the left margin (BDMP12, FT3, fol. 01r), but then he cancelled that addition as well, along with most of the other lines that openly connected the Voice to Woburn in this draft. Except for one phrase: 'cette fois j'y suis...dedans' (FT3, fol. 01r). It survived one more typescript, until even 'dedans' disappeared and the passage was revised to 'c'est la bonne...cette fois je la tiens...j'y suis' (FT5, fol. 01r). With this, all explicit ties between narrator and character had been obscured, or 'denarrated' in Brian Richardson's sense, but then on the genetic level. Richardson describes denarration as 'a kind of narrative negation in which a narrator denies significant aspects of his or her narrative that had earlier been presented as given' (2006, 87). The expression 'j'y suis', which Voice reiterates throughout the radio play, is the only survivor of this theme. It is a heavily condensed contraction that could be interpreted as either an identification of the narrator with the character—in light of the deleted genetic variants—or as the fulfilment of a goal—on the level of the published text. In keeping with this ambiguity, Beckett translated it into English as 'I'm there' (2009a, 87; 89; 92).

Denarrativisation

Having now 'undone' or 'vaguened' the 'Soi 2' element of self-identification in the drafts of Cascando, as S. E. Gontarski (1985) and Rosemary Pountney (1988) have summarised the primary dynamic of Beckett's writing process, he was free to concentrate on what remained. This was the 'Soi 1' element, in which Voice encourages itself to conclude the story, and the relationship of this strand to the 'Histoire' about Woburn, who no longer played an explicit double role as the Voice's fugitive and elusive self. This newfound clarity of purpose gave Beckett an opportunity to shift his attention away from 'denarration' to 'denarrativisation', by which I mean a gradual undoing of the characteristics that make us regard a string of words as 'narrative'. At the same time, he started conceptualising Cascando not just as a text or script but also as a radio play, to be listened to rather than read. In this more advanced stage of the writing process, Beckett took particular care to ensure that Voice never relates the 'Histoire' of Woburn when it can be heard together with Music, but only uses 'Soi' or self-encouraging phrases when Opener activates the two channels simultaneously. As Clas Zilliacus argues, in these moments, 'the words of Voice in Cascando gradually approach the fundamental quality of Music', as 'they rid themselves of their anecdotal content, of the histoire' (1976, 136).

From this point of view, Opener does not so much try to finish the story of Woburn as to liberate the words from their traditional storytelling function by gradually exposing them to music's alleged non-narrativity.[6] Voice in Cascando, restricted to the verbal, always relapses into the teleological story of Woburn. It can only free itself of linearity, and use language in a more dysteleological way, when Opener forces Voice, by opening both channels, to engage in a dialogue with Music, as may be gathered from the following two examples:

> – down ... gentle slopes ... boreen ... giant aspens ... wind in the boughs ... faint sea ... Woburn ... same old coat ... he goes on ... stops ... not a soul ... not yet ... night too bright ... say what you like ... he goes on ... hugging the bank ... same old stick ... he goes down ... falls ... on purpose or not

---

6   This contested assumption has a long history, not just in the field of narratology, but also in musicology and philosophy. For a recent overview, see (Bouckaert, Peeters and Van Nerom 2024).

> ... can't see ... he's down ... that's what counts ... face in the mud ... arms spread ... (Beckett 2009a, 86)
>
> – sleep ... no further ... no more searching ... to find him ... in the dark ...
>
> to see him ... to say him ... for whom ... that's it ... no matter ... never him
>
> ... never right ... start again ... in the dark done with that ... this time
>
> ... it's the right one ... we're there ... nearly ... finish – (89)

In the first example, Voice speaks alone and language is used to propel the story of Woburn. Every word adds new plot details to the narrative, which unfurls in chronological fashion as we follow the sequential journey of the protagonist. When Music joins, as in the second example, the discourse becomes more scattered, with a limited set of phrases being constantly reiterated in a different order, following a pattern that is not random but rhythmic or melodic rather than (teleo)logical or rational. Through this exposure of language to music, the words behave more akin to notes. As Kevin Branigan puts it: 'No longer obliged to hold referential meaning, they may chime as musical units' (2008, 33).

There is only one exception to this neat pattern. *Cascando* concludes with a chain of self-encouraging elements, in a prolonged counterpoint of Voice and Music. Just before the script ends, however, a narrative element from the 'Histoire' creeps in again: 'il s'agrippe' (BDMP12, FT6, fol. 08r)—'he clings on' (Beckett 2009a, 93). This phrase Beckett planted there in the sixth typescript, i.e. the second composite typescript that merges the framework and the speech parts, which gave him an opportunity to consider the radio play as a whole. Language, it seems, no matter how heavily it is 'denarrativised', cannot help but cohere and tell stories, as words remain essentially and irreconcilably different from music. Even when dissonance becomes its structuring principle, language still consists of meaningful units carrying certain denotations, even if that meaning is heavily abstracted and no longer figures within the larger framework of a linear story, but rather a theme. Words would have to be reduced to nonsensical combinations of letters or, if we factor in the acoustic dimension of *Cascando*, mere vocal emissions. Beckett once described his work to American director Alan Schneider as 'fundamental sounds' (1998,

24). He comes quite close to this quality in the French production of the radio play by RTF, where Voice gradually picks up speed, then speaks slower and more silent, almost fading to the point of inaudibility while repeating itself *da capo*, until a long silence marks the end of the broadcast.

Narrative Closure

The disruption of this denarrativisation process at the end of *Cascando*, via the intrusion of a linguistic element from the Woburn story into Voice's self-reflexive discourse, thus distorts the linear progression of the radio play and replaces it with a cyclical structure. The story we are presented with as readers or listeners begins in medias res, was clearly preceded by others and will likely be followed by more still, as Voice's opening words imply:

> – story ... if you could finish it ... you could rest ... sleep ... not before ... oh I know ... the ones I've finished ... *thousands and one* ... all I ever did ... in my life ... with my life ... saying to myself ... finish this one ... It's the right one ... then rest ... sleep ... no more stories ... no more words ... and finished it ... and not the right one ... couldn't rest ... straight away another ... to begin ... to finish ... saying to myself ... finish this one ... then rest ... this time ... it's the right one ... this time ... you have it ... and finished it ... and not the right one ... couldn't rest ... straight away another ... but this one ... it's different ... I'll finish it ... I've got it ... (Beckett 2009a, 85; emphasis added)

There is a potential intertextual allusion in these opening words that draws attention to the concept of narrative closure. The phrase 'thousands and one', in the context of storytelling, points to the *Arabian Nights*, also known as the *One Thousand and One Nights*. In this popular collection of Middle Eastern folktales, the main protagonist of the frame story, Scheherazade, leaves all the stories she tells Sultan Shahriyar unfinished so that she may live to see another day. This phrase, too, has fascinating variants in the genesis of *Cascando*. In the manuscript of the speech parts, Voice merely admits that it has finished 'other' ones before: 'j'en ai fini d'autres' (BDMP12, FM2, fol. 01r). Beckett next altered his wording to 'thousands'—'j'en ai fini ... des milliers' (FT1, fol. 01r)—in the first typescript of the speech parts, and then, in the third typescript, to 'hundreds of thousands' or, more idiomatically, 'huge amounts'—'des mille et ~~des cent~~ ^{une}' (FT3, fol. 01r)—altering it one last time to 'des mille et des une' (FT4, fol. 01r), which is how it appears in the published version (Beckett 2009b, 47). Beckett translated the expression into English, literally rather than idiomatically, as 'thousands and one' (2009a, 85), already in the first draft (EM, fol. 01r) and without variations in any of the five typescripts that followed (ET1–5, fol. 01r). He thus took care to mirror it in both languages, the one being a continuation or repetition of the other.

This reference has not gone unnoticed in Beckett studies, but it has received very little sustained attention. Enoch Brater just notes that 'though this is no *Arabian Nights*, tales in this case also number in the "thousands and one"' (1994, 42), disregarding any substantial affinity between these two texts. In addition to arguing that we can, indeed, consider *Cascando* as an *Arabian Nights* of sorts, I also aim to show that we need to factor in a third text: Proust's *À la recherche du temps perdu*. He evokes the *One Thousand and One Nights* throughout his novel (see Jullien 1989), especially in *Le temps retrouvé*. Beckett marked some of these instances in his own copy of the 16-volume edition by Gallimard's Nouvelle Revue Française imprint, for example the passage in which the transporting effect the sound of a spoon makes against a plate inspires the narrator to make the following comparison:

> comme le personnage de Mille et une Nuits qui sans le savoir accomplit précisément le rite qui fait apparaître, visible pour lui seul, un docile génie prêt à le transporter au loin, une nouvelle vision d'azur passe devant mes yeux (Proust 1929, 10)[7]

> [like the character in the *Arabian Nights* who, without knowing it, performs precisely the ritual which makes appear, visible to himself alone, a docile genie ready to take him far away, a new vision of azure passed in front of my eyes (Proust 2002, 177)]

Here, the reference is to the story of 'Aladdin and the Wonderful Lamp', which links to the magic lantern in Marcel's boyhood bedroom at the beginning of the first book in the series, thus setting the motif in motion, but Scheherazade is also mentioned at other times. As the narrator approaches the end of his magnum opus, he realises that he, too, is

---

[7] Beckett drew a line next to this passage in ink and wrote 'Rev. 9' in the left margin, keeping count of Proust's revelations in the *Recherche* (Van Hulle and Nixon 2013, 72). See https://www.beckettarchive.org/library/PRO-ALA-16.html?page=10&zone=1.

writing against death, much like the narrator of the frame story on the topmost level in the *Arabian Nights*:

> For myself, what I had to write was something different from a dying man's farewell, longer, and for more than one person. Longer to write. In the daytime, at best, I could try to sleep. If I worked, it would be only at night. But I would need a good number of nights, *perhaps a hundred, perhaps a thousand*. And I would be living with the anxiety of not knowing whether the Master of my destiny, less indulgent than the Sultan Shahriyar, when I broke off my story each morning, would stay my death sentence, and permit me to take up the continuation again the following evening. Not that I was claiming in any way to be rewriting the *Arabian Nights*, any more than the *Mémoires* of Saint-Simon, both of them books written at night, nor any of the other books that I loved in the naivety of my childhood [...]. No doubt my books too, like my mortal being, would eventually die, one day. But one has to resign oneself to dying. One accepts the thought that in ten years oneself, in a hundred years one's books, will not exist. Eternal duration is no more promised to books than it is to men. It would be a book as long as the *Arabian Nights* perhaps, but quite different. (2002, 353; emphasis added)

Although this section is unmarked in Beckett's copy (Proust 1929, 254–55), the neighbouring pages are all heavily annotated, and also the phrase 'perhaps a hundred, perhaps a thousand'—'peut-être cent, peut-être mille' (255)—resembles the genetic variant 'des mille et des cent' in the drafts of *Cascando*. So, Beckett may have had this passage in mind when he was writing the radio play. What is more, the verso of the novel's ending, coming just a few pages after this comparison, has a curious annotation in blue crayon that corroborates Beckett's interest in the motif: 'Arabian Nights of the mind' (qtd. in Pilling 1976, 28n85).[8] Beckett read the entire *Recherche* twice, first in 1930 to prepare for his essay *Proust* (1931), followed by a second round in 1932, when he was working on his first novel, *Dream of Fair to Middling Women*, not

---

8 See https://www.beckettarchive.org/library/PRO-ALA-16.html?page=lastpage&zone=1. No edition of the *Arabian Nights* was extant in Beckett's personal library at the time of his death, but in his student copy of A. J. Wyatt and W. H. Low's *Intermediate Text-Book of English Literature, Part 1*, he marked the passage that connects certain elements in Chaucer's 'The Squire's Tale' to it: 'the magic horse, ring, and mirror are frequently found in Eastern tales—e.g. the "Arabian Nights".' (1920, 63) See https://www.beckettarchive.org/library/WYA-INT-1.html?page=63&zone=1.

published until after his death. Dirk Van Hulle and Mark Nixon have surmised that 'the pencil marks seem to be the traces of a first reading, while the comments in ink mark a subsequent reading' (2013, 70). The blue crayon markings are not situated that explicitly in time, but some clearly override the pencil annotations, so they must belong to the later phase or an intermediate one during which Beckett revisited choice passages. If the plan was to use the 'Arabian Nights of the mind' epithet for his essay, then it is remarkable that it does not resurface there. If Beckett was thinking of using it as the premise for one of his own works, then it is equally remarkable that *Cascando*, written some thirty years later, presented him with a first opportunity to do so, in the medium of radio.

As much as the *Recherche* is 'different' as a 'rewriting' of the *Arabian Nights*, so, in turn, is Beckett's, of both his literary models. Sharing '[t]he necessity to survive, to ward off death, and to "create" time to live' with Scheherazade, it is in the 'creation of a suspension of reality, and, perhaps more importantly', influenced by the philosophy of Henri Bergson, in the 'creation of a subjective experience of time' that Proust's *Recherche* distinguishes itself (Van Leeuwen 2018, 123). Aline Carpentier picks up on this theme when she states about Beckett's *Cascando*: 'Comme dans *Les mille et une nuits*, le récit permet au personnage de lutter contre la mort' (2008, 80). This positive or optimistic reading, however, runs counter to the Opener's wishes, and Beckett's idiosyncratic approach to the *One Thousand and One Nights*, which is more negative than Proust's. Unlike Scheherazade, who ends her stories on cliffhangers to go on living, and the narrator of *À la recherche du temps perdu*, who regards his work as both a way to relive his life as well as an afterlife, Opener yearns for death so he can have peace and quiet. The compulsion to tell stories—'I *must* open' (Beckett 2009a, 91; emphasis added)—is a means for him to try (in vain) to express the 'unnarratable' and finally achieve silence, but every word he speaks is always 'not the right one' (85), no matter how hard he tries to deconstruct or 'denarrativise' language—a typically Beckettian double bind familiar from so many of his other works. As such, he, too, can be added to that long list of authors who have revisited the *Arabian Nights* from a twentieth-century perspective. Of course, *Cascando*, at merely nine pages or a running time of approximately 15–20 minutes, is not exactly 'a modern(ist) metamorphosis of the *Thousand and One Nights*' (Van Leeuwen 2018, 121), on a par with Proust's *Recherche* in terms of literary significance. Nevertheless, the radio play revisits this shared source from the perspective of a different medium, thus adding a new element to a long-standing tradition of intertextual engagement.

For example, because it has been recorded, *Cascando* could be replayed ad infinitum, indefinitely postponing narrative closure and replacing it with a mechanically repetitive cycle. There is, in fact, a tension between the sonic or technological dimension of the radio play and its textual nature, which Beckett clearly struggled with on the levels of writing, translation and publication. Particularly the genetic history of the closing direction 'FIN' or 'END' is fraught. Present in all drafts of the French version except the last typescript that was used as a setting copy—where 'Fin' is crossed out in blue ink, presumably by the author, since all the printer's markings are in red ink or grey pencil (FT8, fol. 08r)—it was nevertheless retained for the text as published by Minuit and the magazine *L'VII*. Because the proofs or galleys for these editions have not been found, it is unclear if Beckett authorised its reinstatement. He did 'unend' the radio play again by translating it into English, which resulted in a further six drafts. 'END' is dropped in all of them, leaving only the final direction 'Silence.' One exception is the fifth and last typescript, which was used as a setting copy for the Faber edition. It appears to 're-end' the radio play, as on this version the direction 'End.' returns, now with a full stop (ET5, fol. 06r). To complicate the matter even more, Beckett had sent an earlier draft of his English translation—a sibling of the second typescript (ET2)—to Grove Press in New York, who printed it in the magazine *Evergreen Review* (no. 30, 1963) and also used it as the base text for their paperback edition *Cascando and Other Short Dramatic Pieces* (1968). Neither of these has the closing direction. Until 1984, when Grove adopted the Faber text for their jointly-published *Collected Shorter Plays*, two different English versions of the radio play circulated in print, marred by textual variance and a different sense of closure at the 'end'—one that is inconclusive from a genetic vantage point as well.[9] The word 'FIN' or 'END' is often

---

9   On the Faber galleys—which are not the original document but rather a reconstruction of Beckett's corrections for book collector Alan Clodd on a proof copy of the edition, held at the National Library of Ireland in Dublin—the final stage direction mistakenly reads 'CURTAIN', which Beckett crossed out and replaced with 'END'. While he seems to provide closure after all by reinstating the word, thus settling the matter, we cannot be certain without the actual

a pragmatic and paratextual way of signaling the last page of a work, so that both author and compositor know there are no sheets missing. While at one point it may well have served such a function in the genesis of *Cascando*, its exact purpose remains unclear and ambiguous.

Irrespective of this editorial conundrum, the fact remains that Beckett does not close the frame story in any version of *Cascando*, so that there is no unequivocal narrative closure on the textual or the paratextual level. Unlike the *Arabian Nights*, in which Scheherazade marries the Sultan, or Proust's *Recherche*, in which Marcel resigns himself to death—even if the real-world author passed away before he could revise the final volumes of his masterpiece—we do not revisit the frame story and there is no similar sense of resolve in Beckett's radio play. Opener 'opens' *Cascando* by stating 'It is the month of May ... for me' (Beckett 2009a, 85), and he interrupts Voice and Music from time to time, but the higher-level narrator does not foreground himself again at the end. This invocation of Spring, which Opener elsewhere refers to as 'the reawakening' (90), implies that his death will be deferred, the cyclical pattern of the seasons ousting the linear and finite life course as the main structural principle. Instead, Voice has the final say: 'come *on*' (93; emphasis added). Beckett knew from the very first draft in French, and never changed his mind thereafter, that the last word would be 'allons' (BDMP12, FM2, fol. 05r) followed by 'Silence' (FM1, fol. 05r)—arguably more effective in English, since 'on' is the palindrome of 'no' and means the exact opposite. *Cascando* thus rewrites the frame story of the *One Thousand and One Nights*, using open-endedness as a contradictory or paradoxical—in any case volatile—form of narrative closure: until further notice or until re-opened.

Works Cited

galleys, as Beckett was reconstructing his proof corrections from memory. In any case, Faber failed to heed the author's wishes, as the text appeared with the obviously erroneous theatrical curtain call, which makes no sense for a radio play. It persisted in Faber's editions, including the *Collected Shorter Plays* (Beckett 1984, 144) and *The Complete Dramatic Works* (Beckett 1986, 304), after which it was changed to 'END' by Everett Frost for *All That Fall and Other Plays for Radio and Screen* (2009a, 93). All of the present Grove editions, unfortunately, still have 'Curtain' (2006, 351; 2010, 145).

Beckett, Samuel (1984), *Collected Shorter Plays* (London: Faber & Faber).

Beckett, Samuel (1986), *The Complete Dramatic Works* (London: Faber & Faber).

Beckett, Samuel (1998), *No Author Better Served: The Correspondence of Samuel Beckett and Alan Schneider*, ed. by Maurice Harmon (Cambridge, MA: Harvard University Press).

Beckett, Samuel (2006), *The Grove Centenary Edition*, vol. 3: *Dramatic Works*, ed. by Paul Auster (New York: Grove Press).

Beckett, Samuel (2009a), *All That Fall and Other Plays for Radio and Screen*, prefaced by Everett Frost (London: Faber & Faber).

Beckett, Samuel (2009b), *Comédie at Actes Divers* (Paris: Les Éditions de Minuit).

Beckett, Samuel (2010), *The Collected Shorter Plays* (New York: Grove Press).

Bernaerts, Lars and Jarmila Mildorf, eds. (2021), *Audionarratology: Lessons from Radio Drama* (Columbus: Ohio State University Press).

Bouckaert, Bart, Ann Peeters and Carolien Van Nerom, eds. (2024), *Music and its Narrative Potential* (Leiden and Boston: Brill).

Branigan, Kevin (2008), *Radio Beckett: Musicality in the Radio Plays of Samuel Beckett* (Bern: Peter Lang).

Brater, Enoch (1994), *The Drama in the Text: Beckett's Late Fiction* (New York: Oxford University Press).

Carpentier, Aline (2008), *Théâtres d'Ondes. Les Pièces Radiophoniques de Beckett, Tardieu et Pinter* (Paris: De Boeck).

Gontarski, S. E. (1985), *The Intent of Undoing in Samuel Beckett's Dramatic Texts* (Bloomington: Indiana University Press).

Huwiler, Elke (2005), 'Storytelling by Sound: A Theoretical Frame for Radio Drama Analysis', *Radio Journal: International Studies in Broadcast and Audio Media*, 3.1: 45–59.

Jullien, Dominique (1989), *Proust et ses Modèles. Les Mille et une Nuits et les Mémoires de Saint-Simon* (Paris: Corti).

Mélèse, Pierre (1966), *Samuel Beckett* (Paris: Seghers).

Mildorf, Jarmila and Till Kinzel, eds. (2016), *Audionarratology: Interfaces of Sound and Narrative* (Berlin: De Gruyter).

Pilling, John (1976), 'Beckett's "Proust"', *Journal of Beckett Studies*, 1: 8–29.

Pountney, Rosemary (1998), *Theatre of Shadows: Samuel Beckett's Drama 1956–76. From* All That Fall *to* Footfalls *with Commentaries on the Latest Plays* (Gerrards Cross: Colin Smythe).

Proust, Marcel (1929), *À la Recherche du Temps Perdu, Tome VIII. Le Temps Retrouvé* (Paris: Librairie Gallimard; Éditions de la Nouvelle Revue Française).

Proust, Marcel (2002), *Finding Time Again*, trans. by Ian Patterson (London: Penguin).

Richardson, Brian (1988), 'Point of View in Drama: Diegetic Monologue, Unreliable Narrators, and the Author's Voice on Stage', *Comparative Drama*, 22: 193–214.

Richardson, Brian (2001), 'Voice and Narration in Postmodern Drama', *Literary History*, 32.3: 681–94.

Richardson, Brian (2006), *Unnatural Voices: Extreme Narration in Modern and Contemporary Fiction* (Columbus: Ohio State University Press).

Ryan, Marie-Laure, ed. (2004), *Narrative across Media: The Languages of Storytelling* (Lincoln, NE: University of Nebraska Press).

Ryan, Marie-Laure and Jan-Noël Thon, eds. (2014), *Storyworlds across Media: Toward a Media-Conscious Narratology* (Lincoln, NE: University of Nebraska Press).

Thon, Jan-Noël (2016), *Transmedial Narratology and Contemporary Media Culture* (Lincoln, NE: University of Nebraska Press).

Vandevelde, Tom (2013), '"I open": Narration in Samuel Beckett's *Cascando*', *Samuel Beckett Today/Aujourdhui*, 25: 253–65.

Van Hulle, Dirk (2011), '"Eff it": Beckett and Linguistic Skepticism', *Sofia Philosophical Review*, 5.1: 210–27.

Van Hulle, Dirk and Mark Nixon (2013), *Samuel Beckett's Library* (Cambridge: Cambridge University Press).

Van Leeuwen, Richard (2018), *The Thousand and One Nights and Twentieth-Century Fiction: Intertextual Readings* (Leiden and Boston: Brill).

Verhulst Pim (2021), 'Music, Voice and (De)Narrativization in Samuel Beckett's Radio Play *Cascando*', in: *Audionarratology: Lessons from Radio Drama*, ed. by Lars Bernaerts and Jarmila Mildorf (Columbus: Ohio State University Press), 196–214.

Verhulst, Pim (2024), 'Radio Drama: Between Text and Sound', in: *Comparative History of the Literary Draft*, ed. by Olga Beloborodova and Dirk Van Hulle (Amsterdam: John Benjamins), 514–26.

Wyatt, A. J. and W. H. Low (1920), *Intermediate Text-Book of English Literature, Part I* (London: W. B. Clive University Tutorial Press).

Zilliacus, Clas (1976), *Beckett and Broadcasting: A Study of the Works of Samuel Beckett for and in Radio and Television* (Åbo: Åbo Akademi).

10. A Genetic and Biographical Analysis of Barbara Pym's Companion Character

Jane Loughman

Jessie Morrow, the paid companion of the elderly Miss Doggett, is a prominent character in Barbara Pym's fictional world; she appears in *Jane and Prudence* (1953), in the posthumously published novel *Crampton Hodnet* (1985), and in 'So, Some Tempestuous Morn' from the posthumous short story collection *Civil to Strangers* (1987). The order of publishing differs from the order in which Pym wrote these texts. The first time Pym wrote about Jessie was in a 1939–40 draft of *Crampton Hodnet*. She returned to the character ten years later while writing 'So, Some Tempestuous Morn' around 1950, and then again while writing *Jane and Prudence* in 1951. Pym changes Jessie's personality significantly from her introduction in the *Crampton Hodnet* draft through to her final appearance in *Jane and Prudence,* the only contemporarily published text that features the character. In particular, Jessie is ever less tolerant of her profession and of her spinsterhood. Jessie is not the only companion character that Pym created; twenty-seven companions and governesses appear in her manuscripts (Wyatt-Brown 1992, 162). A 'variant' of Jessie Morrow, Deborah Wilde, appears in an unfinished draft called *Something to Remember* (1940) written just after *Crampton Hodnet*. Ten years later, in 1950, around the same time as Pym's return to Jessie Morrow, Pym also adapted *Something to Remember* into a radio play for the BBC, changing Deborah's name to Edith Gossett. In the span of roughly ten years, Pym's companion character changed across the manuscripts and typescripts of these texts. There is minimal scholarship that examines the transformations, which may be due to the minimal endogenetic material that would be useful in a genetic analysis—drafts, typescripts and sketches—on the companion character in the ten-year period between the first and last iteration of Jessie. Expanding the endogenesis to include Pym's diaries and letters facilitates a study of Pym's creative process. On the 'narrative' level of narratology, the consideration of autobiographic material allows an interpretation of the characterisation changes that Pym made to Jessie and her companion 'variants'. There is a tendency in studies of Pym and of her work to read her characters as stand-ins for Pym herself; Hazel Holt—friend and biographer of Pym—writes that Prudence of *Jane and Prudence* is 'only a slightly distorted mirror image of Barbara herself' (Holt 1990, 165). This chapter postulates that the companion character is not a mirror image of Pym, but rather a persona adopted on-the-page in tandem with the fictive personae Pym adopted off-the-page throughout her life.

From her days studying English at Oxford to her time as a Women's Royal Navy (WRN) officer, Barbara Pym (1913–1980) documented her life and corresponded with acquaintances through various personae that she invented. Biographer Paula Byrne takes note of the many personae that Pym adopted in her daily life, or 'off-the-page' (Byrne 2021). In this way, Pym not only made a life of her fiction, but she also made a fiction of her life. Anthony Kaufman contends that Pym was able to distance herself from her own living experience to gain perspective and to transmute her painful experiences into comedy (Kaufman 1996, 187). The personae complicate biographical readings of Pym as readers of her personal writings may doubt whether the 'real' Barbara Pym is even known, and question if they 'followed the emotional career of a character not entirely fictional, but not entirely Barbara Pym' (Kaufman 1996, 189). While it seems that the personae were designed to provide Pym with detachment from her 'true' self, they nevertheless offer insights into Pym's thoughts and feelings at the times she was writing. Pym herself said: 'even when a novel isn't obviously autobiographical [...] a novelist [...] can hardly avoid putting something of himself into his creations' (Bodleian MS. PYM 98, fol. 66r). While there is a fictionalisation of her life in her autobiographic material, there also is 'something of' Pym in the personae, as she used them to channel the dissatisfactions she felt in her life. Stemming from her obsession with the narrative of Charlotte Brontë's *Jane Eyre*, Pym created the companion character in her fiction, assuming the persona 'on-the-page'. Pym then employed the sentiments of her off-the-page personae to experiment with different versions of the companion persona over the years. There is a symbiotic relationship between the companion characters and her off-the-page personae; the transformation in the companion characterisations aligns with the fluctuating outlooks on life Pym took on from 1938–51 as she used the detachment she derived from her personae to cope with change, heartbreak and spinsterhood.

Pym was a mid-century romantic comedy novelist who had many relationships but never married. Spinsterhood is a key subject of her novels; Pym's romantic heroines are often unmarried women or 'gentlewomen' who keep themselves busy with their jobs or involvement in parish affairs. While some critics, in analysing Pym's social comedies and romantic narratives, have deemed her a 'twentieth-century Jane Austen,' others see such a reading as reductive and as misinterpreting Pym. Margaret Bradham writes: 'It is not about marriage and marriageability that Pym writes, but about spinsterhood and unmarriageability' (1987, 31). The companion, a carer for an elderly person, is a particular kind of spinster Pym was interested in. There are recurring traits between the different 'variants' of the companion character throughout her work, one being that they are overlooked by their employer and others in their social circle. Another shared character trait is their timidity, yet this is a trait which evolves into confidence for the character of Jessie Morrow. In narratological studies, Uri Margolin has asked 'how much can a character change and still remain the same individual [...] in different fictional worlds [...] is it one version per world, or are there rather one original individual and his counterparts in other worlds?" (Margolin 2007, 75). Viewing each Pym text as a different 'world',[1] is Jessie Morrow of *Crampton Hodnet* a completely different character than Jessie in *Jane and Prudence*? Margolin puts forward two answers to this question, one that characters are 'text-bound' and 'cannot be exported across text and world boundaries,' the other being that we can export characters across texts by the same author, that the variations are 'alternative elaborations of one common core' (Margolin

---

1   Although it could be argued that Pym's texts form one fictional world together since characters like Mildred Lathury from *Excellent Women* makes appearances in other texts, I use Margolin's word 'world' to study characterisation changes across genetic drafts through a narratological lens.

2007, 70). The symbiotic relationship between Pym's companions and her off-the-page personae complement the narratological argument that Pym's companion characters are not 'text-bound' but are variants of 'one common core' as their characterisation transformations align with Pym's own changing attitudes. Studying diaries and letters as endogenetic material reveal that characters and personae cannot be static and 'text-bound' but are susceptible to change, just like a person's real-life growth and development. After an overview of the textual revisions to Pym's companion characterisations across the drafts, sketches and typescripts of seven texts, I introduce a biographical reading of Pym to argue that the author's diaries and letters can be used to amend the gaps in the genetic evolution of Pym's companions' characterisation.

The Genetic Evolution of the Companion Character

While Pym was a spinster, she was never a companion, and so there has been scholarly interest in the origin of Pym's fascination for the social role. Janice Rossen and Anne M. Wyatt-Brown have sourced the fascination from Pym's love for *Jane Eyre* by Charlotte Brontë; they see the abundance of companions, governesses, themes of unrequited love and heroines pining after aloof men in Pym's work as hints of both an obsession and grappling with Brontë's gothic romance. Rossen asserts that Brontë's text 'haunted' Pym throughout her life (Rossen 1988, 137), and Wyatt-Brown attests that Pym 'never outgrew her youthful obsession' with the text (Wyatt-Brown 1992, 6), supporting their claims with biographical and genetic evidence. Rossen, for instance, notes that Pym referred to *Jane Eyre* as one of her favourite texts during a talk (Rossen 1988, 155), and that in her diaries she sometimes considered rewriting the text; in 1970, she asks herself if she could write 'A modern version of *Jane Eyre*?' (Pym 1984, 259). However, in their study of the connection between Pym and *Jane Eyre*, neither Rossen nor Wyatt-Brown give very significant consideration to Jessie (or her variant companion characters). Rossen does write convincingly that the 1940 rendition of *Something to Remember*—featuring the companion Deborah—is an attempt to rewrite *Jane Eyre* (Rossen 1988, 139), and Wyatt-Brown does take minor interest in Jessie in her Pym biography. Wyatt-Brown's only conclusion for Jessie's character change, though, is that 'Pym's view of her had changed over the years' (Wyatt-Brown 1992, 80). Despite acknowledging the variations of Jessie as 'spunky' and 'sensible' (80), Wyatt-Brown insists that Pym 'absorbed from *Jane Eyre* a belief that powerless women must inevitably submit to their adored but aloof, Rochester-like men' (40). Wyatt-Brown forgets that Jessie never submits to her Rochester figure, but instead either refuses his half-hearted proposal in *Crampton Hodnet* or takes charge of her own life and seduces him into marriage in *Jane and Prudence*. In this section of the chapter, I track the genetic evolution of the companion characterisation in Pym's work, beginning with a resigned spinster who sticks to what she knows, and evolving to a bold, daring woman who seeks change from her caregiving role. Using the endogenetic material of Pym's fiction, I closely read Pym's textual edits—some of which are excluded from final, published versions—that reveal Pym's intentions behind the characterisations.

Pym began writing *Crampton Hodnet* in 1939, but the typescript was abandoned after 1940 and was only published posthumously 45 years later by Holt. The story follows the tribulations of three pairings in North Oxford, including curate Stephen Latimer's failed proposal to companion Jessie Morrow. While staying at Leamington Lodge with the spinster and her employer Miss Doggett, Stephen makes his proposal on a spur of the moment, inspired by the notion that 'he might do *worse* than marry Miss Morrow' (Pym 2022b, 81). She rejects his proposal since he only regards her with 'respect and esteem' but does not *love* her (116). She sees her standards as so high that she cannot envisage herself in a loving marriage (118) since, as a companion, she believes she is 'looked upon as a piece of furniture' (21). Miss Doggett is often condescending to Jessie, saying she does 'not know the world as' she does (163), which undermines Jessie's 'definite personality' (2). Yet Jessie is 'able to look upon herself and her surroundings with detachment' (2), which allows her to make bold and witty comments that are overlooked. Because of her detachment, she does not suffer heartbreak from the failed proposal, and instead sees herself as a 'lucky woman' to be concerned only with 'the trivial round, the common task' (198). However, in the typescript draft of the novel (Bodleian MS. PYM 10) one can find a line added by Pym to a section in chapter 16 (omitted by Holt in the published edition of the story): 'Miss Morrow began to wonder whether he had fallen in love with somebody, but after racking her brains without success, she decided it must be the thought of Paris that was responsible for his odd behaviour' (Fig. 10.1). This line in the manuscript strengthens a reading of Jessie as covertly preoccupied with romance, accepting her position as an unmarried companion with an air of resignation. Jessie in the final chapter of *Crampton Hodnet* can be understood as having a fatalist view; nothing will ever change for her as she listens to the same romantic programme on the radio that she did at the beginning of the novel (Pym 2022b, 3; 270), and she agrees with Miss Doggett that there is no 'change and decay' at Leamington Lodge (271).

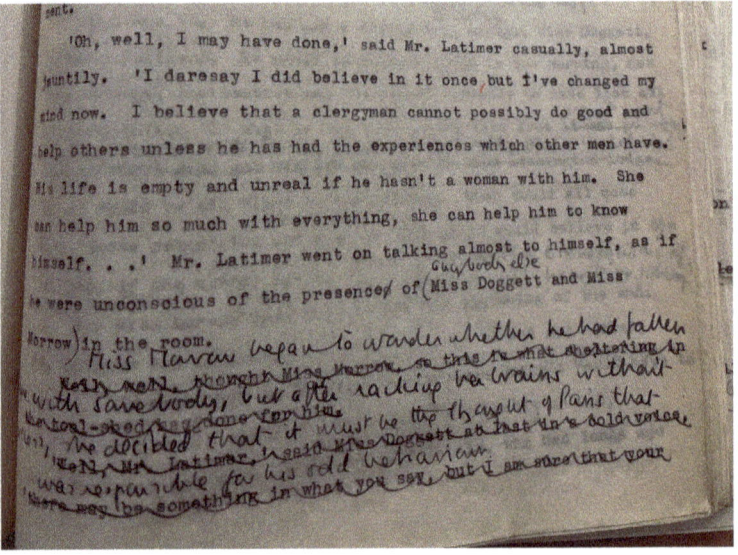

Fig. 10.1 Barbara Pym, *Crampton Hodnet* typescript (1939), Bodleian MS. PYM 10, fol. 213r.

Written in 1940 but incomplete and unpublished, *Something to Remember* (Bodleian MS. PYM 11) features another companion character who accepts her spinsterhood with resignation. Deborah Wilde takes on a new role as 'companion-secretary' to Mrs Otway, although Deborah thinks the title 'too grand' for the post (fol. 07r). As evident from her first-person narration, she has low self-esteem, and complementing that are her low expectations for her life in her new job: 'My life would be uneventful but comfortable […] Oh, yes, I was a lucky woman' (08r). When Deborah ponders on her new job, she realises that 'the thought of being a companion-secretary frightened me now and I didn't want to

10. A Genetic and Biographical Analysis of Pym's Companion Character 175

think about it, ~~so that I~~ and in any case one could hardly imagine that there would be anything exciting about it' (Fig. 10.2). However, Pym crossed this sentence out, and she replaced Deborah's feelings of fright over her new role with: 'I felt rather heavy and resigned, which is perhaps the most suitable feeling a companion can have' (21r). Resignation and heaviness better characterise Deborah as she broods over sad memories, imagines alternate lives and enters bouts of melancholy throughout the text. Deborah believes this is the existence she ought to have: 'When you are past the early twenties, I think you do not any longer rebel against things' (17r). Her resignation carries over into her prospects of love. Deborah still grieves over her failed relationship with Reverend Bernard Hoad, to whom she was once engaged, but who jilted her. Now, she ponders falling in love with Mr Otway, admitting it 'would be like falling in love with one of the stuffed birds', but still 'might be soothing' (68r). After heartbreak, Deborah now seeks comfort, not passionate love, settling for 'soothing' but unrequited love. Mrs Otway sees potential for Deborah as a suitable, 'awfully good clergyman's wife' (69r), but the overall gloom of the unfinished draft does not present hope to the reader.

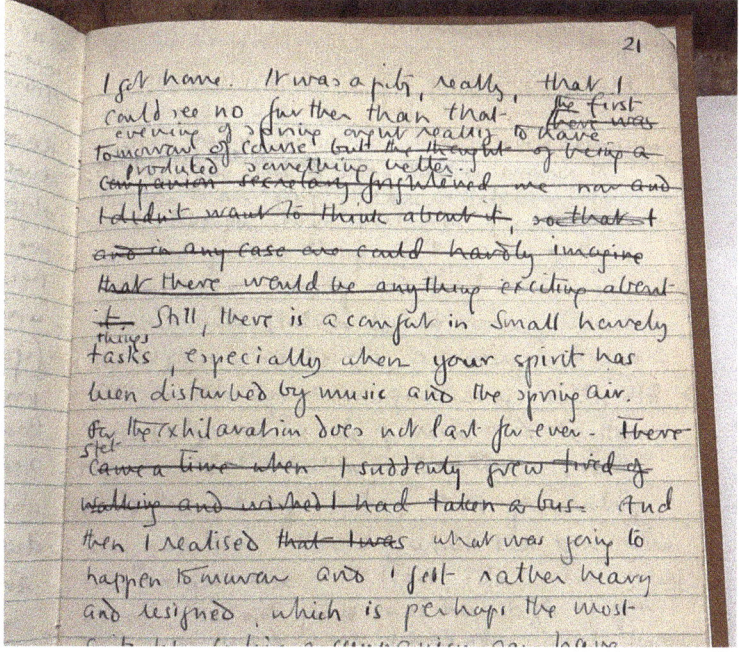

Fig. 10.2 Barbara Pym, *Something to Remember* (1940), Bodleian MS. PYM 11, fol. 21r.

Following Jessie of *Crampton Hodnet* and Deborah, and throughout the war, there are no substantial drafts or typescripts of stories featuring companion characters. The only possibly wartime endogenetic material featuring a companion is an undated Pym notebook (Bodleian MS. PYM 90) where one can find a sketch of a character similar to Deborah. Wyatt-Brown names this notebook 'Notes for a Wartime Novel' in her critical biography (Wyatt-Brown 1992, 165), and it is most likely from 1944 (Pym stated that her heroine is '18 in 1889' and '73 in 1944' [Bodleian MS. PYM 90, fol. 09r]). Beatrice Gossage, or 'Gossy' (09r) looks back on her past as a 'governess and companion' who works for 'Lord Edge' (10r). At 18, she was in love with the eldest son of the Lord's family, 'Julian' (15r). Like Deborah, Gossy is a clergyman's daughter who is melancholic and does not feel a whole sense of self: she relates to the stag's head on the wall of the home 'whose melancholy eyes seemed to ask/cry to her—oh where is the rest of me—a question she had sometimes asked herself' (13r). In 1945, Pym began drafting a second version of what would become her first published novel, *Some Tame Gazelle* (1950). She wrote the first version in the 1930s but returned to the story as the war came to an end to update it and make it 'acceptable' (Wyatt-Brown 1992, 145) In the second version, Pym reuses a character from an earlier story, her 'Home Front Novel,' which she drafted at the beginning of the war but never attempted to publish. The character is Connie Aspinall, who in 'Home Front' is not a companion but Agnes Grote's friend who lives with her (Bodleian MS PYM 8, fol. 15r). Connie is 'meek and wispy about the head' (36r), and while she occasionally feels 'defiant' (28r), she is resigned, but not over a lack of love in her life. She often daydreams of living in Belgravia (61r) and away from her overbearing housemate. Interestingly, in *Some Tame Gazelle*, Connie is a former companion who used to live in Belgrave Square working for Lady Grudge but is now living with her elderly relative Edith Liversidge, away from Belgravia. While she is not named as a companion of Edith, it seems she has adopted the role; Edith calls on Connie 'as if she were a dog' (Pym 2022d, 25). Harriet views Connie as a 'decayed gentlewoman' (10), and Belinda cannot help but see 'something elegiac about poor Connie' as she plays piano with a 'melancholy air' (37). It is evident that she is nostalgic over 'her past glories of her life' in Belgravia (126), so Connie of *Some Tame Gazelle* is similar to Deborah in her melancholic nostalgia. Connie is also close to Jessie of *Crampton Hodnet* in that she is overlooked, yet she strays from Jessie's fatalism and instead accepts a surprising proposal from Bishop Grote (241). Connie was not the bishop's first choice, as he originally proposed to the novel's protagonist, Belinda, and got rejected (225), yet she believes that when he first saw her 'he knew it was to *be*' (241).

In Pym's *Excellent Women* (1952), which Pym began drafting in 1949, there is a minor character, Miss Jessop, who is not explicitly described as a companion but could be interpreted as one as she acts like a subordinate to the elderly Mrs Bone, with whom she lives. She is even more meek than Connie; she does not say a single word throughout the entire text, and only makes a 'quavering sound which might have been a "Yes" or "No"' (Pym 2009, 167). It is interesting that Pym brings in a companion-like character who is so quiet and submissive, as her characterisations of the companion throughout the early 1950s gradually begin to show more rebellion and frustration instead of resignation.

In 1950, Pym adapted *Something to Remember* into a play for BBC Radio, the script of which remains unpublished (Bodleian MS. PYM 96 fols.193–229) and which contains hints of a reference to the 1944 'Gossy' sketch and a similar melancholic air to previous versions of the companion. In the radio adaptation, Edith Gossett, a companion employed by Miss Lomax, is resigned, and she is regarded as part of the furniture: 'She goes with all that delicious Edwardian and Victorian bric-a-brac' (219r). While she is not as formidable as Miss Doggett, Miss Lomax still looks down on Edith enough for it to sting, such as when she implies Edith lacks a 'forceful personality' (223r). However, like Jessie in *Crampton Hodnet*, Edith does have a bold side, seen only when she is talking to Simon Sheldonian: after Simon asks, 'What can I say to that?', Edith replies 'I thought you were going into the Diplomatic Service […] You ought to know what to say' (220r). While Jessie and Connie get proposed to, Edith instead gets an offer from her eligible bachelor to be his mother's companion, much to her surprise: 'Oh, I see' (227r). In *Crampton Hodnet*, Jessie also replies to Stephen Latimer with an 'Oh, I see' when he proposes to her (Pym 2022b, 115); the aloof response reveals how Jessie holds back an overt show of her feelings in her state of detachment. Edith also masks her feelings to Simon, but her appeal to the stag's head shows her disappointment over the lack of a proposal. In their first exchange years before, Edith says 'I suppose I've more feeling than that old stag's head on the wall' (Bodleian MS. PYM 96 fol. 220r), then years later when they reunite, she refers to that stag's head again after Simon asks if she could be his mother's companion

(227r). Simon does not recall the stag's head, nor did he recognise Edith at first when they reunited (225r). Since Edith's memory of their first exchange is stronger, Edith had evidently been more invested in Simon than he had been in her, so she was let down by his job offer. If the Beatrice Gossage sketch from 1944 mentions Beatrice sharing an affinity with a stag's head, perhaps her successor Edith is also 'connected' to her own stag's head, showing a similar detachment style as Jessie from *Crampton Hodnet* by saying 'I don't think the stag's head would have approved of [the job offer]' (227r).

In Pym's handwritten notebooks from the 1950s, there are notes that show Pym's thoughts of returning to Jessie Morrow and Miss Doggett ten years after writing *Crampton Hodnet*. In MS. PYM 41, a notebook dated from 1950, Pym wrote 'New novel. An old lady with a companion, who is blamed for the modern slackening of moral stands' (Bodleian MS. PYM 41, fol. 08v), a call-back to Miss Doggett's treatment of Jessie in *Crampton Hodnet*. A few pages later in the same notebook, among ideas for *Jane and Prudence*, Pym sketched her short story 'So, Some Tempestuous Morn':

> a story about Oxford Love.
> A story ab and North Oxford.
> First of all the companion and the
> peonies too ravaged to
> decorate the church
> 'Ravaged?'—Miss D. frowned (Bodleian MS. PYM 41, fol. 14r).

Pym used elements of this sketch in the short story, which became a retelling of the opening scene of *Crampton Hodnet*, but also remained unpublished until the 1980s. The four typescripts of 'So, Some Tempestuous Morn' (MS. PYM 94, fols. 149r–204r) are undated but are likely to be from 1950 considering the sketch in her 1950 literary notebook. Holt published the version of the story in the fourth typescript in 1987. Like the Jessie of *Crampton Hodnet*, the Jessie of 'So, Some Tempestuous Morn' feels that she is a marginal figure in Oxford life, 'a dim figure on the fringe of the University melting away into North Oxford' (199r). Miss Doggett is still unaccommodating of Jessie's witty remarks in the short story, calling her comments 'little lapses' and altogether unsuitable (193r), but, beyond her sassy comments, Jessie shows more signs of rebellion against Miss Doggett's views than her predecessor. After delivering flowers to the church, Jessie thinks of a place to have morning coffee and cake, an activity Miss Doggett denounces as 'time-wasting and self-indulgent', to purposefully 'waste time and be self-indulgent' (199r). The first typescript and the fourth typescript of 'So, Some Tempestuous Morn' have different endings, and the differences have a significant impact on a reading of Jessie's character as being rebellious. In the first typescript, Pym describes Jessie joining the luncheon crowd in the garden with a 'swaggering air' (158r), suggesting she has built up her self-confidence despite the snide remarks of Miss Doggett in front of the 'strikingly handsome clergymen' (150r). However, in the fourth typescript's ending, and thus in the published version, Jessie follows the crowd 'solemnly round the garden' (204r; Pym 2022a, 338). In this version's ending, she comes across as an even more melancholic, resigned spinster than Deborah or Connie, even though, throughout 'So, Some Tempestuous Morn,' Jessie is antsier over her role than her predecessors. Holt chose to publish the fourth typescript and, thus, the ending that uses the word 'solemnly'. Holt's decision is notable as the confident, arrogant nature of 'swaggering air' from the first typescript speaks more to the final iteration of the Jessie/companion character.

Contemporaneous readers of Pym first met Jessie Morrow in *Jane and Prudence*. There are no drafts of the novel in Pym's archive, but as previously mentioned, Jessie and other *Jane and Prudence* characters appear in Pym's literary notebooks. In a sketch detailing the ending of the novel, Pym wrote:

> At the end a scene where Miss
> Doggett uncovers a scandal—
> Miss Morrow and Fabian have
> been having an affair*—he
> has been running her and
> Prudence at the same time.
> Almost imperceptibly Miss M.
> has taken the place of Constance,
> his late wife.
> *Miss D. is vague—doesn't really
> know all but wishes she did (Bodleian MS. PYM 42, fol. 12r).

As the sketch suggests, the Jessie of *Jane and Prudence* is the most rebellious of all her variants; dissatisfied with her job as a companion, she takes action into her own hands and seduces the widower Fabian

Driver to bag him as a husband. She sees her job as 'outmoded,' especially since Miss Doggett has 'no need' of her (Pym 2022c, 25). As a friend of the late Constance Driver, Jessie knew Constance's husband Fabian well and 'had always loved him' (150) but did not realise so until a year after Constance's passing. According to Fabian, Jessie 'appeared always in [Constance's] shadow, a thing without personality of her own, as neutral as her clothes' (54), resembling Pym's previous characters who are undermined and perceived as lacking in personality. Fabian does understand, however, that Jessie has an 'unexpectedly sharp tongue' (117), which she uses to get his romantic attention. She refuses to remain in her social position as a mere marginal onlooker on society: 'I don't intend to be a distressed gentlewoman' (134). In an act of defiance, she not only lies to Miss Doggett about her whereabouts for her afternoon off, but also wears Constance's old blue velvet dress when she goes to visit and seduce Fabian, asserting her newfound self: 'I wondered [...] if I would have the courage to call on you. Well, I did have, so here I am' (151). Her boldness reaches its peak once Jessie calculatingly decides to spill tea on her competitor for Fabian, Prudence, to make her leave a social gathering (186). Ruthless, sharp, and even frightening to Fabian (215), Jessie of *Jane and Prudence* is very different from Pym's first companion characterisation in *Crampton Hodnet* ten years before.

While she is still underestimated by her wider circle, Pym's companion character finally breaks out of her fatalistic mindset and makes a change to her tedious existence in *Jane and Prudence*. Jessie does not submit to a Rochester figure, departing from Wyatt-Brown's reading, and instead finds a courage inside herself to seduce Fabian. But what prompted the characterisation change, the genetic evolution of a companion from resigned and melancholically nostalgic, to bold, determined and ready to uproot her life? Emily Stockard studies Pym's life and work through themes of change, arguing that Pym adhered to a 'principle of continuity'; she was always in tune with the past, present and future, acknowledging that change, not stasis, is the key to continuity (Stockard 2021, 14). In order to maintain a sense of continuity in times of change, Pym created personae to '[accommodate] herself to major alterations in her life' (63) such as her first love, her time in the WRN and her first major heartbreak, and to channel her true feelings. A study of the off-the-page personae through Pym's letters and diaries illuminates the fluctuating attitudes to life that Pym adopted and which she then applied to the variants of a 'common core', Jessie Morrow. In the following section, I explore Pym's personal archives and biography to track the symbiosis between the changes in Pym's life and the changes in the companion character.

The Fictive Personae of Barbara Pym

The first of Pym's fictive personae was created out of Pym's wish to detach from her 'innocent' self to gain confidence around men (Byrne 2021, 64). 'Sandra,' short for 'Cassandra,' was a flirty, bold, romantic Oxford student (Byrne 2021, 64). Pym recorded her adventures as Sandra in her Oxford diary labelled 'the adventures of the celebrated Barbara M C Pym during the years 1932–1933' (Bodleian MS. PYM 101, inside front cover), in which she documented her life like a story, with Sandra as the main protagonist. For a new term in 1933, she considered taking the opportunity 'to change entirely!!' in 'intoxicating' Oxford (Bodleian MS. PYM 101, fol. 05v), and in her new form she flirted with many Oxford men, including one with whom she would become life-long friends. Henry Harvey, or 'Lorenzo' according to Sandra, dominated her diary, including in her poems from 'Sandra to Lorenzo' (Bodleian MS. PYM 101, fols. 58r–59v). Pym had a tumultuous on-off romance with Harvey (see Byrne 2021), but it was ultimately an unrequited love; Stockard writes that Pym made use of her Sandra persona 'to cordon off and observe with irony the part of her that suffered' (Stockard 2021, 114). Long after their Oxford days, Pym maintained a friendship with Harvey, often writing to (and pining after) him. When Harvey moved to Finland in 1934, Pym started a new diary, and created the persona of 'Pymska', a Finnish version of Barbara (Byrne 2021, 126) and a 'more sophisticated person than Sandra' (Byrne 2021, 159). The Pymska persona, like Sandra, was another means through which to flirt with men and to cope with unreturned feelings from her first significant love, Harvey.[2]

Pymska evolved into 'Paavikki Olafsson',[3] another Finnish role. Pym impersonated Paavikki when meeting Julian Amery in 1937, dropping

---

[2] The persona being Finnish and Harvey being in Finland shows that Pym was still not over Harvey.
[3] The persistence of the Finnish inspiration for the personae reveals an ongoing infatuation with Harvey.

the act almost immediately. Pym became infatuated with Amery, and when they embarked on a fleeting affair, she revealed her habit of acting out roles; he wrote in a letter to her asking 'When am I going to see you again my "vaend at Elske" Vicki [...] will you be a Shropshire spinster? a Finnish student? or just a novelist up to see her publisher?' (Bodleian MS. PYM 147, fol. 01v). The romance with Amery did not last as he left for Spain to work as a war correspondent in the Spanish Civil War in 1938. She kept up the continental Paavikki persona, shortening the name to Vikki, as she moved to Poland in 1938 to be a governess before soon returning to England due to rising tensions (Byrne 2021, 223). In Poland, she started 'a new life' as Vikki (Byrne 2021, 223), wearing her 'Vikki Olafsson macintosh and battered Austrian hat' (Bodleian MS. PYM 104, fol. 135r). Yet she would continue to pine, missing Amery, and was homesick, writing that 'Vikki was temperamental—but after cigarettes, some Mozart and a Brandenburg concerto felt better' (139r). At the same time as she was inhabiting the role of Vikki, Pym adopted the contrasting 'Miss Pym' when writing letters in the style of poet Stevie Smith. Unlike the romantic and charming Sandra, Pymska and Vikki, 'Miss Pym' is a 'spinster lady who was thought to have been disappointed in love' (Pym 1984, 67). In a letter to Harvey and her friend Robert Liddell in 1938, Pym described Miss Pym in a vexed tone as an 'old brown spinster horse' or 'old-stuffed shirt' who is 'all shut up like oyster, or like clam' (71). Despite her recent romance with Amery, Pym persisted with conjuring up Miss Pym as a 'crabby' spinster (71). There is an element of truth to 'Miss Pym', of course, as the letters are 'a study in masking and revealing emotional trauma by means of self-mockery' over Pym's failed romances (Stockard 2021, 134). She used the comedic spinster persona in her writings to help her endure her disappointments of losing Harvey and Amery.

'Miss Pym's' complaints of spinsterhood continued into the war years as Pym pined after Amery and when she was later jilted by another lover, Gordon Glover. As her relationship with Amery faded, she met the married, philandering Glover in 1941, and had an affair with him in 1942 (Byrne 2021, 332). Glover's jilting caused Pym so much heartbreak she destroyed the diaries that had thoroughly documented their time together (Byrne 2021, 332–34). She did capture 'Miss Pym's' thoughts after the fact in a diary: 'And the bewildered English spinster, now rather gaunt and toothy, but with a mild, sweet expression, may hardly know herself' (Bodleian MS. PYM 108, fol. 40r). Prompted by her heartbreak, Pym joined the WRN, or 'Wrens,' in 1943 to 'take a measure of control over her wartime life' (Stockard 2021, 280). She constructed another persona, 'Wren Pym,' which she used as a title on a new page in her diary (see Fig. 10.3). There is a clear divide between Barbara and Wren Pym: on a solitary walk, prompted by the sounds of Bach, she returned to her 'old gothick self—the self that I've had to put off while I've been here' (Bodleian MS. PYM 109, fols. 30v–30r). She noted how easy it was to adopt her alter ego—'in fact I seem to have adapted myself quite happily to this life' (30r)—and later in the diary expressed her excitement in the idea that she 'can do something I thought I couldn't do before' (69v). Even though she was often homesick, Pym's time as Wren Pym begins to encourage her to move on from Glover: the Wrens had 'at least given me a change, less opportunity to think of G […] and the feeling that I am trying to do something about it' (71r–71v). Following the war, despite exhibiting admirable independence in working during the war and taking on a new office job in 1946 (Byrne 2021, 379), Pym's negative 'Miss Pym' mindset regarding spinsterhood remained; in a letter to Harvey, she wrote 'Maybe I shall be able to keep my illusions as it doesn't look like I shall ever get married' (Pym 1984, 180). She did not write about her life very much following her mother's death in 1946. She became a published author in 1950, and, as she began to write *Jane and Prudence* in 1951, had an affair with a married man (Byrne 2021, 426).

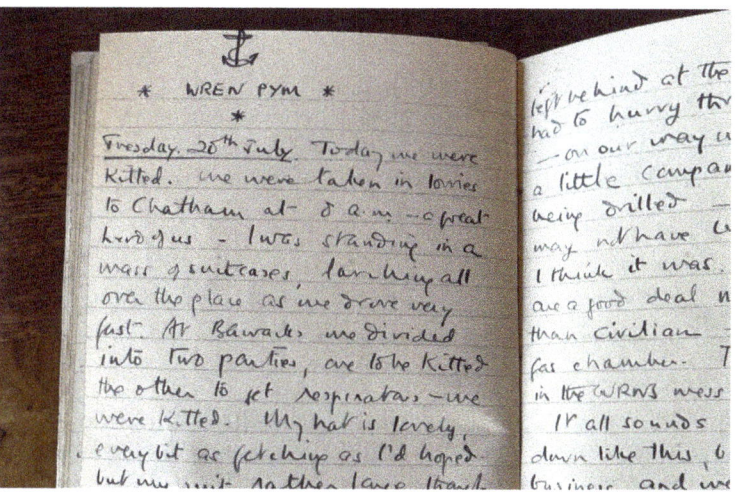

Fig. 10.3 Barbara Pym, Diary (1943), Bodleian MS. PYM 109, fol. 44v.

Pym's adoption of different roles helped her to take control of her life at points of change, to ironically distance herself from herself, and to explore parts of herself she did not know. Stockard writes that, in this way, Pym was aware of the 'relation between the roles one takes on or finds oneself in and the alterations that these roles undergo as consequent to changes in one's life, alterations necessary to form life's continuity' (Stockard 2021, 131). Some of her personae evolved into new versions, such as from Sandra to Pymska, while others were used simultaneously, such as Vikki and Miss Pym; Pym adhered to a principle of continuity, staying in tune with her true self as she inhabited many lives on- and off-the-page. As Kaufman writes, Pym 'feels the emotion and yet at the same time can observe herself with ironic self-awareness and, thoroughly accustomed even this early to viewing herself and her world through literature, can see herself as acting out a fiction' (Kaufman 1996, 191–2). Wren Pym was the most self-aware persona of Pym's fictionalised life, as she laughed at the prospect of 'a grown up person playing a fantastic game' being considered to work overseas: 'You see Reader, I am now completely myself again—the most unlikely person to be in the Wrens' (Bodleian MS. PYM 109, fol. 84v). Yet, I agree with Stockard in that it is Wren Pym that lends Pym an 'expanded sense of herself' (Stockard 2021, 295), a new sense of self that Pym then lends to her on-the-page persona, the companion.

Pym never worked as a companion, but she did fleetingly joke in a letter to Liddell in 1937 that she could work as a companion for Harvey's partner's mother, listing her qualifications: 'I am [...] a gentlewoman, cultured, a good needlewoman, very clean and pleasant-tempered' (Bodleian MS. PYM 153, fol. 190r). As Pym begins to write *Crampton Hodnet* the year following her finding out that Harvey will marry his partner Elsie (Byrne 2021, 195), it is possible to interpret this joke as the origins of the Jessie/companion character. Thus, the companion is a persona Pym took on, more separate from herself than her off-the-page fictive personae, but nonetheless a character influenced by her real-life personae and used to grapple with strong feelings of frustration and loneliness. In *Crampton Hodnet*, Mr Latimer proposes to Jessie on the grounds of 'respect and esteem' (Pym 2022b, 116), a phrase that Harvey used in a letter to Pym (Byrne 2021, 246). Jessie's rejection of the half-hearted proposal and her emotional detachment funnels Pym's wish to move on from her unattainable infatuations of Amery and Harvey and to distract herself from her emotions as 'Vikki.' However, Deborah Wilde's lack of confidence and nostalgia over past loves in *Something to Remember*, written around the same time as *Crampton Hodnet*, captures 'Miss Pym's' continued resignation over her spinsterhood. Channelling the nostalgia of both 'Gossy' from the 1944 sketch and Connie from *Some Tame Gazelle*, as well as the emotional detachment and resignation of Edith from the 1950 radio adaptation of *Something to Remember*, allowed Pym to look back on her own life after heartbreak over Glover while distracting herself as Wren Pym or as a post-war working lady trying to get published. In a 1941 diary entry, Pym felt melancholic and nostalgic, quoting Matthew Arnold's 'Thyrsis': 'So, some tempestuous morn in early June [...]' (Bodleian MS. PYM 146, fol. 24r). Pym returned to the Arnold imagery again in 1950 in 'So, Some Tempestuous Morn' but not to express melancholy: 'Tempestuous morn' speaks to the stormy morning in North Oxford but also to the tempestuous, conflicted feelings of Jessie over her social role across the typescript drafts. Jessie resolved these feelings in *Jane and Prudence* after Pym came to a revelation in her fictionalised life while working as a Wren in the war years: that she could adopt even 'an unnatural or uncongenial role if required' (Stockard 2021, 295). Becoming Wren Pym was a way for Pym to distract herself from Glover, but she came away from the role believing that she could 'do something I thought I couldn't do before', even if she was 'a grown up playing a fantastic game'. Her newfound courageousness as Wren Pym is the key turning point for the characterisation change in Jessie between *Crampton Hodnet* and *Jane and Prudence*; being a companion is what is natural, comfortable and suitable to Jessie, but frustrated after years of being in the margins, she decides to assume a new role in *Jane and Prudence* as a spunky, bold woman who finds love for herself.

Pym's fictive personae, therefore, serve to make up for the lack of endogenetic material on the character of the companion in the war years, and contribute to a fuller image of Pym's fictionalising of her own life. However, the subsequent return to the Miss Pym mindset shows that she was still bitter over Glover. Pym writes Fabian, a 'Gordonish character' (Bodleian MS. PYM 41, fol. 11r) into *Jane and Prudence*, and Jessie seduces him with her newfound sense of self. It is possible that Pym's affair with married man Thomas Kendrick in 1951 (Byrne 2021,

426) led to Pym's adoption of another off-the-page persona, such as the 'Other Woman', who she then channelled into her final iteration of her on-the-page companion persona in *Jane and Prudence*, but there is a lack of personal material that might confirm this reading. We can argue, though, that via the 'principle of continuity', which kept Pym in tune with her past to face change (Stockard 2021, 14), the writer returned to sentiments from the early 1940s that her personae had expressed in *Crampton Hodnet* and *Something to Remember*, and used them for Connie during the war, and Edith Gossett, the Jessie of 'So, Some Tempestuous Morn' and the Jessie of *Jane and Prudence* ten years later. She employed the Miss Pym-esque resignation in the companions of *Some Tame Gazelle* and the *Something to Remember* radio play before transforming it into the Wren Pym-esque ambitious outlook hinted at in the Jessie of 'So, Some Tempestuous Morn' but fully realised by the Jessie of *Jane and Prudence*.

Pym purposefully writes about her life as if it were a novel. She addresses a 'Reader', expecting her personal writing to be read (Bodleian MS. PYM 109, fol. 84v), and structures some diary entries as if they are chapters in a novel: 'I seemed to be thinking of [Gordon] less… But… Tuesday April 6th I spoilt it by dreaming of him' (Bodleian MS. PYM 108, fol. 37v). Her use of personae both in her personal documents and in the endogenetic material of her literary work blurs the lines between her fiction and her reality. Her attempt to fictionalise her life shows her eagerness to live a 'writable' life: she once wrote that 'the novelist has to do a good deal of improving upon life at all stages in a plot. [...] Somethings do not happen at all, but in a novel they must be made to happen' (Bodleian MS. PYM 98, fol. 64r). It is fitting, then, that Pym's narratological techniques for her character variants follow the 'principle of continuity' across texts. While Pym and her companion personae were once resigned, heartbroken, and hopeless about their spinsterhood, they learn to make things happen, to take charge of their lives as if they are the writers of their own stories. The author does more than act in different roles as she plays 'a fantastic game'; she makes a memorable life that complements her memorable fiction.

Works Cited

Amery, Julian, MS. PYM 147 (fols. 1–50), Letters from, and Newspaper Cuttings Concerning Julian Amery, 1937–1948, n.d., Archive of Barbara Mary Crampton Pym, Oxford: Bodleian Libraries.

Bradham, Margaret, C. (1987), 'Barbara Pym's Women', *World Literature Today*, 61.1: 31–37.

Byrne, Paula (2021), *The Adventures of Miss Barbara Pym* (London: William Collins).

Holt, Hazel (1990), *A Lot to Ask: A Life of Barbara Pym* (London: Macmillan).

Kaufman, Anthony (1996), 'A Life like A Novel: Pym's "Autobiography" as Fiction', *Journal of Modern Literature*, 20.2: 187–97.

Margolin, Uri (2007), 'Character', in: *The Cambridge Companion to Narrative*, ed. by David Herman (Cambridge: Cambridge University Press), 66–79.

Pym, Barbara, MS. PYM 8, Unfinished Manuscript Draft of 'Home Front Novel' (*Civil to Strangers*, 1987), written Oct. 1939–Oct 1939, Archive of Barbara Mary Crampton Pym, Oxford: Bodleian Libraries.

Pym, Barbara, MS. PYM 10, Typescript Draft of *Crampton Hodnet* (1985), 1939–1940, Archive of Barbara Mary Crampton Pym, Oxford: Bodleian Libraries.

Pym, Barbara, MS. PYM 11, Notebook Containing Unfinished Manuscript Draft of 'Something to Remember', 14 June 1940, Archive of Barbara Mary Crampton Pym, Oxford: Bodleian Libraries.

Pym, Barbara, MS. PYM 41, Literary Notebook II, 1950, Archive of Barbara Mary Crampton Pym, Oxford: Bodleian Libraries.

Pym, Barbara, MS. PYM 42, Literary Notebook III, 1951–1952, Archive of Barbara Mary Crampton Pym, Oxford: Bodleian Libraries.

Pym, Barbara, MS. PYM 90, Notebooks Containing Miscellaneous Extracts, Notes and Drafts, n.d., Archive of Barbara Mary Crampton Pym, Oxford: Bodleian Libraries.

Pym, Barbara, MS. PYM 94 (fols. 149–204), 'So, Some Tempestuous Morn' (*Civil to Strangers*, 1987), Three Copies of a Draft and Early Version, n.d., Short Stories, Mainly Unpublished and Undated Typescripts and Manuscripts, n.d., Archive of Barbara Mary Crampton Pym, Oxford: Bodleian Libraries.

Pym, Barbara, MS. PYM 96 (fols. 193–229), 'Something to Remember,' Two Copies of a Play, Typescripts of Radio Broadcasts and Scripts Submitted to the BBC, 1948–1978, Archive of Barbara Mary Crampton Pym, Oxford: Bodleian Libraries.

Pym, Barbara, MS. PYM 98 (fols. 56–123), Texts of Autobiographical Talks and Articles with Related Correspondence, 1953–1979, Miscellaneous Papers, 1922–1979, Archive of Barbara Mary Crampton Pym, Oxford: Bodleian Libraries.

Pym, Barbara, MS. PYM 101, Diary, Jan. 1932–Sept. 1933, Archive of Barbara Mary Crampton Pym, Oxford: Bodleian Libraries.

Pym, Barbara, MS. PYM 104, Diary, 1938, Archive of Barbara Mary Crampton Pym, Oxford: Bodleian Libraries.

Pym, Barbara, MS. PYM 108, Diary, Jan.–May 1943, Archive of Barbara Mary Crampton Pym, Oxford: Bodleian Libraries.

Pym, Barbara, MS. PYM 109, Diary, June–Nov. 1943, Archive of Barbara Mary Crampton Pym, Oxford: Bodleian Libraries.

Pym, Barbara, MS. PYM 146, Reflections by Barbara Pym Concerning Herself and Julian Amery, c.1939–1951, Archive of Barbara Mary Crampton Pym, Oxford: Bodleian Libraries.

Pym, Barbara, MS. PYM 153 (fols. 154–97), Letters to J. R. Liddell from Barbara Pym and Ivy Compton-Burnett, 1936–1940, Archive of Barbara Mary Crampton Pym, Oxford: Bodleian Libraries.

Pym, Barbara, et al (1984), *A Very Private Eye: The Diaries, Letters and Notebooks of Barbara Pym* (London: Macmillan).

Pym, Barbara, and Hazel Holt (2022a), *Civil to Strangers* (London: Virago Press).

Pym, Barbara (2022b), *Crampton Hodnet* (London: Virago Press).

Pym, Barbara (2009), *Excellent Women* (London: Virago Press).

Pym, Barbara (2022c), *Jane and Prudence* (London: Virago Press).

Pym, Barbara (2022d), *Some Tame Gazelle* (London: Virago Press).

Rossen, Janice (1988), 'On Not Being Jane Eyre: The Romantic Heroine in Barbara Pym's Novels' in: *Independent Women: The Function of Gender in the Novels of Barbara Pym*, ed. by Janice Rossen (Brighton: Harvester), 137–56.

Stockard, Emily (2021), *The Making of Barbara Pym: Oxford, the War Years, and Post-War Austerity* (Basingstoke: Palgrave Macmillan).

Wyatt-Brown, Anne M. (1992), *Barbara Pym: A Critical Biography* (London: University of Missouri Press).

11. Also for Irony: Historical Realism and the Move of a Chapter for the Final Version of *V.* (1963) by Thomas Pynchon

Luc Herman and John M. Krafft[1]

V. is a historical novel that intersperses chapters set largely in 1956 New York with an almost chronological sequence of chapters set in various locations in Europe and Africa from the end of the nineteenth century onwards. The 1956 storyline centres on the picaresque adventures of ex-sailor, former roadworker, sometime alligator hunter, sometime nightwatchman Benny Profane among an array of other characters including former shipmates, would-be girlfriends and the members and satellites of a group of hedonistic pseudo-bohemian New Yorkers known as The Whole Sick Crew. The other storyline, anchored in the first, centres on Herbert Stencil, the middle-aged son of a British diplomat-*cum*-spy, and especially on his efforts to find out about the reference to a certain V. in his father Sidney's diaries. From 1956, Stencil is trying to trace the supposed role of this mysterious V. in the violent and chaotic events of the twentieth century, from the potentially apocalyptic Fashoda crisis of 1898 as seen from Egypt, to the siege of Malta during the Second World War. The result of Stencil's investigation, so to speak, is the sequence of historical chapters mentioned above, chapters that narrativise his 'findings' about the mysterious V.

The Lippincott first edition of *V.* (like the later Modern Library [1966] and Harper Perennial [1986] editions) consists of 492 pages divided into

---

[1] This essay is based largely on material in our *Becoming Pynchon: Genetic Narratology and V.* (Columbus: Ohio State University Press, 2023), esp. 152–57. Used with the permission of The Ohio State University Press.

sixteen chapters plus an unnumbered epilogue. An untitled typescript (1961) of *V.* acquired in 2000 by the Harry Ransom Humanities Research Center in Austin, Texas, consists of 685 numbered pages divided into thirty chapters. All in all, the published novel has about 25,000 fewer words than the typescript. So, what happened? In the spring of 1962, Pynchon rewrote his novel, following a few suggestions from his editor, Corlies ('Cork') Smith, but the Pynchon-Smith correspondence shows that the author had merely been waiting for these suggestions to expound his own ideas for the revision: Pynchon responded on 13 March with a fourteen-point plan to a 23 February letter in which Smith had made only three remarks.[2] However, Pynchon did address these remarks, so they must have seemed important to him.[3] For instance, in order to avoid the reader's potential confusion at the relatively late moment the typescript switches from New York 1956 to Egypt 1898 for the first of the historical chapters, he moved the chapter forward and added a two-page introduction to it in which he thematises historiography and frames the multiple focalisation in that Egypt chapter as an imaginative way of transcending the vantage point of an individual narrativising character and (by extension) author who is trying to make sense of the twentieth century. The added introduction insists on the creative power of the historical imagination, and—judging from other historical chapters in the published novel, including 'Confessions of Fausto Maijstral' (a long letter to his daughter containing journal entries about the bombing of Malta during the Second World War) and 'Mondaugen's Story' (the rewritten version of the typescript chapter on the 1922 Herero uprising in German South-West Africa)—Pynchon was clearly keen on pushing the boundaries of that imagination. What he does, for instance, with the dreams in the South-West Africa chapter in terms of intersubjective-consciousness evocation is absolutely stunning. In other words, in many historical chapters in *V.* the historical imagination runs riot.[4]

---

2   Facsimiles of these letters have been published in two unauthorised, limited editions: Pynchon, *Of a Fond Ghoul*; rpt. in Pynchon, *The 'C' Section*. Both editions are unpaginated.
3   For more details and an overview comparing typescript and published novel, see Herman and Krafft 2023, 15–38.
4   For more on the Egypt episode, see Herman and Krafft 2023, 39–51; on Maijstral's 'Confessions', passim; on 'Mondaugen's Story', 53–76.

Still, after all the historiographical grandstanding of the so-called 'Stencilized' (Pynchon 1963, 228) chapters ('Stencilized' because they have been narrativised, to various degrees, by Stencil),[5] the book ends on what looks like a relatively simple example of historical realism, a more or less conventional presentation of the past as Georg Lukács found it in the work of Walter Scott and other nineteenth-century authors (see Lukács, *The Historical Novel*). Interestingly, this chapter, 22 in the typescript, which deals with events on Malta in 1919 and is called 'June Disturbances', was moved to the end of the novel in the course of the rewriting in 1962, becoming 'Epilogue 1919'. In what is perhaps the last letter to his editor about the rewriting of *V.* (2 June 1962), a slightly exasperated Pynchon addresses the position of that historical chapter set on Malta: 'I put 1919 at the end primarily because there's nowhere else to put it. Also for irony [...]. If it could go better anywhere else I'd like to know'. The chapter could easily have kept its place in the nearly chronological arrangement of historical chapters, so 'there's nowhere else to put it' sounds merely impulsive. Pynchon's declaration of 'irony', on the other hand, merits further scrutiny, not least because this term can have a number of meanings. In order to elucidate Pynchon's use of the term, we need to say more about the rest of the novel.

In both typescript and published novel, the historical chapters set in Egypt (1898), Florence (1899), South-West Africa (1922) and Paris (1913) are all more or less explicitly narrated by Stencil. Maijstral's 'Confessions' is obviously not, and we don't need Pynchon's 24 March 1962 letter to Smith saying that typescript chapter 22, 'June Disturbances', which became the published novel's 'Epilogue 1919', is not one of those 'in a sense "told" by Stencil' to infer that the chapter is neither narrated by Stencil nor limited to his perspective. And although as late as 2 June Pynchon was still uncertain about the wisdom of having moved his 'favorite chapter' to the end of the novel, we can recognise that one effect of giving the chapter such pride of place is to emphasise the ways it provides outside, even higher-level narratorial support for some elements of Stencil's historical constructs. For example, it confirms a V. figure in the place and role Stencil imagines in the Florence chapter (see Pynchon 1961b, 444–45; Pynchon 1963, 487). That is, we think the

---

5   The term 'Stencilized' does not appear in the typescript but was added during the 1962 revision.

epilogue and, by extension, the novel as a whole, despite Stencil's own anxieties and other characters' criticisms, do more to corroborate than to undermine Stencil's idiosyncratic historiographical project.[6]

'Stencilizing', seeing patterns and making meaning of them, though risky, keeps Stencil from 'resuming [his] prewar sleepwalk' (Pynchon 1961b, 61–2; Pynchon 1963, 54), sinking 'back into half-consciousness' (Pynchon 1961b, 62; Pynchon 1963, 55), a state he both fears for himself and sees 'horrifying[ly]' mirrored in the shallow, merely present-minded Whole Sick Crew (Pynchon 1961b, 63; Pynchon 1963, 56). (Stencil attributes to the Crew the 'hothouse sense of time' [Pynchon 1961b, 65; Pynchon 1963, 57] that many critics attribute, we think wrongly, to Stencil himself.)

If we see the relocated epilogue as to some degree authorising Stencil's project, that is to claim practical use value for his narratives, not truth value. Uncertainty (though less ridicule) remains, and scepticism is still a virtue. The narrator of a 1956 chapter (possibly the same narrator as, or similar to, the epilogue's) tells us that the millions of readers of newspaper headlines in New York City 'read what news they wanted to and each accordingly built his own rathouse of history's rags and straws', *but* that 'Stencil fell outside the pattern': 'he was hard at work creating' a 'grand Gothic pile of inferences' (Pynchon 1961b, 339–40; Pynchon 1963, 225–26). We read a 'grand Gothic pile' (a fair—perhaps self-conscious—description of *V.* itself) as qualitatively superior, but we acknowledge that, as a description of Stencil's construction, it may be just a bigger rathouse.

---

6   Another effect of moving the 1919 chapter to the end of the published novel is to take pride of place away from typescript chapter 30 (originally 'Epilogue', now *V.* chapter 16, 'Valletta'), set on Malta beginning in late October 1956. Even though the ominous aura diminishes somewhat in the second half of chapter 16 (until its very end in 'the abruptly absolute night' [Pynchon 1963, 455; cf. Pynchon 1961b, 685]), the Suez Crisis shadowing it hints that this episode on the novel's present-day axis may also be virtually the latest episode on the crisis-ridden historical axis. With the chapter set on Malta in 1919 now the published novel's epilogue, the seeming convergence of the two axes in what thus becomes the next-to-last chapter is less portentously climactic. The Malta 1919 chapter (which ends with the mysterious sinking of Sidney Stencil's ship) is plenty ominous, to be sure, but the June Disturbances that give it its typescript title subside, and the continuation of uneasy but peaceful metropolis-colony relations from then until the 1956 present is explicitly noted, although the typescript does seem to take a somewhat more jaundiced view of those relations (cf. Pynchon 1961b, 449 and Pynchon 1963, 491–92).

Deletion of the short typescript chapter 16, 'No Man's Land', a present-day conversation between Herbert Stencil and the dentist Dudley Eigenvalue following the Florence episode, strengthens our argument that Pynchon's relocating the epilogue was part of an effort to lend credence to (or lessen doubt about) Stencil's procedures. There (Pynchon 1961b, 312) the typescript Eigenvalue overestimates the wisdom of Sidney Stencil's 'theory' of the 'Situation' (Pynchon 1961b, 286–88, 439–40; Pynchon 1963, 189–90, 483–84), seeing Sidney as not prone, like Herbert, to willful self-projection, even though it is Herbert who has just portrayed Sidney to Eigenvalue and given him not only Sidney's theory but also an example in practice: the imaginary Vheissu plot and the way it was, first, diplomatically negotiated into (fictional) being in all its flagrant comic absurdity (Pynchon 1961b, 294–96; Pynchon 1963, 196–98) and, then, simply abandoned (Pynchon 1961b, 310; Pynchon 1963, 211). We have no reason to think Herbert himself takes the literal existence of the Vheissu plot seriously (see Pynchon 1961b, 249; Pynchon 1963, 155), although its imaginary existence is just as symptomatic, historically indexical, as his V. construct is. In the (un-Stencilized) epilogue, Sidney's partner in espionage, Demivolt, praises their bureaucratic superiors' 'guesswork [that] draws from a really first-rate intuitiveness' and claims the 'hunch' that '"something [was] wrong"' in Florence 'was right' about 'symptoms' if not about 'whatever the disease [was]' (Pynchon 1961b, 426; Pynchon 1963, 473), and Sidney does not demur. We are sceptical (as Demivolt is not) of 'all elaborate games of this sort' (Pynchon 1961b, 426; Pynchon 1963, 473) and of the people who play them precisely because they can get things as absurdly and catastrophically wrong as the Stencilized Florence episode shows they did.

What, then, does it mean to be right about symptoms and wrong about the disease, and how does the distinction bear on Herbert's view of V. as a 'symptom' (Pynchon 1961b, 588; Pynchon 1963, 386)? We do not read Demivolt's credulity as a reflection on the younger Stencil that necessarily compromises the latter. Still, we take Roony Winsome's denunciation of his fiction-writing wife as 'smart enough to create a world but too stupid not to live in it' (Pynchon 1961b, 554–55; Pynchon 1963, 360) to be cautionary, and we understand that it serves as a warning about the risks involved in Stencil's (hi)story-making as well. So whatever his potential as a historian may be, perhaps it is just as well that Stencil is not, 'like his father, inclined toward action' (Pynchon 1961b, 340; Pynchon 1963, 225).

If the Stencilization of history has its risks in terms of action, it might also have its limits as a type of discourse about the past that testifies to the powers of the imagination and is not so much tied to the facts as inspired by them. The 'irony' of moving the 'June Disturbances' chapter in the typescript to the end of the novel could then refer to the fact that after all the historiographical grandstanding of the Stencilized chapters—notably in the reworked South-West Africa chapter, with its fancy evocations of consciousness—the book ends on what looks like a relatively simple example of historical realism. Pynchon wonders in his 24 March 1962 letter to Smith whether he 'shouldn't just keep [the names and places] historical and "realistic" as in the June Disturbances chapter'.

As a method of historical evocation, what we call 'historical realism' includes the construction of a narrative situation (similar to the ones developed in nonhistorical realism from, at the latest, Jane Austen to Arnold Bennett and beyond) in which a mostly unobtrusive narrator uses a limited degree of internal focalisation to show us characters whose thoughts and actions will be recognisable even to an audience that isn't familiar with the historical circumstances at hand. The emphasis in this narrative situation is on measure: historical realism avoids a spectacular evocation of the past that would draw attention to itself, but instead goes in for a relatively detached creation of the illusion of historical reality that easily allows readers to draw their own conclusions about past and present from the supposed 'truth' of what is shown. Lukács's insistence on realism as the only correct mode of representation for the past was accompanied by a requirement for authors to provide a Marxist interpretation of historical events and developments, but the postmodernist reaction against historical realism led by Linda Hutcheon (see, for example, her *Poetics of Postmodernism*) has pushed this ideological aspect into the background, probably because Hutcheon's 'historiographic metafiction' wanted to claim its own progressive potential. Stripped of its ideological load, historical realism became an ideal whipping boy because of its alleged simplicity and lack of literary invention.

With Pynchon's relocated epilogue, we have, at first sight, come full circle in terms of historical representation—not to the published novel's first historical chapter (the Egypt episode we have already mentioned), because the multiple focalisation there is already a decisive step away from convention, but rather to the original version of that chapter in Pynchon's short story 'Under the Rose' (1961). An apprentice (even boyish) tale about scheming secret agents, set against the background of the Fashoda crisis in 1898, the earlier story-version of the chapter does already contain a character, Bongo-Shaftsbury, who has an electric switch sewn into his skin and could thus undermine verisimilitude; but otherwise it displays all the hallmarks of historical realism as just described: brief instances of the characters' perspectives are repeatedly included in the presentation of their thoughts; the narrator is very much in control and avoids any showboating that would undercut his required detachment; and the plot offers a clear truth in that it foreshadows the possibility of an all-out war.

As we have suggested, the published novel's epilogue is also geared to historical realism, but, just as in the case of Bongo-Shaftsbury's electric switch, at least two (but see note 7 below) small yet important elements may well indicate that Pynchon is quite aware of the artificial normality of conventional historical representation to which he seems to be 'ironically' returning after all his fancy historiographic footwork—'ironically', in our reading, because the epilogue's relative clarity and simplicity expose that footwork as extravagant and perhaps somewhat hollow. Importantly, one of the elements we have just brought up even has a genetic dimension, which perhaps reinforces the significance of the decision to turn the typescript's 'June Disturbances' chapter into the novel's epilogue.

To begin with, the skipper who brings Stencil senior to Malta, Mehemet, has mythological proportions. Mehemet claims to '[belong] to the trade routes of the Middle Ages' (Pynchon 1961b, 408; Pynchon 1963, 459), and he tells a tale of the legendary Maltese sorceress Mara (a being with explicit similarities to the novel's V. figure) and of her role in breaking the Turkish siege of 1565. This tale at the outset of the novel's epilogue doesn't entirely break its realist mould, but it does foreground a kind of historiography that is much more majestic and convoluted than the coordinates of historical realism ordinarily allow. This aspect of the published novel's epilogue is already there in the typescript, but it does connect rather nicely with the work of the somewhat grandiose historians (James Frazer, Robert Graves and Henry Adams) who are explicitly mentioned in the introduction added to the Egypt chapter, thus creating another full circle, if you will, this time within the boundaries of the novel itself.

The other antirealist element in the epilogue consists of a set of eight small images of a hand with a pointing index finger (Pynchon 1963, 471–72). These manicules precede consecutive short descriptions of various discontented factions on Malta. Although this set of images threatens the realistic illusion created by the narrator, we do not read it as signalling Pynchon's forthright rejection of historical realism. Rather, given their sudden appearance and equally abrupt disappearance, we prefer to read the manicules as signalling Pynchon's awareness of the constructedness of what usually passes for historical verisimilitude—a tenuous illusion rather than the objective narrativisation of historical truth of the kind so admired and even prescribed by Lukács.

Interestingly, the manicules are not present in the typescript (see Pynchon 1961b, 424–25), and neither does the typescript provide an indication that they should be included in print. The manicules are also absent from the galleys, but they do appear in the advance reading copy of the novel. We have no evidence to date of who came up with the idea of inserting the manicules, but that doesn't prevent us from speculating about their presence. Having explicitly pondered (in the pages added to the Egypt chapter during the rewriting of *V.*) the force of the historical imagination, Pynchon may have wanted (or must at least have agreed, if it wasn't his own idea) to include the manicules even later in the composition process to reinforce his hint (through the mythological skipper) at the insufficiency of historical fictions that feign an allegiance to the facts of the past to get their own purported truth across to readers. As we have already suggested, the return to historical realism in the epilogue is ironic because it suggests the limits of 'Stencilization' as an extremely imaginative type of historiographic discourse, but Pynchon's sly practice of that realism at the end of the novel also suggests that he does not mean to offer it as the perfect alternative. Moving the 'June Disturbances' chapter to the end of the novel would then be ironic because Pynchon is not actually committed to an unqualified historical realism.

Taken together, in a chapter that otherwise avoids anything that might be disparaged today as postmodernist showboating, the mythological character of Mehemet and the manicules create what we would call an enhanced historical realism.[7] They reveal an author using the final pages of his historical novel to show that it doesn't take much to undo the objectivity the narrators of classical historical realism *seem* to practice. But far from entirely negating the historical truth on offer, Pynchon augments it with an insight into its relativity, thus perhaps reinforcing what we might call the powers of the historical imagination he has displayed earlier. Of course, it remains to be seen which historical truths the reader will want to take away from either form of historical evocation, but the way Pynchon relates them to each other in *V.* gives us a very young author in complete control of the genre he is performing.

Works Cited

Herman, Luc, and John M. Krafft (2023), *Becoming Pynchon: Genetic Narratology and V.* (Columbus: Ohio State University Press).

Hutcheon, Linda (1988), *A Poetics of Postmodernism: History, Theory, Fiction* (New York: Routledge).

Lukács, Georg [1937] (1962, 1983), *The Historical Novel*, trans. by Hannah and Stanley Mitchell (Lincoln, NE: University of Nebraska Press).

Pynchon, Thomas [1961a] (1984), 'Under the Rose', in: *Slow Learner* (Boston: Little, Brown), 99–137.

Pynchon, Thomas, (1961b), untitled draft of *V.*, Harry Ransom Humanities Research Center, The University of Texas at Austin, MS-03358: R14802.

Pynchon, Thomas (1963), *V.* (Philadelphia: Lippincott).

Pynchon, Thomas (1990), *Of a Fond Ghoul: Being a Correspondence between Corlies M. Smith and Thomas Pynchon* (New York: Blown Litter).

Pynchon, Thomas (2015), *The 'C' Section*, ed. by Andrew Boese (Phoenix, AZ: Optics Press).

---

7   Another subtle antirealist element in both typescript and published novel is the hint that V. (an avatar of the sorceress Mara or vice versa: see, for instance, Pynchon 1961b, 590, 412; Pynchon 1963, 388, 462) may have 'reach[ed] out' (Pynchon 1961b, 416; Pynchon 1963, 465) from Malta to sink the departing Sidney Stencil's ship with a waterspout (Pynchon 1961b, 450; Pynchon 1963, 492).

12. You Don't Get Scared of Monsters, You Get Scared for People: Creating Suspense across Versions in Stephen King's *IT*

Vincent Neyt

The world may view Stephen King as a horror novelist, but he regards himself as a suspense novelist. 'A suspense novel is basically a scare novel', he told an interviewer in 1979; 'I see the horror novel as only one room in a very large house, which is the suspense novel' (Underwood and Miller 1989, 91). Suspense, according to King, can be seen as 'diluted horror' (81): a horrific scene can amplify the readers' emotional state from 'tense' to 'terrified' by triggering deep-rooted fears or phobias in addition to their anxiety, hopes and fears for the characters involved. As to 'what makes a good horror story', King said in 1980:

> Character, I think. [...] I want you to feel that the characters are people that you care about, that they are real, and that they are doing real things. You must feel that the characters are deep. And I don't mean deep in the sense that they have a lot of deep thoughts. They must have thickness. Do they stand off the page? Then the writer puts them into a position where they can't get out. You don't get scared of monsters; you get scared for people. (79)

In this essay, I will explore this central position assigned by King to the characters he places in harm's way.

The study of suspense traditionally has two main focuses: the narrative that creates suspense, and the reader, viewer or listener who experiences it (Bálint 2020). I propose to widen the text-oriented focus to include a genetic approach, to study the drafts of such captivating texts. Authors of suspense-driven narratives revise their work with the goal of enhancing the reader's experience in suspenseful episodes or of strengthening the reader's engagement with the narrative, resulting in a more intense overall experience. King has referred to the craft of rewriting as 'a nuts-and-bolts kind of operation', like 'adjusting the carburetor [...] to make it right' (Underwood and Miller 1989, 169). His valuable insights into the mechanics of suspense shine through in the adjustments he makes 'under the hood'.

From *On Writing*, his memoir of the craft, it becomes clear that King is an intuitive writer who requires minimal preparation to begin a new work. He starts from what he calls a 'situation', which usually arises in the form of a 'what if' question (King 2012, 190). The situation that King explored in his epic novel *IT* (1986), the test case of this genetic analysis, can be formulated in its simplest form as: 'what if a group of children came face to face with a monster at the age of eleven, and were then forced to face that same monster again as adults?'

After the 'what if' question, King explains, 'the characters—always flat and unfeatured, to begin with—come next. Once these things are fixed in my mind, I begin to narrate' (ibid.). From here, he moves forward solely on instinct. The plan is to put the characters in a predicament and watch them try to work themselves free (189) and he goes about this without any outlining or plotting beforehand. 'For a suspense novelist', King adds,

> this is a great thing. [...] [I]f I'm not able to guess with any accuracy how the damned thing is going to turn out, even with my inside knowledge of coming events, I can be pretty sure of keeping the reader in a state of page-turning anxiety. (King 2012, 190)

In the eighties, King imposed a high tempo of writing on himself. Six pages a day, no more, no less (Underwood and Miller 1989, 75), with no rereading or revising of what was written the day before, *ever* moving the story forward until it's complete. This is necessary 'to keep up with my original enthusiasm and at the same time outrun the self-doubt that's always waiting to settle in' (King 2012, 249). For each work, King habitually does 'two drafts and a polish' (248). In this polish (which sometimes becomes a third draft), he is mainly concerned with language, with giving the work a unified stylistic feel.

King wrote three drafts of *IT* between 1980 and 1986: the first on a typewriter, the second and third on a personal computer.[1] The original typescript of the first draft is missing, but there are photocopies. The second draft, however, is nowhere to be found. Two printouts of the third draft are kept at King's archive. Because of the missing link in the dossier, it's impossible to tell whether the variants between the first and third drafts entered the text at the second or third draft stage. So, as a shorthand, I will speak of changes in 'the second/third draft', taking the two together out of necessity. Chuck Verrill, King's editor, gave his editorial feedback both on the first draft and the third (after King had submitted it for publication in early 1986). Verrill primarily raised issues in chronology and continuity, suggesting cuts and revisions regarding language and overall pace. On his set of proof pages, King made only cosmetic changes.

In the following two sections, I present a concise overview of relevant methodological publications on suspense theory and the narratological concepts of pace, characterisation and focalisation. The section 'Revising *IT* for Suspense' describes four patterns of revision discovered in King's work on *IT* across versions, and the section 'Meeting Pennywise' combines these patterns in the analysis of a passage from the first chapter of the novel.

1. Suspense Theory

From studies in the cognitive (reader-based) approach (Zillman 1980; Gerrig and Allbritton 1990; Vorderer et al. 1996; Beecher 2007; Smuts 2008; Hakemulder et al. 2017) the consensus has arisen that an equivalent-to-reality representation of events in a narrative can trigger suspense, which is a pleasurable experience that has an emotional component (interest, hope, fear, thrill, anxiety, restlessness, empathy, sympathy) and a cognitive component (uncertainty, anticipation, prospection, gap-filling, the dynamic calculation of possible outcomes and the probability of these competing scenarios). Without the emotional component, there can be no suspense.

---

[1] The drafts and proofs mentioned are stored at Stephen King's personal archive in Bangor, Maine. In what follows, I mainly quote from the first draft (King 1981).

Foundational to the text-oriented approach in suspense theory is the work of Meir Sternberg (Sternberg 1978; 2003a; 2003b). He discerns three 'universals of narrative', three narrative techniques that produce enjoyment in readers: suspense, curiosity and surprise. Suspense and curiosity both derive from a lack of information, drawing the reader's attention forward (Sternberg 1978, 65). They differ in that suspense is the emotion experienced with regard to temporary gaps in story events situated in what Sternberg calls the 'narrative future', and curiosity is the emotion with regard to events from the 'narrative past' that have not yet been related in the narrative (65). A third category is surprise, where a hidden gap is opened and the reader discovers retrospectively, at the point of closure, that there was a gap or an ambiguity (244). The three lines of narrative interest in Sternberg's model can occur simultaneously, and usually do, on all textual levels.

Brewer and Lichtenstein based their influential 'structural-affect theory of stories' on Sternberg's universals. They turned suspense, curiosity, and surprise into three separate 'discourse structures' that account for the 'entertainment force' of stories, and they state that these structures will produce three different affect curves in readers (Brewer and Lichtenstein 1982).

The 'suspense discourse organisation' must contain an initiating event, early in the narrative text, an event which could lead to significant consequences (either good or bad) for a character. The initiating event causes the reader to become concerned about the consequences for the relevant character and this produces suspense, which is later resolved by the outcome event. Between the initiating event and the outcome event, there is 'additional discourse material', or 'outcome delay' (what Sternberg calls 'retardation'), to encourage the build-up of the suspense. Chronological narration is prevalent, with the exception of the technique of foreshadowing (482). In addition to the narrative-spanning suspense and resolution structure, there are 'mini' suspense and resolution episodes along the way, which, in the case of a long narrative, results in an affect curve that makes 'a saw-toothed climb towards a climax' (Brewer 1996, 116).

The initiating event is important in engaging the reader. The protagonist must by this point be characterised as likable and good and the event itself must have a considerable impact on both protagonist and reader. As a result, the reader will empathise (feel with the character) or sympathise (feel for the character) and become concerned, which is experienced as a 'clash of hope and fear' (Sternberg 1978, 65).

Stephen King's *IT* adheres to the macro-organisation of Brewer and Lichtenstein's 'suspense discourse structure'. In the horror genre, suspense is the dominant line of narrative interest, with most stories moving chronologically towards a final confrontation between the protagonist and the monster. Curiosity comes into play when, in order to successfully defeat the monster, the protagonist must first discover its true nature, where it came from, and how it can be killed.

Noël Carroll states that what drives readers forward is their desire to find answers: an early scene will raise a question which is then answered in a later scene, which he calls 'erotetic narration' (Carroll 1990, 130). Suspense, in his view, 'is generated as an emotional concomitant of a narrative question that has been raised by earlier scenes and events in a story', a question that must have only 'two possible, opposed answers which have specific ratings in terms of morality and probability' (137). The suspense is highest when the morally just outcome is the least likely (138). It can easily be seen, Carroll concludes, how horror narratives trigger suspense in readers. Monsters are irredeemably evil, are generally immensely powerful and often operate in secret. Almost from the onset the odds are stacked heavily against the human protagonist(s) in the inevitable confrontation, and 'the situation is ripe for suspense' (139). Horror narratives typically will spend more time on establishing the improbability of the humans being successful against the monster than on establishing the monster's evilness (142), suggesting that improbability—not morality—is the more important factor in suspense creation.

Suspense has also been studied at the smallest textual level. Richard Gerrig (Gerrig 1996) describes an experiment on triggering suspense through a single sentence. From the results he distils two categories that proved successful. First, sentences that suggest a lack of knowledge, either on the part of the narration, the character, or the reader, are suspenseful because they activate the problem-solving cognitive mechanism (99). A second category is 'classic suspense schemas' (98). Concepts that recurred in the suspenseful sentences were danger, darkness, potential physical harm, doors, fear and despair. Words associated with these concepts, Gerrig believes, evoke 'prototypical scenes in which readers are likely to have experienced suspense in the past' (98). This dovetails nicely with the results of Mark Algee-Hewitt's project 'Suspense: Language, Narrative, Affect' at the Stanford Literary Lab, which traced suspense at the word level. They found that 'suspenseful passages were characterised by words relating to the imagination (e.g., "thought"), the senses ("saw"), and movement ("struggled") and topics such as "assault", "guns", "crime", and "dramatic weather"' (Ueda 2016). The presence of words that convey how things appear to be rather than how they really are, such as 'seemed', 'perceived', or 'observed', generate 'epistemological uncertainty', which translates into suspense (Ueda 2016).

2. Suspense and Narratology

In view of the structuralist division of the study of narrative texts into three levels, story, narrative and narration (Herman and Vervaeck 2019, 43), it is apparent from the preceding research that suspense is triggered by elements at all levels. An initiating story event puts the protagonist in harm's way and a series of discovery and confrontation events leads to a climactic event in which good triumphs over evil against great odds. Mieke Bal states that suspense is mainly evoked in readers on the level of the narrative; by how story material is manipulated into a narrative sequence (Bal 2009, 76). It is not so much the action of the confrontation that is suspenseful, but the build-up to the action (the outcome delay), and this is where the manipulations occur. A good deal is also achieved through the narration itself, in the actual phrasing, as the studies on suspense at the smallest textual level have shown.

Pace

In the case of the narrative aspect of time, the manipulation lies in the speed with which the narrator goes through the story events, in the text's 'pace' or 'pacing'. Brian Gingrich gives the most comprehensive definition of the concept in his PhD dissertation 'The Pace of Modern Fiction': 'large-forward-rhythmic-shifting-dynamic-temporal narrative movement' (Gingrich 2018, 6). Pace is akin to rhythm (a pattern of varying units of narrative speed), but not identical to it: 'what distinguishes pace from rhythm in general is that it moves forward toward senses of endings (projected moments of closure, climax, or nonnarratable resolution)' (9).

In terms of the relationship between the duration of the narrative (reading time) and the duration of the narrated events (story time), one would expect the action in confrontations to be narrated in scenic mode, and the reading time in the suspenseful build-up to these confrontations to be longer than the story time, either by narrating a scene in slow-down, 'a sort of scene in slow motion' (Genette 1980, 95), or by retarding a scene by inserting descriptive pauses—two options that are often hard to distinguish from each other. Gérard Genette states that pauses in scenes can be 'concealed' by presenting them through the perception of a character (107): a room is described as a character sees it. Story time does not stop but runs on as the character is looking around. Alfonso de Toro proposes to distinguish between 'static descriptions', given by the narrator, interrupting the sequence of narrated events; and 'dynamic descriptions', given by a character, which only insignificantly affect the narrative sequence in its flow (de Toro 2011, 133).

Karin Kukkonen provides an additional approach to the dynamics of time in narrative texts with her notions of 'plot speed', 'storyworld speed' and 'discourse speed' (Kukkonen 2020). Two episodes might be narrated in the same scenic mode; for instance, a tranquil conversation scene transitioning suddenly into a high-speed car-chase scene, but the reader will experience this transition as an acceleration, purely on the basis of verbs like 'rushing', 'running', 'chasing' and so on. For this experience of the reader that 'the novel is speeding up', Kukkonen uses the term 'storyworld speed'. Readers can have a similar experience of acceleration when a page-filling paragraph with long sentences and difficult words is followed by a series of simple one-sentence paragraphs, which is a change in 'discourse speed', defined as: 'readers' sense of how swiftly they get through a stretch of narrative in relation to its perceived length in terms of mediation' (75). 'Plot speed' has to do with readers' expectations or predictions. Changes in plot speed arise when events 'make a projected outcome more likely (acceleration) or less likely (deceleration)' (77).

Characterisation

Relevant to suspense are also the narratological aspects of characterisation and focalisation. Fotis Jannidis defines characterisation as 'the process of ascribing properties to names which results in agents having these properties in the storyworld' (Jannidis 2013, paragraph 3). A character's traits can be described directly by the narrator; the reader can indirectly deduce them from the character's actions, discourse and other metonymic elements; or characterisation can be done through analogy (Rimmon-Kenan 2002, 59–70). Philippe Hamon distinguishes four different principles that work together in the dynamic process of constructing a character throughout a narrative text. The first presentation of a character is typically followed by: the continuous repetition of its most relevant traits; an accumulation of traits that together form a whole; relations to other characters, in the form of similarities and contrasts; and transformations that a character undergoes on the level of its traits (Hamon 1977, 128).

The process is equally dynamic from the reader's perspective. When experiencing the representation of a character in a narrative, Ralf Schneider states, readers dynamically form (and update) a mental model of that character, a process that is 'a complex interaction of what the text says about the characters and of what the reader knows about the world in general, specifically about people and, yet more specifically, about "people" in literature' (Schneider 2001, 608). The model is fed bottom-up from the text and top-down from the reader's knowledge. When readers first meet a character, they may form a mental model of it based on categorisation (when they recognise it as a stock character or stereotype) or a personalised model, which 'is constructed more laboriously in the bottom-up mode, and the result will be a more complex structure that is kept "open" for a longer time to allow for the integration of further, potentially conflicting information' (Schneider 2013, 123). Categorised models may transition into personalised models (which Schneider calls 'individuation'), and the opposite transition is possible as well ('de-personalisation'). In Schneider's analysis, only characters in the personalised category can trigger the emotions in readers that are necessary for them to experience suspense (124).

Focalisation

Focalisation, according to Mieke Bal, is the storyteller's most effective tool in creating suspense: the manipulation of the information we receive by restricting it to the perception and cognitive functions of particular characters at particular times (Bal 2009, 76). Despite extensive critical attention (Genette 1980; Jahn 1996; Fludernik 1996; Bal 2009; Schmid 2010; Niederhoff 2011), focalisation has remained a 'complex and elusive' phenomenon of narrative texts (Niederhoff 2011, paragraph 18). In the combination of an extradiegetic narrator with an internal focaliser[2] for instance (as is the case predominantly in *IT*), statements that are not explicitly linked by the narrator to the focalising character's perception, such as 'the house was hidden behind a tree', are ambiguous as to whether the perceiving agent is external to the storyworld (the narrator) or internal to it (the focalising character). This uncertainty can be exploited to generate tension.

3. Revising *IT* for Suspense: Four Patterns

Most striking in King's revision campaigns of *IT* is that he expanded the first half of the book. He added more detail to the suspense scenes in the opening chapters, the amount of added text gradually decreasing as he approached the midway point.[3] The scenes in which there is little or no tension in the first half of the novel were similarly lengthened. He saw less need for expansion in the second half of the book; merely streamlining the scenes by revising for style and internal consistency.

---

2   Genette, who coined the term 'focalisation' (1980, 189), objected to Mieke Bal's use of the term 'focaliser' (meaning the 'agent that sees' in a given focalisation) with regard to a character in the storyworld (Bal 2009, 149) on the grounds that only a narrator can narrow and widen the focus, 'to talk about characters as focalisers is to confuse focalisation and perception' (Niederhoff 2011, paragraph 16). However, the term 'focaliser' has been adopted in works of narrative theory (eg. Rimmon-Kenan 2002, 74; Herman and Vervaeck 2019, 78) and I will also use it in this essay.

3   The first such scene, when George Denbrough faces his fears to fetch something from the cellar, is 40% longer in its published form than in the first draft. That percentage steadily decreases in the suspenseful scenes that follow (although there are a few outliers along the way). From chapter 13 onwards (the halfway point), most suspenseful scenes remain more or less equal in length or are reduced by a few percentage points.

Overall, King added almost no story events in his rewrite of the first half; the additions are mainly in dialogue and character descriptions. In my opinion, as a mechanic looking under the hood of his first draft text, King believed the key to sustaining his readers' engagement in such a long novel would depend on the characterisation of its protagonists: lowering the pace of the chapters by giving more attention to the physicality, the character traits, the direct speech and the thoughts and emotions of these 'paper people'.

The suspense structure of the novel was already firmly in place in the first draft. King made no changes to the overall suspense and resolution curve, nor to the tempo with which the pendulum swings between low tension and high tension; between confrontations and breather episodes; between scenes and summaries.

On the level of the suspenseful scene, however, particularly the early ones that were expanded, there are interesting patterns to be discerned in the revisions.[4] Added text, of course, extends the reading time, sustaining the tension longer before the suspense is resolved. To create this extra length, the majority of King's additions deal with how the focaliser experiences the danger. In the rest of this section, I will argue this in more detail.

Sensory Impressions

To the narration of story events King added (or expanded) the character's sensory impressions. He added indications of internal focalisation to neutrally narrated descriptions of danger by presenting them through the perception of the focalising character. '[The clown's] face was deeply lined' (King 1981, 156), for instance, becomes 'Ben could see the clown's face clearly. It was deeply lined' (King 1986, 214). 'The house, brooding and silent, drew closer' (King 1981, 225) becomes 'It did not seem as if his feet were moving; instead the house itself, brooding and silent, seemed to draw closer to where he stood' (King 1986, 311). In its

---

4   In my working definition, a 'suspenseful scene' starts when protagonists feel themselves to be in danger (or when the narrator indicates that there is danger), either because the monster is near or because there is a real-world danger (e.g., from the bully Henry Bowers or from Beverly Marsh's abusive father). The scene ends when the character is no longer in danger (or dead).

first draft state, this sentence contains the troubling description of an unnatural occurrence (a house drawing closer), and in its revised state the same thing is presented through the consciousness of a frightened eleven-year-old boy. King's addition of the word 'seemed' (twice) confirms Algee-Hewitt's remarks that verbs that relay how things appear can be used to generate epistemological uncertainty, leading to increased suspense.

Many such small changes occur throughout King's revision campaigns of the suspense scenes in the first half of the book. To make the scenes more effective and to increase the reader's engagement with the events, King placed the reader inside the body of the character in the dangerous situation, more so than in the first draft. Expanding the text with simple phrases pertaining to the sensory experience of the protagonist turns static descriptions to dynamic and adds diegetic outcome delay (on the micro-level) that slows down readers (by lowering the discourse speed) without giving them the impression that the action is being halted for description.

King regularly inserted details of the smells, sounds and tactile sensations that the protagonists experience in their predicament. In a scene where It terrorises Bill and Richie by making the pages of a photo album turn on their own, King revised 'When [Bill] stopped turning [the pages], they turned themselves' (King 1981, 251) to 'He gave up after a minute, but the pages did not. They turned themselves, flipping slowly but steadily, with big deliberate riffling sounds' (King 1986, 336). Further on, King added: 'The inside of Richie's mouth suddenly felt as dry as dust and as smooth as glass' (337).

Similar in nature are King's edits in the episode where young Eddie Kaspbrak is chased by the monster in the guise of a leper. The differences between the first draft and the published text are visualised in the following quote with omitted text struck through and added text in superscript:

> Eddie raced for his bike. It was the same race as before, only ~~now~~ it ^now^ had the quality of a nightmare, where you can only move with ^the most^ agonizing slowness no matter how hard you try to go fast…and ^in those dreams^ ^didn't^ you ~~can~~ ^always^ hear ^or feel^ something, some It, gaining on you.? ^Didn't you always smell Its stinking breath, as Eddie was smelling it now?^ (King 1981, 229; King 1986, 314)

As suggested here by the additions of 'feel' and 'smell', King devoted conscious attention to the sensory experience of the focaliser across versions. The revision also lengthens reading time and story time, while giving the reader no information on the threat that lies behind the boy as he runs for his life.

Inner Life

Complementary to the focus on sensory experiences (transporting the reader into the character's body), in his second/third draft King chiefly expanded these suspense scenes by adding the protagonist's inner life, transporting the reader into the character's conscious mind.[5] The previous example can also serve as an illustration here. In the next paragraph the narrator informs us that, for a moment, Eddie felt 'a wild hope' that he was indeed having a nightmare, which clarifies that the narrator was expressing Eddie's thought that his race had the quality of a nightmare, complete with sounds and smells. The revision from 'you can always hear something' to 'didn't you always hear or feel something' (and the subsequent repetition of 'didn't you always') turn the passage into more of a direct transcription of Eddie's thoughts than narration by an external narrator.

King made heavy use of this technique in his revision of the first section of chapter 3, 'Six Phone Calls', in which Patty Uris tries to fight off panic when she realises that her husband Stan has locked himself in the bathroom and doesn't answer her calls. The suspenseful scene follows the classic schema of 'the horror that lies behind the closed door'. King expanded the text by 32% from its first draft form, slowing down the pace primarily by diving deeper into Patty's panicked mind, as in this passage:

> Now she could remember dropping the beer can outside the bathroom door and pelting headlong back down the stairs, ~~but she could only remember it vaguely.~~ *thinking vaguely: This is all a mistake of some kind and we'll laugh about it later. He filled up the tub and then remembered he didn't have cigarettes and went out to get them before he took his clothes off –*
>
> Yes. Only he had already locked the bathroom door from the inside and because it was too much of a bother to unlock it again he had simply opened the window over the tub and gone down the side of the house like a fly crawling down a wall. Sure, of course, sure— (King 1981, 26; King 1986, 56; italics are King's)

---

5   By 'inner life' I mean the information the narrator supplies on the focalising character's emotions, cognitive functions, imagination and psychology.

After having fetched a spare key, Patty forces herself to walk, not run, back to the bathroom to stave off panic, because, she thought, 'running made the panic want to come back' (57). In his second/third draft, King extended this paragraph considerably by adding:

> Also, if she just walked, maybe nothing would be wrong. Or, if there was something wrong, God could look down, see she was just walking, and think: *Oh, good—pulled a hell of a boner, but I've got time to take it all back.* (ibid.)

Having arrived at the door with the key, Patty is afraid to use it because it is 'somehow too final' (58). King added: 'If God hadn't taken it back by the time she used the key, then He never would. The age of miracles, after all, was past' (ibid.). The insertions more accurately evoke the story time involved in Patty's walk back upstairs and hesitation at the door. The choice to expand this classic suspense scenario with Patty's inner life instead of with new minor events, descriptions of setting or character physicality reveals King's poetics on how best to amplify the tension.

Feeding Patty's internal panic throughout the scene is an external sound coming from behind the bathroom door—the sound of dripping water: 'Plink...pause. Plink...pause. Plink...pause' (55). The sound motif, already present in the first draft, was further expanded. When Patty is standing by the phone, thinking about who to call and what to say, King replaced 'someone had to know that Stan didn't answer, because he was unconscious, or dead. *Someone* had to help her. Maybe it wasn't too late yet' (King 1981, 26), rational considerations on Patty's part, with '[how did you tell someone] that the steady sound of the water dripping into the tub was killing her heart? *Someone* had to help her' (King 1986, 57). The incessant drip of the faucet leaves no room in her mind for rationality or hope of a good outcome.

In the climax of the scene, King revised the description of Stan's body in the bathtub from static to dynamic, presenting it through Patty's perception, and added a concluding repetition of the sound motif. He expanded 'Patty Uris at last found her voice, and staring into her husband's dead and sparkling eyes, she began to scream' (King 1981, 28) to:

> Another drop fell into the tub.
> *Plink.*
> That did it. Patty Uris at last found her voice. Staring into her husband's dead and sparkling eyes, she began to scream. (King 1986, 59)

The change in discourse speed (from one compound sentence to five short sentences spread over three paragraphs) is meant to evoke the story time of the final drop falling and unravelling Patty's composure completely.

In summary, King chose to heighten the tension of this scene by amplifying Patty's inner life and the sound dynamics between her shouts to her husband and the excruciating 'plink...pause...' which is the only reply she receives.

Character Traits

A third way in which King lowered the pace of suspenseful scenes was by adding repetitions of character traits of the protagonists. After having intuitively discovered the traits of the seven protagonists while writing his first draft, King used all subsequent stages of revision to paint the characters with a thicker brush. He did so most extensively in the low-tension episodes, but this pattern of revision is also present in high-tension scenes.

Richie Tozier was the character that underwent the most expansive rewrite, with a significant amount of new text devoted to him in the second/third draft. The eleven-year-old Richie loves doing comical voices and talking about rock 'n' roll music. In the first draft, young Richie grew up to be a lawyer who no longer did impressions. King's most significant alteration to a character in the novel was transforming adult Richie from a lawyer into a radio deejay who had gained success and fame by performing voice impressions between songs.

King inserted references to these character traits into several of the suspense scenes in which Richie is the focaliser. In the scene where Richie is attacked by It in the guise of a giant plastic statue of Paul Bunyan (a landmark in the town of Derry), King slows down a sentence containing straight-forward action:

> ~~There was another earth-shaking thud, seemingly right at his heels, as Paul Bunyan's~~ The earth shook. Richie's upper and lower teeth rattled against each other like china plates in an earthquake. He did not have to look to know that Paul's axe had buried itself ~~hilt-deep~~ haft-deep in the ~~earth.~~ sidewalk inches behind his feet.
> Madly, in his mind, he heard the Dovells: *Oh the kids in Bristol are sharp as a pistol When they do the Bristol Stomp....*

(King 1981, 504; King 1986, 586)

Again, the revisions reposition the narrator's chosen perspective from an external to one much more internal to the focaliser, adding a sound (teeth rattling like china plates) and sensory verbs (look, heard). The result—which shares only a few words with the text of the first draft—gives more detail about how Richie experienced the danger in body and mind. The progression of the action is halted in the middle of a high-tension confrontation for twenty-four words of direct characterisation of Richie's inner life as a young music aficionado.

Although the extra length undeniably lowers the discourse speed of an actional passage (during which the reader will be anxious to find out what happens next), the storyworld speed is still high (because of the words 'shook', 'rattled', 'earthquake', 'buried', 'madly' and 'Stomp'). Adding references to popular culture is another revision pattern in the second/third draft of IT, and although the other children also like rock 'n' roll music, King singled it out as a distinguishing trait for Richie because of the change from lawyer to deejay.

Dialogue

Lastly, King lowered the pace of the suspense scenes in the first half of the novel by inserting more dialogue, notably by putting more words into the mouth of Pennywise the Dancing Clown. As the antagonist, Pennywise is always the focalised object, never the focaliser; it is only at the beginning of chapter 21 that we are taken inside the mind of the monster for the first time. In the many scenes that build up to that moment, King worked on his villain by expanding the external characteristics only, and the increase in dialogue is the most notable revision pattern. When Pennywise tries to lure young Ben Hanscom towards him, for instance, King's modifications in the speech contain a repetition of one of Ben's character traits, his love of books:

> *You'll like it here, Ben*, the clown ~~said, and now~~ said. Now it was close enough so ~~that~~ Ben could hear the *clud-clud* sound ~~of~~ its funny shoes ~~on~~ made as they advanced over the uneven ice. *You'll like* ~~it, yes, there are all sorts of things to be here; so~~ it here, I promise, all the boys and girls I meet like it here because it's like Pleasure Island in Pinocchio and Never-Never Land in Peter Pan; they never have to grow up and that's what all the kiddies want! So come on! See the sights, *have a balloon,* ~~come with me, run away with the circus,~~ *feed the elephants,* ~~see the world, Ben, oh, Ben,~~ ride the Chute-the-Chutes! Oh you'll like it and oh Ben *how you'll float*—(King 1981, 155; King 1986, 213)

Similarly, when Pennywise menacingly invites Richie Tozier to return to the sewers to seek him out, he reminds Richie of his childhood fear of the movie 'The Crawling Eye': 'We've got the Eye down here, Richie... We've got the Crawling Eye down here' (King 1981, 509), which King revised to resemble a radio advert:

> We've got the eye down here, Richie... you hear me? The one that crawls. If you don't want to fly, don't wanna say goodbye, you come on down under this here town and give a great big hi to one great big eye! (King 1986, 591)

4. Meeting Pennywise: Combining the Four Patterns of Revision

The changes made across versions in the first physical description of Pennywise, in the novel's opening chapter, illustrate many of the patterns of how King revised for suspense. The chapter is focalised by George Denbrough, an innocent, vulnerable and likable six-year-old boy whose older brother Bill is the novel's protagonist. George's violent murder by Pennywise is the initiating event (cf. Brewer and Lichtenstein) that sets up the narrative-spanning suspense arc: the first chapter introduces and endears Bill and George to readers and after George is killed readers instinctively know that what this novel is heading towards is a confrontation between Bill and Pennywise.

With the importance of the impact of this first atrocious murder in mind, King meticulously rewrote the chapter, increasing its length by a quarter, thus lowering the pace.[6] The character of George Denbrough is developed further (his fears about going into the cellar, his relationship with his brother, his love of movies and television); additional insights into Bill's character are gleaned indirectly through Georgie's perspective; the playful dialogue between the brothers is enriched possibly with the intention of enhancing the reader's emotional reaction to George's subsequent death; and foreshadowing references were added to the events of the book's climax (necessary because of King's intuitive first

---

6   The chapter contains 4279 words in first draft, and 5426 in its published form. King retained 3068 words of the first draft verbatim and added or changed 2358 words. 57% of the chapter in second/third draft form equals the first draft, and 43% of it was revised.

draft writing practice). Small adjustments are made throughout from external to internal focalisation, such as the change from '[George] put on speed, and did almost in fact catch the boat' (King 1981, 8) to '[George] put on speed, and for a moment he thought he would catch the boat' (King 1986, 12).

After George's paper boat has just disappeared into a stormdrain, he hears a voice speak his name. He peers inside:

~~Barely visible in the shadowy hole, he could see a clown. He~~ There was a clown in the stormdrain. The light in there was far from good, but it was good enough so that George Denbrough was sure of what he was seeing. It was a clown, like in the circus or on TV. In fact he looked ~~a bit~~ like ~~Bozo, who had been on TV until last year; his~~ a cross between Bozo and Clarabell, who talked by honking his (or was it her?—George was never really sure of the gender) horn on Howdy Doody Saturday mornings—Buffalo Bob was just about the only one who could understand Clarabell, and that always cracked George up. The face of the clown in the stormdrain was white, there were funny tufts of red hair on either side of his bald head, and there was a big clown-smile painted over his mouth. If George had been inhabiting a later year, he would have surely thought of Ronald McDonald before Bozo or Clarabell. ¶7 He held a bunch of balloons like gorgeous ripe fruit in one hand. ¶ In the other he held George's boat. (King 1981, 9; King 1986, 13)

This descriptive paragraph has been quite heavily extended, from 72 to 175 words. The word 'clown' has been moved to the front in a much simpler sentence, suggesting that King found this phrasing to be more effective as the slap in the readers' face that initiates the tension in the scene. King added three repetitions of the word 'clown' in the paragraph. The observation that it was dark inside the hole, needed for verisimilitude, is moved, and expanded along the lines of the revision patterns discussed above.

The change from a casual mention of Bozo to three references from popular culture (Bozo, Clarabell and Ronald McDonald) is remarkable. In the first draft the scenic mode is not interrupted: it would only take George a few seconds to think of Bozo as he is making sense of what he is seeing. But in its rewritten form, the narrator distinctly pauses the scene when he chooses to digress into George's thoughts on Clarabell's gender and on Buffalo Bob. It is unclear whether George is thinking all of this as he is looking into the drain or if the narrator pauses here

---

7   The '¶' symbols here and after the next sentence signify that King added paragraph breaks there in his second/third draft.

for a flashback. Of note is that King again opted to insert the focalising character's inner life to slow down a high-tension passage.

The straightforwardly descriptive sentence ('funny tufts of hair' and 'a big clown smile') is left largely unaltered, and it is followed by an addition in which the narrator suggests that Ronald McDonald is a closer resemblance than Bozo or Clarabell. To do so, the narrator is forced to give up the internal focalisation, adding 'If George had been inhabiting a later year', because the mascot for McDonalds was only introduced in 1963 and this scene is situated in 1957. Intriguingly, by giving up the internal focalisation in this addition, King breaks the empathic link between George and the reader by temporarily letting the narrator focalise a part of the paragraph, which is at odds with the revision patterns described above.[8]

The paragraph in its revised form contains no extra information about Pennywise's appearance. The changes mainly add to the characterisation of George, a typical child of 1950s America who watches TV. As readers we realise, one additional time, how young and innocent he is, and how great the danger is that he finds himself in now. Meanwhile, the pressing questions that readers have, at this point, about the nature and the intentions of the clown creature are purposefully left unanswered.

King turned a medium-sized descriptive paragraph into a long, lulling read that is dominated by a digression into George's thoughts about *The Howdy Doody* show, slowing down the discourse speed, which then accelerates again in the two short one-sentence paragraphs that follow. The one-sentence paragraphs raise the tension, slapping readers awake with two new disturbing facts: Pennywise is holding a bunch of balloons in one hand, and George's boat in the other. The balloons become a distinguishing trait for Pennywise throughout the novel.

5. Conclusion

Stephen King's intuitive and fast-paced writing practice, in the case of *IT*, resulted in a first draft text that is likewise fast-paced. During the

---

[8] I can only speculate about the intended effect of this addition by King. Upon rewriting, King might have wanted to include a more recent (and current, at the time of publication) reference to popular culture; the addition might have been meant as criticism of the fast-food chain; or King might have decided that Pennywise most closely resembled Ronald McDonald.

revision process, he made the necessary adjustments to align the text with his views on creating optimal suspense. The genetic dossier shows that only minimal alterations were required to the story events or their sequencing, but that King increased the length of the suspenseful scenes in the first half of the novel (albeit to a lesser extent as the narrative progresses).

There are clear patterns in the revisions (in both modified and added text), and they are fully in line with King's statement that 'you don't get scared of monsters, you get scared for people'. In King's view, it is the readers' connection with the protagonist in body and mind that grabs them and keeps them engaged. If its place in the narrative sequence allows it, a scene that puts a character in danger can be made more suspenseful by immersing readers in what the protagonist is thinking, feeling and sensing. Such elements delay the outcome of the episode in a way that does not feel digressive or retardatory—on the contrary, it strengthens the reader's empathy for the character, which also has a favourable effect on sustaining interest to the end.

The added repetitions of already established character traits show that even in suspense scenes King worked on what he called the 'thickness' of his characters (as quoted above). In a sense, those characters undergo a process of what Schneider called 'individuation' across versions. The unnaturalness and grotesqueness of the monster is most effectively conveyed to the reader if it is mediated internally through the perception and the bodily experiences of the protagonists rather than described by the narrator directly. Interestingly, most of the alterations made to the presentation of Pennywise mainly contribute to the characterisation of the person in danger. The additions that Pennywise speaks of Ben's love of books, or that Richie is a radio deejay, for instance, have the effect that those characters (and readers along with them) realise the monster's god-like knowledge and powers and, consequently, that their odds of besting the creature are very low indeed.

As King undertook the 'nuts-and-bolts operation' of rewriting his first draft of *IT*, he saw many opportunities for small edits that would put his readers more directly in touch with the harrowing experiences of his protagonists, to access not their fear of the monster but their concern for the people in danger.

Works Cited

Bal, Mieke (2009), *Narratology: Introduction to the Theory of Narrative*, 3rd edition (Toronto: University of Toronto Press).

Bálint, Katalin E. (2020), 'Suspense', in: *The International Encyclopedia of Media Psychology*, ed. by Jan Van den Bulck (Hoboken, NJ: John Wiley & Sons, Inc). https://doi.org/10.1002/9781119011071.iemp0178.

Beecher, Donald (2007), 'Suspense', *Philosophy and Literature*, 31.2: 255–79.

Brewer, W.F. (1996), 'The Nature of Narrative Suspense and the Problem of Rereading', in: *Suspense: Conceptualizations, Theoretical Analyses, and Empirical Explorations*, ed. by Peter Vorderer et al. (Mahwah, NJ: Erlbaum), 107–27.

Brewer, W.F., and E.H. Lichtenstein (1982), 'Stories Are to Entertain: A Structural-Affect Theory of Stories', *Journal of Pragmatics*, 6.5–6: 473–86.

Carroll, Noël (1990), *The Philosophy of Horror or Paradoxes of the Heart* (New York: Routledge).

de Toro, Alfonso (2011), 'Time Structure in the Contemporary Novel', in: *Time: From Concept to Narrative Construct: A Reader*, ed. by Jan Christoph Meister and Wilhelm Schernus (Berlin: De Gruyter), 109–42.

Fludernik, Monika (1996), *Towards a 'Natural' Narratology* (London and New York: Routledge).

Genette, Gérard (1980), *Narrative Discourse*, trans. by Jane E. Lewin (Ithaca, NY: Cornell University Press).

Gerrig, Richard, and David W. Allbritton (1990), 'The Construction of Literary Character: A View from Cognitive Psychology', *Style*, 24.3: 380–91.

Gerrig, Richard J. (1996), 'The Resiliency of Suspense', in: *Suspense: Conceptualizations, Theoretical Analyses, and Empirical Explorations*, ed. by Peter Vorderer et al. (Mahwah, NJ: Erlbaum), 93–106.

Gingrich, Brian (2018), *The Pace of Modern Fiction: A History of Narrative Movement in Modernity* (Princeton, NJ: Princeton University Press). http://arks.princeton.edu/ark:/88435/dsp012f75rb738.

Hakemulder, Frank, Moniek M. Kuijpers, Ed S. Tan, Katalin Bálint, and Minura M. Doicaru (2017), *Narrative Absorption* (Amsterdam: John Benjamins Publishing).

Hamon, Philippe (1977), 'Pour un Statut Sémiologique du Personage', in: *Poétique du Récit*, ed. by Roland Barthes et al. (Paris: Seuil), 115–80.

Herman, Luc, and Bart Vervaeck (2019), *Handbook of Narrative Analysis*, 2nd edition (Lincoln, NE: University of Nebraska Press).

Jahn, Manfred (1996), 'Windows of Focalization: Deconstructing and Reconstructing a Narratological Concept', *Style*, 30.2: 241–67.

Jannidis, Fotis (2013), 'Character', in: *The Living Handbook of Narratology*, ed. by Peter Hühn et al. (Hamburg: Hamburg University). https://www-archiv.fdm.uni-hamburg.de/lhn/node/41.html.

King, Stephen (1981), *IT* (first draft photocopy), Stephen King's personal archive in Bangor, box 70, folders 4–5.

King, Stephen (1986), *IT* (New York: Viking).

King, Stephen (2012), *On Writing: A Memoir of the Craft* (London: Hodder).

Kukkonen, Karin (2020), 'The Speed of Plot. Narrative Acceleration and Deceleration', *Orbis Litterarum*, 75: 73–85, https://doi.org/10.1111/oli.12251.

Niederhoff, Burkhard (2011), 'Focalization', in: *The Living Handbook of Narratology*, ed. by Peter Hühn et al. (Hamburg: Hamburg University). https://www-archiv.fdm.uni-hamburg.de/lhn/node/18.html.

Rimmon-Kenan, Shlomith (2002), *Narrative Fiction: Contemporary Poetics*, 2nd edition (London: Routledge).

Schmid, Wolf (2010), *Narratology: An Introduction* (Berlin and New York: De Gruyter).

Schneider, Ralf (2001), 'Toward a Cognitive Theory of Literary Character: The Dynamics of Mental Model Construction', *Style*, 35.4: 607–40.

Schneider, Ralf (2013), 'The Cognitive Theory of Character Reception: An Updated Proposal', *Anglistik: International Journal of English Studies*, 24.2: 117–34.

Smuts, Aaron (2008), 'The Desire-Frustration Theory of Suspense', *The Journal of Aesthetics and Art Criticism*, 66.3: 281–90.

Sternberg, Meir (1978), *Expositional Modes and Temporal Ordering* (Baltimore, MD: Johns Hopkins University Press).

Sternberg, Meir (2003a), 'Universals of Narrative and Their Cognitivist Fortunes (I)', *Poetics Today*, 24.3: 297–395.

Sternberg, Meir (2003b), 'Universals of Narrative and Their Cognitivist Fortunes (II)', *Poetics Today*, 24.4: 517–638.

Ueda, Akemi (2016), 'Stanford Literary Lab uses Digital Humanities to Study Why We Feel Suspense', https://news.stanford.edu/2016/02/18/literary-lab-suspense-021816/.

Underwood, Tim, and Chuck Miller, ed. (1989), *Bare Bones: Conversations on Terror with Stephen King* (New York: Warner Books).

Vorderer, Peter, Hans J. Wulff, and Mike Friedrichsen, ed. (1996), *Suspense: Conceptualizations, Theoretical Analyses, and Empirical Explorations* (Mahwah, NJ: Erlbaum).

Zillman, Dolf (1980), 'Anatomy of Suspense', in: *The Entertainment Functions of Television*, ed. by P. H. Tannenbaum (Hillsdale, NJ: Lawrence Erlbaum Associates), 133–63.

13. Genetic Narratology and the Novelistic Cycle across Versions

Lars Bernaerts

The novelistic cycle is one of the most ambitious literary forms. In many cases, it requires and is accompanied by a process of careful planning: the narrative arc of a novelistic cycle is often so vast that the author has to rely on extensive notes, sketches, drawings and so on to organise this narrative complexity. For literary scholars, too, these material traces offer insights into the narrative poetics of the cycle. In that respect, a genetic narratology (Bernaerts, Martens and Van Hulle 2011; Bernaerts and Van Hulle 2013) can not only be an aid in the narrative analysis of the cycle but also a way of recognising the 'conceptual art' of the novelistic cycle. In order to do justice to the scale and nature of the cycle, I propose an exploration in two movements. The first one considers a particular case in which the unusual genesis of the cycle materialises in the novel and is fictionalised in the narrative. The second one zooms out to the general narrative features of the cycle and its genesis, beaconing a text-genetic narrative analysis of the cycle. Together, the two movements demonstrate how at the intersection of genetic criticism and narratology, a better understanding of the novelistic cycle as narrative can emerge.

The Dossier and the Cycle: *Slow Light*

In 2010, the Dutch author Herman Franke published the novel *Slow Light* (*Traag licht*, 2010), not just the final novel of his oeuvre, in the year of his decease, but also the final novel of a cycle called *Beyond Me and True* (*Voorbij ik en waargebeurd*, 2007–2010). *Slow Light* was not supposed to be the final novel in the series. When it became clear to the author that his illness was terminal, however, he decided to incorporate the process in the product, the genesis in the work, the unfinished workplan in the published work. As a result, the playful, funny and metafictional ensemble of novels about a portraitist—a man who fashions written portraits—ends with a bang, a cluster bomb of stories, sketches, portraits, but still with a clear story frame about the anonymous portraitist and his personal mission, his family and his relationships. In an interview Franke explains that he had planned to write a novel for the cycle every single year from a certain point on, but then he changed tack and started to include the notes for those novels in the final volume of the cycle (2010, 246). Indeed, not only does this novel contain stories that could have grown into novels, it refers to the looming death of the actual author and fictionalises this authorial figure.

How does this incorporation of the genetic dossier affect the narrative structure of the novel and how does genetic narratology come into the picture? First, the rhetoric of the narrator has a text-genetic dimension. The metafictional opening of the novel introduces a narrator who depends on his terminally ill 'boss':

> Ongeneeslijk ziek. Niet lang meer te leven. Dat is verschrikkelijk voor de baas, maar wat moet ik daarmee? Goed, hij heeft me geschapen. Moet ik me daarom door hem laten afmaken? Ik begon net lekker op gang te komen. Ik ben nog lang niet klaar met mezelf en met al die anderen in me. Ik rekende op wel tien delen. (Franke 2010, 7)

> [Terminally ill. Not long to live anymore. That is awful for the boss, but what am I supposed to do about that? Alright, he created me. Should I let him finish me off then? I was just beginning to pick up steam. I am not done with myself and with all these others in me. I was expecting ten volumes at least.]

On the one hand, the opening directs the reader's attention towards the reality of the cycle, the author's illness, and the writing process. The reality claim is corroborated by the paratextual publisher's note that precedes the opening, in which the death of the author is mentioned as the reason for the unfinished state of the novel. On the other hand, the opening *fictionalises* the author as a character who controls the life of the narrator. As long as the boss is alive, the narrator can continue telling his stories. By referring to this predicament in his narration, the narrator keeps the genesis of the text on the reader's radar.

Second, the ambiguous—real and fictionalised—presence of the cycle's genesis is strengthened by the insertion of notes between square brackets. The brackets index their temporary and unfixed status as a note by the author, a reading that is triggered by the paratextual information mentioned earlier. Sometimes the notes are like the stage directions in a script, the type of fascinating self-addressed instructions you can often find in modern manuscripts, as in 'finish this' (Franke 2010, 84), or 'maybe add something here about the work of David Claerbout' (193).[1] They become part of the narrator's discourse, where they are at once process and product.

For a narrative analysis of the notes from a genetic and narratological perspective, let us turn to one of those passages. When the anonymous first-person character meets his friend Ilonka in present-day Brussels, she reveals that she knows about his secret quest for a nineteenth-century female prostitute he knows from a picture. Then, suddenly, the text is interrupted and at the same time continued in the interruption (2010, 84):

[Afmaken. Ze heeft in New York een vriendje, een hackertype, dat mijn googlegedrag heeft weten te achterhalen. Ze weet dus niet alleen dat ik op zoek ben naar ene Mathilde, maar nog veel meer, ook dat ik heel vaak haar naam heb gegoogled (…)] (The ellipsis is mine, LB.)

[Finish this. She has a boyfriend in New York, a hacker of sorts, who managed to trace my google searches. Not only does she know that I am looking for Mathilde, but she knows much more, also that I have frequently googled her name (…)]

Immediately below this note between brackets is another one:

[Goed, nu ligt de baas weer in het ziekenhuis. (…) nu wordt het wel erg moeilijk het alleen maar over mezelf en al die anderen te hebben]. (The ellipsis is mine, LB.)

[Fine, now the boss is in the hospital again (…) now it becomes really difficult to only talk about myself and all the others].

A narrative analysis and a genetic narratology are instrumental in making sense of this passage. At first sight, these notes are clearly

---

1   David Claerbout is a contemporary Belgian video artist.

separated from the main text. They are put between brackets, set in another typeface (a sans-serif letter) and in a smaller font size. In that way, they are visually rendered as provisional and severed from the main text. The first word of the note ('Afmaken' ['Finish this']) suggests that the narrator of the note is the author who is instructing himself. This is the reading elicited paratextually in the preface, on the jacket blurb and in the interview added at the end of the novel. However, as the note continues, it is clear that the 'I' is still the character-narrator, the portraitist, who explicitly distinguished himself from the 'boss' in the opening of the novel. In the above note, the narrator mentions the boss again, drawing him further into the story: he explains that Ilonka knows about the imminent death of the boss. In the second note, the boss is about to die and he is in hospital again. Again, it is clear from the note that the narrrator can only go on as long as the boss is alive. When he dies, the narrator has to quit as well.

The postmodern metafiction in this narrative situation is obvious, but it works as metafictional play because it also refers to the actual genesis of this novel and the cycle. If we read the narrative situation as *communication*—a conventional option but by no means the only one—then we can discern multiple channels and layers. Through the lens of rhetorical narratology and in James Phelan's terms (2017), we can see how the novel assumes an authorial audience that is cognizant of the author's predicament, while the narrative audience accepts the unusual relations between the narrator and the boss as a given. For the actual reader, the fun as well as the gravity of the narration lies in that double communication.

On my reading, the boss is the fictionalised flesh-and-blood alter ego of Herman Franke, quite literally reduced to flesh and blood, while the autodiegetic first-person narrator is his writing alter ego. In introducing a boss character, the narrator fictionalises the author, putting him on the same ontological plane as himself. Somehow the narrator knows how the boss is doing, so the boss is part of the same fictional world, but their relationship is also 'unnatural', as unnatural narratology would call it (see below). This means that it cannot be reduced to real-world parameters. The narrator emphasises that he depends upon the boss's survival. Calling him a 'boss' implies that the author-character has a certain power, while at the same time the narrator inverts the power relations by creating him as a character. It is only in the narrator's words that this character takes shape.

This is a conventional metafictional gesture at first sight, but it gains special meaning from a genetic perspective. The self-instruction in the first sentence adds to the rhetorical and narrative complexity. To invoke Phelan's rhetorical definition of narrative, there is 'someone telling somebody else on some occasion for some purpose that something happened' (1996, 218). In this case, the first sentence is not retrospective (it is not the recounting of something that already occurred); instead it is an imperative, oriented towards the future. It has a silent narratee. The message in 'Finish this' is directed towards the extratextual author if we simply read the note as a document from the genetic dossier, but it is addressed to the narrating self who is writing the story if we consider the entire narrative context of the note. What is more, the initial sentence changes the status of what follows. 'She has a boyfriend in New York', seems to be simultaneous narration, but in fact, 'Finish this' indicates that the story of what Ilonka knows about the portraitist still has to be written, still has to be narrated in the future. The narrational act is ambiguous in this case. In Phelan's view, narrative is an action shaped by the narrator as well as the narrative audience (2018, 2). In this case, the action is telling the authorial and narrative audience that something happened but also telling the narratee along with the authorial audience that something has to be told.

The latter point reveals the cognitive function of the note as a note. It is a reminder, a placeholder, for something that will never come; it fills a gap in the text *and* it *creates* further gaps by suggesting possible additional volumes for the cycle. For the author, these notes are part of the 'extended mind' that is so characteristic of the creative process (Van Hulle 2014). The cognitive processes or planning, thinking ahead, developing ideas, remembering decisions about narrative progression and character development, are not just recorded on paper. They also emerge from the interaction between the author and the written traces, if we follow the logic outlined by the philosophers Andy Clark and David Chalmers in their pioneering article about the extended mind (1998).

For the reader, the notes enable the projection of stories, worlds and further volumes in the cycle. Prompted by the paratext, readers may activate their knowledge of the cycle as a whole to fill in the gaps and imagine how the brief notes would have been expanded into novels. 'Would have been': arguably, this cognitive response engenders an experience of potentiality as well as loss. The alternative possible world the reader is invited to imagine is one in which Franke would have written several more books. In mentally responding to the cues in the novel, the reader is thus confronted with existential questions: what is the meaning of writing when life is ending, what does it mean to finish a cycle of novels that accompanies a writer's life, what is the role of the reader in retrieving those lost imagined worlds?

The previous paragraphs suggest that rhetorical and cognitive narratology help us to account for the powerful metafiction in this novel. Along the way, though, we notice that the narrative situation cannot be reduced to a natural communicative situation or a mimetic structure. Our text-genetic narrative approach can thus also benefit from unnatural narrative theory, developed by Jan Alber, Brian Richardson and other narratologists. Rather than simply explaining away this unnatural dimension, we should integrate it in our reading and consider how it supports narrative meaning-making. Illuminating in this respect are the reading strategies distinguished by Alber in *Unnatural Narrative: Impossible Worlds in Fiction and Drama* (2016, 47–57). In this case, the logical impossibilities of the narrative situation can be understood through 'the Zen way of reading'—accepting the unusual nature of this narrative aspect—or 'foregrounding the thematic': in *Slow Light* the metalepsis asks whether the intrusive reality of the human body (the boss figure) can trump the power of literary imagination.

All these narratological angles, which enrich the reading of the novel, can also feed into a genetic narratology. At stake here is the diachronic aspect of the writing process and the genetic story not just of the novel but of the entire cycle. The case of Franke leads us to a few broader points about genetic narratology and the cycle across versions. First, the example reminds us that works are, on some level or another, never finished and that the unfinished has an aesthetic value and a tradition in itself. In painting and sculpture, the deliberately unfinished style, which foregrounds the process of creation, is known as the *non finito*. In the case of the cycle, and certainly that of Franke, the constitutive relationships between parts and whole elicit reflections upon the possibility and impossibility of finishing a work. Second, the writing process is emphatically present in Franke's novel. If one studies versions of literary works, however, one realises that the process is always also part of the product, and sometimes it can break through the barriers of the textual world. Again, the cycle offers a special case: until the final volume is published it leaves questions open by its nature, and remains 'process'. Third, on a methodological level, a functional genetic narratology integrates narrative concepts available in a range of narratologies today, such as, in this case, rhetorical, unnatural and cognitive narratology.

The Cycle's Narrative Complexity from a Genetic Perspective

In the second part of this chapter I want to zoom out from Franke's cycle to genetic narratology and the novelistic cycle across versions. What can genetic narratology do for the study of the novelistic cycle? How do the defining narrative features of the cycle evolve from one version to another? Clearly, the most interesting answers to these questions come from close readings of individual cycles, which is what the previous section suggests. However, there are some general insights we can glean from a broader comparative analysis of cycles and their genetic dossiers. In three respects, the study of the cycle and genetic narratology can cross-fertilise: a narratological approach to the genetic dossier can shed light on the narrative building blocks of the cycle's complex construction; theoretical frameworks in narratology can be refined and developed in the study of the cycle's genesis; and narratology offers an ideal vantage point to examine text-genetic narratives, i.e. the telling of stories about the writing process.

First of all, in view of the size and scope of many novelistic cycles, it is evident that planning and global structure become very important.[2] Material traces such as sketches, notes, drafts, even drawings and maps are vital in the process. An excellent example is Emile Zola's *Les Rougon-Macquart* (1871–93), the cycle of twenty novels that centers around a family during the Second Empire and sketches the social conditions of

---

2   More accurately, the cycle emerges from a creative interplay between planning, coincidence and revision.

the family and the hereditary relations between one generation and the next. Zola's preparatory materials, which are accessible online as well as offline (Becker 2003-2013),[3] contain notes, sketches and drawings related to the plot, settings and characters of his cycle.[4] The narratologist and genetic critic Philippe Hamon among others has examined how these narrative aspects develop across versions and in which ways the avant-texte shapes the published version (Hamon 1983; Hamon 1997), showing how they serve to support, reflect and advance the narrative and cognitive complexity of the cycle.

A particular type of complexity defines the novelistic cycle. It consists of a number of volumes that are perceived as autonomous narrative units, but at the same time contribute to the same overarching narrative. The cycle emerges from the manifold narrative relations between its parts, such as recurring settings, the continuation of plot patterns or the return of the same narrator—but also discontinuities such as temporal shifts, shifts from one main character to another one and so on. This combination of continuities and discontinuities creates a narrative complexity that goes hand in hand with a cognitive complexity. Just consider the challenge of the cycle for the reader as well as the author when it comes to long-term memory, to activating and re-activating the relevant mental schemata for recurring characters, their backstories, for a setting familiar from volume 1 and evoked again in volume 4 published ten years later.

In the genetic dossier, this complexity often materialises. For some novelistic cycles, the genetic dossier contains elegant lists, drawings, or tables which summarise the envisaged logic of the cycle. In some cases, the cycle is a form of conceptual art, one could argue: the artistic value already lies in the concept, in its graceful and neat design, in the instructions for its execution. This is another analogy with the visual arts, where conceptual art is widely recognised. In sum, to the extent that the notes, sketches, manuscripts are available, they give us an image of the type of narrative ambition and the scope of the ambition that goes into the cycle. The genetic dossier often visualises the narrative complexity

---

3   Manuscripts and other materials are accessible at the Bibliothèque nationale de France through Gallica (https://gallica.bnf.fr).

4   For a view from genetic criticism, see e.g. (Leduc-Adine 2002) and (Lumbroso and Mitterand 2002).

that results from relations between the parts and between the parts and projected whole. The experimental *Alpha Cycle* (1963–79) by the Belgian author Ivo Michiels, for example, displays the conceptual ambition of breaking down narrative and language step by step.[5] Each volume contributes to that goal, each volume represents a step in that process. In a series of notes and what the genetic critic Pierre-Marc de Biasi calls the 'precompositional and compositional schemata and sketches' (1996), Michiels creates a conceptual blueprint for the cycle,[6] in which each volume develops a certain concept: doubt, interchangeability, imprisonment, communcation and death. Each volume also correlates to an autobiographical phase, a historical episode, and certain formalistic principles (such as rhythm and dialogue). The result is a complex grid of relations on which the narrative (and anti-narrative) of the four books is grafted.

From the perspective of the cycle as an ambitious conceptual and narrative art we can study the cycles across versions. An important recent impetus for this endeavour has been given in a special issue of *Genesis*,[7] edited by Alain Pagès and Olivier Lumbroso, and devoted to the genetic criticism of the novelistic cycle. In France, the discipline of *critique génétique* has had a strong tradition since the 1960s (Van Hulle 2007, 11), the modern tradition of the novelistic cycle is particularly influential, and the theory of the novelistic cycle is well developed. The special issue acknowledges the legacy of *La Comédie humaine* (Balzac), *Les Rougon-Macquart* (Zola), *À la recherche du temps perdu* (Proust), *Les Thibault* (Roger Martin du Gard) and *Les Hommes de bonne volonté* (Jules Romains). These cycles and *romans-fleuves* open up a special space in genetic criticism, the editors argue, in the sense that they require a view that transcends an individual work and considers the macrotext, i.e. the artistic project of the ensemble. In their contributions to the issue,

---

5 The first two volumes were translated into English by Adrienne Dixon (Michiels 1979).

6 Undated notes on paper, kept in the archives of the Letterenhuis, Antwerpen. The status of the notes remains uncertain: it is plausible that they were made when Michiels had already started writing the first volumes. In any case, the blueprints do not yet mention the volume *Samuel, o Samuel* (1973), which was added as volume 3 ½ in the early seventies.

7 A more recent issue on serial writing (issue 54, 2022) is also relevant to this discussion. It examines popular seriality across versions, for example in crime fiction or the *Harry Potter* franchise.

Thomas Conrad, Aude Leblond and Christophe Pradeau, who helped develop a theory of the cycle in previous work (Conrad 2016; Leblond 2015; Pradeau 2000), demonstrate the importance of the genetic dossier for a theoretical and narratological understanding of the cycle. Their essays reveal how the narrative features that define the cycle as a cycle are foregrounded in the *avant-texte*. Building on this, a genetic narratology can provide a touchstone for the analysis of those features. We can distinguish four narrative parameters that typify the cycle (but that do not necessarily occur to the same extent in particular examples): (1) the return of characters; (2) the fundamental relationship between temporal structure and the theme of time; (3) the way in which closure is distributed, with weak closure in individual volumes and strong closure for the complete cycle; and (4) the principle of cyclicity that complicates narrative linearity.[8] The genetic dossier offers insight into the conceptual narrative art of the cycle and the conceptual role played by these narrative aspects, which are the core business of the cycle. A few examples may illustrate this point. The role of recurring characters and temporality as theme and structure, for example, clearly surfaces in the genetic dossiers of novelistic cycles that I have been able to look into. In varying degrees, they are clearly given narrative priority during the writing process, for example in the *Gangreen Cycle* by Jef Geeraerts, published between 1967 and 1977, a semi-autobiographical cycle of four novels. The available documents suggest that Geeraerts organises the novels and the relations between the novels around characters which he lists and supplements with anecdotes and character traits, and also around moments in time. For each volume of the cycle there are a number of sheets with a chronological order and then a sketch for the narrative for the relevant years.[9] Figure 13.1 is an example from *Gangreen IV*, which shows the procedure Geeraerts already uses in *Gangreen I*: each bit of narrative information is tied to a date or brief period in time ('March-April', 'May-June', '8/7/1963').

In the first volume, the most rudimentary structure is a list of women who then represent episodes in time. Figure 13.2 shows one of the sheets from that dossier. Leaving aside the intriguing stylistic self-instructions

---

8   The studies that argue for these aspects as fundamental are Aranda 1997, Bernaerts 2022, Besson 2004, Conrad 2016, Pradeau 2000.

9   The author's archives are kept at the Letterenhuis in Antwerp.

13. Genetic Narratology and the Novelistic Cycle across Versions   231

('cool observation', 'control', 'cold irony'), we can see that list of women on the left as the narrative skeleton for *Gangreen I*. In the third volume, there is an interesting shift from character to setting in that phase: setting becomes more important as a structuring device. Figure 13.3 shows a list of locations from the author's childhood, which will structure the novel. Visually and conceptually, the note prioritises settings over characters: the characters are associated with the setting on this sheet.

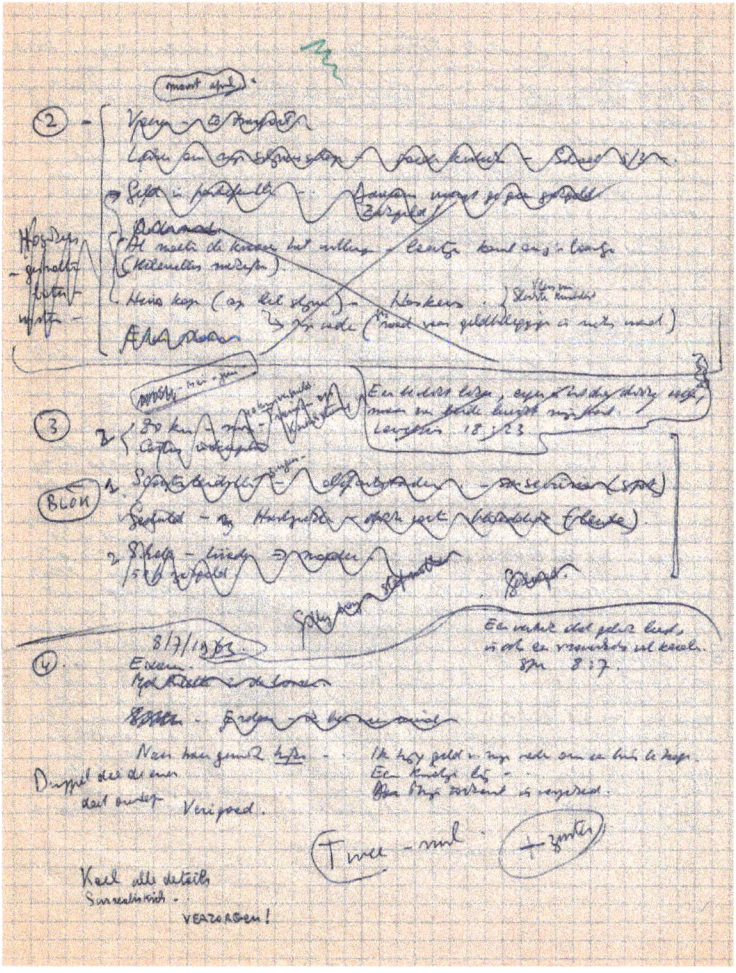

Fig. 13.1 Jef Geeraerts, notes for *Gangreen IV* (1977). Collectie Stad Antwerpen, Letterenhuis.

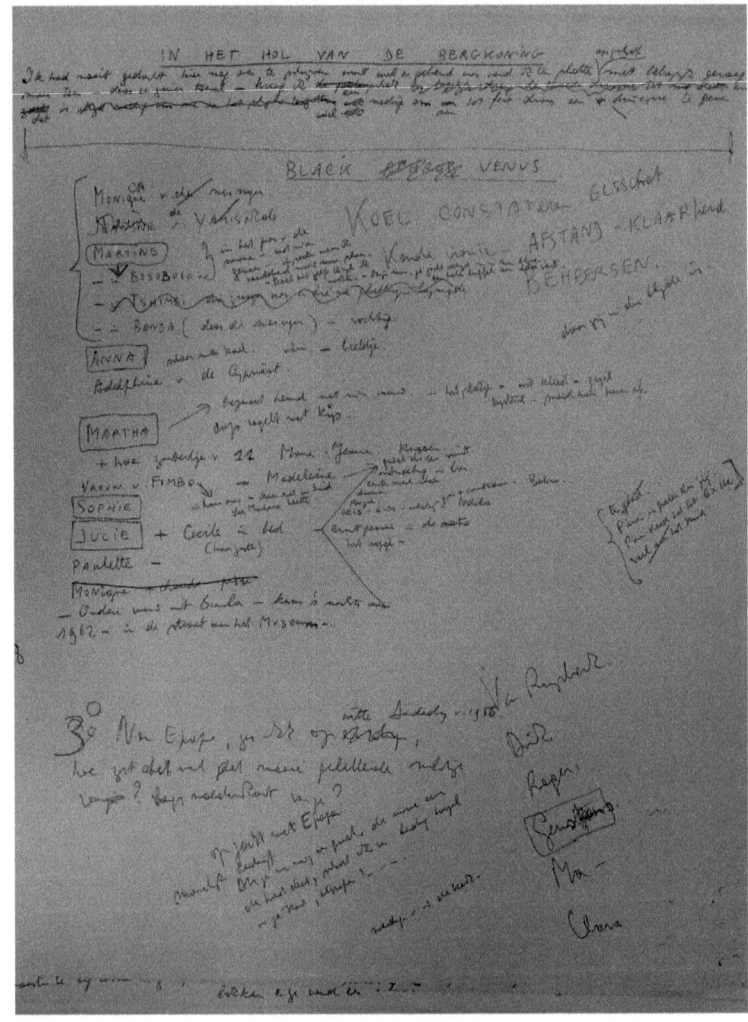

Fig. 13.2 Jef Geeraerts, notes for *Gangreen I* (1968). Collectie Stad Antwerpen, Letterenhuis.

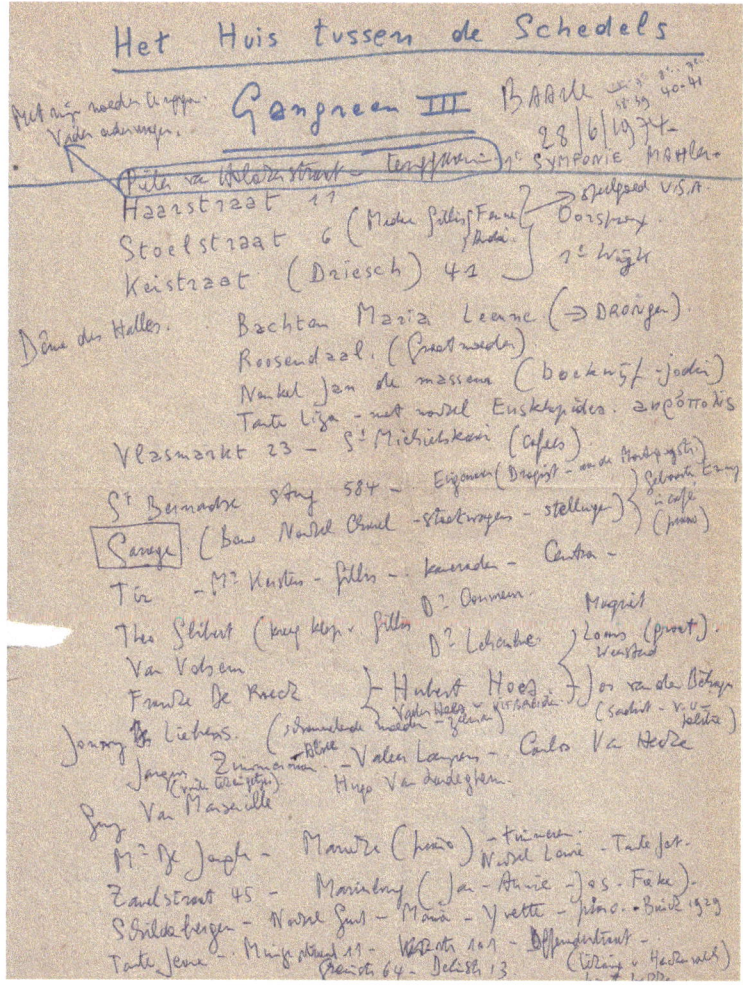

Fig. 13.3 Jef Geeraerts, notes for *Gangreen III* (1975). Collectie Stad Antwerpen, Letterenhuis.

The first novel, *Gangreen I: Black Venus*,[10] famously deals with the erotic escapades of a colonial official in the Belgian Congo from 1955 until the battle for independence in 1960. The narrative stands out for the combination of a monologous flowing narrational style and an episodic structure. The episodes are mainly tied to the women

---

10 The novel was first published in 1967 and translated into English by Jon Swan in 1975 (Geeraerts 1975).

with whom the Belgian colonial officer hooks up. It is this structure that the preparatory notes already make visible. In the novel itself, the textual genesis and the relations between novel and cycle crop out in a telling note: '....I skip the period of 22 April until 16 March 1960. Perhaps later I will write about it, or maybe not...' (Geeraerts 2003, 185: my translation, LB). In a way similar to the example of *Slow Light*, the note interrupts the flow of the narrative, foregrounds the narrator's and the author's writing process and emphasises the temporal and thematic coherence of the novel. For the main character, the deleted period is a period of battle and violence. The first volume of the cycle, however, foregrounds themes of vitality and sexuality. It is only in the second volume, centring around violence, that this episode will be narrated.

Another example is a four-part cycle by Walter van den Broeck, *The Siege of Laeken* (1985–92). The author's archive contains a number of documents, drawings, sketches, diagrams, and timelines that show and support the narrative complexity of the cycle. In particular, again, the temporality and the distribution of characters are conceptually planned ahead. Van den Broeck uses timelines in and across the volumes to pre-structure his narrative. Figure 13.4 shows such a timeline for the second volume of the cycle, *Gek leven na het bal!* (1989), in which the narrator looks back on his relationship with his German friend Ursula and his trip to her hometown Paderborn. In Figure 13.5, the timeline exceeds the boundaries of the individual volume. It visualises the narrative arc of the entire cycle, from 'moorddroom' ['murder dream'] to 'droommoord' ['dream murder']: the two palindromes indicate how the beginning and the ending of the cycle mirror each other, emphasising the cyclical nature of the ensemble of novels. In the cases of Geeraerts, Van den Broeck and others, the narrative core business of the novelistic cycle is materially prominent in the genetic dossier.

13. Genetic Narratology and the Novelistic Cycle across Versions   235

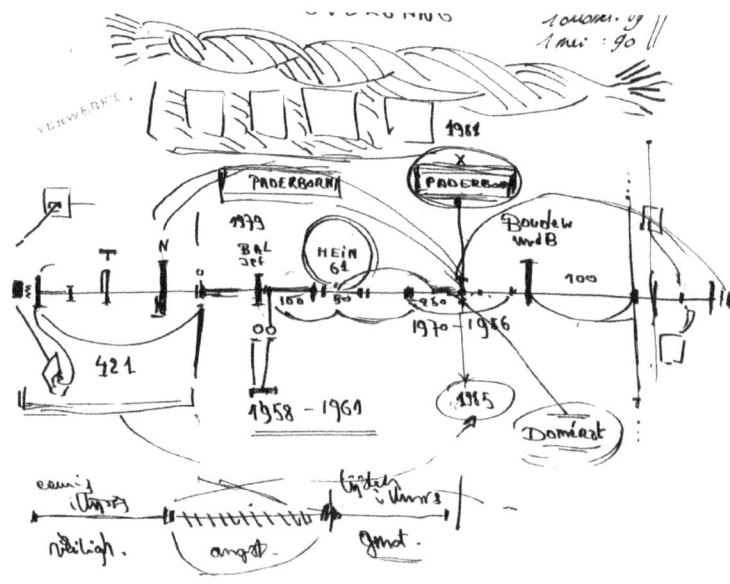

Fig. 13.4 Walter van den Broeck, timeline for *Gek leven na het bal!* (1989). Collectie Stad Antwerpen, Letterenhuis.

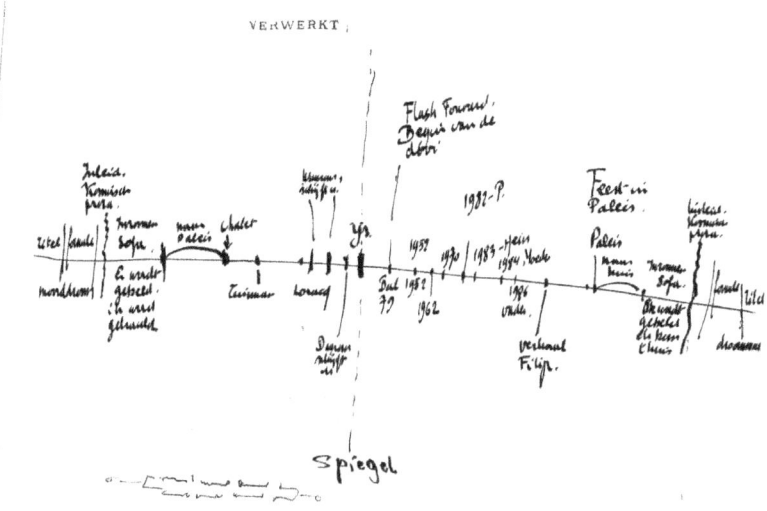

Fig. 13.5 Walter van den Broeck, timeline for *The Siege of Laeken*. Collectie Stad Antwerpen, Letterenhuis.

The second point is that our theoretical understanding of narrative can be advanced by the study of the cycle's genesis. It can be a catalyst in the development of theory. Key works in narratology took interest in the novelistic cycle. Philippe Hamon examines the system of characters in Zola's cycle while at the same time contributing to a theory of characters in *Le personnel du roman* (1983). The equivalent for 'time and temporality' is Gérard Genette in *Narrative Discourse* (1972). He analyses temporal relations in *À la recherche du temps perdu*, laying bare the chronology, the complex anachronies, the amount of acceleration and deceleration, the significance of iterative narration. It is telling that in Genette's pioneering work the narrative analysis transcends the boundaries of an individual work, and this in fact made the model possible. For the narrative theory of character and time, it has proven valuable to turn to the cycle across versions.

Third and finally, genetic narratology has a role in analysing and demystifying the genetic narrative itself, the story about the writing process and the genesis of a literary work. The novelistic cycle is one of those literary phenomena that give rise to elaborate and successful genetic narratives. Those genetic narratives are often but not always told by the authors themselves. Sometimes they acquire the status of a myth. These myths refer to material processes but become infused with ideas about creation and creativity, authorship and readership, craftsmanship and visionary qualities. They can be analysed as narrative discourse with referential traces in the genetic dossier. A.F.Th. Van der Heijden is the author of *The Toothless Time* (1983-present), a novelistic cycle that is not finished yet but already consists of nine parts (about twenty books) and more than 6000 pages. At several points in his career, he narrativises his own working process and the genesis of the cycle in essays, interviews and letters. In that genetic narrative the always expanding cycle goes back to a manuscript he started writing around 1967, when he was sixteen years old, in which he fictionalises the main themes of his life (De Roder 1986, 58). A few years later, he wrote a novel which would be repeatedly revised until it became *The Toothless Time* (see e.g. Van der Heijden 2003, 93; Van der Heijden 2006). That narrative is not only created in interviews and egodocuments, but also integrated in the cycle itself. As in the case of Franke, the genetic process is fictionalised in Van der Heijden's work. Genetic narratology can examine the strategies of narrativisation involved, the material traces that back up or belie the story and the way genetic stories are integrated in fiction. In that sense, genetic narratology provides the tools to debunk the myth, to analyse the actual material traces and the transformation into the narrative told by authors, publishers, critics, fans and scholars.

Conclusion

As part of the aesthetic value of novelistic cycles often already lies in its design, the cycle is a conceptual art. Since the novelistic cycle is not just a conceptual but also a narrative art, we need a narrative theory geared towards those material traces of the design, to the diachronic dimension inherent in it, and also to the intricacies of the cycle. Genetic narratology can contribute to the understanding of the cycle, first in the development of a narrative theory of the cycle—which is still fragmented –, second as a touchstone for narrative analysis and third for the research into the story of a work's genesis, the genetic narrative.

The narrative analysis of cycles across versions also benefits from particular narratological frameworks for a better understanding of the mentioned narrative and cognitive complexity. As the case of Herman Franke demonstrated, a combined cognitive, rhetorical and unnatural narratology illuminates the powerful and playful rhetoric of the cycle in *Slow Light*, where the genetic narrative becomes part of the narrative text and adds another layer in the narrative communication. Along those lines, we can refine, combine and expand the available narratological concepts to improve our understanding of the large-scale narrative projects we call cycles.

Works Cited

Alber, Jan (2016), *Unnatural Narrative: Impossible Worlds in Fiction and Drama* (Lincoln, NE and London: University of Nebraska Press).

Aranda, Daniel (1997), *Le retour des personnages dans les ensembles romanesques* (Paris: Université de la Sorbonne Nouvelle).

Becker, Colette (2003-2013), *La Fabrique des Rougon-Macquart. Édition des dossiers préparatoires*, par Colette Becker, avec la collaboration de Véronique Lavielle (Paris: Champion).

Bernaerts, Lars and Dirk Van Hulle (2013), 'Narrative across Versions: Narratology Meets Genetic Criticism', *Poetics Today*, 34.3: 281–326.

Bernaerts, Lars, Gunther Martens and Dirk Van Hulle (2011) 'Narratologie en Tekstgenese. Een Terreinverkenning', *Spiegel der Letteren*, 53.3: 281–309.

Bernaerts, Lars (2022), 'Totaalpakketten. De Romancyclus in de Nederlandse Literatuur—een Verkenning in Theorie en Praktijk', *Tijdschrift voor Nederlandse Taal- en Letterkunde*, 138.2: 130–56.

Besson, Anne (2004) *D'Asimov à Tolkien. Cycles et Séries dans la Littérature de Genre* (Paris: CNRS).

Clark, Andy and David Chalmers (1998), 'The Extended Mind', *Analysis*, 58.1: 10–23.

Conrad, Thomas (2016a), *Poétique des cycles romanesques de Balzac à Volodine* (Paris: Classiques Garnier).

Conrad, Thomas (2016b), 'Du Cercle Fermé au Réseau Ouvert. Les Treize comme Avant-Texte de La Comédie Humaine', *Genesis*, 42: 65–73, https://doi.org/10.4000/genesis.1630.

De Rover, Frans C. (1986), 'Een Wraakneming op de Verloren Tijd. Het Schrijverschap van A.F.Th. van der Heijden', in: *Jan Campertprijzen 1986* ('s-Gravenhage: BZZTôH), 52–71.

Franke, Herman (2010), *Traag licht* (Amsterdam: Podium).

Geeraerts, Jef (1975), *Gangrene*, trans. by Jon Swan (London: Weidenfeld and Nicolson).

Geeraerts, Jef (2003), *Gangreen, de Cyclus* (Amsterdam and Antwerpen: Meulenhoff; Manteau).

Hamon, Philippe (1983), *Le Personnel du Roman. Le Système des Personnages dans les Rougon-Macquart d'Emile Zola* (Genève: Droz).

Hamon, Philippe (1997), 'Échos et Reflets: L'Ébauche de *La Bête Humaine* de Zola', *Poétique*, 109: 3–16.

Leduc-Adine, Jean-Pierre (2002), *Zola: Genèse de l'Oeuvre* (Paris: CNRS Editions).

Leblond, Aude (2015), *Sur un monde en ruine: Esthétique du roman-fleuve* (Paris: Honoré Champion).

Leblond, Aude (2016), 'Genèses du Roman-Fleuve: Réduire le Cycle à l'Opus?', *Genesis*, 42: 53–64, https://doi.org/10.4000/genesis.1626

Lumbroso, Olivier and Henri Mitterand, eds. (2002), *Les Manuscrits et les Dessins de Zola: Notes Preparatoires et Dessins des Rougon-Macquart* (Paris: Editions textuels).

Michiels, Ivo (1979), *Book Alpha and Orchis Militaris*, trans. by Adrienne Dixon (Boston: Twayne Publishers).

Pagès, Alain (2016), 'Pour une Génétique des Cycles Romanesques', *Genesis*, 42: 7–16, https://doi.org/10.4000/genesis.1265

Phelan, James (1996), *Narrative as Rhetoric* (Columbus: Ohio State University Press).

Phelan, James (2017), *Somebody Telling Somebody Else: A Rhetorical Poetics of Narrative* (Columbus: Ohio State University Press).

Phelan, James (2018), 'Authors, Resources, Audiences: Toward a Rhetorical Poetics of Narrative', *Style*, 52.1–2: 1–34.

Pradeau, Christophe (2000), *L'Idée de Cycle Romanesque: Balzac, Proust, Giono* (Paris: Université Paris-VIII).

Pradeau, Christophe (2016), 'La Beauté Ajoutée Cyclique', *Genesis*, 42: 37–51, https://doi.org/10.4000/genesis.1621.

Van den Broeck, Walter (2006), *Het Beleg van Laken* (Amsterdam: De Bezige Bij).

Van der Heijden, A.F.Th. (2003), 'Brieven aan Helga van Beuningen', *De Revisor*, 30.5–6: 84–155.

Van der Heijden, A.F.Th. (2006), 'Van Oerboek tot Eindboek. De Papyrusrol in de Hondenkennel', *Literatuur. De Groene Amsterdammer*, 30 November 2006.

Van Hulle, Dirk (2007), *De Kladbewaarders* (Nijmegen: Vantilt).

Van Hulle, Dirk (2014), *Modern Manuscripts: The Extended Mind and Creative Undoing from Darwin to Beckett and Beyond* (London: Bloomsbury).

14. 'Indolence, interruption, business, and pleasure': Narratological Rupture in *The Last Samurai*

Kaia Sherry

1. The Circle Line Begins

> We are now sitting in front of Bellini's Portrait of the Doge. L is reading Odyssey 18, consulting Cunliffe at intervals—*infrequent* intervals. I have been looking at the Portrait of the Doge—*somebody's* got to. I have brought things to read myself but the room is so warm I keep falling asleep and then jerking awake to stare. In a half-dream I see the monstrous heiskaihekatontapus prowling the ocean bed, pentekaipentekontapods flying before it.
>
> —Helen DeWitt, *The Last Samurai* (2000)

A mother sits in London's National Gallery—she is named Sibylla, after the epigraph from T.S. Eliot's 'The Waste Land'. Barely able to stay awake, Sibylla is even less able to afford the central heating that the National Gallery provides. As her precocious son Ludo reads a Homeric lexicon, a portrait of interruption begins to emerge from the text, balancing a tension between an extraliterary lineage and the conditions that occlude it. Like the tonal gradation of Leonardo Loredan in Bellini's poplar, these disturbances occur both syntactically and from within the narrative: the epistrophe of dashes, the stilted Greek prefixes, Ludo's 'infrequent intervals', Sibylla's half-dreams and 'jerks' of consciousness and Ludo's referent of 'L'—itself an affectionate truncation of his namesake. Later, when Ludo and Sibylla ride the Circle Line for hours on end to keep warm, they are interrupted by a deluge of commentary regarding

Ludo's prodigy. The novel stochastically maintains this disorder, primarily through what Toril Moi calls a barrage of 'capital letters, broken-off sentences, lists of numbers, and words in many different alphabets' (2021, 34). Together, these constructs reflect Sibylla's internal focalisation: the guilt, disorder and alienation imbued in teaching a five-year-old Greek syllabary from books she cannot afford.

Therefore, painting a metafictional portrait of producing art under capitalism, Helen DeWitt's *The Last Samurai* poses formal rupture as an extension—and attempted remediation of—narrative distress (Konstantinou 2022, 48). DeWitt, often paired with the 'post-postmodernism' of David Foster Wallace and Thomas Pynchon, consciously blocks the ongoing narrative in continuance of an ancillary one—the chaos of capital made real on the page. Spanning throughout the text, these insertions typically manifest as either extramedial references (e.g. Akira Kurosawa's *Seven Samurai* and Roemer's *Aristarchs Athetesen in der Homerkritik* as hypotext) or the capricious fits expected of a young child. Although Moi contends that DeWitt is 'fascinated by creativity voluntarily imposing strict yet random rules on it', her formal implosions actually invert the methodologies of avant-garde movements like *l'Ouvroir de Littérature Potentielle* [the Workshop of Potential Literature], or OuLiPo (34; Baetens 2019, 408). *The Last Samurai* revels in the dissolution of formal borders, rather than the constraints or procedure of a movement like OuLiPo. In this sense, DeWitt experiments with the duality inhered in twentieth-century 'process-oriented art' as an aesthetic category, '[inviting] us into the workshop to witness the experiment as it unfolds', but also to witness the interruptions that preclude such unfolding (Bray et. al 2015, 2). These interruptions may be as material as a 'genius' child in the form of 'the Infant Terrible', or as diffuse as the exigencies of capitalism; each disruption takes on a quality of self-referentiality, as it necessarily extends to the analysis of the genetic process.

As the genetic dossier reveals, DeWitt's irruptive elisions are the result of 'progressive alteration' rather than initial epiphany (qtd. in Bernaerts and Van Hulle 2013, 282). Like the superseded *pentimenti* of a Bellini, DeWitt's drafts intonate a version of Sibylla's homodiegetic voice that Lee Konstantinou hears as 'linear, coherent, [and] forceful', but 'lifeless on the page' (2022, 4). Although Sibylla is initially named

'Ruth' in earlier drafts, Eliot's allusion to the Sibyl's divine circumstance of Petronius's *Satyricon* is far more fitting: a 'body withered away' by the incessant, capitalist grind, 'leaving behind only her voice' as her first-person narration (Konstantinou 2022, 5). But as seen through the progression of DeWitt's drafts, even this narration is subject to interruption, as DeWitt herself was during the tumultuous publication process with Talk Miramax Books. Sibylla's voice is further diminished by the end of the novel, her internal focalisation replaced by Ludo's burgeoning consciousness. By fictionalising her own circumstance, DeWitt dereifies form as a means of withholding narrative agency.

A genetic narratological approach, in which 'the appeal to versions is [...] one way of reconciling incongruities in a narrative', is thus well-suited for elucidating the formal disjunction of *The Last Samurai* (Bernaerts and Van Hulle 2013, 288). In particular, Bernaerts and Van Hulle emphasise the utility of this framework for examining experimental work that 'emphatically resists or challenges literary conventions', as DeWitt does by resisting literary convention itself. Recently, this approach has been effectively used to re-evaluate DeWitt's 'post-postmodern' contemporary Thomas Pynchon in *Becoming Pynchon: Genetic Narratology and V.*, examining genre as performance against the grain of cognitive narratology. In comparison, this essay will construe formal breakage as intervention, postulating DeWitt's alterations of her drafts as a narrative contingency of this intervention.

With regard to the available material, *The Last Samurai*'s extant drafts are on fifty-two floppy discs beginning from the year 1991. A number of the discs are defective, while others contain only downloadable software. Although the original manuscript and accompanying drafts were handwritten, the boxes were stolen from DeWitt's apartment fourteen years ago, owing to a broken cellar lock—but as DeWitt writes in her letter 'LAURA', 'let's not think of boxes'. DeWitt, through Lee Konstantinou at the University of Maryland, College Park, has generously provided what remains of *The Last Samurai*'s drafts. The data, providing the literary-critical foundation for this essay, was extracted at the Oxford Duplication Centre. Available as WordPerfect files, the drafts are divided into seven folders labelled as follows:

Folder Name	Files
7S9	7s9.1, 7s9.4, 7s9.5, 7s9.6, 7s9.7, 7s9.12, 7s9.13, 7s9.21, 7s9.31, 7s9.32, 7s9. 33, 7s9.42, 7s9, and Notes on 7S9
09-07-96	7S1.8, 7S3.2, 7S3.2C, 7S3.2E, 7S3.3, 7S3.4, and 7S5.3
20-04-98	csm, cv2610, ind, richard2, and woolf
Backup Liberace 7-6-96 + 1Liberac (Very Early)	1LIBERAC, 7S1.8, 7S2.2, 7S3.2, 7S4.2A, 7S4.2B, 7S4. 2C, 7S5.3, 7S6.2, 7S7.2, 7S8
Mary.WPD (Orig. Beg.)	Notes on Disk Mary Orig Beg
Notes 17.5.97	ADVENT, CHIAKI, CHILD, FOREST, INUIT, KUROSAWA, LAURA, LAURA2, NME, SCHOEN, SKARP, SKARP2, WIENER, WITTE
Story of 7s	7s2.0, 7s2.0a, 7s2.2a, 7s2.10, Notes on Disk

According to the metadata of the provided documentation, the genetic lineage of *The Last Samurai* seems to span from September 1991 to July 1996, barring any missing material. Certain files (e.g. Notes on Disk Mary Orig Beg) are corrupt, yielding a blank document with 'file could not transfer', while others are irrelevant to a genetic narratological undertaking—I have become intimately familiar with DeWitt's tax returns, as well as her CVs from 1998. While the files' numerical suffix indicates chapter and subsection, the universal prefix '7S' is in reference to the novel's original title *The Seventh Samurai*, a direct homage to the Kurosawa film it eponymises. Again, signalling interruption as extradiegetic to the text, DeWitt was impelled to change the manuscript title after the Kurosawa estate permitted her to use quotations from the film, but not its title. As such, this essay will comprise two sections, beginning with an evaluation of aesthetic and paternal rupture in '1LIBERAC'. The second section, referencing the drafts '7S3.2' (in *09-07-96*), '7S3.2' (in *Backup Liberace*) '7S3.2c', '7S3.2e', '7S3.3' and '7S3.4', will elucidate two separate scenes: an argument between Ludo and Sibylla regarding his oft-contested paternity, and an encounter at Tesco with a character initially named 'the Meddler'. This section will contend with interruption as transmedial, examining DeWitt's added interjections with respect to Marie-Laure Ryan's concept of 'narrative across media'.

2. '1LIBERAC'

The first line of '1LIBERAC' reads: 'Precocity is not genius, nor genius precocity'. DeWitt's chiasmus is serviceable, evenly balanced and imbued with a tonal stiffness appropriate of Sibylla (and DeWitt's) Oxford background. The amended line reads quite differently. Punctuated by frantic ampersands and anaphora as interior mantra, Sibylla's thoughts unroll with a dialogic intensity: 'Not every genius is a prodigy & not every prodigy is a genius & at 5 it is too soon to tell' (DeWitt 2000, 27). In Konstantinou's view, the initial version alludes towards Ruth as 'a model of assurance', with a controlled clause balanced on either side (2022, 6). Meanwhile, the parataxis of the second reifies Sibylla's maternal anxieties regarding Ludo's education. By intensifying every phrasal constituent, and using abbreviation in service of elongation ('&' versus 'and'), DeWitt's shift to parataxis allows her to recall what Gerald Bruns sees as 'the freedom of schizophrenic language from operations of instrumental reason', in which 'reason' is literalised as Sibylla's mental faculty (2018, 74). Sibylla, a woman obsessed with reason above all, is made capable of irrationality—and consequently, made to be like the rest of us.

In these lines, the post-postmodernist valence comes through in its intensification of postmodernist tendencies: a hyperfixation upon formal authenticity, a return to 'subjective emotion', and resistance against late-stage capitalism (Smith 2011, 424). Ruth, bolstered by the confidence of her syntax, is high-functioning within this model. Sibylla, in contrast, is swept along by the undercurrent of her own deluge, working as a typewriter while raising, if not a 'genius', a verifiable 'prodigy'. As Jeffrey Nealon contends, post-postmodernism is not 'a difference in kind' from its predecessor, but a 'difference in intensity', viscerally aware of the 'collapse of cultural production into the logic of economic production, and vice versa' (2012, x; 51). Through the avant-texte, this collapse becomes articulated through the logic—or illogic—of DeWitt's interruption.

These fissures are evident through DeWitt's restructuring of the text, the 'structures' and 'patterns' of a Jamesian formalism (Gallagher 2000, 231). '1LIBERAC' is linear in execution: it begins with the incipit of Sibylla's parents' artistic failures, and traces the sequence of events to her one-night stand with Ludo's father (derisively called Liberace) and subsequent pregnancy. The '1LIBERAC' draft ends with Sibylla attempting to gain a work permit to stay in the country as a typewriter, having become disillusioned with Oxford:

> Meanwhile, meanwhile—oh, meanwhile I was living in a bedsit and had to find a bigger place. [...] It was very rundown, and the rent was very low, so it seemed I would not have to type too much.

This passage is not in the final edition. Rather, DeWitt replicates it sporadically, through the bombardment of phrasal elements—'work permit' inhabits the text as it does Sibylla's thoughts, while references to her 'typing' and 'rent' are split up metadiegetically, interrupted by secondary narratives. Again, DeWitt makes lavish use of parataxis:

> I walked up and down and I tried to think of an artist who might need an assistant.
> I walked up and down and I thought that perhaps it would be easier to think of an artist if I were already in London or Paris or Rome. (DeWitt 2000, 25)

In proper post-postmodernist fashion, DeWitt gestures towards the pressure of capital upon the artist through form. The steady, parataxic rhythm mirrors the observance of 'clock and calendar' that governs Sibylla's hourly-waged day, and Ludo's when he is forced to attend school for the requisite five days a week (Anderson 2016, 24). Evoking Walter Benjamin's 'homogenous, empty time', this temporal and rhythmic governing is perpetuated by '1LIBERAC', which itself is a 'complex gloss on the word meanwhile' through its repetition of the word (Benjamin 2019, 261; Anderson 2016, 24). Its linearity is followed through by the repetition of 'meanwhile, meanwhile—oh, meanwhile', embodying the endlessness of capital, even when in resistance to it. In contrast, the final edition is erratic, jumping between temporal instances, resisting reconstruction to represent events as 'fuzzily or indeterminately ordered' (Herman 2016, 62–62). As Christian Metz and Michael Taylor write, 'one of the functions of narrative is to invent one time scheme in terms of another time scheme' (2007, 18). Accordingly, DeWitt's instantiation of time through the architecture of thought splices together 'the time of the thing told' and 'the time of the narrative' (Metz and Taylor 2007, 18). The two temporal instances are conveyed simultaneously, because Sibylla simply does not have enough time. The looming phrase 'work permit' appears at least once on each page within the sequence, interrupted by interjections that are both internally and externally focalised: dialogue from *Seven Samurai*, a college formal at Oxford, maternal anxieties about Ludo and a tantrum from Ludo himself. In this way, form is simultaneously representation and resistance to Sibylla's anxieties of survival, à la the post-postmodernism of Zadie Smith or Percival Everett (Kowalik 2023, 7).

The next '1LIBERAC' section solidifies this cultural-capitalist anxiety within the lineage of Sibylla's 'geniuses', pontificating upon Albert Einstein, Glenn Gould, Wolfgang Amadeus Mozart, Gianlorenzo Bernini and Paul Cézanne. In the draft, it is proffered as a single, prolonged paragraph, with no breaks beyond the standard indentation. For the purposes of a genetic narratological analysis, I have rendered the '1LIBERAC' draft as unbolded text, while DeWitt's subsequent additions are in bold. In Gérard Genette's terms, the textual genealogy is represented by the 'old analogy' of the palimpsest, in reference to the way DeWitt's changes do 'not quite conceal but allow to show through' (1997, 398–99). Any further deletions are crossed out:

And Cezanne? Paul Cezanne (1839-1906) was a French painter of genius, associated with the Impressionist

treiskaihexekontasyllabic

school of painting []. He taught himself to paint when in his 20s. He was inarticulate: people called him the Bear. He worked very slowly and with

oktokaihexekontasyllabic enneakaihexekontasyllabic HEBDOMEKONTASYLLABIC

difficulty. He is most famous for his landscapes and still lifes. His method was to apply blocks of paint to the canvas, often with a palette knife rather than a brush. He worked so

heptakaihebdomekontasyllabic

slowly that even fruit could not

OGDOEKONTASYLLABIC

stand still enough: it rotted

[...]¹

treiskaiogdoekontasyllabic tessareskaiogdoekontasyllabic pentekaiogdoekontasyllabic

before he was done. He used

oktokaiogdoekontasyllabic enneakaiogdoekontasyllabic ENENEKONTASYLLABIC

wax fruit instead. ~~I don't know why I tht he started to paint at the age of 40. I must have been thinking of someone else, but if I was thinking of someone else it can't be someone I admire as much as I do Cezanne.~~

Key points of critical intervention coincide with DeWitt's formal intervention: Ludo's temperamental, multisyllabic experimentation with Greek prefixation, but less obviously, the syntactic point at which DeWitt chooses to place these interruptions. On a formal level, Ludo's precocity creates what Konstantinou calls 'a tempo of agitation and interruption not only for the mother but also for the reader', invoking the 'mind-relevance' of cognitive narratology (2022, 5). Konstantinou's choice of 'tempo' implies a metronomic stability, a narrative progression that falls forward like the notes on sheet music. Erich Auerbach speaks of this stylistic effect as 'a process of complex and periodic development'; DeWitt's additions confuse this temporal coincidence, with Ludo's indiscernible Greek adjectives signalling 'repeated returns to the starting point' (2013, 105). In Auerbach's terms, DeWitt's 'halting, spasmodic, and juxtapositive' method obscures the 'causal, modal, and even temporal relations' of the text, making progression impossible (2013, 105). Konstantinou interprets this intervention as 'the difference between writing without interruption and writing while having to do other work'—extending this logic to the *avant-texte*, each version is a representation of these subjectivities. Their combined palimpsest creates a mode of simultaneity in which the possibility of the first subjectivity is interrupted by the next one.

---

1 The bracketed ellipses ([...]) indicate sections I excluded for the sake of brevity. They are not central to this essay's analytical considerations.

Each intrusion is also defined by its placement within the textual economy. Comparing '1LIBERAC' and the final text, she puts Ludo's syllabic cries between the phrases: 'Impressionist school', 'with difficulty', 'so slowly', 'rotted before' and 'used wax'. Ludo's obtrusions slow the act of reading down, as the narrative can only become 'actualised' through the way it is 'consumed' (Genette 1979, 34). In the same way Ludo 'agitates' the reader in tandem with Sibylla, the subjectivity of the reading experience is elongated with respect to its form. Many of the interruptions bifurcate the temporal referent ('slowly', 'before') from the act it is amending, reproducing Cézanne's languid pace in the architecture of the text. Further, Genette's phrasing of 'consumption' conveys the secondary valence of Nealon's 'consumption-based capital' (2012, 90). Forcing a juxtaposition between Sibylla and Cézanne, DeWitt's later version shows the way in which capitalism totalises the working process. While Cézanne's 'genius' is inculcated by his ability to work 'slowly', Sibylla's sense of time is fragmented by her *in*ability to do the same—bound to a typing speed of £6.25 an hour. The question of 'genius' becomes less a matter of innate, 'unparalleled talent' than one of time and who has access to it ('1LIBERAC' 3). As such, '1LIBERAC' is impersonal in narration, with Cézanne's section relayed biographically; functionally, the narrative only becomes Sibylla's once it is interrupted.

As Sibylla continues to deliberate the nature of the 'genius', she veers into a paternal genealogy reflective of the textual one. Considering Bernini and the parental lineage that precipitates his 'genius', Sibylla gestures towards her anxieties about Ludo's father, a 'self-regarding' travel writer with 'a terrible facility and a terrible sincerity' (DeWitt 2000, 77). The faculties of Bernini and Ludo dovetail in this passage:

You say it, and I tht thought it; but the fact is that a clever man so seldom needs to think that he loses the knack of it.

What's a syllabary? A syllabary is a set of phonetic symbols each representing a syllable

he gets out of the habit.

[...]²

---

2   This bracket is a continuation of Ludo's interrogation on syllabary, and Sibylla's attempts to answer him.

And who was Bernini? Gianlorenzo Bernini (1598-1680) was 'the greatest genius of the Italian Baroque', who moved to Rome at the age of seven and was taught by his father

EIKOSASYLLABIC

Pietro, a sculptor. Rudolf Wittkower (German art historian, refugee from the Nazis [**where to begin?**], author of Art & Architecture (*title italicised in final edition*) in Italy 1600-1750) compares him to Michelangelo (( )) ([1475–1564]),

enneakaieikosasyllabic

TRIAKONTASYLLABIC

painter, poet, sculptor of genius...) in his capacity for superhuman

oktokaitriakontasyllabic enneakaitriakontasyllabic

TESSARAKONTASYLLABIC

concentration. 'But unlike the terrible and lonely giant of the sixteenth century, he was a man of infinite charm, a brilliant and witty talker, fond of conviviality, aristocratic in demeanour, a good husband and father, a first-rate

enneakaitessarakontasyllabic PENTEKONTASYLLABIC

heiskaipentekontasyllabic

organizer, endowed with an unparalleled talent for creating rapidly and with ease.

In this case, the placement of each interruption reveals how Sibylla's relationship with Liberace is mapped onto her relationship with cultural production. This is demonstrated by the separation of these phrases in the final edition: 'think he', 'father Pietro', 'Michelangelo ([1475–1564]) painter', 'superhuman concentration' and 'first-rate organizer'. As described by Konstantinou, the interruptions channel the mental duress of Sibylla's 'unpaid reproductive labor'; her 'superhuman concentration' is disrupted on a literal narrative level, as well as a formal one (2022, 5). Sentences ('think he') are visualised as trains of thought incapable of completion. Further, in the same way that 'Impressionism' is split from 'school of painting' in Cézanne's passage, nominal signifiers ('Pietro', 'Michelangelo') are often separated from the clarifying noun.

Maurice Blanchot distinguishes between the act of composition and that of juxtaposition; here, DeWitt defers to the latter by 'respecting and preserving this exteriority and this distance as the principle' (1993, 308). The added syntactic distance between 'father' and 'Pietro', for instance, reflects that Ludo does not know his father's name.

Second, still projecting Sibylla's voice, it formalises the disparity between Pietro and Liberace as father figures, as only the former can fulfil the paternal ideal in '[existing] as an ideal point of reference' (Namiki 2020, 2132). In her view, Liberace's commercial success as a mediocre travel writer, couched in the post-postmodernist 'logics of globalization and capital', is antithetical to the higher artistic providence symbolised in Pietro as a father (Nealon 2012, 42). Yet, as the changes from '1LIBERAC' suggest, Ludo is not subject to the continuity of a bloodline. 'Pietro, a sculptor' can occupy a separate line from Bernini, as Ludo can choose his own father. Even Ludo's name, Latin for 'I play', is at odds with the capitalist motivations of Liberace's career. As such, the interruption of lineation doubles as one of lineage, reinforcing the novel's theme that 'the paternal, or authority, is subjective'—not subject to genealogical determinism or continuity (Namiki 2020, 2137). Or, in Moi's words: 'elective affinities beat biological families every time' (2021, 37). The syntactic difference between versions thus places what Blanchot calls the 'disjunction or divergence' of form as 'the infinite centre from out of which, through speech, relation is to be created'—literally forming the relation of Sibylla's post-nuclear family (1993, 308). On its broadest level, DeWitt's interruption of a paternal lineage extends to the 'favoured hypotexts' of modernity (Genette 1997, 397). In 'emptying the position of the father' from '1LIBERAC', DeWitt negates a literary economy in which this aesthetic lineage is privy to Genette's version of 'the realistic "father" [...] and the invocation of a few privileged uncles and ancestors' (Frow et. al 2020, 1905; 1997, 397). Consequently, DeWitt broadens the text's thematic underpinnings to construe 'genealogy' as double-pronged, having meaning beyond the narrative level of *familial*.

3. '7S3.2'

In the third chapter, Ludo and Sibylla begin to argue about this *familial* paternity: the identity of his father, whom Sibylla will not reveal due to

Liberace's perceived mediocrity. Fed up with Ludo's line of questioning, Sibylla retreats to watch *Seven Samurai*, referred to in facetious longhand as 'one of the masterpieces of modern cinema' (2000, 280). Despite the obvious homage to Kurosawa, the interjections of *Seven Samurai* are not present in the drafts '7S3.2' (in *09-07-96*), '7S3.2' (in *Backup Liberace*) '7S3.2c', '7S3.2e', '7S3.3', or '7S3.4'. DeWitt's notes in the folder *17.5.97*, which include transliterated descriptions of the film in 'KUROSAWA' and 'CHIAKI', indicate that these incursions were added about a year after the 1996 drafts. To best represent the significance of these changes, this section will directly compare DeWitt's earliest draft ('7S3.2' in *09-07-96*) to its final instantiation. Again, DeWitt's additions to the draft are rendered in boldface:

> She said: If you don't need me for anything I'm going to watch 7S Seven Samurai for a while.
>
> **She turned off the computer. It was about 11:30. So far she had spent about 8 minutes typing which at £6.25 an hour meant she had earned about 83p.**
>
> **She picked up the remote and pressed ON and PLAY.**
>
> ***40 bandits stop on a hill above a village in Japan. They decide to raid it after the barley harvest. A farmer overhears.***
> ***A village meeting is held. The farmers despair.***
> ***Rikichi leaps to his feet with burning eyes.***
> ***Let's make bamboo spears! Let's run 'em all through!***
> ***Not me, says Yohei.***
> ***Impossible, says Manzo.***
>
> I used to take her word for it. But what if she's wrong? A new book by the author of the magazine article came out last month. According to the reviews he is one of the greatest writers of our time.

DeWitt's additions signal two distinct levels of interruption: the numeric addendum of her hourly wage, keeping with the post-postmodernist authenticity of the text, and the transmedial narrative of *Seven Samurai*. First, DeWitt's added invocation of numerical values yokes Sibylla's experienced time to Benjamin's 'homogenous, empty time'. In contrast, '7S3.2' links leisure (watching *Seven Samurai*) to an abstracted notion of time ('a while') not beholden to the metric of the workday—8 minutes can be quantified as 83p, while 'a while' cannot (2000, 261). By juxtaposing these two temporalities between versions, DeWitt narrativises the way in which capital occludes leisure, representing it on the page anaphorically. The time Sibylla spends watching *Seven Samurai* is now parsed in terms of lost capital. Relatedly, Bernaerts and Van Hulle argue that Cohn and Pountney's integrated approach to Beckett's *Lessness* simultaneously 'applies' and 'exposes' narrativisation through the way they interpret human imposition on time (2013, 310). Extrapolating this critical logic to *The Last Samurai*, DeWitt 'applies' narrativisation by linking it to a casual sequence of events, yet 'exposes' it by indicting the framing of capitalism as a naturalised 'model of coherence' (qtd. in Bernaerts and Van Hulle 2013, 309). Considering *Seven Samurai* within this post-postmodernist framework, the seamless integration of film into text represents the place where cultural and economic production meet. By reducing the filmic valence to the level of text, *pace* Baudrillard's *Simulations* via Nealon, the reality of the narrative 'isn't becoming indistinguishable from the movies; it has become indistinguishable' (2012, 176). DeWitt's conflation of medium (e.g. film and text) further reinforces this interpretative liminality.

As such, on the transmedial level, Marie-Laure Ryan's 'medium-independent definition of narration' is useful in conceptualising DeWitt's repudiation of medium coherence, insofar as it 'relies on literary narrative as a comparative standard but does not limit itself to the literary form' (Bay 2005; Ryan 2004, 721–22). Ryan contends that there are 'other ways of evoking narrative scripts' beyond language; *The Last Samurai* complicates this discursive gap by rendering cinematic media *as* language, both transmedial and not (2004, 13). While '7S3.2' (in *09-07-96*), '7S3.2' (in *Backup Liberace*), '7S3.2c', '7S3.2e', '7S3.3' and '7S3.4' straightforwardly cast watching the film as a narrative action carried out by Sibylla, the later version plays it as if on videotape. *Seven Samurai* forms a dialectic, interrupting the text while continuing its narrative thread. Rikichi's 'burning eyes' become a transmedial motif, reproduced in Sibylla during times of duress. For example, when Ludo pesters her about his father, she looks at him with the same 'burning eyes' (280). The film's line-up of Rikichi, Yohei, Manzo and the other five samurai comprise Sibylla's 'eight male role models' for Ludo. Demanding narrative attention through disruption of the text, they also parallel the male role models Ludo seeks outside the transmedial space of *Seven Samurai*. As Yuki Namiki points out, Ludo re-enacts these scenes whenever he meets a potential father, resembling Kambei, 'who is recruiting master-less yet authentic Samurai to join his band' (2020, 2136). The hypotext, rather than being mapped beneath the textual economy, is mapped chaotically atop it.

After Ludo's argument with his mother, they take a mundane grocery trip to Tesco, where they run into a 'mild fat woman' whom Sibylla 'had hoped never to see again' (2000, 396). The woman is referred to as 'The Meddler' in earlier drafts, reminiscent of Ludo's nickname 'The Infant Terrible', and later amended to simply 'the woman'. It is revealed the woman once saved Sibylla's life, though the circumstances are unclear. While this scene occurs immediately after Ludo's argument in '7S3.2' (in *09-07-96*), '7S3.2' (in *Backup Liberace*) '7S3.2c', '7S3.2e', '7S3.3' and '7S3.4', it is ultimately moved to the last quarter of the book, after an unsuccessful meeting with the potential father HC. Additionally, the interruption in this passage is excerpted from Hamlet's soliloquy and significantly pared down in the final version from '7S3.2'. Rather than an overt breakage of narrative like *Seven Samurai*, the soliloquy is voiced diegetically through Sibylla, ventriloquising her suicidal ideation. As Konstantinou elucidates, Sibylla, 'a character named after a victim of divine abuse' at the hands of Apollo, *'wants to die'* (2022, 6). Sibylla's chosen Shakespearean verse reflects this ideation:

> If the woman opposite was capable of thought, something for which we had as yet no evidence, her thoughts were certainly opaque to her companions. I could see Sibylla's thoughts circling her mind like goldfish in a bowl. ~~She was fighting a powerful urge to say that I was tubercular, or had sickle-cell anaemia, or leukaemia, or cancer, that my every waking hour was a torment, and that I could not draw breath without anguish.~~ At last ~~my mother~~ she spoke.
>
> > To be or not to be, that is the question:
> > Whether 'tis nobler in the mind to suffer
> > The slings and arrows of outrageous fortune
> > Or to take arms against a sea of troubles
> > And by opposing, end them. To die, to sleep—
> > No more and by a sleep to say we end
> > The heart-ache and the thousand natural shocks
> > That flesh is heir to; 'tis a consummation

> ~~Devoutly to be wished~~
>
> ~~So far she had spoken with a slow, natural gravity, as if there cd be no need for words of her own when the poet had expressed her very thought. But now, as she went on, her voice by its very stress seemed to emphasise her rejection of the words:~~
>
> [...]³
>
> ~~If one does not believe in the afterlife, said my mother, one's course wd appear to be clear.~~
>
> The ~~Meddler~~ woman glanced aghast at the small fat crew and was at once relieved, for it was clear enough that they had not understood a word of this.
>
> Well, of course we all have our cross to bear, she said cheerily.
>
> ~~My mother~~ Sibylla gazed down, eyes blazing, at a tin of baked beans.

In contrast to the transmedial interjections of *Seven Samurai*, the excerpted soliloquy is fully narrativised as dialogue that Sibylla conveys to another character, creating a tension between dieges es. This tension is foregrounded by the onus of interpretation falling to the woman, in the same way that it falls to the reader with *Seven Samurai*—as if asked to prove we too are 'capable of thought'. In changing her name from 'the Meddler' in '7S3.2' to simply 'the woman', DeWitt further aligns her with a *role*, rather than a character with any focal interiority beyond her capacity to interpret Sibylla's opacity. As David Herman writes, the burden of evaluating meaning in experimental literature 'quite often seems to shift from teller to interpreter' (2016, 49). DeWitt complicates this dichotomy by posing 'interpretation' on the level of both the narrative (why is she reciting Shakespeare in the Tesco bread aisle?) and the text (the soliloquy itself). Through this interpretative tension, DeWitt tests the extent to which her interpolated fragments 'can become a narrative sequence if the spectator supplies common agents and logical connections', as David Bordwell and Kristin Thompson have

---

3   This bracket, which DeWitt took out in the final iteration of the text, is a continuation of Hamlet's soliloquy beginning from 'to die' and ending at 'puzzle the will'.

contended (qtd. in Ryan 2004, 11). The woman, in responding to Sibylla, inadvertently narrativises what is initially intertextually incompatible.

Further, while '7S3.2' transcribes nearly the entire speech, the final version interrupts itself before its logical and syntactic conclusion—"'tis a consummation' stands on its own, while 'devoutly to be wished' is rendered to subtext. Hamlet's deliberation about the afterlife, and any ambiguity that may 'puzzle the will', is conspicuously removed (Shakespeare 2019, 78). Again, Sibylla *'wants to die'*, but can only express it obliquely, as the focalisation has shifted to Ludo (Konstantinou 2022, 6). As she expresses in a line cut from '7S3.2', there is 'no need for words of her own when the poet had expressed her very thought', narrativising the two texts into coherence. In Ryan's sense, the soliloquy's hermeneutic utility 'resides neither in the concrete circumstances nor in the particular social function of the narrative act but in the context-transcending nature of this act' (2004, 5). Released from its initial context, the soliloquy resupplies Sibylla her voice.

4. The Circle Line Ends

> I said: Aren't you supposed to be typing *The Modern Knitter*?
> Indolence, interruption, business, and pleasure; all take their turns of retardation, said Sib. I'm up to 1965.
>
> —Helen DeWitt, *The Last Samurai* (2000)

In DeWitt's collection *Some Trick*, her critique of the publishing industry and its larger, institutional fatuity is hardly veiled. In fact, in execution, it is far more overt than *The Last Samurai*. One story, 'My Heart Belongs to Bertie', offers itself as punchline to a cynical set-up: what happens when a mathematician and a literary agent walk into a diner? DeWitt answers: nothing. The mathematician will walk out, and the literary agent will remain a creature of convention, uninterested in accurately publishing his opaque binomials. As Moi writes, *Some Trick* agonises over publishers 'who are only too ready to "love" writers they haven't read and to travesty the artist's vision in order to make money off her creativity' (38–39). *Some Trick* could consequently be called semi-autobiographical, bitterly adducing DeWitt's own battle with Talk Miramax Books.

Similarly, while the extant floppy disks of *The Last Samurai* contribute to an avant-texte of the work itself, they also form one which catalogues

DeWitt's unending struggle to publish it (Ramsden 2022, 39). The folders *Notes 17.5.97* and *20-04-98* feature a slew of letters to editors, friends and employers from DeWitt, seemingly 'nothing but apologies and missed deadlines' ('woolf'). Most of the letters entail work, albeit not work on *The Last Samurai* manuscript, but the exterior work that would allow her to. As endless as the Circle Line itself, DeWitt writes of her secretarial job: 'I'll be working days (and days and days) until the end of the month the way things are going' ('LAURA'). She considers quitting and moving in with her mother to write full time, describing the exigencies of white-collardom as 'like putting my mind in a little box; at the end of the day it hardly seems worth taking it out of the box' ('LAURA'). Meanwhile, the originating conceit of 'My Heart Belongs to Bertie' becomes obvious in DeWitt's dealings with Talk Miramax Books. As Konstantinou details, the publishing company prioritised convention over stylistic expressiveness, changing DeWitt's intentionally experimental use of restrictive clauses, capital letters and rendering of numbers—all choices that consciously inform the mechanics of rupture examined in this essay. After all, in the words of DeWitt herself: 'These rules are not handed down by God', and to experiment with these rules and their interstices is 'what makes literary language literary in the first place' (qtd. in Konstantinou 2022, 58). As the genetic narratological findings of this essay suggest, the diachrony of DeWitt's versions poses *The Last Samurai* as 'more a dynamic work in progress than a static oeuvre' (Bernaerts and Van Hulle 2013, 311). In moving to eschew the standards of copyediting, DeWitt's dynamism is a quest for the originality of language, mirroring Ludo's quest to find a father.

DeWitt supplies one last meditation on language. In a document titled 'How I would improve the Sunday Review' in *20-04-98*, she writes that book reviews should provide extracts, as 'some books don't show to good advantage in reviews, because the best thing about them is the use of language' ('ind'). *The Last Samurai* does not offer itself up for appraisal, extracted or otherwise. Deviating from what easily shows to good advantage, DeWitt aligns herself with a desire beyond that of institutions like Talk Miramax Books or the Sunday Review—choosing instead to break with language to best use it.

Works Cited

Auerbach, Erich [1946] (2013), *Mimesis: The Representation of Reality in Western Literature* (Princeton, NJ: Princeton University Press). https://doi.org/10.2307/j.ctt3fgz26.2.

Baetens, Jan (2019), 'Critical Fictions: Experiments in Writing from Le Nouveau Roman to the Oulipo', in: *Introducing Literary Theories*, 404–10.

Bay, Jennifer (2005), 'Narrative across Media: The Languages of Storytelling (Review)', *MFS Modern Fiction Studies*, 51.3: 721–24, https://doi.org/10.1353/mfs.2005.0050.

Benedict, Anderson [1983] (2016), *Imagined Communities: Reflections on the Origin and Spread of Nationalism* (London: Verso).

Benjamin, Walter [1968] (2019), *Illuminations*, with an introduction by Hannah Arendt (Boston: Mariner Books; Houghton Mifflin Harcourt).

Bernaerts, Lars, and Dirk Van Hulle (2013), 'Narrative across Versions: Narratology Meets Genetic Criticism', *Poetics Today*, 34.3: 281–326, https://doi.org/10.1215/03335372-2325232.

Blanchot, Maurice [1969] (1993), *The Infinite Conversation* (Minneapolis, MN: University of Minnesota Press).

Bray, Joe, et al (2015), *The Routledge Companion to Experimental Literature* (London: Routledge).

Bruns, Gerald L. (2018), *Interruptions: The Fragmentary Aesthetic in Modern Literature* (Tuscaloosa, AL: The University of Alabama Press).

DeWitt, Helen (1996), 3.5" floppy disk labelled '09-07-96', in a file called '7S3.2'.

DeWitt, Helen (1998), 3.5" floppy disk labelled '20-0-.98', in a file called 'ind'.

DeWitt, Helen (1998), 3.5" floppy disk labelled '20-04-98', in a file called 'woolf'.

DeWitt, Helen (1996), 3.5" floppy disk labelled 'Backup Liberace 7-6-96 + 1Liberac (Very Early)', in a file called '1LIBERAC'.

DeWitt, Helen (1998), 3.5" floppy disk labelled 'Notes 17.5.97', in a file called 'LAURA'.

DeWitt, Helen (2000), *The Last Samurai* (New York: Talk Miramax Books).

Frow, John, et al. (2020), 'The Bildungsroman: Form and Transformations', *Textual Practice*, 34.12: 1905–10, https://doi.org/10.1080/0950236x.2020.1834692.

Gallagher, Catherine (2000), 'Formalism and Time', *Modern Language Quarterly*, 61.1: 229–51, https://doi.org/10.1215/00267929-61-1-229.

Genette, Gérard (1979), *Narrative Discourse: Gerard Genette* (Oxford: Blackwell).

Genette, Gérard [1982] (1997), *Palimpsests: Literature in the Second Degree* (Lincoln, NE: University of Nebraska Press).

Herman, David (2016), 'Toward a Transmedial Narratology', in: *Transmedial Narratology and Contemporary Media Culture* ed. by Jan-Noel Thon (Lincoln, NE: University of Nebraska Press), 1–32, https://doi.org/10.2307/j.ctt1d8h8vn.6.

Konstantinou, Lee (2022), *The Last Samurai Reread* (New York: Columbia University Press). https://doi-org.ezproxy-prd.bodleian.ox.ac.uk/10.7312/kons18582.

Kowalik, George (2023), 'Post-Postmodernism, the "Affective Turn", and Inauthenticity', *Humanities*, 12.1: 7, https://doi.org/10.3390/h12010007.

Metz, Christian, and Michael Taylor [1974] (2007), *Film Language: A Semiotics of the Cinema* (Chicago: University of Chicago Press).

Moi, Toril (2021), *B-Side Books: Essays on Forgotten Favorites* (New York: Columbia University Press).

Namiki, Yuki (2020), 'It's a Wise Child Who Knows His Own Father: The Figure of the American Family in *The Last Samurai* and *Extremely Loud and Incredibly Close*', *Textual Practice*, 34.12: 2131–43, https://doi.org/10.1080/0950236x.2020.1834701.

Nealon, Jeffrey Thomas (2012), *Post-Postmodernism: Or, the Logic of Just-in-Time Capitalism* (Redwood, CA: Stanford University Press).

Ramsden, Maureen A. (2002), 'Jean Santeuil and the Notion of Avant-Texte: A Case for an Extension of the Term?', *Dalhousie French Studies*, 58: 39–53, http://www.jstor.org/stable/40836979.

Ryan, Marie-Laure (2004), *Narrative across Media: The Languages of Storytelling* (Lincoln, NE: University of Nebraska Press).

Shakespeare, William [1603] (2019), *Hamlet* (Charlotte, NC: Spark Publishing).

Smith, Rachel Greenwald (2011), 'Postmodernism and the Affective Turn', *Twentieth-Century Literature*, 57.3–4: 423–46, https://doi.org/10.1215/0041462x-2011-4008.

15. Nanogenetic Econarratology: Where Narratology Meets Keystroke Logging Data

Lamyk Bekius

1. Introduction: Genetic Narratology Without Versions?

Genetic narratology introduces various drafts or versions to the study of narratives (Bernaerts and Van Hulle 2013; Van Hulle 2022). The rise of home computers from the 1980s and literary authors adopting them to write their novels creates uncertainty concerning this specific type of narrative analysis, as the digital writing environment complicates the concept of version. What is, for instance, the probability that the author working in a digital environment consistently saves intermediate versions of the text under a different name? Apart from when the Track Changes function has been used, additions are mostly visualised by the Graphical User Interface (GUI) as inline text production while deleted text 'disappears' from the screen. Common traces of the writing process are replaced by clean, formatted texts in default fonts. In the absence of digital versions, genetic narratology seems hardly possible for texts written in the Digital Age. Are we therefore forced to return to studying these narratives only in their final and published form?

Such far-reaching consequences are no more than doomsday scenarios. The work of Matthew Kirschenbaum (2008), Thorsten Ries (2017; 2018), Veijo Pulkkinen (2023) and the *Derrida Hexadecimal* project led by Aurèle Crasson (Crasson 2023) demonstrates how digital forensics methods and tools can be applied to recover deleted text files and reveal genetic layers that are not visible in the conventional GUI of word processors. These digital forensic methods show promising results for the genetic study of narratives that have already been written, mostly on, but not limited to, legacy devices. In this essay, I discuss another method that scholars can use—in collaboration with living authors—to provide a solution to the challenges posed by the shift to a digital writing environment: the use of keystroke logging to log the writing process from the first character typed to the last revision. This entails a form of 'pre-custodial' archiving, meaning that it takes place in the period before the actual acquisition of the literary archive (Weisbrod 2016). More precisely, the decision to use a keystroke logger must be made before the actual writing of the text. The resulting keystroke logging data offer a wealth of possibilities for genetic criticism and can enrich genetic narratology by including an enhanced temporal dimension into the analysis, which I have termed the nanogenesis (Bekius 2021; 2023).

No doomsday scenario for genetic criticism so far, but it is in fact possible to investigate the creation of a story that engages with a doomsday scenario. The story 'Mondini', written by the Flemish poet and author David Troch (1977–), is set in a world after environmental collapse and its writing process was logged with the keystroke logger Inputlog. With the keystroke logging data of this narrative engaging with the effects of climate crisis, we therefore have the unique opportunity to examine the writing process from an econarratological perspective.

Econarratology examines 'the mechanics of how narratives can convey environmental understanding via building blocks such as the organization of time and space, characterization, focalization, description, and narration' (James and Morel 2020, 1). To explore the possibilities of introducing keystroke logging into the field of econarratology, this essay examines the visible dynamics of writing as Troch integrated details of narrative space into his story. For a fruitful interdisciplinary combination of genetic criticism and narratology, this essay addresses two focal points: the principle of minimal departure and genre.

First, Marie-Laure Ryan's 'principle of minimal departure' suggests that readers project their knowledge of the real world onto the world represented by the text, unless the text dictates otherwise. In addition, as I will show, it can also be used as a framework for understanding authorial decisions. Second, according to Astrid Bracke, '[a]n econarratological approach to genre provides a useful starting point for exploring which forms, registers, structures, and tropes tend to feature in narratives of environmental crisis' (2020, 165). By examining the writing process from an econarratological perspective, I explore the relationship between genre and narrative space in particular. With a focus on these two points, the essay assesses the usability of keystroke logging data to enhance the study of (eco)narratology.

2. Keystroke Logging the Creation of an Alternative Possible World

The opportunities keystroke logging offers for studying the digital literary writing process within genetic criticism and writing studies have been investigated within the project Track Changes: Textual Scholarship and the Challenge of Digital Literary Writing (2018–24).[1] For this project, Dutch and Flemish authors have been asked to log the writing process of a short story with the keystroke logger Inputlog (Leijten and Van Waes 2013). While activated, Inputlog logs every keystroke and mouse-movement in Microsoft Word, as well as outside the word processor (e.g. the switches to different windows and websites). Additionally, the tool saves the digital document at the start of each writing session as well as at the end of the session in a folder containing the date and number of the writing session—the 'session-versions' (Bekius 2021; 2023). The most fine-grained level of output provided by Inputlog is a tabular representation of keystroke data, in which every row represents one log event, such as a keystroke or a mouse movement, in combination with the position in the text and a timestamp. This output is not well-suited for a text genetic analysis, which aims to study the revisions and text production within the context of the text that has already been

---

[1] The analysis of Troch's writing process in this essay contains revised parts of my analysis of this writing process in my PhD dissertation *Behind the screens: the use of keystroke logging for genetic criticism applied to born-digital works of literature* (2023). These parts are taken from chapter 5.3.1 and chapter 6.1.3. For this essay, the analyses are incorporated into an econarratological framework. The project 'Track Changes' is a collaboration between Huygens Institute (Royal Netherlands Academy of Arts and Sciences, Amsterdam) and the University of Antwerp (Antwerp Centre for Digital Humanities and Literary Criticism) and is funded by the Dutch Research Council (NWO).

written—the text produced so far. For this reason, I have encoded the writing actions as present in the keystroke data into the session versions and made visualisations that allow for seeing all the modifications made within one writing session at a glance and replaying the writing session (Bekius 2021). These visualisations are publicly accessible on Nanogenesis Digital.[2]

Through these visualisations of the keystroke logging data, the writing process can be examined at an unprecedented level of granularity, including the way the author moved through the text and the sequentiality of text production and revision. Through this focus on the nanogenesis, the movement of writing can be highlighted in a way that has not been feasible before.

David Troch was one of the authors willing to record their writing process with Inputlog. Troch wrote 'Mondini' in eight days—from mid-August until mid-September 2020—during which he logged 20 writing sessions. The genetic dossier thus comprises 20 Word documents and the keystroke logging data, with a total duration of 27 hours, 48 minutes and 24 seconds. As mentioned above, the story offers a glimpse into a world heavily affected by global warming. The first-person narrator has fled from the drought and heat caused by climate change and lost his partner and daughter along the way. He narrates how he is now trying to survive on his own, in a small apartment in the mountain village named Mondini in Italy. The narrator describes his daily whereabouts and how he tries not to lose his mind. In the meantime, he describes the changes in the environment and society, and the impact it has on his personal life. 'Mondini' therefore presents the reader with a worst-case scenario of climate crisis. An econarratological perspective can therefore provide useful guidance for analysing the writing process in which this world is created.

Richard Kerridge identifies 'providing an all-out apocalyptic vision of catastrophe, to shock and scare us deeply' as one of the functions of literature from an eco-critical perspective (2014, 372). A crucial factor regarding these narratives is, according to Kerridge, 'the extent to which the apocalyptic plot is combined with elements of literary realism, giving

---

[2] Nanogenesis Digital is my digital scholarly edition platform that hosts visualisations of digital writing processes based on keystroke data. It is publicly available at: https://nanogenesis-digital.github.io.

us characters and events that seem consistent with real possibility' and 'the degree of compatibility with what is scientifically understood to be possible' (372). This means that in order to achieve this effect of shock and anxiety, the reader must be able to immerse themselves in the (in this case apocalyptic) world presented by the text. This concept is described by Marie-Laure Ryan as 'recentering', which is the process that 'pushes the reader into a new system of actuality and possibility' (1991, 22). In other words, it places the reader into an alternative possible world.

In the framework of possible world theory within literary theory, the text is understood as presenting an alternative possible world (APW)—or in this case the textual actual world (TAW)—that stands in relation to the actual world (AW). Ryan distinguishes nine accessibility relations from the AW that are involved in the construction of a TAW—and thus show the similarity/difference between the AW and the TAW. These include that the TAW is accessible from the AW if 'the objects common to TAW and AW have the same properties' (A/properties), if they 'are furnished by the same objects' (B/same inventory), 'if TAW includes all the members of AW, as well as some native members' (C/expanded inventory), 'if it takes no temporal relocation for a member of AW to contemplate the entire history of TAW' (D/chronology), 'if they share natural laws' (E/natural laws), 'if both worlds contain the same species, and the species are characterised by the same properties' (F/taxonomy), 'if both worlds respect the principles of noncontradiction and of excluded middle' (G/logic), 'if objects designated by the same words have the same essential properties' (H/analytical) and 'if the language in which TAW is described can be understood in AW' (I/linguistic) (Ryan 1991, 32–33). Based on these nine types of accessibility relations, Ryan has delineated a typology for differentiating genres.

For example, from the genres discussed by Ryan, anticipation novels—and I will return to this below—are most relevant for our discussion of the TAW in 'Mondini'. As Ryan points out, '[t]he point of anticipation novels is to show what may become of the actual world given its present state and past history' (36). To achieve this, the only relations that may be severed are B/same inventory and D/chronology (36).

Ryan argues that readers always rely on their own (knowledge of the) world and environment as a starting point for their understanding of the

TAW, which she refers to as 'the principle of minimal departure' (Ryan 1991). This principle states that we reconstrue the central world of the textual universe 'as conforming as far as possible to the representation of AW' (Ryan 1991, 51). This means that we will project on a fictional world 'everything we know about reality, and we will make only adjustments dictated by the text' (Ryan 1991, 51). We will thus always imagine the textual actual world with snippets of the actual world when we are reading fiction that engages with climate crisis, and—it appears—also while writing it.

The principle of minimal departure is mostly used for the part of the reader, but in the process of writing the same principle can apply to the author *constructing* the TAW. In fiction, 'the writer relocates to what is for us a mere possible world, and makes it the center of an alternative system of reality' (Ryan 1991, 24). Since the AW is where the author is located (Ryan 1991, 24), this will of course also be their starting point during the writing process, especially in its initial stages. As Trexler points out, the first hurdle faced by an author writing about climate change 'is to construct a fictional space where climate change presents itself as an immediate problem' (78). The keystroke logging data now enables us to reconstruct how Troch invented his climate-change-affected TAW, step by step.

3. Authorial Minimal Departure

In narratives engaging with climate crisis, narrative space naturally plays a fundamental role. The narrative space, at its most fundamental level, is the environment in which the characters of the story move and live (Buchholz and Jahn 2005, 552). One of the parameters by which it is marked is the (friendly/hostile) living conditions, including climatic and atmospheric, that it provides (Buchholz and Jahn 2005, 552). Writing about climate change thus involves imagining the living conditions in a world affected by environmental collapse. In his descriptions of the TAW in 'Mondini', Troch eventually deals with widely represented transformations of global climate change, as described by Trexler: direct heat, arctic switches and floods (2018, 78). Since the keystroke logging data allows for a detailed reconstruction of the writing process, the principle of minimal departure can be used to describe the way authors come to write narrative spaces affected by climate change. In this case, the principle is useful to illustrate how Troch constructed his TAW that is dictated by transformations of global climate change. Based on the reconstructions of the writing process, we can examine how ideas for this TAW emerged from aspects of the AW and how other ideas were triggered by other aspects of the TAW.

In the first session in which Troch starts working on the story (Session 2, 10 August 2020)—he types the approximately 700-word long opening sentence. In this version, the first-person narrator is already hiding out in a desolate mountain village, but Troch does not yet provide any information about the exact reason *why* he is hiding. The world the first-person narrator inhabits still has running water and electricity, and although he tries to avoid people, when he does meet others, they are rather friendly—too friendly for his liking:

> maar als je dan toch iemand tegenkomt, heeft die zo goed als altijd zin om je staande te houden voor een praatje en de praatjes vrolijken me niet bepaald op, want veel diepgang kennen ze niet, er worden geen vragen gesteld, men durft de huidige toestand niet aan de kaak te stellen en dat zou men nochtans beter soms wel eens doen, [...] (Session 2)

> [but when you do meet someone, they almost always want to stop you for a chat and the chats don't exactly cheer me up, because they don't go in depth, no questions are asked, people don't dare denounce the current situation and they should do that sometimes, [...]]³

In this world, people still want to talk to each other, preferably about light-hearted topics. The reference to 'the current situation', however, seems to imply that there is something going on in the world, but *what* is not explicated. The first-person narrator acts as if he is 'de laatste mens op deze godvergeten planeet' ['the last human being on this godforsaken planet'], but for the reader, this world still resembles the AW—except for the part where the narrator believes that there will be no more snow in this mountain village where people used to go skiing.

The TAW already changed a bit in the fourth session, which took place only a couple of hours later. Whereas in the previous version it was only very unlikely that it would snow again, skiing is now something from

---

3   Unless otherwise indicated, all the translations of quotations from the Dutch original are mine (LB).

the 'distant past'. Also, all appliances that run on electricity have lost their practical use. As the first-person narrator puts it: 'We zijn terug naar het stenen tijdperk geworpen. Wat er van we nog overblijft' ['We have been thrown back to the Stone Age. Whatever is left of we']. People no longer form a community; they are all on their own. People no longer talk to each other; they just look at each other cautiously from a distance before finally running away. Troch is thus already describing a tiny shift in worldview, one that affects human interaction.

At the end of the text, Troch writes a conceptual note suggesting that the story is set in a world in which there seems to be no life. How did the narrator get there and what is he saying about the past? These two questions can be interpreted as questions that Troch wants to explore in the short story. However, they can also be interpreted as questions that Troch is asking himself—he needs to think about these questions before he can continue writing the story. Troch has not yet fully conceived his dystopian world; his knowledge of the TAW he is creating still needs to develop as he writes.

As mentioned above, Troch had written in the fourth session that all appliances that run on electricity have lost their practical use, which means that there is no more electricity. In the following session, Troch writes that the first-person narrator tries to maintain a pattern in his days, and in describing this pattern we see the principle of minimal departure. Since many people start their day with a shower, this was probably also one of the first things Troch thought of when writing about how the narrator starts his day as he writes: 'De dag begint met een douche' ['The day begins with a shower'] (n186).[4] Then he adds 'Zolang er stromend water is, is er hoop' ['As long as there is running water, there is hope'] (n187–189). He then probably remembers that he had previously mentioned that there is no electricity, and realises that it is very unlikely that there would be running water without electricity, so he adds: 'Hoe het komt dat er geen elektriciteit maar nog wel stromend water is' ['How come there is no electricity but there is still running water'] (n190–196). This, again, can be interpreted both

---

[4] The number refers to the numbers given to the writing actions in my reconstructions of the writing sessions. In this case, the sentence production was the 186th encoded writing action of this session (see Bekius 2023 for a detailed description of the way the writing sessions were reconstructed).

as a reminder to address this in the story and as a question he is asking himself. A little later he does a Google search to find out if it is possible to have running water without electricity: 'kan er stromend water zijn zonder elektriciteit' ['can there be running water without electricity'] (n203). This leads him to the webpage 'Leven zonder stromend water en elektriciteit' ['Living without running water and electricity'] (n204). Eventually, Troch clarifies the situation by explaining that the narrator has to go outside to get water; it no longer comes out of the tap. In this way, there is still a physical compatibility between the TAW and the AW, while—on the other hand—the difference between this world and the AW is also highlighted.

The examples above show the authorial principle of minimal departure. In the first writing sessions, Troch did not yet fully conceive how the TAW differs from the one we know. This indicates that in the construction of this TAW, Troch's reference point remained the AW. Slowly, however, 'Mondini' begins to take place in a world where environmental disaster has already occurred, which makes it relevant to consider what genre the story is becoming, and how Troch's choices during the writing process influence this matter of genre.

4. Alternating Between Genres

As mentioned above, of the genres discussed by Ryan, 'Mondini' most closely resembles the genre of anticipation fiction. After all, the story shows 'what may become of the actual world given its present state and past history' (Ryan 1991, 36) regarding environmental crisis. However, it is in fact this specific engagement with environmental crisis that the genre of anticipation novels does not do justice to, while understanding 'the workings of genre as a significant element in narrating environmental crisis' has been considered relevant to econarratology (Bracke 2018, 165). Since the genre was still variable during the writing process, it is worth reviewing the genres that could apply to 'Mondini' as the writing process proceeded.

The world in 'Mondini' could, in the first instance, be described as post-apocalyptic, yet, as E. Ann Kaplan notes 'this term assumes some sudden event takes place to bring on the end' (14). Astrid Bracke—quoting Greg Garrard (2011)—also deems the term *apocalypse* problematic, since it has the 'tendency to reduce complex issues to "monocausal crises involving conflicts between recognizably opposed groups"' (Bracke 2018, 24). Moreover, she argues that post-apocalyptic narratives are too much associated with 'the fictions of disaster films or science fiction', which distances people from the sense of urgency regarding climate crisis (2018, 4). In 'Mondini', the environmental condition of the TAW did not develop overnight but was the result of gradual and cumulative environmental changes. Moreover, Troch seems well aware of the associations of apocalypse and addresses it in the story: for example, the narrator states that the 'reality would make up for a fine film scenario'. As a result, the story seems to transcend the apocalypse genre.

Given her aforementioned objection to the term *apocalypse*, Kaplan opts for using the term *dystopia* for the worlds depicted in her corpus of pretrauma climate cinema: '[g]iven the gradual and subtle shifts in ecosystems damaged by humans, rather than a Big Bang sort of event, *dystopia* seems best to convey what this genre depicts' (14). What, then, are the distinguishing features of a dystopian text? Mattison Schuknecht states that literary utopia and dystopia are difficult to place within Ryan's typology and suggests adding a 'new accessibility relation that can distinguish utopian/dystopian texts from science fiction and anticipation novels': 'non-a/meliorate' (2019, 234). This relation 'would maintain if the possible world presented through the fictional text does not systematically ameliorate or deteriorate the state or conditions of our actual world' (234). According to Schuknecht, utopian and dystopian texts abandon this rule, as they 'represent possible worlds that are significantly better or worse than the reader's AW' (234). Then, taking on the internal perspective of the textual universe, a distinction can be made between utopian/dystopian fictional worlds. For this purpose, Schuknecht uses Doležel's system of modalities: 'alethic, deontic, axiological, and epistemic' (238). He proposes that 'utopian and dystopian texts engage with the deontic system (permitted, prohibited, and obligatory)' (234). In this respect, he argues, 'dystopian texts contain extensive conflict between the modalities of the deontic system, while utopian texts contain a substantial degree of harmony between the same modalities' (234). In other words, deontic conflict is maximised in dystopian worlds, and minimised in utopian worlds (234).

'Mondini' meets these parameters for being a dystopian story: the TAW represented is significantly worse than the AW, as—among other things—the high temperatures make it unbearable to be outside. Moreover, the relentless search for water and cooling creates a deontic conflict. The dystopian TAW in 'Mondini', however, contains one aspect not accounted for in Schuknecht's discussion of dystopias, namely that the natural, physical laws are no longer compatible with the AW. For example, the hydrological cycle is broken in the TAW, and even when it rains, the rain is warmer than 'de heetste waterstraal die vroeger, lang, lang geleden uit de douche kwam' ['the hottest jet of water that used to come out of the shower a long, long time ago']. This means that the TAW contains elements common in climate fiction. Whereas utopia/dystopia are compatible with the accessibility relation 'E/natural laws' (physical compatibility with the AW), climate fiction novels—but not all—draw exactly on these aspects: 'climate crisis has circumstances that have worsened so much that old laws no longer apply or new ones kick in' (Bracke 2020, 175).

However, there are also reasons why Mondini does not fit into the genre of climate fiction. One is that it is set in the future, although not very far in the future. According to Bracke, *cli-fi* is set so close to the present that it makes readers 'barely [...] able to distinguish between the near future and the present of the actual world', and is therefore compatible with the AW (175). 'Mondini' is set in the near future, indicated by, among other things, the fact that the narrator's parents could go on a skiing holiday in Mondini (compatible with the AW), but that before the narrator's birth snow no longer fell in the mountains surrounding the village (not compatible with the AW). Additionally, the TAW is introduced to the reader from the beginning as clearly distinct from the AW by, for example, stating that electrical appliances—which are not described as being more advanced than in the AW—no longer work.

Bracke chooses the term *environmental collapse* for narratives in which climate crisis has led to 'extensive and irreversible environmental, societal, economic and political changes' (2018, 9)—and thus describe a world different from the AW. Regardless of these circumstances, 'one or several people survive [in these narratives], allowing for the story of what happens after the collapse to be told' (Bracke 2018, 25). This genre seems relevant for 'Mondini' as well—in particular for some of the intermediate versions. Yet, I consider the final version of 'Mondini' to be an eco-dystopia. These narratives highlight the environmental aspects of the significantly worse TAW relative to the AW, reflect on the deontic conflict created by these circumstances and 'imagine near futures in which the environment has been damaged, perhaps irreparably— usually by human population growth, pollution, new technologies, and the unchecked cycle of production and consumption' (Griffin 2018, 273). Both the genres of environmental collapse narrative and eco-dystopia seem applicable to 'Mondini'.

4.1. Environmental Collapse or Eco-Dystopia?

Through a nanogenetic analysis, we can see the dynamics at work that allow us to trace Troch's alternation between the genres of environmental collapse narrative and eco-dystopia. From Session 5 onwards, as we have seen above, it becomes increasingly clear that the TAW differs from the AW: there is no electricity nor running water and it is stiflingly hot in the Northern Hemisphere even in January. In Session 6 (12 August 2020), Troch writes a part of the backstory that briefly summarises how the world changed due to climate change, in particular the consequences of the ever-increasing heat. Troch mainly focuses on the effects of the heat on the world, resources and the well-being of the people. This session-version thus clearly contains key aspects of narratives of environmental collapse.

A couple of hours later, in Session 7, he elaborates this passage mainly by describing how people's behaviour changed. With these revisions he includes a whole new level of consequences, introducing the deontic conflict:

> Eerst stegen de temperatuurgemiddelden gestaag, toen exponentieel. Groen gras werd zeldzaam, niet al te voedzaam voor vee. [68]Koeien kalveren niet meer. Alsmaar minder plekken werden leefbaar. [127]De voede[128] [129]selketen kwam stil te vallen. [130]De econono[131] [132]mie. [133]Het bruto nationaal product van elk k[134+135]land kelderde. [136]De beurs[137-138]zen crashten. [139]Plunderingen. [140]Het was[141] [142]Een pretje was het allemaal niet. [149]Ik verschanste me onder bruggen leegst[150] [151]verlaten panden i[152153]doodde als ik moest doden. [143]Ik weet niet waaraan ik het verdiend heb om het te

vo¹⁴⁴ ¹⁴⁵overleven. Ik weet niet hoeveel levens ik heb maar dit is wellicht het laatste.¹⁴⁷ Men probeerde zijn heil elders te zoeken. ⁶⁹Natuurlijk kwam daar handgemeen van. ¹²⁶Men ging om het minst met elkaar op de vuist. ⁷¹Men moorde elkaar uit. ⁷⁰Beschaafd is men nooit geweest. Men zocht koelte. Die was haast niet te vinden. Er sneuvelden er velen van uitputting en uitdroging. ⁷²Men sneed elke⁷³ ⁷⁴aar de keel door en at elkaar vervolgens op. ⁷⁵Tot op het bot. Men viel bij bosjes. Men vocht om drinkbaar water. Om een plek in de schaduw. Ook ik. (Session 7)⁵

[First, temperature averages rose steadily, then exponentially. Green grass became rare, not too nutritious for cattle. ⁶⁸ Cows no longer calved. Fewer and fewer places became habitable. ¹²⁷The foodh¹²⁸ ¹²⁹chain came to a standstill. ¹³⁰The econono¹³¹ ¹³²my. ¹³³The gross national product of eacho¹³⁴ ¹³⁵county plummeted. ¹³⁶The stockmarkets¹³⁷ ¹³⁸s crashed. ¹³⁹Lootings. ¹⁴⁰It was¹⁴¹ ¹⁴²None of it was any fun. ¹⁴⁹I holed up under bridges empty¹⁵⁰ ¹⁵¹abandoned buildings I¹⁵² ¹⁵³killed if I had to kill. ¹⁴³I don't know the reasons why I deserve to us¹⁴⁴ ¹⁴⁵survive. I don't know how many lives I have, but this might be the last.¹⁴⁷ People tried to seek refuge elsewhere. ⁶⁹Of course scuffles ensued. ¹²⁶ People clashed with each other for the least. ⁷¹ People killed each other. ⁷⁰People were never civilised. People looked for some cooling. This was almost impossible to find. Many died from exhaustion and dehydration. ⁷²People cut eachi⁷³ ⁷⁴other's throats and then ate each other. ⁷⁵To the bone. People were dropping like flies. People fought for drinkable water. For a place in the shade. So did I.]

The effects of climate change forced people to seek refuge elsewhere, they began to fight, kill and resorted to cannibalism. The nanogenesis indicates that Troch came to write this change in morality by interacting with the text produced so far: because he had first described how the environment changed, he could later add how this also affected the behaviour of human beings. First, he wrote about the environmental collapse (a hostile climatic narrative space), then turned it into an eco-dystopia (a hostile climatic and social narrative space).

The anarchy caused by the effects of climate change generates a large-scale conflict. As Schuknecht points out, in anarchy 'deontic conflict

---

5   The numbers in this citation refer to the chronological numbering of the writing actions in the reconstructions of the writing process; the purple text indicates new text production; the pink text indicates immediate deletions; the brown text indicates typos; and the dark blue text indicates that the sentence has been copy-pasted from another location in the text.

occurs not between one or more person and a totalitarian government but between one or more character and the void of governing authority created after its collapse' (2019, 240). This is even more emphasised as Troch continues expanding this specific paragraph, for he also focuses on the narrator's behaviour, who even *killed* when he could. And this last addition, that the narrator also had to kill, leads to the addition elsewhere in the text that the narrator keeps hearing the death rattle of his partner: 'en toch blijk ik maar haar doodsreutel horen' ['and yet I keep hearing her death rattle'] (n154–156). Because of this temporal connection between the two revisions, we can ask what the connection is between the narrator's having to kill and his partner's death. Something in this description must have triggered an idea for Evelina's death. At this point in the writing process, the idea seems to emerge that there is a causal relation between the deontic conflict and the narrator's personal loss.

In Session 12—still on 12 August—Troch moves this backstory to a place near the end of the document. It is no longer part of the text but can later be consulted for similar descriptions. Now it is by means of the references to the world in the fictive present that the extent to which the world has changed becomes clear. These references are constantly elaborated on and altered. They emphasise the opposition between inside (the apartment), which is safe, and outside, which is unsafe. By reducing the description of deontic conflict in the TAW, this session version becomes more related to the narratives of environmental collapse—with a focus on how one survives in a world dictated by extreme elements, especially of severe heat.

4.2. Consequences of Heat or of Deontic Conflict

The backstory is addressed again in Session 23 (27 August) as Troch inserts a passage that both describes how the consequences of climate change had an impact on the environment and the interaction between people as well as how this led to the loss of the narrator's partner and daughter. In the TAW, people's behaviour again becomes geared towards self-protection, no matter the sacrifice. As such, Troch re-inserts the deontic conflict. During the writing process for this paragraph, Troch

shifts between whether it was this change in behaviour—the violence—
or the climate change itself that caused most of the deaths.

Troch begins with the first-person narrator describing how there was little left of the North and South Pole when they tried to escape. Rising sea levels forced everyone in low-lying areas to pack their bags. This changed people's behaviour: they became more violent towards each other.

> Het probleem van veel volk op een beperkte ruimte loste de mens zelf op met menig handgemeen (After n71)[6]
>
> [The problem of too many people in too little space was solved by people themselves with lots of scuffles]
>
> veel te veel volk op een beperkte ruimte; problemen lost de mens graag op met menig handgemeen en lynchpartijen. (After n102)
>
> [far too many people in a limited space; people like to solve problems with lots of scuffles and lynchings.]
>
> veel te veel volk op een beperkte ruimte; de mens die een probleem graag oplost met een handgemeen of een lynchpartij. (After n116)
>
> [far too many people in a limited space; people like to solve a problem with a scuffle or a lynching.]

The above versions show how Troch is constantly exacerbating the impact of climate change on human behaviour. At first it just causes a 'handgemeen' ['a scuffle'], then a 'lynchpartij' ['lynching']. Next, he adds that this led to a thinning of the population, which was made worse by the extreme temperatures:

> veel te veel volk op een beperkte ruimte; de mens die een probleem graag oplost met een handgemeen of een lynchpartij; en als dat onvoldoende was om de bevolking uit te dunnen zorgde de onmenselijke temperaturen er wel voor dat er slachtoffers bij bosjes vielen. (After n140)
>
> [far too many people in a limited space; people like to solve a problem with a scuffle or a lynching; and if that wasn't enough to thin out the population, the inhumane temperatures ensured that people were dropping like flies.]

---

6 This number indicates that this is the version of the sentence as it was after writing action 71 in the reconstructions of the writing session.

de mens die een probleem graag oplost met een handgemeen of een lynchpartij. De onmenselijke temperaturen werkten de uitdunning van de wereldbevolking alleen maar in de hand. (After n159)

[people like to solve a problem with a scuffle or a lynching. The inhumane temperatures only accelerated the thinning of the world's population.]

de mens die een probleem graag oplost met een handgemeen of een lynchpartij. Maar de onmenselijke temperaturen zorgden voor de echte genocide. (After 188)

[people like to solve a problem with a scuffle or a lynching. But the inhumane temperatures caused the real genocide.]

Yet in the end, it is not man but climate change that causes most deaths. During this implementation of the backstory, Troch also starts to focus on Evelina and Lily, respectively the partner and daughter of the first-person narrator, and what happened to them. The versions below indicate that Troch started with the idea that it was the severe heat that became fatal for them—'[D]e hitte is onverbiddelijk' ['[T]he heat is relentless'] (After n175) –, also for Evelina and Lily (After 196; After 207), and they became victims of the 'onmenselijke temperaturen [die] zorgden voor de echte genocide' ['inhumane temperatures [that] caused the real genocide'] (After n196).

We wisten uit handen van bendes te blijven, maar de hitte is onverbiddelijk. (After n175)

[We managed to stay out of the hands of gangs, but the heat is relentless.]

We wisten uit handen van bendes te blijven, maar al volgden we zoveel mogelijk waterwegen, de hitte is onverbiddelijk. (After n180)

[We managed to stay out of the hands of gangs, but even though we followed as many waterways as possible, the heat is relentless.]

De onmenselijke temperaturen zorgden voor de echte genocide. Ook Evelina en Lily zijn een van de slachtoffers. (After n196)

[The inhumane temperatures caused the real genocide. Evelina and Lily are also among the victims.]

De onmenselijke temperaturen zorgden voor de echte genocide. Ik vond het wijs, het was wijs om langs zoveel mogelijk waterwegen te verplaatsen en toch bleek de hitte ook voor Evelina en Lily onverbiddelijk. (After n202)

[The inhumane temperatures caused the real genocide. I thought it was wise, it was wise to move along as many waterways as possible and yet the heat proved relentless even for Evelina and Lily.]

Het leek mij het verstandigst om langs zoveel mogelijk waterwegen te verplaatsen, om te drinken, om te verfrissen en toch bleek de hitte ook voor Evelina en Lily onverbiddelijk. (After n207)

[It seemed most sensible to move along as many waterways as possible, to drink, to refresh, and yet the heat proved relentless even for Evelina and Lily.]

The insertion of 'om te drinken' ['to drink'] (After n207) leads to the insertion of new text: everybody wanted to drink. The revision that included the drinking of water thus prompted the idea to bring back the possibility of human involvement in the death of Evelina and Lily:

Iedereen zocht verfrissing, iedereen wilde drinken, drinken, drinken. Evelina, Lily en ik waren niet de enigsten die zich zoveel mogelijk langs waterwegen verplaatsten. Ze hebben het niet gehaald hoe ik ook mijn best heb gedaan, ze hebben het niet gehaald. (After n219)

[Everyone was looking for refreshment, everyone wanted to drink, drink, drink. Evelina, Lily and I were not the only ones moving along the waterways as much as possible. They didn't make it no matter how hard I tried, they didn't make it.]

At the end of the session, the paragraph does not yet provide a clear answer for Evelina and Lily's cause of death, although the large number of people moving along the waterways seems to be related to it. The writing actions of the following session make clear that Troch had not resolved this question either. First, he added that the first-person narrator tried to quench their thirst. This shows that the climate (the heat and drought) was eventually fatal for them. Troch then deletes this and instead adds that they screamed for mercy, describing how the first-person narrator tried to defend them too. As such, it is more likely that a human action killed them, rather than the heat:

Zij, mijn twee oogappels, hebben het niet gehaald, hoe ik ook mijn best heb gedaan, hoe ik ook gepoogd heb hun dorst te lessen, [235][236] hoe hard ze ook om genade hebben ²³⁸ ge²³⁹gild en²⁴⁰⁻²³⁷hoe ik hen ok²³³²³²ok met hand en tand heb verdedigd ²³⁴zij hebben het niet gehaald. (Session 24)

[They· the two apples of my eye· didn't make it no matter how hard I tried· no matter how I tried to quench their thirst ²³⁵²³⁶ no matter how hard they²³⁸ have²³⁹ screameding²⁴⁰ for mercy, ²³⁷no matter hw²³³²³²ow I fought tooth and nail, ²³⁴they didn't make it.] (Session 24)

In Session 25 (27 August) Troch expands the paragraph even further, going into detail about the fatal event. The narrator remembers that they were travelling with about seven people, but that these people suddenly started pulling, pushing and shouting. Before they realised it, the family had ended up in a brawl. The narrator tried to defend them, but before he could get hold of everyone, it was too late; they had already grabbed Evelina and Lily. In the end, it was not the climate that took Evelina and Lily's lives, but the way the climate made people behave: the merciless TAW of an eco-dystopia.

5. Concluding Remarks: Dynamics of Constructing a Textual Actual World

This essay set out to provide the first steps in assessing how genetic criticism applied to keystroke logging data can enhance the study of (eco)narratology. It has shown that by means of the keystroke logging data, we can trace the development of the TAW. The nanogenesis showed Troch's quest for how much the TAW differed from the AW—the environment as well as people's behaviour—due to climate change. At first, we could see the principle of minimal departure during the writing process, as Troch's major point of reference in the creation of the TAW was the AW. In making decisions about the TAW, Troch then also started to interact with the text produced so far, which reminded him of previously described features of the TAW and helped him to further develop his ideas.

Troch also alternated during the writing process between making 'Mondini' a story best classified as a narrative of environmental collapse and turning it into an eco-dystopian narrative. The keystroke logging data revealed his decision-making process, wondering whether it was the heat or the change in people's behaviour—the violence and deontic conflict—that led the narrator to survive alone. Moreover, the keystroke logging also proved that Troch made a connection between deontic conflict (that people have been driven to kill each other) and the death of Evelina at an early stage in the writing process. Even though he was not working on a description of Evelina, text production regarding the changes in the world prompted the addition that the narrator still hears her death rattle.

Nanogenetic narratology, where narratology meets keystroke logging data, therefore offers a unique glimpse into the dynamics at play at the moment a story is written. We can see the invention of a TAW, as if we are looking over the author's shoulder. It offers the genetic scholar a utopia for researching the genesis of a dystopia.

Works Cited

Bekius, Lamyk (2021), 'The Reconstruction of the Author's Movement Through the Text, or How to Encode Keystroke Logged Writing Processes in TEI-XML', *Variants*, 15-16: 3–43, https://doi.org/10.4000/variants.1245.

Bekius, Lamyk (2023), *'Behind the Screens'. The Use of Keystroke Logging for Genetic Criticism Applied to Born-Digital Works of Literature*, PhD Dissertation in Literature (University of Amsterdam and University of Antwerp).

Bracke, Astrid (2018), *Climate Change and the 21st-Century British Novel* (London and New York: Bloomsbury Academic).

Bracke, Astrid (2020), 'Worldmaking Environmental Crisis. Climate Fiction, Econarratology, and Genre', in: *Environment and Narrative: New Directions in Econarratology*, ed. by Erin James and Eric Morel (Columbus: Ohio State University Press), 165–82.

Bernaerts, Lars and Dirk Van Hulle (2013), 'Narrative across Versions: Narratology Meets Genetic Criticism', *Poetics Today*, 34.3: 281–26, https://doi.org/10.1215/03335372-2325232.

Buchholz, Sabine and Manfred Jahn (2005), 'Space in Narrative', in: *Routledge Encyclopedia of Narrative Theory*, ed. by David Herman, Manfred Jahn and Marie-Laure Ryan (London: Routledge), 551–55.

Crasson, Aurèle, Jean-Louis Lebrave, Jérémy Pedrazzi and Laurent Alonso (2022), 'Le Toucher Touch/to Touch Him: Étude Forensique de Données Numériques de Jacques Derrida L'archive Numérique et Les Modalités de Son Appréhension Pour La Recherche', *Genesis*, 55: 121–36, https://doi.org/10.4000/genesis.7747.

Griffin, Dori (2018), 'Visualizing Eco-dystopia', *Design and Culture*, 10.3: 271–98, https://doi.org/10.1080/17547075.2018.1514573.

Kaplan, E. Ann (2016), *Climate Trauma. Foreseeing the Future in Dystopian Film and Fiction* (New Brunswick, NJ and London: Rutgers University Press).

Kerridge, Richard (2014), 'Ecocritical Approaches to Literary Form and Genre: Urgency, Depth, Provisionality, Temporality', in: *The Oxford Handbook of Ecocriticism*, ed. by Greg Garrard (Oxford: Oxford University Press), 361–76.

Kirschenbaum, Matthew G. (2008), *Mechanisms: New Media and the Forensic Imagination* (Cambridge, MA: MIT Press).

Leijten, Mariëlle and Luuk Van Waes (2013), 'Keystroke Logging in Writing Research: Using Inputlog to Analyze and Visualize Writing Processes', *Written Communication*, 30.3: 358–92, https://doi.org/10.1177/0741088313491692.

Pulkkinen, Veijo (2023), 'Kirjallisuudentutkijan näkökulma syntysähköisten käsikirjoitusten arkistointiin', *Kirjallisuudentutkimuksen Aikakauslehti Avain*, 20.1: 48–65, https://doi.org/10.30665/av.122368.

Ries, Thorsten (2017), 'Philology and the Digital Writing Process', *Genrehybriditeit in de Literatuur, Cahier voor Literatuurwetenschap*, ed. by Reindert Dhondt and David Martens, 9: 129–58.

Ries, Thorsten (2018), 'The Rationale of the Born-Digital Dossier Génétique: Digital Forensics and the Writing Process: With Examples from the Thomas Kling Archive', *Digital Scholarship in the Humanities*, 33.2: 391–424. https://doi.org/10.1093/llc/fqx049.

Ryan, Marie-Laure (1991), *Possible Worlds, Artificial Intelligence, and Narrative Theory* (Bloomington and Indianapolis: Indiana University Press).

Schuknecht, Mattison (2019), 'The Best/Worst of All Possible Worlds? Utopia, Dystopia, and Possible Worlds Theory', in: *Possible Worlds Theory and Contemporary Narratology*, ed. by Alice Bell and Marie-Laure Ryan (Lincoln, NE and London: University of Nebraska Press), 225–46.

Trexler, Adam (2015), *Anthropocene Fictions. The Novel in a Time of Climate Change* (Charlottesville, VA and London: University of Virginia Press).

Troch, David (2021), 'Mondini', unpublished.

Van Hulle, Dirk (2022), *Genetic Criticism: Tracing Creativity in Literature* (Oxford: Oxford University Press).

Weisbrod, Dirk (2016), 'Cloud-Supported Preservation of Digital Papers: A Solution for Special Collections?' *Liber Quarterly*, 25.3: 136–51, https://doi.org/10.18352/lq.10114.

16. On the Value of Variants and Textual Genesis for Interpretation: Some Remarks on a New Relationship between Historical-Critical Editing, Genetic Criticism and Narratology

Rüdiger Nutt-Kofoth

1. On Possibilities of an Interaction between Scholarly Editing, Genetic Criticism and Narratology

As the subject of this essay focuses on scholarly editing, genetic criticism and narratology,[1] it seems to be dealing with three different and independent scholarly fields: scholarly editing as a field of care for *preserving* the cultural and—in our case—mainly literary heritage by special means of presenting a literary work in all expressions of its transmission; genetic criticism as a field of *interpreting* the different steps or stages of the genesis of a literary work by—particularly in the original French tradition—looking at the manuscripts as representations of the so-called 'avant-texte' ('pre-text', i.e. all handwritten stages before print);

---

1   A preliminary remark to the following German-oriented approach to the topic of this volume: when in the following narratology and genetic criticism are brought into a relationship with editing, the English term 'scholarly editing' is used for the latter because there is no suitable English translation for this broader field of studies of what forms the basis here: namely the German 'Editionswissenschaft' [literally translated: 'editorial scholarship'] which includes both the theory and method as well as the practice of editing, i.e. rather a mixture of what functions in Anglo-American as textual scholarship and as scholarly editing (Greetham 1992; Greetham 1995).

and finally narratology as a field of *examining* the structure of narrative of—mostly but not only—literary texts. But indeed, these scholarly fields are suitable for interacting with each other. The most important reason for this is the non-ignorable correlation of edition and interpretation. This does not only mean that each editorial operation includes at least a certain, albeit often only small, share of interpretation, a fact that Hans Zeller once summed up in the image of the editor's inescapable shadow, which he or she casts over the editorial presentation (Zeller 1966, 15), but this relationship is also effective in reverse since every interpretation is dependent on its specific editorial textual basis. Only a scholarly edited text provides a precise basis for scholarly interpretation, which also means that all edited textual or non-textual material can be used for interpretation.

The last remark is important because scholarly editions offer extensive material that enables a variety of different interpretative approaches and insights. This concerns in particular the concept of the 'historical-critical edition' in the German speaking world. In the last century, the focus of German historical-critical editing has shifted from the presentation of a critically constituted text as a representation of the work to the overall presentation of all genetic steps and stages of the work, i.e. to a presentation of the genesis of the work. This shift was first called for exactly one hundred years ago by Reinhold Backmann, when he announced in an article on his Grillparzer edition in 1924: 'Die Klarlegung der Entwicklung gibt dem Apparat erst seinen selbständigen Wert gegenüber dem Textabdruck, ja sie gibt ihm, wenn sie in der rechten Weise erfolgt, ein Übergewicht an Bedeutung über den letzteren' ['The clarification of the genesis gives the apparatus its independent value compared to the text [of one version, e.g. an authorised print version], and, if done in the right way, gives it a preponderance of meaning over the latter'] (Backmann 1924, 638).[2] Subsequently, German historical-critical editions became increasingly concerned with textual genesis and developed different models of its representation, which was accompanied by intensive discussions about the precision and appropriateness of the respective models and procedures (overviews: Zeller 1986; Zeller 2003; see also Zeller and

---

2   Unless otherwise indicated, the English translations are mine, RNK.

Martens 1998; Nutt-Kofoth 2005; Bosse and Fanta 2019). Precisely in the spirit of its name, the historical-critical edition is concerned both with the chronological sequence of the development of a work (the 'historical' element) and its textual presentation with the means of textual criticism (the 'critical' element). In the sense of Backmann's demand, this equal duality of tasks concerning the 'historical' and the 'critical' dimension actually led to the fact that, on the one hand, the complete presentation of the work's genesis (as far as can be ascertained from the surviving documents) was understood as a critical presentation of the work's text in its entirety, and that, on the other hand, the presentation of a single version or several selected versions as reading texts was merely an addition to this, only a further editorial offer. Depending on the user's interest, this offer is no less valuable than the extensive presentation of the textual genesis. However, it is evident not only in print editions but also in digital editions that the presentation of the textual genesis occupies the most extensive space within the edition. Thus, two ('Archive', 'Genesis') of three central accesses (the third is 'Text') of the digital historical-critical edition of Goethe's *Faust* (2018–) contain the description of the transmission (metadata), thousands of scans of the documents (manuscripts and prints) and their transcriptions and genetic representations, while the 'Text' section 'only' provides the text-critically constituted reading text as the author's final authentic version of the work.

All in all, this means that the concept of the German historical-critical edition encompasses a large part of the tasks that genetic criticism—in the originally French (Grésillon 1994/2016, 1999) as well as in the younger English orientation (Van Hulle 2022)—also claims to solve, namely the presentation of all phases of the genesis of a literary work with precise indexing, differentiation and referencing of all processes of the formation of variants and versions. In this sense, genetic criticism does indeed in most cases involve basic editorial steps, at least the presentation of facsimiles of the manuscripts studied accompanied by their transcriptions. The important difference, however, is that scholarly editing does not aim at interpreting the manuscript, which is a central further step in genetic criticism. The German historical-critical edition, in contrast, leaves the actual interpretation of the text and the textual genesis—beyond all the unavoidable subjective parts of editorial work, which should be made as clear as possible—to literary studies and sees itself primarily as a documentary activity that does not interpret texts in a similar way, but creates the basis for literary studies' interpretation.

While it is true that scholarly editing deliberately leaves the interpretative handling of the editorial results to literary studies, it is again to be noted that literary studies often does not take note of the extensive material indexed and presented in the edition or does so only very selectively. This finding, which had already been noticed in many cases through general observation, was substantiated by an empirical study some ten years ago. For this purpose, three central academic journals in German studies (*Zeitschrift für deutsche Philologie*, *Euphorion* and *Deutsche Vierteljahrsschrift für Literaturwissenschaft und Geistesgeschichte*) were examined for the period of more than ten years (2000–13) with regard to the use of historical-critical editions in the journals' articles by their authors. The result was this: if an historical-critical edition is available for a literary author, two-fifths of the literary critics use this edition, three-fifths—i.e. more than half—ignore it. If an historical-critical edition is used, nine-tenths of the interpreters are interested in the edited text, a good tenth also in the commentary and only about five per cent in the variants or the textual genesis (Nutt-Kofoth 2015, 242). Beyond the deplorable fact that only less than half of the interpreters use existing historical-critical editions at all, it is particularly noteworthy that only an extremely small proportion of these then also includes the results of the text-genetic representation in the interpretation. This also means that only a small number of interpreters make use of the most laborious and often most extensive part of an historical-critical edition. This result, which was collected a decade ago, has probably not changed much to date.

Although this is a long-standing fundamental problem, this discrepancy should be remedied in the sense of broadening scholarly knowledge. A reflection on the recently promoted concept of 'reader-facing editions' (Eggert 2019, 89) could be of some help here. This includes, on the one hand, the necessity for interpreters to engage in the reading of genetic representations, even if this also means having to deviate from the usual linear reading habits, because genetic representations work not only linearly, but also with spatial representations and various information-containing diacritical marks. On the other hand, it might be necessary that editors as well as genetic critics show the interpreters ways in which genesis and variants can have epistemological value for the interpretation, because editors and genetic critics often already have the comprehensive meaning structure of the variants in mind from their concrete work with the material.

In the German-speaking world, it has—unsurprisingly—been editors who have considered the possible function of variants for the interpretation of the literary work. Initially, the *identifying function* was raised to a standard of variant use, as presented, for example, by Friedrich Beißner, the editor of the Stuttgart Hölderlin edition (1943-85), which was pioneering in terms of editorial methodology from the 1940s to the 1960s:

> Der Leser also, der sich bemüht, den in erster, unmittelbarer Begegnung empfangenen Eindruck zu läutern, das erste, noch dunkel ahnende und tastende Verständnis zu gründen und zu vertiefen, gerät oft in die Lage, daß er zwischen zwei Deutungsmöglichkeiten schwankt. Wie oft hilft ihm in solcher Lage die Lesart eines Entwurfs! (Beißner 1969, 212)

> [The reader, therefore, who endeavours to purify the impression received in the first, direct encounter, to establish and deepen the first, still darkly foreboding and groping understanding, often finds himself in the situation of vacillating between two possible interpretations. How often does the reading of a draft help him in such a situation!]

This was later countered by the *differentiating function* of variants, which became established in the term 'negative Ersatzprobe' ['negative substitute test'], represented by the Schiller editor Herbert Kraft (e.g. Schiller 1971; Schiller 1982; Schiller 2000):

> *Varianten bestimmen negativ die Semantik desjenigen Textes, von dem sie abweichen.* Mit ihrer Hilfe wird Erkenntnis gewonnen gerade nicht durch Identifizieren, sondern durch Unterscheiden und Ausschließen. In dem, was *nicht* gemeint ist, ist das Gemeinte als Verweisung enthalten; keineswegs ist in den Varianten das Gemeinte positiv vorhanden [...]. (Kraft 2001, 100)[3]

---

3   See also the further discussion and the examples ibid., 100–6; the term 'negative Ersatzproben' ['negative substitute tests'] ibid. in the chapter title, 93.

[*Variants negatively determine the semantics of the text from which they deviate.* With their help, knowledge is gained precisely not by identifying, but by distinguishing and excluding. In what is *not* meant, what is meant is contained as a reference; in no way is what is meant positively present in the variants [...].]

The Celan editor Beda Allemann (Celan 1990-2017) connected to this position not only by calling for a separate discipline of 'Textgenetik' ['textual genetics'], which—as can be assumed—could offer a German-language analogy to genetic criticism, but also by making it clear from a structuralist-semiotic perspective that textual genetics is not primarily concerned with an investigation of individual variants per se, but rather with the correlation of structural variant processes of alteration and modification within the development of the work:

> Sie [die 'Textgenetik'] muß über die Semantik einzelner Wörter und Wendungen und jener ihres 'Ersatzes' im Laufe des poetischen Arbeitsprozesses hinaus vordringen in jene Dimension der strukturellen Bezüge und ihrer Verschiebung im Prozeß der Artikulation [...]. (Allemann, qtd. by Bücher 1994, 334).
>
> [It [i.e. 'textual genetics'] must progress beyond the semantics of individual words and phrases and that of their 'replacement' in the course of the poetic working process into the dimension of structural relations and their shift within the process of articulation [...].]

If textual genesis is understood in this sense as a process of transformation of structures of the literary work, as a process of work-restructuring, this applies to all literary works, regardless of their genre. However, with narratology there exists an established field of research that, due to its original structuralist basis, seems particularly suitable to serve as an example of the profit that can be drawn from the textual genetic consideration of a narrative work. The fact that narratology itself has hardly ever dared to build this bridge to textual genetic research and scholarly editing may be surprising, but if you take a closer look at this field of investigation it can become a model for the additional benefit of such a previously unnoticed branch of research.

2. On the Interrelation of Narratology and Scholarly Editing by Means of Text-Critical and Genetic Research

Although we have to note—as mentioned above—that narratology and scholarly editing did not interact at all or maybe hardly until today, there have been some single scattered remarks on a possible relationship in a few studies, especially those by Gabriele Radecke (2002), Lars Bernaert/ Dirk Van Hulle (2012), Michael Scheffel (2021), Dirk Van Hulle (2022, 149–63) and Luc Herman/John M. Krafft (2023). In addition to these discussions on the topic, which have become more frequent in recent years, a Wuppertal conference in 2022 may also be mentioned, which explicitly dealt with the relationship between narratology, scholarly editing and literary history, and which will result in a forthcoming book with articles emerging from the conference lectures.[4] It could be helpful to place a systematic orientation alongside these rather isolated beginnings. To this end, the following series of systematically ordered examples drawn from the German discourse is intended to offer a further step forward.[5]

---

[4] Produktion des Erzählens, Varianten des Erzählten. Narratologische, editionswissenschaftliche und literarhistorische Perspektiven auf die Genese von Erzähltexten ['Production of Narrative, Variants of the Narrated. Narratological, editorial and literary-historical perspectives on the genesis of narrative texts']. International Conference at the Bergische Universität Wuppertal, Germany, 17–19 November 2022, organised by Matthias Grüne and Rüdiger Nutt-Kofoth, in cooperation with Zentrum für Erzählforschung (ZEF), Interdisziplinäres Zentrum für Editions- und Dokumentwissenschaft (IZED), Bergische Universität Wuppertal, the Wuppertal DFG-graduate school 'Dokument—Text— Edition. Bedingungen und Formen ihrer Transformation und Modellierung in transdisziplinärer Perspektive' and the 'Kommission für allgemeine Editionswissenschaft' of the 'Arbeitsgemeinschaft für germanistische Edition'.

[5] The following second section of this article is a shorter English version of the more comprehensive German version which appears in the anthology based on the conference mentioned above. An earlier version was given a decade and a half ago as a lecture at the workshop *Text—Kontext—Erzählen* [*Text—Context—Narrative*], Bergische Universität Wuppertal, 30–31 January 2009 (organisation: Andreas Bödorn, Rüdiger Zymner). It was then revised, updated and presented again at the conference (mentioned in the previous footnote) and subsequently in a shorter English version at the Workshop *Genetic Narratology*, University of Oxford, 23–24 February 2023 (organisation: Dirk Van Hulle).

2.1. Hypotheses about the Narration as a Precondition for Editorial Decisions

The critical constitution of a text is the oldest task of the editor: text constitution on the basis of textual criticism, i.e. after strictly examining and evaluating the transmission. This becomes somewhat more difficult if there is no form of the text that has been declared finished by the author, i.e. authorised in the narrow sense of the word. It is particularly difficult, however, if the text has not been completed at all, i.e. if it has remained fragmentary. The prime example of this case is Franz Kafka's novel fragment *Der Process* [*The Trial*]. As is well known, in addition to the opening and closing chapters, Kafka wrote a whole series of other chapters, mainly in 1914/15, some of which he himself did not complete, and none of which he put in any kind of order. Thus, Kafka's friend Max Brod, who published the text in 1925, a year after Kafka's death, had to arrange the chapters himself, chapters which had been handed down in individual loose-leaf units, and in doing so he left out in particular the chapters that were very fragmentary or that he could not integrate into the plot (Kafka 1925). In later editions of *Der Process*, Brod published these chapters in an appendix, so that the status of the text as a fragment became recognisable. Subsequently, there were various scholarly proposals for the overall order of the chapters, which were based on the assumed type of narration (Uyttersprot 1957; Uyttersprot 1966; Elema 1977; Eschweiler 1989; Kafka 1990). In particular, arguments concerning the chronology of the plot played a role. However, none of these proposals could resolve all contradictions. For the historical-critical Kafka edition of *Der Process* published in 1997, the editor Roland Reuß therefore used a radically different presentation method compared to all previous editions. Reuß abandoned the search for narrative sequence and offered the chapters of Kafka's novel in separate booklet units, not arranged in any order, loosely set in a slipcase (Kafka 1997).[6] He therefore reproduced the state of transmission instead of establishing a fixed editorial suggestion

---

6 Cf. ibid., Franz-Kafka-Hefte 1, 10–15 and 33–36 the discussion of the earlier proposals on the chapter order; ibid., 15–16 the explanation of the text presentation in the Historisch-Kritische Kafka-Ausgabe and its consequences.

for the readers. In this way, he made it possible for, or left it up to, the reader to order the chapters. For Kafka philology, in any case, the point was reached at which the edition no longer saw itself in a position to produce a stable text of *Der Process* with narratological considerations due to the difficulties of the transmission.

Narratologically-based considerations can play an important role not only for questions of textual order in the context of editorial text constitution, but also for difficult individual passages, namely those that are suspect of errors from a text-critical perspective. An example of different text-critical conclusions can be found in editions of Annette von Droste-Hülshoff's oeuvre. The penultimate sentence in Droste-Hülshoff's novella *Die Judenbuche* [*The Jew's Beech*] was first printed as follows in the journal *Morgenblatt für gebildete Leser* [*Morning Journal for Educated Readers*] in 1842, the only authorised printing of the text, and also in the historical-critical Droste edition in 1978: 'Dieß hat sich nach allen Hauptumständen wirklich so begeben im September des Jahrs 1788' ['According to all the main circumstances, this really did happen in September 1788'] (Droste-Hülshoff 1978, 42). This passage, however, contradicts other statements in the 'histoire' of the novella, for the man hanged at the end of the story returned to the village of B. on the '24sten December 1788' (Droste-Hülshoff 1978, 35), as stated some paragraphs before. Most of the earlier editors resolved the contradiction by changing the year at the end of the novella from 1788 to 1789, thus intending to correct the narrative chronology. In contrast, Heinz Rölleke in his 1970 edition of *Die Judenbuche* retained the final date of September 1788 and instead changed the date of homecoming from December 1788 to December 1787, on the assumption that Droste had deliberately let her novella end in the year before the French Revolution, thus situating the diegesis in the pre-revolutionary, pre-modern world (Rölleke 1970, 49; 58; 177). The 1978/84 historical-critical Droste edition argues once more differently with reference to the period of 28 years, which plays a special role in the novella by being mentioned three times. The interval between the murder of the Jew Aaron in 1760 and the return or death of the real or alleged murderer is therefore preserved in several places while retaining the year 1788, and thus also the temporal structure of the novella that proves to be a direct intertextual connection to the pattern of the genre *'Schicksalstragödie'* ['tragedy of fate'], namely Zacharias Werner's drama *Der vierundzwanzigste Februar* [*The Twenty-Fourth of February*, from 1815] with its plot intervals of 28 years (Droste-Hülshoff 1984, 199 and 246–8).

In addition to the reconstruction of textual order and the text-critical question of emendation or conjecture of a single passage narratological considerations can also have editorial relevance if a text is available in different versions. The editor is then faced with the question of how to present these versions. Particularly if two versions have a special aesthetic or literary historical relevance, it may be that an editorial presentation in the sense of presenting one version as a full text and the other in the variant apparatus, reduced to its differing passages, is not sufficient. Through the procedure of parallel presentation of the full versions' text, the editor decides in particular to communicate the difference between the versions visually. For Goethe's novel *Die Leiden des jungen Werther* [*The Sorrows of Young Werther*], with its two versions from 1774 and 1787, this procedure has become established. Important recent editions of *Werther*, such as those by Erna Merker, Waltraud Wiethölter or Matthias Luserke (Goethe 1954; Goethe 1994; Goethe 1999), paralleled the text of the versions on the left- and right-hand pages. This not only makes clear the massive text expansion of the second version, which the reader immediately perceives visually through the corresponding blank parts of the left-hand page, but if the reader then looks a little more closely, it quickly becomes apparent which passages have been expanded, namely in particular those of the narrative arrangement. As is well known, the fictional intra-narrative 'Report of the Editor', which begins in the middle of the second part of the novel, only reveals itself at this late point as the organising voice of the novel, thus bringing about a decisive change of focus in the novel, which until then had been told purely intra- and autodiegetically. The increased importance of this narrator in the second version is immediately apparent in the parallel presentation. The edition makes the narrative difference between the two versions visible through the editorial way the text is presented.

2.2. Editorial Representations as a Basis for Narratological Work

What can be discussed in the *Werther* edition as a question of text constitution based on narratological interests can be understood in a different way as a question of what scholarly editing offers narratology. Versions of a work can be understood as frozen states of the textual genetic process. The reconstruction of the textual genesis now shows the text in its dynamic course of formulation and reformulation, of writing and alteration, text and variant. But if textual genesis enables studies on the *making of the text*, it might prove promising if this interest of scholarly editing were to be taken up by narratology, which is interested in *how the text is made*. The presentations of the genesis of a literary text, which can be found in great detail in historical-critical editions, should provide narratology with plenty of material for its own interests in the literary text.

Franz Kafka's novel fragment *Das Schloss* [*The Castle*] from 1922 can serve as a particularly good and probably well-known example, so that it is only briefly touched upon here, because following Dorrit Cohn's essay (Cohn 1968) this case has been cited several times in basic narratological works as an example (for instance Stanzel 2008, 206–07; Bode 2011, 182–89; Van Hulle 2022, 158; 161–62). And in fact, it can be used to study how a complete reconstruction of the narrator's position functions during the writing process itself, because in the middle of writing down the third chapter Kafka revised the whole text already written and substitutes the first-person narrator or, in other terminology, the homo-/autodiegetic narrator by a heterodiegetic narrator, but one who is bound to the protagonist by a personal narrator or, in other terminology, through internal focalisation. From a narratological point of view, the fact that the change almost only affects the personal, possessive and reflexive pronouns, as an examination of the variant apparatus of Malcolm Pasley's critical edition from 1990 shows, makes it possible to study the linguistic—and in this case primarily grammatical—means by which this subsequent change of the narrator's position is possible over a long stretch of text, amounting to 67 pages in the critical edition (Kafka 1990).

By initially different means, the author's working method can be reflected in the use of sources and the production of additional textual records, which are significant from a narratological point of view as intertextual references and motors of textual genesis. Once again, an example in Kafka (cf. Plachta 2013, 127–29) can illustrate the importance of the textual genesis for understanding narration and the narrated world, the diegesis. At the beginning of the novel fragment *Der Verschollene* [*The Man Who Disappeared*, mainly written in 1912], when the protagonist Karl Roßmann enters New York harbour, the first thing he sees is the Statue of Liberty: 'Ihr Arm mit dem Schwert ragte wie neuerdings empor' ['The arm with the sword reached aloft'] (Kafka, 1983, Textband [7]). As is well known, however, the real Statue of Liberty does not carry a sword but a torch. And a sword as an attribute of the Statue of Liberty is also not to be found in Kafka's source text, Arthur Holitscher's travelogue *Amerika: Heute und morgen* [*America: Today and Tomorrow*] from 1911/12, which opens with the image of the Statue of Liberty. However, Holitscher does describe the Statue of Liberty as a 'menschliche Gestalt von ungeheuren Proportionen' ['human figure of immense proportions']; and the silhouette of Manhattan then looks like a 'Hand, die sich schmal und langsam in die Höhe streckt, man weiß nicht zum Willkomm oder wie eine Drohung' ['hand stretching trimly and slowly upwards, one does not know whether as a welcome or as a threat'] (Holitscher 1912, 39).[7] The attributes of the powerful and the threatening are now united in the text of *Der Verschollene* to form the Statue of Liberty as a sword-bearer, a symbol of the America of the novel fragment in which Karl Rossmann will succumb to the circumstances up to the point of de-individualisation. A look at the genesis of the text shows how much Kafka wanted to emphasise the difference from reality. The description of the sword-bearing Statue of Liberty was initially followed by the following sentence: 'Er [Karl Roßmann] sah zu ihr auf und verwarf das über sie Gelernte' ['He [Karl Rossmann] looked up at it and rejected what he had learned about it'] (Kafka, 1983, Apparatband, 123). But Kafka deleted this sentence without replacement. This changes the narrative function of the sword-bearer symbol. After this deletion, there is no longer an intradiegetic difference between the torch-bearing and the sword-bearing statue in the narrated world of *Der Verschollene*, which was evoked by the original formulation as a comparative reference

---

7   Holitscher's travelogue was first printed in the magazine *Neue Rundschau* in 1911/12.

for the protagonist. In the end, the sword-bearer remains the only truth of the narrated world: its narrative symbolic value is thus increased.

The development of the narrative form of a text can be studied particularly well when—unlike in Kafka's case—more extensive preliminary stages have been preserved. Again Annette von Droste-Hülshoff's novella *Die Judenbuche* [*The Jew's Beech*] is a good example. In it, various shifts within the structure of the narrative can be detected. A particularly striking one can already be seen in the paratextual location, namely in the title. Thus, the most extensive of the early drafts, manuscript H^2, was entitled 'Friedrich Mergel, eine Criminalgeschichte des 18ten Jahrhunderts' ['Friedrich Mergel, a Criminal Story of the 18th Century'] (Droste-Hülshoff 1984, 258).[8] When Droste sent the novella to Cotta's journal *Morgenblatt* in 1842, it bore the completely different title, which later became the subtitle: 'Ein Sittengemälde aus dem gebirgigten Westphalen' ['A portrait of morals in hilly Westphalia'] (Droste-Hülshoff 1978, 1). But with that, the genre had changed. The focus now was not on the criminal case and not only on the psychologising portrayal of the character Friedrich Mergel, for example in continuation of the pattern of Friedrich Schiller's story *Der Verbrecher aus verlorener Ehre* [*The Criminal from Lost Honour*, 1786/92], but on the regional narrative focusing on the history of society's mentality. The fact that Hermann Hauff, the editor of the *Morgenblatt*, invented an additional and final title for the novella, 'Die Judenbuche', which Droste accepted, only contributes to this genre shift of the text.

A final example illustrates how the narratological evaluation of textual genesis can enable insights into *literary history* beyond the individual text. Gabriele Radecke's aforementioned monograph from 2002 should be consulted here. It is already paradigmatically titled for a narratological perspective on textual genesis: *Vom Schreiben zum Erzählen: Eine textgenetische Studie zu Theodor Fontanes 'L'Adultera'* [*From Writing to Narrating: A text-genetic study of Theodor Fontane's 'L'Adultera'* [*'The Adulteress'*]], a German novel from 1880. Radecke's aim is to show the development of Fontane's narrative process in *L'Adultera* by reconstructing the writing process. In this respect, Radecke's study stands under the guiding question: 'Wie entsteht poetische Fiktionalität?' ['How is poetic

---

8   On the printing history of the *Die Judenbuche* and the question of the title see Droste-Hülshoff 1984, 207–08.

fictionality created?'] (Radecke 2002, 9). Using the example of the palm house, the location of the central twelfth, the adultery chapter entitled 'Unter Palmen' ['Under Palms'], for which Fontane had collected a wide variety of material, especially on the large Palm House in the Royal Botanic Gardens in Kew near London, Radecke can show that 'the historical models also played a role as text-constituting elements', but that subsequently 'the processes of textualisation are accompanied by a loss of external descriptive features, which limits or completely blurs the relationships to the real places. This process of dissolution corresponds to the construction of ambiguous layers of meaning'.[9] Such a 'blurring of echoes of extra-literary models' is thus accompanied by an 'increase in constructed references to reality'.[10] In this respect, Radecke can also show the value that the analysis of textual genesis can have for narratological insights by presenting an author's writing process as an exemplary model of a textualisation strategy, the result of which corresponds to or co-constitutes the epoch-specific literary style—in this case the German literary epoch 'Poetischer Realismus' ['Poetic Realism'] in the second half of the nineteenth century.

3. Conclusion and Perspectives

Hopefully, the cases presented above have been able to give an indication of the extent to which narratology and scholarly editing can be interdependent. Summing up, narratology can be of importance to scholarly editing in two central editorial areas, namely (1) the text-critical constitution of the text, that means (a) the general question of textual order and (b) the specific question of a possible textual error, as well as (2) the editorial presentation of versions. Scholarly editing, in turn, can enrich narratology, if the latter, for example, takes greater account of the editorial representations of variance and textual genesis, in order to (1) gain insights into the linguistic and literary

---

9   'die historischen Vorbilder auch als textkonstituierende Elemente eine Rolle gespielt haben' – 'mit den Textualisierungsvorgängen ein Verlust von äußeren Beschreibungsmerkmalen einhergeht, der die Beziehungen zu den realen Orten einschränkt oder ganz verwischt. Mit diesem Auflösungsprozeß korrespondiert andererseits der Aufbau mehrdeutiger Sinnschichten' (Radecke 2002, 129).
10 'Verwischen von Anklängen an die außerliterarischen Vorbilder'—'Zunahme von konstruierten Wirklichkeitsbezügen' (Radecke 2002, 150).

means used for (a) the creation of a certain narrative perspective, (b) the characterisation of the diegesis, (c) the basic structure of the development of the plot (a detailed example is omitted for reasons of space) or (d) the assignment to a genre. In addition, the genesis of the text (2) can point out from a literary-historical point of view which narrative methods are used to ascribe a text to the style of a specific literary period.

In any case, it can be said that it is relatively easy to build direct and indirect, but above all meaningful and necessary bridges between narratology and scholarly editing. And precisely because narratology and scholarly editing have fundamental tasks within literary studies, it might be a good idea to make their relationship clearer—with a hoped-for exemplary effect—within a network of literary studies. An essential tool for this is without doubt the examination of textual genesis and thus the research field of genetic criticism.

Works Cited

Beißner, Friedrich (1969), 'Hölderlins letzte Hymne' [first 1948/49], in: Friedrich Beißner, *Hölderlin: Reden und Aufsätze*, 2nd, rev. edn. (Köln and Wien: Böhlau) (first 1961), 211–46 and 282–83.

Bernaerts, Lars and Dirk Van Hulle (2013), 'Narrative across Versions: Narratology Meets Genetic Criticism', *Poetics Today*, 34.3: 281–326.

Bode, Christoph (2011), *Der Roman. Eine Einführung*, 2nd, expanded edn. (Tübingen and Basel: A. Francke).

Bosse, Anke and Walter Fanta (eds., 2019), *Textgenese in der digitalen Edition* (Berlin and Boston: De Gruyter) (Beihefte zu editio, 45).

Bücher, Rolf (1994), 'Beda Allemann über Textgenese', in: *Die Genese literarischer Texte: Modelle und Analysen*, ed. by Axel Gellhaus, Winfried Eckel, Diethelm Kaiser, Andreas Lohr-Jasperneite and Nikolaus Lohse (Würzburg: Königshausen & Neumann), 327–38.

Celan, Paul (1990–2017): *Werke: Historisch-kritische Ausgabe*, ed. by Beda Allemann, Rolf Bücher, Axel Gellhaus and Stefan Reichert (Frankfurt a.M.: Suhrkamp).

Cohn, Dorrit (1968), 'K. enters *The Castle*: On the Change of Person in Kafka's Manuscript', *Euphorion*, 62: 28–45.

Droste-Hülshoff, Annette von (1978–2000), *Historisch-kritische Ausgabe: Werke, Briefwechsel*, ed. by Winfried Woesler (Tübingen: Niemeyer).

— (1978), vol. V,1: *Prosa: Text*, ed. by Walter Huge (Tübingen: Niemeyer).

— (1984), vol. V,2: *Prosa: Dokumentation*, ed. by Walter Huge (Tübingen: Niemeyer).

Elema, Hans (1977), 'Zur Struktur von Kafkas "Prozeß"', *Sprachkunst*, 8: 301–22.

Eggert, Paul (2019), *The Work and the Reader in Literary Studies: Scholarly Editing and Book History* (Cambridge: Cambridge University Press).

Eschweiler, Christian (1989), 'Zur Kapitelfolge in Franz Kafkas Roman-Fragment "Der Prozeß"', *Wirkendes Wort*, 39: 239–51.

Goethe, Johann Wolfgang (1954), *Werke*, ed. by Deutsche Akademie der Wissenschaften zu Berlin, vol.: *Die Leiden des jungen Werthers*, 1: *Text: Erste und zweite Fassung*, ed. by Erna Merker (Berlin: Akademie-Verlag).

Goethe, Johann Wolfgang (1994), *Sämtliche Werke: Briefe, Tagebücher und Gespräche*, 40 vols, ed by Friedmar Apel et al., section I, vol. 8: *Die Leiden des jungen Werthers, Die Wahlverwandtschaften, Kleine Prosa, Epen*, in cooperation with Christoph Brecht ed. by Waltraud Wiethölter (Frankfurt a.M.: Deutscher Klassiker Verlag).

Goethe, Johann Wolfgang (1999), *Die Leiden des jungen Werthers: Studienausgabe. Paralleldruck der Fassungen von 1774 und 1787*, ed. by Matthias Luserke (Stuttgart: Reclam).

Goethe, Johann Wolfgang (2018–), *Faust: Historisch-kritische Edition*, ed. by Anne Bohnenkamp, Silke Henke and Fotis Jannidis in cooperation with Gerrit Brüning, Katrin Henzel, Christoph Leijser, Gregor Middell, Dietmar Pravida, Thorsten Vitt and Moritz Wissenbach (Frankfurt a.M., Weimar, Würzburg), Version 1.3 RC from September 2023, https://faustedition.net.

Greetham, D.C. (1992), *Textual Scholarship: An Introduction* (New York and London: Garland Pub.).

Greetham, D.C. (ed., 1995), *Scholarly Editing: A Guide to Research* (New York: The Modern Language Association of America).

Grésillon, Almuth (1994), *Eléments de critique génétique: Lire les manuscrits modernes* (Paris: Presses universitaire de France; 2nd edn. Paris: CNRS Editions, 2016); German version: Almuth Grésillon (1999), Literarische Handschriften: Einführung in die "critique génétique", trans. by Frauke Rother and Wolfgang Günther, rev. by Almuth Grésillon (Bern et al.: Lang) (Arbeiten zur Editionswissenschaft, 4).

Herman, Luc and John M. Krafft (2023), *Becoming Pynchon: Genetic Narratology and 'V.'* (Columbus: Ohio State University Press).

Hölderlin, [Friedrich] (1943–1985), *Sämtliche Werke: Große Stuttgarter Ausgabe*, ed. by Friedrich Beißner [and Adolf Beck]. 8 vols. in 15 (Stuttgart: Kohlhammer).

Holitscher, Arthur (1912), *Amerika: Heute und morgen. Reiseerlebnisse* (Berlin: Fischer).

Kafka, Franz (1925), *Der Prozess: Roman*, [ed. by Max Brod] (Berlin: Die Schmiede) (Die Romane des XX. Jahrhunderts).

Kafka, Franz (1982–), *Schriften Tagebücher Briefe: Kritische Ausgabe*, ed. by Jürgen Born, Gerhard Neumann, Malcolm Pasley and Jost Schillemeit with the advice of Nahum Glatzer, Rainer Gruenter, Paul Raabe and Marthe Robert (Frankfurt a.M.: Fischer).

— (1983), *Der Verschollene*, 2 vols.: [Textband]/Apparatband, ed. by Jost Schillemeit (Frankfurt a.M.: Fischer).

— (1990), *Der Proceß*, 2 vols.: [Textband]/Apparatband, ed. by Malcolm Pasley (Frankfurt a.M.: Fischer).

Kafka, Franz (1997), *Historisch-Kritische Ausgabe sämtlicher Handschriften, Drucke und Typoskripte*, ed. by Roland Reuß and Peter Staengle, vol.: *Der Process*, ed. by Roland Reuß, in cooperation with Peter Staengle (Basel and Frankfurt a.M.: Stroemfeld), 17 unnumbered booklets in slipcase, including as editorial report and documentation: Franz Kafka-Hefte 1.

Kraft, Herbert (2001), *Editionsphilologie*, 2nd, rev. and expanded edn. with contributions by Diana Schilling and Gert Vonhoff (Frankfurt a.M. et al.: Lang).

Nutt-Kofoth, Rüdiger (2005), 'Textgenese: Überlegungen zu Funktion und Perspektive eines editorischen Aufgabengebiets', *Jahrbuch für Internationale Germanistik*, 37.1: 97–122.

Nutt-Kofoth, Rüdiger (2015), 'Wie werden neugermanistische (historisch-) kritische Editionen für die literaturwissenschaftliche Interpretation genutzt? Versuch einer Annäherung aufgrund einer Auswertung germanistischer Periodika', in: *Vom Nutzen der Editionen: Zur Bedeutung moderner Editorik für die Erforschung von Literatur- und Kulturgeschichte*, ed. by Thomas Bein (Berlin and Boston: De Gruyter) (Beihefte zu editio, 39), 233–45.

Plachta, Bodo (2013), *Editionswissenschaft: Eine Einführung in Methode und Praxis der Edition neuerer Texte*, 3rd, augmented and updated edition (Stuttgart: Reclam).

Radecke, Gabriele (2002), *Vom Schreiben zum Erzählen: Eine textgenetische Studie zu Theodor Fontanes 'L'Adultera'* (Würzburg: Königshausen & Neumann) (Epistemata, Reihe Literaturwissenschaft, 358).

Rölleke, Heinz (1970), *Annette von Droste-Hülshoff: Die Judenbuche* (Bad Homburg v.d.H. et al.: Gehlen) (Commentatio: Analysen und Kommentare zur deutschen Literatur, 1).

Scheffel, Michael (2021), 'Wege zu einer genetischen Narratologie oder Von der Geburt und dem Abenteuer der Geschichten am Beispiel von Werkgenesen des Autors Arthur Schnitzler', *Diegesis: Interdisziplinäres E-Journal für Erzählforschung / Interdisciplinary E-Journal for Narrative Research*, 10.1: Why Narratology?, 49–72.

[Schiller, Friedrich] (1943–), *Schillers Werke: Nationalausgabe*, [...] ed. [...] by Lieselotte Blumenthal and Benno von Wiese resp. Norbert Oellers and Siegfried Seidel resp. Norbert Oellers (Weimar: Böhlau).

— (1971), vol. 11: *Demetrius*, ed. by Herbert Kraft (Weimar: Böhlau).

— (1982), vol. 12: *Dramatische Fragmente*, in cooperation with Klaus Harro Hilzinger and Karl-Heinz Hucke, ed. by Herbert Kraft (Weimar: Böhlau).

— (2000), vol. 5, new edn.: *Kabale und Liebe, Semele, Der versöhnte Menschenfeind, Körners Vormittag*, ed. by Herbert Kraft, Claudia Pilling and Gert Vonhoff in cooperation with Grit Dommes and Diana Schilling (Weimar: Böhlau).

Stanzel, Franz K. (2008), *Theorie des Erzählens*, 8th edn. (Göttingen: Vandenhoeck & Ruprecht).

Uyttersprot, H. (1957), *Eine neue Ordnung der Werke Kafkas? Zu Struktur von 'Der Prozeß' und 'Amerika'* (Antwerpen: de Vries, Brouwers).

Uyttersprot, H. (1966), 'Franz Kafka und immer noch kein Ende. Zur Textgestaltungsfrage', *Studia Germanica Gandensia*, 8: 173–246.

Van Hulle, Dirk (2022), *Genetic Criticism: Tracing Creativity in Literature* (Oxford: Oxford University Press).

Zeller, Hans (1966), 'Edition und Interpretation. Antrittsvorlesung', *Zürcher Student*, 43.7, January: 15 and 19.

Zeller, Hans (1986), 'Die Typen des germanistischen Varianten-Apparats und ein Vorschlag zu einem Apparat für Prosa', *Zeitschrift für deutsche Philologie*, 105, special issue: *Editionsprobleme der Literaturwissenschaft*, ed. by Norbert Oellers and Hartmut Steinecke, 42–69.

Zeller, Hans (2003), 'Die Entwicklung der textgenetischen Edition im 20. Jahrhundert', in: *Geschichte der Editionsverfahren vom Altertum bis zur Gegenwart im Überblick: Ringvorlesung*, ed. by Hans-Gert Roloff (Berlin: Weidler) (Berliner Beiträge zur Editionswissenschaft, 5), 143–207.

Zeller, Hans and Gunter Martens (eds., 1998), *Textgenetische Edition* (Tübingen: Niemeyer) (Beihefte zu editio, 10).

Index

Adams, Jonathan 59
Ahnlund, Knut 57
Alber, Jan 92, 226
Allemann, Beda 286
Andersen, Vilhelm 58
Andrews, Molly 39

Backmann, Reinhold 282–283
Bal, Mieke 11, 112, 124, 204, 207
Balzac, Honoré de 11, 229
Barthes, Roland 43–44
Beckett, Samuel 8–11, 14, 31–32, 151–152, 154–164, 253
Behrendt, Flemming 57–58, 65–66
Beißner, Friedrich 285
Bekius, Lamyk 7, 261–264, 268
Bennett, Alan 6
Bergson, Henri 162
Bernaerts, Lars 2, 7, 14, 91–92, 155, 221, 230, 242–243, 253, 257, 261
Bernini, Gianlorenzo 247, 249–251
Bernini, Marco 22, 31
Biasi, Pierre-Marc de 7, 18–19, 22, 37, 76, 229
Blanchot, Maurice 251
Blin, Roger 155
Bödorn, Andreas 287
Borchsenius, Otto 67
Bouckaert, Bart 157
Bracke, Astrid 262, 269–271
Bradham, Margaret 171
Branigan, Kevin 158
Brater, Enoch 160
Brewer, W.F. 202–203, 214
Brod, Max 288
Brontë, Charlotte 17–20, 23–32, 170, 172
Bryant, John 19–20
Buchholz, Sabine 266
Burrows, Rachel 11

Byrne, Paula 170, 181–185

Campe, Rüdiger 29
Carpentier, Aline 162
Carroll, Noël 203
Caxton, William 134, 137, 140–141, 143
Celan, Paul 286
Chalmers, David 225
Chatman, Seymour 3, 38, 92
Chaucer, Geoffrey 134, 140, 161
Clark, Andy 22, 225
Clodd, Alan 164
Cohn, Dorrit 2, 5–6, 62–63, 92, 253, 291
Crasson, Aurèle 261

Dannenberg, Hilary P. 38
Debray Genette, Raymonde 19, 102, 137
Derrida, Jacques 141, 261
Didion, Joan 61
Doležel, Lubomír 270
Dostoevsky, Fyodor 11
Douglas, Lawrence 77, 80, 84
Droste-Hülshoff, Annette von 289–290, 293
Duccio, Agostino di 1
Du Maurier, Daphne 91–107

Ferrer, Daniel 24, 116, 128
Fforde, Jasper 17
Flaubert, Gustave 19–20, 43, 137
Fludernik, Monika 13, 40, 43–44, 47–49, 95, 97, 207
Fontane, Theodor 13, 35–44, 46–52, 293–294
Forster, E.M. 74–75
Franke, Herman 221–224, 226–227, 236–237
Frost, Everett 164

Gao, Timothy 27
Gaskell, Elizabeth 28
Geeraerts, Jef 230–234
Genette, Gérard 3, 6, 62, 92, 205, 207, 236, 247, 249, 251
Gerrig, Richard 201, 203–204
Gide, André 11
Gilbert, Sandra M. 28–29
Gingrich, Brian 204
Gjellerup, Karl 57
Goethe, Johann Wolfgang 283, 290
Gontarski, S.E. 157
Gottlieb, Katja 57–58, 67
Griffin, Dori 272
Grillparzer, Franz 282
Grüne, Matthias 7, 13, 35, 44, 287
Gubar, Susan 28–29

Haarder, Jon Helt 58
Hamburger, Käte 48
Hamon, Philippe 3, 92, 206, 228, 236
Hanks, Lucy 20, 23
Hayford, Harrison 7, 73–74, 76, 79, 82, 84, 86
Hay, Louis 12
Hehle, Christine 40
Heritage, Barbara 20, 24, 29–30
Herman, David 3, 64, 92, 97, 246, 255
Herman, Luc 3, 7, 11, 87–88, 189–190, 204, 207, 287
Herring, René 59
Hettche, Walter 51
Hilfling, Josefine 6, 55
Hölderlin, Friedrich 285
Holitscher, Arthur 292
Holt, Hazel 170, 173, 178–179
Hutcheon, Linda 194
Huwiler, Elke 155

Iser, Wolfgang 11
Ishiguro, Kazuo 6, 120

Jahn, Manfred 207, 266
James, Henry 3, 38, 47, 51, 92
Johnson, Barbara 77, 83–84

Joyce, James 111–116, 118–126, 128–129
Jullien, Dominique 160

Kafka, Franz 2, 5–6, 62, 92, 288–289, 291–293
Kaplan, E. Ann 269–270
Kaufman, Anthony 170, 184
Kerridge, Richard 264
Kielberg, Esther 57
King, Stephen 13, 199–201, 203, 207–217
Kinzel, Till 155
Kirschenbaum, Matthew G. 261
Kittler, Friedrich 29
Krafft, John M. 7, 189–190, 287
Kraft, Herbert 285
Kukkonen, Karin 4, 7, 17, 21, 26–27, 30–32, 38, 44, 92, 205

Larkin, Peter 59
Lebrave, Jean-Louis 12
Leijten, Mariëlle 263
Lichtenstein, E.H. 202–203, 214
Loughman, Jane 7, 169
Low, W.H. 161
Lukács, Georg 191, 194, 196
Lumbroso, Christine 228–229
Luserke, Matthias 290

Margolin, Uri 171
Marin, Ileana 23, 30
Martens, Gunther 2, 221, 283
Mascia, Charles 7, 13, 73
Mauthner, Fritz 154
McGillen, Petra S. 36
Meister, Jan Christoph 3
Mélèse, Pierre 155
Melville, Herman 7, 13, 73–88
Merker, Erna 290
Michelangelo 1–2, 250
Mildorf, Jarmila 155
Miller, Lucasta 29, 199–200
Murray, Janet H. 27

Neyt, Vincent 7, 13, 199
Niederhoff, Burkhard 63, 207
Nixon, Mark 160, 162
Nutt-Kofoth, Rüdiger 7, 281, 283–284, 287

Olson, Charles 75

Pagès, Alain 229
Pain, Nesta 6
Parker, Hershel 73, 75, 77–79, 81–82, 84–86, 88
Pasley, Malcolm 291
Peeters, Ann 157
Phelan, James 61, 66, 224–225
Phillips, Joshua 7, 13, 133, 136
Pilling, John 161
Pontoppidan, Henrik 6, 55–59, 62, 64–68
Pountney, Rosemary 157, 253
Prince, Gerald 8, 63, 112, 123–124
Proust, Marcel 3, 92, 151, 160–164, 229
Pulkkinen, Veijo 261
Pym, Barbara 169–186
Pynchon, Thomas 189–197, 242–243

Qu, Claire 7, 91
Quiller-Couch, Sir Arthur ('Q') 91–107

Radecke, Gabriele 36, 287, 293–294
Rasmussen, Krista Stinne Greve 57–58, 67
Ratchford, Fannie Elizabeth 27
Reuß, Roland 288
Richardson, Brian 8, 65, 151, 154, 156, 226
Ries, Thorsten 261
Rölleke, Heinz 289
Rømhild, Lars Peter 57
Rossellino, Antonio 1
Rossen, Janice 172
Ryan, Marie-Laure 155, 245, 253, 256, 262, 265–266, 269–270

Scheffel, Michael 36, 287
Schiller, Friedrich 285, 293
Schmid, Wolf 38, 207
Schneider, Ralf 206, 217
Schuknecht, Mattison 270–271, 273
Sealts, Merton M. 7, 73–74, 76, 79, 82, 84, 86
Shelley, Mary 6
Shen, Dan 56
Sherry, Kaia 7, 241
Silver, Brenda 133
Skjerbæk, Esther 59
Skjerbæk, Thorkild 57, 59
Skov Nielsen, Henrik 56, 63, 65
Springer, Olga 25, 30
Stangerup, Hakon 56
Stanzel, Franz Karl 2, 37–38, 47–48, 51, 92, 291
Sternberg, Meir 202–203
Stewart, H.F. 98
Stockard, Emily 180–186

Thon, Jan-Noël 155
Trexler, Adam 266
Troch, David 262–264, 266–270, 272–279

Valera, Éamon de 10
Van den Broeck, Walter 234–235
Van der Heijden, A.F.Th. 236
Vandevelde, Tom 155
Van Hulle, Dirk 1, 4, 7, 14, 17, 19–20, 22, 35, 56, 63, 76, 92, 95, 102, 113, 115, 117, 120, 126, 129, 145, 154, 160, 162, 221, 225, 229, 242–243, 253, 257, 261, 283, 287, 291
Van Leeuwen, Richard 162–163
Van Nerom, Carolien 157
Van Waes, Luuk 263
Vasari, Giorgio 1
Verhulst, Pim 7, 14, 151–152
Verrill, Charles (Chuck) 201
Vervaeck, Bart 3, 11, 87–88, 92, 97, 204, 207

Watt, Ian 9
Weaver, Raymond 73, 114, 123
Weisbrod, Dirk 262
Weller, Shane 14
Wenke, John 7, 76, 78–81, 83, 86–88
Werner, Zacharias 290
White, Hayden 48
Wiethölter, Waltraud 290
Wittkower, Rudolf 250
Woolf, Virginia 3, 13, 92, 133–145

Wyatt, A.J. 161
Wyatt-Brown, Anne M. 169, 172–173, 176, 180

Zeller, Hans 282
Žiliukas, Joris 7, 111
Zilliacus, Clas 157
Zillman, Dolf 201
Zola, Émile 3, 92, 227–229, 236
Zymner, Rüdiger 287

About the Team

Alessandra Tosi was the managing editor for this book.

Sophia Bursey and Lucy Barnes proof-read this manuscript. Lucy Barnes compiled the index.

Jeevanjot Kaur Nagpal designed the cover. The cover was produced in InDesign using the Fontin font.

Cameron Craig typeset the book in InDesign and produced the paperback and hardback editions. The main text font is Tex Gyre Pagella and the heading font is Californian FB.

Cameron also produced the PDF and HTML editions. The conversion was performed with open-source software and other tools freely available on our GitHub page at https://github.com/OpenBookPublishers.

Jeremy Bowman created the EPUB.

Raegan Allen was in charge of marketing.

This book was peer-reviewed by Prof. Michael Scheffel, University of Wuppertal and Dr. Janina Jacke, Institut für Neuere deutsche Literatur und Medien Christian-Albrechts-Universität zu Kiel, Germany. Experts in their field, these readers give their time freely to help ensure the academic rigour of our books. We are grateful for their generous and invaluable contributions.

This book need not end here...

Share

All our books — including the one you have just read — are free to access online so that students, researchers and members of the public who can't afford a printed edition will have access to the same ideas. This title will be accessed online by hundreds of readers each month across the globe: why not share the link so that someone you know is one of them?

This book and additional content is available at
https://doi.org/10.11647/OBP.0426

Donate

Open Book Publishers is an award-winning, scholar-led, not-for-profit press making knowledge freely available one book at a time. We don't charge authors to publish with us: instead, our work is supported by our library members and by donations from people who believe that research shouldn't be locked behind paywalls.

Join the effort to free knowledge by supporting us at
https://www.openbookpublishers.com/support-us

We invite you to connect with us on our socials!

BLUESKY
@openbookpublish
.bsky.social

MASTODON
@OpenBookPublish
@hcommons.social

LINKEDIN
open-book-publishers

Read more at the Open Book Publishers Blog
https://blogs.openbookpublishers.com

You may also be interested in:

Text Genetics in Literary Modernism and Other Essays
Hans Walter Gabler

https://doi.org/10.11647/obp.0120

Genetic Inroads into the Art of James Joyce
Hans Walter Gabler

https://doi.org/10.11647/obp.0325

Prose Fiction
An Introduction to the Semiotics of Narrative
Ignasi Ribó

https://doi.org/10.11647/obp.0187

Text and Genre in Reconstruction
Effects of Digitalization on Ideas, Behaviours, Products and Institutions
Willard McCarty (Ed.)

https://doi.org/10.11647/obp.0008

www.ingramcontent.com/pod-product-compliance
Lightning Source LLC
Chambersburg PA
CBHW040324300426
44112CB00021B/2863